FLIGHT FROM MONTICELLO

 MONTICELLO

THOMAS JEFFERSON AT WAR

Michael Kranish

OXFORD
UNIVERSITY PRESS

2010

OXFORD
UNIVERSITY PRESS

Oxford University Press, Inc., publishes works that further
Oxford University's objective of excellence
in research, scholarship, and education.

Oxford   New York
Auckland   Cape Town   Dar es Salaam   Hong Kong   Karachi
Kuala Lumpur   Madrid   Melbourne   Mexico City   Nairobi
New Delhi   Shanghai   Taipei   Toronto

With offices in
Argentina   Austria   Brazil   Chile   Czech Republic   France   Greece
Guatemala   Hungary   Italy   Japan   Poland   Portugal   Singapore
South Korea   Switzerland   Thailand   Turkey   Ukraine   Vietnam

Published by Oxford University Press, Inc.
198 Madison Avenue, New York, New York 10016

www.oup.com

Oxford is a registered trademark of Oxford University Press

For more information about this title and its author,
please visit www.michaelkranish.com.

Library of Congress Cataloging-in-Publication Data
Kranish, Michael.
Flight from Monticello : Thomas Jefferson at war / by Michael Kranish.
    p. cm.
Includes bibliographical references.
ISBN 978-0-19-537462-9
1. Jefferson, Thomas, 1743–1826. 2. Jefferson, Thomas, 1743–1826—Adversaries.
3. Henry, Patrick, 1736–1799. 4. Virginia—History—Revolution, 1775–1783.
5. Virginia—Politics and government—1775–1783.
6. United States—Politics and government—1783–1809.
7. Governors—Virginia—Biography.
8. Presidents—United States—Biography. I. Title.
E332.4.K736 2010
973.4'6092—dc22
[B]   2009018156

1   9   8   7   6   5   4   3   2   1

Printed in the United States of America
on acid-free paper

IN MEMORY OF DAD AND IN APPRECIATION OF MOM, who took me along these roads of history, and in gratitude to Sylvia, Jessica, and Laura, who traveled them with me

CONTENTS

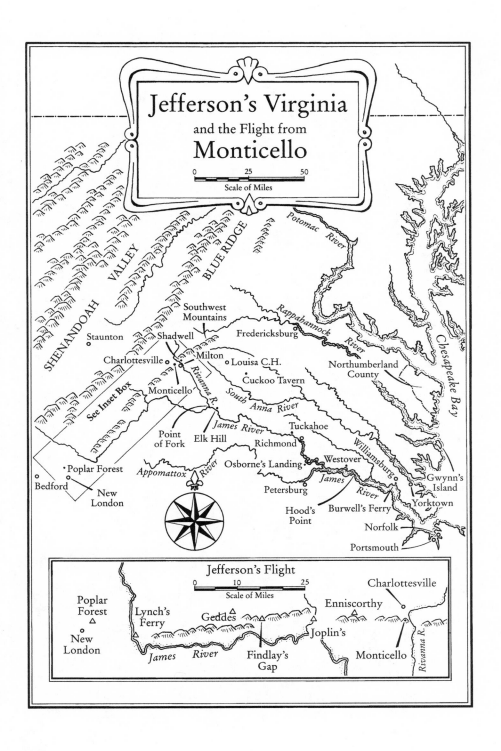

Jefferson's Virginia
and the Flight from
Monticello

0   25   50
Scale of Miles

SHENANDOAH VALLEY

BLUE RIDGE

Potomac River

Southwest Mountains

Staunton

Shadwell

Fredericksburg

Rappahannock River

Charlottesville

Milton

Louisa C.H.

Northumberland County

Monticello

Rivanna R.

Cuckoo Tavern

South Anna River

See Inset Box

Chesapeake Bay

James River

Tuckahoe

Point of Fork

Elk Hill

Richmond

Williamsburg

Poplar Forest

Appomattox River

Osborne's Landing

Westover

Gwynn's Island

Bedford

New London

Petersburg

James River

Burwell's Ferry

Yorktown

Hood's Point

Norfolk

Portsmouth

Jefferson's Flight

0   10   25
Scale of Miles

Poplar Forest

Lynch's Ferry

Geddes

Charlottesville

Enniscorthy

New London

Joplin's

Monticello

James River

Findlay's Gap

Rivanna R.

ON JULY 4, 1781, the fifth anniversary of the adoption of the Declaration of Independence, Thomas Jefferson had retreated to the safety of a small cabin at a remote plantation in the southwestern foothills of Virginia. Three columns of British forces had invaded the state during the last six months of Jefferson's term as governor. One force was led by Benedict Arnold, a former ally turned traitor. The second was headed by Major General William Phillips, who until recently had been Jefferson's favored guest at Monticello. A third general, Lord Cornwallis, arrived with a massive army and set up headquarters at another home owned by Jefferson. The rebellion that Jefferson had helped set in motion seemed in danger of turning decisively to the British as thousands of enemy troops overran Virginia. The British had chased Governor Jefferson from the capital of Richmond and they had come within minutes of capturing him in his study at Monticello. Jefferson vacated the governorship, fled his beloved mountaintop, galloped through forests, forded rivers, and climbed through passes to reach the remote fields of his Poplar Forest plantation. There, in the overseer's cramped home, Jefferson hoped he and his family were safe.

In his refuge, Jefferson received a letter blaming him for everything that had occurred since the British invaded Virginia in January 1781 and informing him that an inquiry would be made into his wartime conduct. He had failed to stop the intruders. He had fled as Richmond was set aflame. He had left the state militia in tatters. Patriots were on the run. The slaves were in flight. British troops were squeezing Virginians in a pincer that Jefferson should have anticipated.

If the worst was believed, Jefferson would be formally censured and punished by the Virginia legislature. His political career would be over, his legacy forever tarnished.

Almost as stinging, Jefferson suspected the man behind the inquiry was someone he had known since he was seventeen, and whose revolutionary fervor had inspired him: Patrick Henry. Henry's cry of "Give me liberty or give me death" had helped galvanize the colonies to take on the British. Jefferson had stood mesmerized in the doorway of the colonial House of Burgesses as Henry suggested that the king of England might suffer the same fate as Caesar, leading Jefferson to compare Henry's oratory to Homer. For years Jefferson had helped Henry personally and even financially. They had debated everything from the punishment for treason to the finer points of the fiddle. Now it seemed Henry was working to ruin him.

In the five years following the adoption of the Declaration of Independence—including two crucial years as governor of Virginia—Jefferson often seemed to be battling the citizenry as much as the British. Many Virginians refused to fight the British, insisting their priority was to protect their home and family. But now Jefferson was blamed for Virginia's being overrun.

Both in the following weeks and over the years, Jefferson sought to respond to every accusation about his conduct during the war. Having to do so made him certain he wanted nothing more to do with politics. He had authored the Declaration of Independence; he had not expected to lead the fight for it on the battlefield. Henry's charges would turn out to be the first of many attacks on Jefferson's actions as governor. His enemies would allege that he had put his personal safety above his duty to the people. The accusations would be used to try to block his election to the presidency, and even to discredit his role in history. Year after year, Jefferson composed documents that outlined his actions in minute detail. "I had been suspected & suspended in the eyes of the world without the least hint then or afterwards made public which might restrain them from supposing that I stood arraigned for treasons of the heart and not merely weakness of the head," Jefferson wrote about the investigation into his conduct. "I felt that these injuries . . . had inflicted a wound on my spirit which will only be cured by the all-healing grave."[1]

The beginnings of the story can be traced to a joyous Christmas party, when a young Thomas Jefferson first befriended the man he would blame for such torment.

Williamsburg

The Gentleman Has Spoken Treason

AS THE SUN DIPPED toward Virginia's great Blue Ridge, Thomas Jefferson liked to walk from his childhood home near the banks of the Rivanna River, slip a canoe into the water, and paddle to the other side. Securing the canoe at the shoreline, he ascended the gentle slope, a half hour's walk at brisk pace, to the hilltop that would be the site of Monticello.[1] The 850-foot hill reigned at the crossroads of British America's east and west, where the gradual rise of the Piedmont gave way to loftier mountain chains. The plateau provided a view of Jefferson's early world: the ribbon of the Rivanna, which passed his childhood home at Shadwell, and a scattering of homes amid the lands that would become the town of Charlottesville. With a small telescope, Jefferson could eye the vast plantation fields, the distant hollows, and the scattered settlements running to the Tidewater country. The dome of Carter's Mountain rose to the southwest, the Southwest Mountains rolled northeastward, and the peaks of the Blue Ridge provided a western curtain. Even as a boy, Jefferson had committed himself so deeply to his little mountain that he and best friend, Dabney Carr, pledged that they would one day be buried near each other under a spreading oak on the hill's western flank.

His father, Peter Jefferson, had inspired him with tales of surveying the land to the west and with stories of primeval forest, bears, and a vast territory tracked mostly by Indians. Thomas would be a thinker and writer, but he also retained the strength, cunning, and confidence that were essential to thrive in these remote surroundings. He was a powerful swimmer, could run in great strides, galloped on horseback for hours, and climbed mountains in the fading light and returned in darkness.[2] Jefferson was fourteen when his father died, leaving an inheritance that included the hill that he so loved. Two years later, in 1759, Jefferson left the backcountry, telling a friend he was anxious to have a more "universal acquaintance" of people and knowledge at the College of William and Mary in Williamsburg.[3] Gangly, sandy-haired, and freckled, Thomas saddled his horse and headed east toward the capital along rough clay roads and forest trails. He envisioned living comfortably within the British colonial hierarchy; he would be a fiddler and philosopher, a lawyer and legislator, a learned gentleman of the land.

The countryside that spread before Jefferson on this winter day rolled gently, watered by creeks and sheltered by towering trees. As Jefferson moved closer to the fall line, where the uplands met the piney woods of the coastal plain, he stayed abreast of a stream called the South Anna River. Here and there, a plantation home stood on a rise, perched over barren fields where tobacco soon would be planted. In sparsely settled Hanover County, about halfway between Jefferson's home at Shadwell and Williamsburg, Jefferson stopped at a plantation festively decorated with holly and mistletoe for the Christmas holiday, with a week of celebration to include dances, games, and perhaps a fox hunt. Inside, logs crackled in the fireplaces and the tables would have been spread with turkey, ham, goose, and fish.

The host was a leading member of the gentry named Nathaniel West Dandridge, whose family had been granted valuable spring-fed lands by British royalty. Dandridge reflected the past and future of the colonies. His father-in-law had been a royal governor of Virginia. His niece, Martha, had recently married a promising colonel named George Washington, who had served with the British fighting the French and Indians. Now that war was near an end and the British soon would control much of North America. No colony would gain more land and power than Jefferson's homeland. Virginia—British Virginia— would bustle with prosperity unlike anything seen before in the colonies, and few would be better positioned to take advantage than those attending this Christmas party.

Jefferson noticed that one guest stood out. He was seven years older and attired somewhat coarsely, yet danced elegantly and chatted easily. He would inspire, confound, and later torment Jefferson as their fates intertwined in the decades to come. Yet as Jefferson sized up Patrick Henry for the first time, there was much that did not impress him. Years later, Jefferson told of this first encounter with Henry in a comment dripping in sarcasm and a touch of jealousy: "His manners had something of coarseness in them; his passions were music, dancing and pleasantry. He excelled in the last, and it attached everyone to him."[4]

Jefferson, a budding intellect already trained in languages and sciences, with an air of superiority about him, could hardly wait to get to Williamsburg, where he could pursue his studies in Greek, Latin, and mathematics. He already read French, played the violin, and danced the minuet. Although his ancestry was not quite as grand as that of the gentry's greatest families, his inheritance of three thousand or so acres of rolling hills and fields was a solid financial foundation.

Henry came from more modest stock. At nineteen, he had married a sixteen-year-old neighbor, Sarah Shelton, inheriting six slaves and six hundred acres on a farm prosaically called Pine Slash. The couple struggled for years. Twice Henry had run a store, but both times it closed because he was too generous with credit. He similarly failed at farming despite helping to tend the fields himself, a task wealthier Virginians left to slaves. His house was destroyed in a fire, requiring the Henrys to move into a small dwelling. He had no aspirations of going to college. Still, at twenty-three, when he and Jefferson met, Henry had the sunniest outlook. "Mr. Henry had, a little before, broken up his store, or rather it had broken him up; but his misfortunes were not to be traced, either in his countenance or conduct," Jefferson remembered years later.[5]

Henry was thinking of becoming a lawyer. He was intrigued by those who practiced at the Hanover County courthouse, across the road from where his father-in-law had established a tavern, at which Henry sometimes helped out (leading Jefferson to conclude that he was a barkeeper). Henry was convinced that his oratorical skills could make up for his lack of familiarity with the finer points of jurisprudence and that he could join the profession with just a few months of study. It was, a cousin later wrote, "a last effort to supply the wants of his family."[6]

During the weeklong Christmas holiday, Jefferson and Henry talked every day. Henry said "the strangest things in finest language, but without logic," Jefferson later wrote. In time, after they had spent tumultuous years at each other's side, Jefferson would say that Henry was both "the greatest orator that ever lived" and a man who was "avaritious and rotten-hearted."[7] What united them was their heritage in these Virginia hills, where the rumbling of revolutionary thoughts could already be felt. After the days of celebration at the Dandridge home, Jefferson and Henry said their goodbyes. Henry would use his oratory to find financial success, while Jefferson prepared to begin his education. Yet both men would wind up on the same path—lawyers, governors of Virginia, indispensable leaders of the rebellion, and eventually bitter rivals.

JEFFERSON SOON TRAVELED farther east toward the colonial capital, passing the great plantations of Tidewater country, with fields reaching to the landings of the broad James River. The Williamsburg Jefferson entered in early 1760 was a city of eighteen hundred or so people and consisted of a muddy main thoroughfare, Duke of Gloucester Street, lined with taverns, stores, and dwellings. Regal yet sometimes riotous (qualities shared by many of its residents), Williamsburg was practically an island of England, a world apart from the Piedmont backcountry where Jefferson had grown up. The clomp of horses echoed in the air, the calls of merchants filled the streets. Gentry were accompanied by black slaves in distinctive livery. The taverns were busy with customers who talked of tobacco prices and distant princes.

Three great brick buildings dominated the scene, each among the most impressive edifices in all of the colonies: the College of William and Mary's Wren Building, the Governor's Palace, and the Capitol. The Wren Building overlooked the western edge of Duke of Gloucester Street; it featured a pair of two-story wings extending from either side of the three-story central hall, creating three of the four sides of what was once intended to be a quadrangle. One wing housed an elegant, wood-beamed chapel and the other a baronial-style dining hall. The Wren Building would not have looked out of place in Oxford or Cambridge. Jefferson would live for two years on the third floor in the east-facing section, often studying more than twelve hours a day.

As he made his way east along Duke of Gloucester Street, Jefferson would have passed a small building housing a saddler and the sturdy brick Bruton Parish Church. To his left was the rectangular Palace Green, which swept to the north. At the end of the green stood the Governor's Palace, completed three decades earlier, and the most visible and imposing sign of British rule. Rising two and a half stories, topped by redbrick chimneys, a rooftop balustrade, and a tall cupola, it was home to the highest representative of the crown. The royal governor had the power to make laws, dissolve the legislature, and call out a small army. Inside, the chambers were lined with neat rows of swords and muskets, more reminders of royal power. Farther east on Duke of Gloucester Street was the Magazine, an octagonal redbrick structure rising two and a half stories that contained many more armaments as well as dozens of kegs of gunpowder. And at the other end of Duke of Gloucester Street, after shoemakers, blacksmiths, a printer, several taverns, a courthouse, a jail, and pillory, was the House of Burgesses, about a mile from the Wren Building. The rectangular redbrick structure, which replaced an elaborate building that had been destroyed by fire, looked more like a plantation house than a legislative institution. It featured a two-tiered portico that may have been inspired by designs of the Italian architect Andrea Palladio.

Jefferson looked on much of Williamsburg's architecture with disdain. The Governor's Palace was "not handsome without" but was "capable of being made an elegant seat." The college was a "rude, mis-shapen" pile that, if not for the roof, would have been mistaken for a brick kiln. The whole town bore the burden of "barbarous ornaments" and lacked architects who knew "the first principle of the art." One can imagine Jefferson stewing over the architectural shortcomings of Williamsburg as he continued down Duke of Gloucester Street. Only the Capitol was "pleasing," and he would later transfer elements of its design to his home, his escape from the mundane, his obsession: Monticello. First, however, he had to decide how to use his time in the capital of the colony to achieve his ambitions.[8]

NOT LONG AFTER JEFFERSON BEGAN his first classes at the College of William and Mary, Patrick Henry visited his third-floor lodging in the Wren Building. Henry, still dressed in his country clothing, said he had been studying law for the previous six weeks or so and was ready to take his examination. Jefferson, in contrast, expected to have two years of broad education and would spend many months reading legal texts and learning at the side of his favorite teacher, George Wythe. Henry became a frequent visitor to Williamsburg and sometimes stayed with Jefferson. On one such visit, Henry examined Jefferson's impressive library and asked to borrow two volumes of Hume's *Essays.* Jefferson later recounted that when Henry returned them, he declared "he had not been able to go further than twenty or thirty pages in the first volume."[9]

The essays included Hume's famous treatise on monarchy and revolution. While Hume said absolute tyranny is problematic, he believed the creation of a republic would lead to factionalism and, ultimately, civil war. "This may teach us the lesson of moderation in all our political controversies," Hume wrote. It is the type of essay that Jefferson would have devoured, debating it with his teachers and colleagues. Jefferson had his problems with London, but he was still inclined to work within the system. He was hardly ready for revolution. Henry, meanwhile, was already preparing to take on the monarchy and did not need a dense essay to convince him of the need to remove its manacles.

HENRY'S TRANSFORMATION from a failed shopkeeper and farmer into one of the most popular lawyers in Virginia and a leader in the rebellion resulted from a 1763 case he seemingly could not win. It pitted him against the local representatives of the Church of England, ministers, and members of his own family. Henry's direct target in the case was the Reverend James Maury, who happened to have been a teacher and mentor to young Thomas Jefferson. Maury ran a small school of "classical education" north of Charlottesville, where he had bookcases filled with some four hundred volumes. Jefferson often stayed at Maury's house and felt indebted to the man who had read to him in Latin and Greek and given him an appreciation for the classics, from Homer to Cicero. Maury's classes had been one of Jefferson's joys, particularly because he attended them with his best friend, Dabney Carr. Maury often would vent his anger against the legislators in Williamsburg, who he felt were cutting his church salary. This may have led, unintentionally, to the most far-reaching lesson that Jefferson gained from his beloved tutor.

Maury represented a system of religious order that was an increasing cause of tension in the colony. He was a member of the Anglican Church, the official church of Virginia as well as of England. The church's policy was that non-Anglicans such as Baptists and Presbyterians were "dissenters." This policy was becoming especially unpopular in Jefferson's region of western Virginia, where Baptists and Presbyterians were settling in greater numbers. Catholics were, for the most part, unwelcome. When a member of the House of Burgesses took his oath of office, the legislator not only promised "faithful and true allegiance" to the king of England but also swore that he did "abhor, detest and abjure as impious and heretical that damnable doctrine" of Catholicism and the "foreign prince," meaning the pope.[10] Virginia authorities imposed severe limitations on non-Anglican ministers, requiring dissenters such as Baptists to get a license to preach in the colony. The alternative was jail.

Virginians paid taxes that went to support the Anglican Church and thus paid the salaries of ministers such as Maury. It did not matter whether Virginians attended the Anglican Church or were members of a different denomination; they were forced to pay taxes to the Anglicans. It was the highest tax paid by many Virginians at the time. The local Anglican hold on power as well as the British control on Virginia's legislators were already under strain when Reverend Maury decided to take his case to court. The case became known as the "Parson's Cause," and, in the view of some historians, it provided an early test of revolutionary spirit in Virginia.

The Maury case arose after the Virginia House of Burgesses passed legislation in 1758 that was intended to end a system in which every Anglican minister was paid an annual salary of sixteen thousand pounds of tobacco, the value of which fluctuated. The burgesses had become particularly concerned that the 1758 tobacco shortage had caused the price of tobacco to soar, so they sought to stabilize the payment to Anglican ministers, paying them the value of the tobacco in currency and fixing the rate at two pence per pound (about one-third the market value during that year's tobacco shortage). This legislation became known as the "Two-Penny Act." Jefferson remembered Maury's anger, writing that in between his lessons he often heard Maury inveigh against the act.

Maury and other Anglican ministers protested, and King George vetoed the Two-Penny Act. Many burgesses were outraged, believing that the king was usurping their authority to set local tax rates and address a local economic crisis. Maury, meanwhile, seized upon the king's action to sue for three years of back wages, worth £400.

In November 1763 the case came before the Hanover County court. Maury thought he had a friendly Anglican judge in Colonel John Henry, the father of Patrick. Judge Henry ruled in Maury's favor, deciding that the king's veto of the Two-Penny Act was valid and that Maury should be compensated. Then the case took a twist that, some argue, changed the course of history. The loser was a colonial official who collected taxes that were to be paid to the ministers. For the phase of the trial in which damages would be determined, he hired a new lawyer to represent him: the judge's son, Patrick Henry.[11]

Like his father and uncle, Patrick was raised Anglican. However, Henry's mother, Sarah, was among a large number of Virginians who left the Anglican Church during the Great Awakening, swayed by itinerant ministers who preached a fiery and theatrical evangelistic form of religion. Their message of salvation inspired many Virginians at a time when death by disease was an everyday fear. Such preaching also attracted those who were disenchanted by the gentry-dominated structure of the Anglican Church. A key tenet of the Awakening was the revolutionary concept that all worshipers were equal in the eyes of God and had the freedom to believe as they chose. Henry's mother, like many others in the Piedmont country, embraced the idea and became a follower of the famed evangelical Presbyterian minister Samuel Davies, who had attracted large crowds across Virginia. As a child, Henry was taken by his mother to hear Davies speak and was influenced by his style of oratory.[12] Now Henry took on the Maury case, focusing on whether the British government was usurping the rights of Virginians to control their own fate and set their own taxes. His argument was, in effect, the prelude that would be followed by Jefferson in the appeal for independence. "A King, by disallowing Acts of this salutary nature, [changes] from being the father of his people, degenerated into a tyrant, and forfeits all rights to his subjects' obedience," Henry told the court, according to an account written shortly afterward by Maury.[13]

"The gentleman has spoken treason, and I am astonished that your Worships can hear it without emotion, or any mark of dissatisfaction," protested Maury's lawyer, Peter Lyons. But the presiding justice, John Henry, let his son proceed.[14]

Patrick Henry then went after the Anglican clergy in a way that few others would dare:

> We have heard a great deal about the benevolence and holy zeal of our reverend clergy, but how is this manifested? . . . Instead of feeding the hungry and clothing

the naked, these rapacious harpies would, were their powers equal to their will, snatch from the hearth of their honest parishioner his last hoe-cake, from the widow and her orphan children their last milch cow! the last bed, nay, the last blanket from the lying-in woman![15]

In another time or place, such words would have led to Henry's imprisonment or even death. But Henry's audacity was timed perfectly, coinciding with a rising resentment against the colonial system in a county where such ideas had the greatest support. Despite his strong words against the clergy, Henry remained an Anglican throughout his life. He had deftly used a court case about the compensation of clergy to launch the broader constitutional argument against British governance that would dominate his career. Maury was outraged, contending later that Henry had apologized to him, and confessed he had taken the case only as a means to increase his popularity. The jury considered Henry's argument for all of five minutes, then ruled that Maury should receive damages, but in the lowest possible amount: one penny.

Henry, who received 15 shillings for his work, was viewed as having won the case of his career, and his law business blossomed. He would soon be elected to the House of Burgesses in Williamsburg.

Jefferson was less than impressed by Henry's success against his former mentor. While Jefferson was putting in endless hours at the College of William and Mary studying intricacies of the law, Henry could succeed only in "mere jury causes" at the county level that depended on oratory. The case was a blow to the power of the local church and the British government. The dissenters, as well as Anglicans such as Jefferson who advocated religious freedom, eventually would play a crucial role in the revolution. At the time of the Maury case, however, colonial power still reigned supreme in Virginia.

Nowhere was this colonial grip on Virginia more evident than on the great plantations that lined the banks of the James River. It was there that the family of William Byrd III oversaw a vast fortune and worked in concert with the royal authorities in Williamsburg to keep the British in power.

BYRD WAS JUST TWENTY-ONE when in 1749 he inherited one of the wonders of British America, the estate of Westover. By virtue of birth, he was one of the wealthiest and most powerful men in Virginia. He would become a central player in the drama of the revolution, a counterweight of loyalism to the revolutionary zeal of Jefferson and Henry. But that was in the years to come. For now, the young man reigned at his palatial home. A Georgian masterpiece of soft red brick, towering chimneys, and shimmering panes of glass, Westover stood on a bluff overlooking the broad James River, situated about halfway between Richmond and Williamsburg. The James flowed in front at a peaceful measure, the broad sheet of water smoothed from its rapid descent from the mountains, its hurtle down the roiling falls of Richmond, and its spirals around serpentine bends. The river teemed with herring and shad; the sky buzzed with eagles, herons, ospreys, ducks, and geese. The water ran deep enough that one could board a sailing vessel at Westover's dock and not stop until reaching England.

There was something about the marriage of the riverfront setting, sheltering trees, emerald lawn, and elegantly executed architecture that set Westover apart from every other manor of the colony. The three-story main house was shouldered by smaller twin annexes, set on opposing sides of the manse. One annex housed a kitchen with a large fireplace; the other held the library, with Byrd's collection of four thousand books, and was often used for entertainment, having enough space for a spinet, a harpsichord, and ten dancing couples. From the sweeping riverfront lawn, the view eastward would have revealed a procession of sailing vessels, including sloops filled with Byrd's crops, headed toward Williamsburg and the port city of Norfolk. To the west lay the lands of Richmond and the interior wilderness, vast amounts of which belonged to the Byrd family.

All of this—the setting, the house, the land, the slaves, the imported furnishings, the gilded accoutrements—bespoke a life that few beyond the plantations strung along Virginia's rivers could imagine. At its height the Byrd wealth consisted of 179,423 acres of forest, fields, and swamp, 1,652 hogs, 951 cattle, 137 horses, and hundreds of slaves. There were wagons and gigs, sloops and ferries, warehouses, townhouses, plantation houses, slave quarters, and icehouses. There were more people living at Westover—family, indentured servants, and slaves—than in most towns across Virginia.[16]

Byrd's grandfather, William, had arrived from England in 1670 and built upon property in the colony inherited from an uncle. Byrd's father, also William, inherited the family fortune in 1704, and it was he who built Westover. The second William assembled a vast fortune selling tobacco and marketing it as a medical marvel, even as he exemplified the worst traits of the time in his hatred of Catholics and exploitation of slaves. His place in history was secured because he left behind an extraordinary legacy of diaries, letters, journals, and books filled with vivid descriptions of plantation life. "I have no bills to pay and a half crown will rest undisturbed in my pocket for many moons. Like one of the Patriarchs I have my flocks and my herds ... we sit securely under our vines and fig trees."[17] He used his fortune to help create Virginia's future, assembling the land that would become Richmond, naming the town after Richmond upon Thames in England, and selling lots to prospective settlers. Similarly, he founded Petersburg, predicting the two towns would someday rise like "cities in the air."

Upon the death of his father in 1744, William Byrd III was sixteen, five years short of the age of inheritance. The young master prevailed upon his mother to send him to England. He did not catch smallpox, as the family feared, but instead acquired another disease that would be equally destructive—an addiction to gambling. "It was his misfortune that he so early inherited his father's property, and that his mother gave him the use without restriction of his resources in England," one of Byrd's granddaughters later wrote. "Gambling was at that time the vice of the fashionable world, and William Byrd, while just an inexperienced youth, was thrown into the dissipated society of Carlton House and yielded to temptation." Carlton House was one of the most ornate buildings in London, located along Pall Mall and adjacent to St. James Park. As Byrd's granddaughter told the story, Byrd was at Carlton House one night, gambling as usual. He and his fellows were playing for such high points that "diamond loops taken from their tri-cornered hats were lost and won. Finally, 10,000 Guineas was staked. Byrd lost and a bystander with a sneer said that 'the Colonial youth can never pay that!' " But a check was promptly sent by Byrd's banker, later returned "honored and cashed."[18]

A portrait of Byrd from the time reveals a sallow-looking man with a rounded face framed by the curls of a white periwig, arched eyebrows, and an angular nose that hangs over pursed lips. He wears a regal-looking embroidered jacket over a shirt with lacy, ruffled sleeves, his right hand tucked partly inside his vest. A fringed tricornered hat—perhaps the one from which diamond loops were wagered and lost—rests at his side.

UPON BYRD'S RETURN TO AMERICA, he promptly took a step that helped make up for his losses. On April 14, 1748, the twenty-year-old Byrd married seventeen-year-old Elizabeth Hill Carter, who had grown up five miles away at Shirley plantation, one of the few estates in the colonies on a par with Byrd's Westover. The uniting of the Byrd and Carter families was akin to a royal wedding, and widely approved. Byrd soon was appointed to the Governor's Council, a position that tightly allied him with the British authorities and the local royal governor.

At the time, Byrd was increasingly consumed with debts from gambling, land schemes, and poor crops. He also apparently was consumed with a dislike of his wife. So in 1756, Byrd all but abandoned Elizabeth in order to command the Second Virginia Regiment under British authority, becoming one of two men to lead a Virginia regiment in the French and Indian War. The other was George Washington, who commanded the First Virginia Regiment. Byrd arranged for his three oldest sons, ages four, six, and eight, to go to school in England, with only the two youngest remaining at home with Elizabeth. For about two years, Washington and Byrd commanded their separate Virginia regiments in the war but worked together occasionally, including a joint expedition in the Shenandoah Valley. After Washington resigned his position in 1758, going to Mount Vernon to manage his plantation, Byrd continued in command of his regiment for nearly three more years, putting him in one of the most high-profile military positions in the colonies. "Col. Byrd was in some respects the superior of General Washington, and in none his inferior," wrote Byrd's neighbor, David Meade.[19]

At first, Byrd's military adventure went well. He rendezvoused in 1758 with the Cherokees, keeping them in the British fold, or so it seemed. Then in March 1760, when Jefferson was just beginning his university studies, Byrd was deep in the wilderness, commanding six hundred men. His mission was to help relieve a two-hundred-man force under siege by Cherokees at Fort Loudon, near what would become Knoxville. Byrd failed to advance far enough to help the soldiers, and most of them were massacred. Byrd's four years of military adventure seemed for naught. In August, Elizabeth Byrd, age twenty-nine, died under mysterious circumstances; her death was variously attributed to an accident, suicide, or "brain fever." William Byrd III now was a widower with a decidedly mixed military record. Yet just two months later, he was in Philadelphia and had met one of the city's most captivating women, Mary Willing. Her father was Philadelphia's former mayor, Charles Willing. Her godfather was Benjamin Franklin, who had taken an active interest in making Mary worldly and wise, sending her historical magazines and recommending to her the works of Milton and others. She also had a first cousin, Peggy Shippen, who would marry a general named Benedict Arnold.

Just six months after Elizabeth's death, on January 29, 1761, Byrd married Mary Willing, and he built an elegant redbrick town house at 110 Third Street in Philadelphia, near the Willing family home. Mary was assertive and independent, while he was "a generous Husband, disposed to indulge her affections to the utmost," a family history recorded. Eventually the couple left

Philadelphia and moved to Byrd's vast Virginia plantation. Mary was en-
thralled with Westover—the mansion, the library, the outbuildings, and the
woods that spread beyond the riverbank.

"This," Mary wrote of her new home on the James River, "is the most de-
lightful place in the world."[20]

A Determination Never to Do What Is Wrong

TWICE A YEAR, the prim little town of Williamsburg, the "seat of intelligence, refinement and elegance," took on a wholly different character.[1] No longer was it the province of the students of the College of William and Mary, the supplicants of the royal governor, and the merchants of Duke of Gloucester Street. The lawyers and politicians had come to town—and with them the gamblers, the thieves, the drunkards, and lately the revolutionaries. It was the semiannual meeting of the General Court, a twenty-four-day session during which Virginians could bring all manner of suits before the judiciary. Anyone who could afford a lawyer, and many who could not, would arrive in Williamsburg in search of quick fortune, doubling or tripling the village's population nearly overnight.

Young Jefferson was still a loyal British subject, more concerned with courting the beauties of Williamsburg than troubling over dictates of the general court. "Devilsburg," Jefferson called the capital when telling a friend about a failed effort at romance with a young lady named Rebecca Burwell. He danced at the Apollo Room of the Raleigh Tavern and attended puppet shows, magic acts, and horse races. His favorite activity seemed to be going to a theater that was built in 1760 near the Capitol and was frequented by local players as well as a British troupe. The ensembles would perform Shakespearean works such as *The Merchant of Venice* and *Othello* as well as John Gay's *The Beggar's Opera*, an opus about class, crime, and corruption that seemed particularly well suited for study in the chaotic milieu of Williamsburg. As Jefferson's education intensified, he was often accompanied by two close friends. One was his childhood companion Dabney Carr. The other was John Page, a descendant of one of the most influential Virginia families, which controlled a great estate called Rosewell Plantation in Gloucester County. Jefferson and Page were "like brothers for almost half a century," sharing confidences from their teens to old age.[2] In the coming years, it would be Page, as much as anybody, who urged on Jefferson's revolutionary impulses. The young men bonded through their membership in what would become the first college fraternity in North America, known at the time simply as the Brothers of the F.H.C., which stood for *fraternitas, hilaritas, cognito*. But another name stuck: the Flat Hat Club. The Flat Hatters often communicated in Latin, conducting informal seminars during the day and parties late into the night at what they called their "temple of mirth and hilarity." Jefferson spent countless hours in philosophical discussions with his friends, questioning the absolutes of his day, following a credo espoused by the English politician and philosopher Lord Bolingbroke: "No hypothesis ought to be maintained if a single phenomenon stands in direct opposition to it."[3]

At the same time, Jefferson was close to the British royal governor, Francis Fauquier, with whom he dined often at the Governor's Palace along with other members of the gentry. Jefferson usually brought his violin, on which he accompanied Fauquier in a musical ensemble. The close connection between Jefferson and Fauquier was further solidified when on March 30, 1763, Fauquier provided a grant to Jefferson of 950 acres in Albemarle County at the fork of the Rivanna River.[4]

Jefferson's conclaves at the Governor's Palace were often joined by two teachers who deeply influenced him. William Small, who Jefferson said was "to me as a father," instilled the lessons of the Enlightenment, spoke with "an enlarged and liberal mind," and encouraged Jefferson to be skeptical of authority and to question the status quo. Small, in turn, introduced Jefferson to George Wythe, a legal mentor who would become a fellow signer of the Declaration of Independence. In these prerevolutionary days, Jefferson and his two mentors would join Fauquier to form a "*partie quarée*" at the Palace, an intellectual feast at which Jefferson years later recalled he "heard more good sense, more rational and philosophical conversations, than in all my life besides."[5] Fauquier was like Williamsburg itself: all order and sophistication on the outside, but with darker impulses evident just beneath the surface. It was said that as a young man in England, Fauquier had lost his inheritance in a game of cards. Luckily for Fauquier, the man who defeated him was in a position to help Fauquier become Britain's representative in Virginia, where Fauquier once again indulged in heavy gambling.

Jefferson saw both sides of Williamsburg, confiding years later to a grandson that he had been alternately attracted and repulsed by the capital's attractions. "I was often thrown into the society of horseracers, cardplayers, foxhunters, scientific and professional men, and of dignified men," Jefferson wrote. "Many a time have I asked myself, in the enthusiastic death of a fox, the victory of a favorite horse, the issue of a question eloquently argued at the bar, or in the great council of the nation, 'Well, which of these kinds of reputation should I prefer—that of a horsejockey, a foxhunter, an orator, or the honest advocate of my country's rights?'"[6]

One witness to the wilder side of Williamsburg was a French government agent, an adventurous traveler and exacting diarist who visited the capital in the spring of 1765, as Jefferson continued his legal studies and Patrick Henry arrived for his first session as a newly elected member of the House of Burgesses. "Never was a more Disagreeable place than this at present," wrote the Frenchman, whose name remains unknown. "In the Daytime people hurrying back and forwards from the Capitol to the taverns, and at night, Carousing and Drinking in one Chamber and box and Dice in another, which Continues till morning Commonly."

With Virginians arriving from all over the colony to plead their cases to the General Court or profit from the accompanying circuslike atmosphere, the Frenchman searched up and down Duke of Gloucester Street for a place to stay, finally finding lodgings just behind the Capitol on Waller Street, settling into Jane Vobe's tavern, where he was told "all the best people resorted."

The bustling tavern was filled with legislators, justices, and lawyers, many of whom were drinking Madeira or a punch made with Jamaican rum. In short order, the Frenchman was introduced to William Byrd III, who was in town due to his service on the Governor's Council. Byrd was at a table covered with the finest Mogul playing cards and sets of dice. He was seated with his friends and fellow gentry, including Sir Peyton Skipwith, who lived near Petersburg. For years, the story would be told that Skipwith won thousands of acres from Byrd during a marathon three-day poker game. Byrd was never happy unless "he has the box and Dices in hand," the Frenchman wrote. "This Gentleman from a man of the greatest property of any in America has reduced himself to that Degree by gaming, that few or nobody will Credit him for Ever so small a sum of money." To pay his debts, Byrd was "obliged to sell 400 fine Negroes." The Frenchman became so "heartily sick" of the endless hours of gambling at the tavern that he hired a carriage to visit nearby Jamestown.[7] Looking back on his youth in Williamsburg, Jefferson concluded that he had avoided its darker side because he had attached himself to a handful of good teachers. Whenever he faced "temptations and difficulties," Jefferson would ask himself what his mentors would do. "What course in it will ensure me their approbation?" He called it a "self-catechizing habit," which he said gave him "a determination never to do what is wrong."[8] He chose a path that he hoped would not bring him to the financial precipice toward which Byrd was headed. But Jefferson was not yet ready to travel along the revolutionary road that Patrick Henry intended to construct as he arrived in Williamsburg.

As the month of May 1765 came to a close, Jefferson was looking forward to witnessing a session of the House of Burgesses, hoping to hear the speech of the newly elected Henry. But first the clerk of the House, Nathaniel Walthoe, had to attend to a hanging. Walthoe had accused three black slaves of breaking into his home. The trial took place on May 18, 1765, at the York County Court, which had jurisdiction over part of Williamsburg. Under a royal court of arms, five justices took their seats, including Thomas Nelson Jr., a future signer of the Declaration of Independence and owner of four hundred slaves who would become governor of Virginia. Another justice was Dudley Digges of Yorktown, who would be a prominent legislator. In their typical dress of "satin waistcoats, fine ruffled shirts, velvet breeches and wigs," the justices would have been a striking contrast to the three slaves, who wore manacles.[9]

The court, His Majesty's Commission of Oyer and Terminer, was called to order. The justices professed their loyalty to the king and swore that they did not subscribe to the Catholic Church. Prosecutor Benjamin Waller told the court that the accused had entered Walthoe's house "with force and arms." He alleged they stole a day's apparel: one pair of silk stockings, one frieze coat, one cloth waistcoat, and one pair of velvet breeches, each valued at 30 shillings. They also allegedly stole £350 worth of Treasury bills of the colony.

The accused were Sam, a slave of John Brown; Charles, a slave of John Carter Gent; and Tom, a slave of William Wilkinson. Each entered the same plea: not guilty. The court noted that "sundry witnesses were Sworn and examined and the said Sam, Charles, and Tom heard in their defence." The record does not reflect what the three said to defend themselves. The judges then declared the three guilty and asked the slaves had anything more to say. "They said they had nothing but what they had before said," the record noted. Indeed, in 115 York County cases from this period, not one slave responded positively when asked if they had anything further to say, according to one study.[10]

The justices then made their customary evaluation, finding that each slave was worth £70. Slave owners would usually insist on being compensated for slaves that were executed. Typically, a bill would be introduced after the hanging of a slave, and Virginia's taxpayers would be required to reimburse the masters for the loss of their "property."[11] The men were taken to the gallows and hanged.

Such punishment troubled Jefferson. He would wonder "whether the slave may not as justifiably take a little from [his master] who has taken all from" the slave. Was not slavery a "violation of property" as well? Jefferson wondered.[12] But if such thoughts bothered the York justices, they did not demonstrate such concern. The bodies of the slaves were left to twist on high, a warning to others.

The three slaves were still swinging from the gallows as Jefferson left his quarters in Williamsburg on May 30, 1765. The residents of the capital opened their doors, sweeping out the dust that gathered after nearly three months with little rain. Planters and their slaves rumbled down Duke of Gloucester Street in their horse-drawn conveyances, picking up supplies. Tavern keeper Jane Vobe cleared her tables and prepared for the arrival of the burgesses and gamblers.

Walthoe, having seen to the execution of the slaves, arrived at the House to open the day's session. The burgesses had been droning on for days about predictable issues, but this day's session promised to produce something unusual. Only 39 of 116 burgesses were in attendance, barely enough to constitute the one-fourth of the membership required for a quorum. The chamber was buzzing with talk about Henry, who had joined the House two weeks earlier. Tradition called for new members to stick to the back bench and to say little. Henry cared little for such precedent. As the scattered members conducted their conversations, Jefferson, watching from the doorway, saw Henry rise to his feet and ask for recognition.

The topic was incendiary. The British had imposed the Stamp Act, which taxed everything from dice to newspapers. Facing a financial crisis, the British government was convinced that the Americans were underpaying the cost of what Britain was doing for the colony, especially during the expensive French and Indian War. The Stamp Act passed the British House of Commons by a vote of 294–42, was then approved by the House of Lords, and was signed into law by the king on March 22, 1765, to go into effect six months later. A proponent of the Stamp Act, Charles Townshend, had told the House of Commons that it was time for the Americans, "planted by our care, nourished up to strength and opulence by our indulgence," to pay their fair share of taxes. Not everyone agreed.

Colonel Isaac Barre, who had served in the colonies, scolded the British rulers for sending governors to America who abused their power and "caused the blood of those Sons of Liberty to recoil within them." Barre's speech and his use of the term "Sons of Liberty" were prophetic. Notably, Lord Cornwallis, who later would invade Virginia, was one of four lords to oppose the measure.

So the stage was set as word of the Stamp Act reached Williamsburg and the burgesses assembled at the Capitol. At first it seemed they would merely discuss and deplore the act but do nothing about it. The House was still firmly in the grasp of more conservative members of the Tidewater elite, such as Benjamin Harrison and his brother-in-law, Peyton Randolph. The gentry had tried to walk a fine line for the last year, expressing their dislike of British-imposed taxes while still professing their "ever loving" loyalty to the crown. They had protested politely, with the burgesses assuring the king of England of their "firm and inviolable attachment to your sacred person and government."[13]

Henry, like the country lawyer he was, felt no such attachment and did not bother with political pleasantries. The ruling gentry had come mostly from the

Tidewater, where 140 families controlled a great portion of the lands. Tobacco was the crop of the colony, and it had long been the practice that a number of burgesses got their position according to how much tobacco they grew and how much money they made. Henry represented the yeoman, the frontiersman, and the farmer, all of whom had their grievances against the crown. The Stamp Act taxes would hit such men especially hard.

Many of the burgesses did not know what to make of Henry. He was recognized for his work on the Parson's Cause case, and there was a recollection of him appearing earlier in Williamsburg as "an ill-dressed young man sauntering in the lobby" of the Capitol, appearing as if he had just arrived from a hunt in the woods. Some had been told of his eloquence, but few had heard him speak until now.[14] Henry had written seven proposed resolutions on a sheaf of paper, which he had stuffed in his pocket before entering the chamber, awaiting his moment to challenge the king. He was convinced that he alone had the courage to stand up against the tax. "All the colonies, either through fear, or want of opportunity to form an opposition, or from influence of some kind or other, had remained silent," Henry wrote later, in a document that he instructed be read upon his death. "I had been for the first time elected a Burgess a few days before; was young, inexperienced, unacquainted with the forms of the House and the members that composed it." The "men of weight" of the colony, Henry continued, were "averse to opposition" and were willing to let the tax take effect. Given that no one else "was likely to step forward," Henry decided to step forward, and said he did so "alone, unadvised, and unassisted."[15]

The twenty-two-year-old Jefferson stood rapt with attention, anxious about how Henry, who had celebrated his twenty-ninth birthday just the day before, would introduce his legislative proposals. Jefferson was well aware of the complaints that had led to this moment of confrontation. In addition to complaints about the Stamp Act, many Virginians disliked London's effort to contain the colonies to the area east of the Appalachian Mountains. With 1.5 million people living in British America, settlement in the west had been increasing, leading to new conflicts with Indians. The British government wanted to stop those conflicts by prohibiting settlement west of the crest of Appalachians and ordering those already there to return. This upset many Virginians who wanted to expand their colony. Jefferson, whose father had performed the surveys in anticipation of the expansion of Virginia, had long looked west from his Appalachian lands with an eye toward America's great growth. That was where the future lay, not east toward England. The combination of the taxes and the barriers to settlement was gradually radicalizing the colonists.

Henry rose to give voice to the complaints. King George III could be compared to leaders who had been killed or executed, Henry said. "Tarquin and Caesar had each his Brutus; Charles the First his Cromwell; and George the Third—"

"Treason!" cried Speaker of the House John Robinson. "Treason! Treason!" echoed the handful of conservative members who remained in the chamber.

"—may profit from their example," Henry continued, seeming to find a way out of his own rhetorical trap. He chose his next words and emphasis carefully, suggesting he had the right to voice his opinion: "If *this* be treason, make the most of it!"[16]

Jefferson later recalled it distinctly: "I well remember the cry of treason, the pause of Mr. Henry at the name of George III, and the presence of mind with which he closed his sentence, and baffled the charge vociferated."[17]

The first four resolutions were not much different from what had already been voiced even by the conservative gentry. They resolved that Virginians had the same liberties as the people of Great Britain, including those born in England, and that the right to taxation was derived from the consent of the taxed. The fifth resolution, however, went further, saying that only the General Assembly of Virginia could tax Virginians. Any attempt to do so by those outside the colony's legislature would "destroy British as well as American Freedom."

The opponents failed to defeat the resolution by one vote. Burgess Peyton Randolph, whom Henry had convinced five years earlier to grant him a license to become a lawyer, swept angrily out of the chamber. Brushing by Jefferson, Randolph declared: "By God, I would have given five hundred guineas for a single vote!" George Wythe, Jefferson's teacher—and one examiner of four who initially had sought to bar Henry from becoming licensed as a lawyer—also thought Henry had gone too far. Virginia was not ready for revolution. The next day, the old guard of the House had recalled enough members to use a parliamentary procedure and rescind the fifth resolution.

But the damage had been done. Moreover, word leaked out that Henry had planned to introduce two more resolutions that indeed would have amounted to treason. One said that colonists were "not bound to yield obedience to any law or ordinance whatever, designed to impose any taxation whatsoever upon them, other than the laws or ordinances of the General Assembly aforesaid." The other said that anyone other than members of the General Assembly who sought to impose taxation "shall be deemed an enemy to His Majesty's Colony."

Henry's proposals created a sensation. Virginia had long been considered a conservative colony with close ties to London; if its burgesses had passed or even seriously considered such inflammatory resolutions, colonies with weaker ties to England could be expected to follow. Governor Fauquier was outraged by the actions of the "young, hot and giddy" House members, who he said had acted in "rash heat," and he dissolved the session.[18] The royal governor did his best to keep the matter quiet, pressuring the *Virginia Gazette* not to publish word of the resolutions. While the publishers of the *Gazette* obeyed Fauquier's wishes, newspapers outside Virginia soon published their content.

Jefferson, still committed to the British way of things, had watched with amazement as a man he initially viewed as a coarse person of little education and "idle disposition" used language so artfully to stoke a revolution. He was evolving in his view, growing more sympathetic to Henry's arguments. He had to admit that Henry "gave the first impulse to the ball of Revolution" in Virginia.[19]

A few days after Henry's orations, the French traveler remained in town, hoping to take in the spectacle of the celebration of King George's birthday. "I went there in Expectation of seeing a great Deal of Company, but was Disappointed for there was not above a dozen people," the Frenchman wrote. The Stamp Act controversy left few Virginians in the mood to pay fealty; instead, it was to Henry that many raised a toast. The French visitor spent a few days west of Williamsburg in Hanover County and found "there was a great deal said about the Noble Patriot Mr. Henery, who lives in this County. The Whole inhabitants say publicly that if the least Injury was offered to him they'd stand by him to the last Drop of their blood."[20] Months later, the British government repealed the Stamp Act, which may have forestalled the Declaration of Independence for nearly a decade. An accompanying piece of legislation gave London authority over the colonies in "all cases whatever," but it was soon to be flagrantly disobeyed.

THE REVOLUTIONARIES OF VIRGINIA could not have dreamed up a better antagonist than John Robinson. The Speaker of the House of Burgesses, who had cried "Treason!" at Henry's speech, was perhaps the most dominant political figure in Virginia apart from the British governor. Overseeing myriad estates and four hundred slaves, Robinson viewed the House as yet another plantation to control. He was compared to a pasha of the Ottoman Empire, presiding in his opulent high-backed chair in the Capitol as if upon a throne.[21] As Speaker, Robinson usually decided what measures passed and failed, and he uniformly backed the wishes of the British government. He was also the treasurer of Virginia, a dual role rife with conflict of interest. His financial and family ties spread throughout the Tidewater. The conservative planters were allied with him, while the "hot and giddy" faction was appalled at his power. Jefferson, who considered Robinson "an excellent man, liberal, friendly & rich," was somewhere in the middle, inclined to side with Robinson but increasingly uneasy with his policies.

Henry saw a darker side to Robinson's power. He was appalled that Robinson had come up with a plan to have Virginia's taxpayers refinance the debt of land-rich but cash-poor planters. Henry accused Robinson of trying to reward those who had lived extravagantly and gone deeply into debt by filling their pockets with money from less wealthy Virginians. Henry's assault helped kill the proposal, greatly angering not just Robinson but also many planters who were on the brink of bankruptcy and had been counting on Robinson to rescue them. Jefferson was impressed by Henry's attack, noting how his friend had "crushed" the plan at its birth, which boosted Henry's popularity among average Virginians.[22]

Robinson, undeterred, came up with a secret plan to use Virginia treasury funds to help his planter friends. He kept in circulation some of the colony's cash that he was supposed to destroy as treasurer. He loaned the cash to a roster of elite Virginians and didn't collect most of the debts, an enormous sum of £109,000. The scheme became known only when Robinson died, on May 11, 1766, a year after the debate on the Stamp Act. Many of the most powerful men in Virginia were implicated; the scandal exposed the weakness of the plantation economy and revealed a level of corruption unknown to many Virginians. Many planters could not afford to repay the loans and faced bankruptcy. It was a crisis that would play a major role in shaping the revolution to come. No one owed more money than William Byrd III, whose debt stood at an astonishing £14,921, nearly three times as much as anyone else. (Patrick Henry, by contrast, had borrowed only £11 and Jefferson nothing.)

The scandal exploded further when it became known Robinson had been a major financial backer of one of the most important commercial ventures of the time, the Chiswell Lead Mines, located on the New River about three hundred miles west of Williamsburg. The mines were operated by Robinson's father-in-law, John Chiswell, a member of the House of Burgesses who had a house near the Capitol on Francis Street. The mine's financial backers included Governor Fauquier and Byrd. The officials had hoped to sell lead from the mines to the government at the same time they profited from the venture. But Chiswell had gone deeply into debt to finance the mines, and some of that debt was connected to Robinson's loan scheme. As the financial house of cards supporting the mine venture collapsed, all of Williamsburg was abuzz with rumors about how many members of the aristocracy would be ruined.

THREE WEEKS AFTER ROBINSON'S DEATH, Chiswell stopped for dinner at Benjamin Mosby's tavern in Cumberland County. During his meal, he encountered a Scots merchant named Robert Routlidge. The *Virginia Gazette* would later describe Routlidge as "a worthy blunt man, of strict honesty and sincerity, a man incapable of fraud or hypocrisy."

Routlidge and Chiswell engaged in a conversation that dwelled upon the debts facing many Virginians. Chiswell blamed Scots traders, saying they had provided costly loans while paying low prices for tobacco. Chiswell accused Routlidge for being one of those responsible for the crisis, calling him "a villain who came to Virginia to cheat and defraud men of their property, and a Presbyterian fellow." A fight ensued. Routlidge angrily tossed a glass of wine at Chiswell's face. Chiswell tried to throw a bowl of toddy at Routlidge, but someone intervened. Chiswell next picked up a candlestick holder and a pair of fireplace tongs, but again someone prevented the objects from being hurled in Routlidge's direction. Chiswell left briefly, only to return dangling a sword in his hands. Chiswell told Routlidge to leave the room or face death, as he was "unworthy to appear in such company." Routlidge seemed unconcerned, but a friend nudged him toward the door. Chiswell waved his two-foot-long sword as Routlidge passed by, with only a small table separating the two. Suddenly Chiswell "stabbed him through the heart across the table," and Routlidge "instantly expired, without uttering a word."

"He is dead, and I killed him," Chiswell said, according to an account later published by the *Gazette*. "He deserves his fate, damn him. I aimed at his heart and I have hit it."[23]

Chiswell and his gentleman friends quickly came up with a story: the drunken Routlidge somehow impaled himself on the sword, and thus the act was not murder. A local court ordered Chiswell jailed without bail even though it was unusual for an aristocrat to be imprisoned. Chiswell was to be tried before the General Court, which included members of the Governor's Council. Chiswell hired a lawyer named John Wayles to argue his case for bail. An agent for slave traders and a debt collector, Wayles would be remembered in history as the father of Martha Wayles Skelton, who would marry Thomas Jefferson in 1772. Wayles was among those who had borrowed from Speaker Robinson, owing him £445. Wayles appealed to the judges on the General Court to release

Chiswell on bail until a trial could be held. The judges included Byrd, who was a partner in Chiswell's mine. Byrd and the other judges promptly acceded to Wayles's request and granted bail, allowing Chiswell to return to his Williamsburg home.

THE DECISION TO LET a suspected murderer out on bail outraged many average Virginians. Robert Bolling, a member of a venerable Virginia family, pseudonymously published a letter in the *Gazette* asking whether the judges were acting illegally. Bolling also took aim at Wayles, saying the lawyer's deposition about Chiswell's action was a "mockery." Bolling demanded that an inquiry be held and warned that otherwise a mob might descend upon the judges.[24] The readers of the *Gazette* seemed delighted that the publisher was willing to run such critical letters. An anonymous subscriber, calling himself "Tit for Tat," wrote: "I am a dear lover of newspapers, for this, among many other reasons, that it is a ready way for a man to convey thoughts to the publick." Another subscriber wrote that Chiswell's case would have more impact than Henry's effort to repeal the Stamp Act because it highlighted "the more dreadful consequences" of giving unbridled power to the few.[25]

One reader who did not appreciate such freedom of the press was Byrd. He sued Bolling and the printers of the *Virginia Gazette* for libel. Wayles also sued the *Gazette*. When the cases were sent to a grand jury, Byrd urged Governor Fauquier to use his influence to "punish the Licentiousness of the Press," Bolling wrote.[26] But the jury, emboldened by public outrage over the matter and the murkiness of libel law, dismissed the case.[27]

It was a significant step forward for freedom of the press. Subscribers had attacked the entire power structure, from Fauquier to Byrd to Wayles. The printers had published the complaints. A Maryland newspaper was so impressed that it published the names of the eighteen grand jury members and called them "good men and true friends to LIBERTY." All of Williamsburg now awaited the day on which Chiswell would go on trial for murder.

VIRGINIANS AWOKE TO STUNNING NEWS on the day of the trial: Chiswell was dead. The cause was given as "nervous fits, owing to constant uneasiness of mind."[28] Many citizens suspected Chiswell had surreptitiously slipped out of Virginia, perhaps to board a ship to England, but authorities insisted he had died at home. He was to be buried on property that belonged to his disgraced son-in-law, John Robinson. The property was known as Scotchtown, in Hanover County. So many people doubted Chiswell was dead that a mob awaited the arrival of the coffin on the grounds of Scotchtown, demanding that the casket be opened. The lid was removed, revealing a decomposing body. Was it Chiswell? A trusted Chiswell cousin, William Dabney, was called upon to examine the body. It was Chiswell, Dabney asserted. The crowd was mollified, the coffin closed.

Chiswell—presumably it really was he—was buried in an unmarked grave on the grounds of Scotchtown. It was later widely believed that he had hanged himself in order to avoid facing trial and an ignominious end at the Williamsburg gallows. Suicide was becoming more common among men who faced huge debts or humiliation, in hopes that the debts would die with them. A few years later, in order to pay off some of Robinson's debts, the lands of Scotchtown were sold, including the ground in which Chiswell was buried. The eventual buyer was none other than Patrick Henry.

WHILE CHISWELL'S MURDER OF ROUTLIDGE was roundly decried, many planters, including Jefferson, echoed Chiswell's condemnation of British control over tobacco prices and loans. When the price of tobacco plummeted, the planters could not repay the loans, and British traders sought either to seize property or to ratchet up interest rates. To stave off the British loan collectors, many of the planters had turned to Robinson for cash. Robinson's money bridge had prevented an all-out financial crisis, but with his death the entire charade collapsed, leaving many of Virginia's elite facing ruin.

The Robinson scandal made a deep impression on Jefferson. Jefferson had learned that some of the most eminent men of Williamsburg were corrupt and cared little for average Virginians. But at the same time, Jefferson was part of the plantation system. Although aghast at Robinson's scheme, he was among those angry about the way British traders had induced Virginians to go so deeply into debt. Jefferson believed that these British traders were conspiring to give "good prices and good credit to the planter, till they got him more immersed in debt than he could pay without selling his lands and slaves." The British then reduced the price they paid for tobacco but refused to discount the debt owed by planters. Thus, Jefferson wrote, many planters could never be free of debt to Britain, passing the encumbrance by inheritance to future generations "so that the planters were a species of property annexed to certain mercantile houses in London."[29] Like many Virginians, Jefferson also believed the root of the problem was that Britain refused to allow the colonists to repay debts in Virginia currency; only commodities were acceptable. This undermined the financial framework of the colonies and, all told, led to huge debts across Virginia. The seeds of Jefferson's rebellion against British policies and the power structure in Williamsburg were firmly planted.

With Robinson and Chiswell dead and their financial machinations exposed, the most indebted Virginians faced a crisis, no one more so than Byrd. His finances were in tatters, as was his honor. Seething with anger, and in disbelief that the grand jury had declined to allow the prosecution of Bolling for libel, Byrd challenged Bolling to a duel. Bolling had a firearm at the ready. Byrd bought a pistol from a local merchant. However, word leaked out, and the "two Heroes were arrested." The pair was set free by authorities on promise of good behavior. Byrd would keep his pistol for another day.[30]

What Is to Become of Children—Divided?

NINE YEARS AFTER HE ARRIVED in Williamsburg, Jefferson walked into the Capitol as the newly elected representative from Albemarle County and took his place on a back bench. He was twenty-six years old, ramrod straight, rail thin, six feet and two and a half inches, with a long face and a dominant nose. Jefferson was noted for his eloquent speech in small settings, in which he impressed visitors as inquisitive, serene, and confident. Amidst a crowd, while often quiet, he was still engaged; his head always seemed to be tilted slightly forward on his long neck as he listened intently to the oration of others. He had achieved a pair of ambitions: he was a member of the House of Burgesses and a lawyer qualified to practice before the General Court, composed of the royal governor and his councilors.

Henry, meanwhile, was thirty-three years old and had served four years in the House of Burgesses, hammering away at British authority. Henry, too, practiced before the General Court, having earned that distinction without the years of legal training acquired by Jefferson, but with the experience of taking hundreds of suits in local courts. Despite their disparate upbringing and differing background in education, they represented similar interests in their respective upland counties of Hanover and Albemarle, where sentiment was tilting against the crown and the elite Tidewater class. "The exact conformity of our political opinions strengthened our friendship," Jefferson wrote.[1]

Jefferson was alternately charmed and repulsed by Henry's native spirit. "His great delight was to put on his hunting-shirt, collect a parcel of overseers and such-like people, and spend weeks together hunting in the 'piny woods,' camping at night and cracking jokes round a light-wood fire."[2] Yet St. George Tucker, who observed Henry closely in Williamsburg, wrote that "you would swear he had never uttered or laughed at a joke . . . his manner was so earnest and impressive, united with a contraction or knitting of his brows which appeared habitual, as to give his countenance a severity sometimes bordering upon the appearance of anger or contempt suppressed."[3] Another observer, Roger Atkinson, called Henry "in religious matters a saint; but the very [devil] in politics—a son of thunder."[4]

For several years, the revolutionary flame flickered, and Jefferson and Henry worked with some of those closest to the crown, including Byrd. Jefferson knew Byrd well, having appeared before him at the General Court. Byrd must have been impressed, because he wound up hiring Jefferson as his attorney in a number of cases. Jefferson made a notation in his account book: "Employed by Colo. Byrd to do his business generally." At one point, he visited Westover and studied Byrd's library, counting 3,486 volumes and estimating their worth at 1,219 pounds.[5]

Byrd hired Jefferson to regain some of his lost fortune. Byrd once had entrusted his financial affairs to John Robinson, among others. Byrd said that the managers of Robinson's estate and another trustee each owed him £15,000 as a result of their stewardship of Byrd's financial affairs. It was probably an impossible case. Jefferson would in effect be working on behalf of one nearly bankrupt man, Byrd, who was suing the estate of another man, Robinson, who had died deeply in debt. The case dragged on for decades without resolution. Byrd came up with several other schemes to rescue his finances. He devised a lottery to sell tickets for much of his property, but the measure failed to bring in enough revenue. Then, under pressure to pay his British creditors more than £5,000, Byrd mortgaged much of the silver from Westover. Finally, Byrd took out a second and more extraordinary mortgage, handing over the title to 159 of his slaves, including 43 children. Among those who served as witness to the mortgaging of the slaves was Byrd's neighbor, John Wayles, Jefferson's future father-in-law.[6]

Byrd still had considerable power, retaining his seat at Westover and his standing as a member of the Governor's Council. But his financial situation was precarious. He tried to get help from Henry, telling him that the Cherokee Indians had offered him some of their "Land on the Waters," an area on the Holston and Clinch rivers in Powell Valley in what would become Tennessee. Henry initially said he would be a partner, but later he backed out amid signs the colonies would be going to war against Britain.[7] Byrd's bankruptcy now seemed inevitable.

JEFFERSON'S LEGAL BUSINESS, meanwhile, was thriving. Much of his work relied on the unique combination of his knowledge about western Virginia land deals and his standing as a practitioner before the General Court. He specialized in challenging land patents in which the owner had not fulfilled the obligations of a claim. Thousands of Virginians had paid nominal taxes to acquire land on the condition that they occupy or farm it. The system was intended to spur settlement but many of those who agreed to settle the land failed to do so. That encouraged a new round of speculators to stake claims on the land. Some speculators arranged for a friend to file a claim challenging their own claim, which had the effect of stopping anyone else from claiming the land, and usually helping them avoid the necessity of paying new fees. The result was that property was tied up for years at little or no cost, giving claimants the opportunity to benefit from a rise in land prices. Huge profits were possible at little expense. Jefferson profited by agreeing to be a cog in this questionable arrangement. He represented those who wanted to protect property in this way, and he arranged for a friend to file claims on some of his own property. In one case, he arranged for his mother to file a claim on land in Bedford County, tying up the property for several years, thus enabling the land to increase in value without further investment from him or competition from others. Henry also got in on the scheme. He and his father-in-law hired Jefferson to file claims on hundreds of acres of property claimed by Henry's half-brother. Jefferson charged his old friend half his usual fee.[8]

The royal government of Virginia finally had enough of these tactics by Jefferson and other lawyers, proposing a law to end the practice and, slyly, sending the matter for consideration by a legislative committee on which Jefferson sat. Jefferson eventually gave in, and his dubious but profitable land claim business dried up.

BRITISH RULE IN VIRGINIA was changing. Governor Fauquier died in 1768 and was replaced by Norborne Berkeley, the fourth Baron Botetourt, who died in 1770. Then, after the office was held on an interim basis by Yorktown planter William Nelson, in 1772 Virginia came under the leadership of its last British governor, a Scot named John Murray, the fourth Earl of Dunmore and Viscount Fincastle.

Dunmore, as he was known, would turn out to be the best possible inducement to rebellion. He had served as the British governor of New York, and came to Virginia with a boisterous reputation. One story had it that Dunmore had left his palace with some drunken companions at midnight, destroying the coach of the chief justice and shaving the tails off his horses. A personal friend of King George, with whom he shared a tutor, and a regular at the Court of St. James, Dunmore was a man of the monarchy. A portrait shows him dressed in full Scottish regalia and embracing a scepter as he strolls upon the stormy moors, his eyes gazing at some distant scene.

Shortly after Dunmore's arrival, allegations began to surface that he had had an illicit relationship with a woman named Kitty Eustace Blair. She had married Dr. James Blair of Williamsburg, but the marriage foundered almost immediately and rumors surfaced about her alleged liaison with the royal governor of Virginia. Within weeks of the marriage she moved out to a nearby boarding-house and filed suit against her husband, seeking financial support. Dr. Blair hired Jefferson to mount a defense.

The case initially revolved around the question of whether Dr. Blair could divorce his wife. At the time, there was no precedent in Virginia for a court granting a divorce, even it if involved adultery. Nonetheless, Jefferson began to research the possibility of winning a divorce case by a special act of the legislature.[9] His notes on the case can be read, in part, as a precursor to his argument for natural rights and the pursuit of happiness. In researching the case, he relied on some of the same philosophers and their works that he used in drawing up the Declaration three years later. Jefferson took out a sheaf of paper and outlined the arguments on divorce.

PRO

Cruel to continue by violence by [a] union made at first by mutual love, now dissolved by hatred ... to chain a man to misery till death.

Liberty of divorce prevents and cures domestic quarrels.

Preserves liberty of affection (which is natural right).

End of marriage is Propagation & Happiness. Where can be neither, should be dissolved ...

CON

What is to become of children—divided? ...

We are formed to submit readily to Necessity, and soon lose inclination which we know is impossible to be gratified ...

When divorces most frequent among Romans, marriages were most rare ...[10]

Shortly after Jefferson began drawing up the arguments, however, Dr. Blair died. The focus of the case shifted to whether Kitty Blair should inherit part of her late husband's estate. Jefferson, a friend of Blair's brother, agreed to help represent the Blair estate without charging a fee, while letting two other lawyers present the argument to the court. Mrs. Blair, meanwhile, hired Patrick Henry as her attorney.

The case of *Blair v. Blair* came before the General Court, whose judges included William Byrd III and Lord Dunmore. The presence of Dunmore doomed Jefferson's case from the start. It would hardly be prudent to argue that Mrs. Blair had committed adultery when her alleged lover, the governor, himself a married man, was sitting as a judge in the case. "The suspicions of adultery were with Lord Dunmore, who, presiding at the court at the hearing of the case, might be the reason why those suspicions were not urged," wrote Jefferson, who took copious notes at the trial.

An argument was delicately advanced about whether, as Dr. Blair had claimed before he died, the marriage had not been consummated. Kitty Blair was represented in this argument by Jefferson's cousin, the attorney general of Virginia, John Randolph, who suggested that she might have consummated her marriage physically but not in her mind. "Mrs. Blair has said . . . she was a vestal, but she means . . . as Lucretia did," Randolph said. This was a reference to Shakespeare's *The Rape of Lucrece,* in which the victim says that while she was "stained with this abuse, immaculate and spotless is my mind."

Next, Henry, formally dressed in a black suit and tie-wig for the court appearance, rose in his role as co-counsel for Mrs. Blair. Jefferson watched with his usual combination of fascination and disdain for his old friend. "Henry for the plaintiff avoided, as was his custom, entering the lists of the law, running wild in the field of fact," Jefferson wrote. Jefferson nonetheless acknowledged that Henry had added "one new and pertinent observation," asserting that if the Blairs had said their vows and retired to their "nuptial bed," then the marriage would be considered consummated and the inheritance rightfully belonged to Mrs. Blair. Henry directly addressed the allegation that the marriage had never been physically consummated, saying the doctrine of "tender and refusal" applied, meaning that Mrs. Blair had offered herself "but that there was a want of readiness in the doctor." In other words, Henry was arguing, the doctor was impotent.[11]

Henry's argument helped win the case for Mrs. Blair and, no doubt, greatly pleased Lord Dunmore. The allegation of adultery was moot. Kitty Blair's mother was ecstatic, writing the day after the verdict that "my worthy friend Henry . . . shined in the cause of justice."[12] The defense team, with Edmund Pendleton presenting the arguments that Jefferson had helped prepare, was abashed and confused, she wrote. Jefferson, meanwhile, had taken valuable lessons from the case not just of the rights of man but of the character of one man in particular, Lord Dunmore.

The case of *Blair v. Blair* seemed a most unlikely venue in which these principal players of the revolution in Virginia gathered. But it foreshadowed much of what was to come on a greater scale: the argument for divorce from Britain.

THE BLAIR CASE was among the last that Jefferson would work on before transferring his legal business to a friend and cousin, Edmund Randolph, the son of John Randolph. In 1773, Jefferson and Henry had joined four other lawyers in placing an ad in the *Virginia Gazette* announcing that they would no longer give opinions or take on cases unless they were at least partly paid beforehand. By 1774, with revolution in the air, the fight against the British would cause the legal work of Jefferson and Henry to diminish dramatically. Their livelihood would henceforth depend on profits from their farms and investments—and a successful revolt against their colonial masters. Jefferson, for his part, was disgusted with lawyering. "The Mob of the profession get as little money & less respect, than they would by digging the earth . . . the lawyer has only to recollect, how many, by his dexterity, have been cheated of their right and reduced to beggary."[13] Being a legal scholar would prove more satisfactory. He would, in a manner of speaking, become the lawyer for the revolution.

SANDY WAS THIRTY-FIVE YEARS OLD, stout, left-handed, a shoemaker, carpenter, and "something of a horse jockey." His behavior was described as "artful and knavish." He was, it was said, "greatly addicted to drink" and could be insolent and disorderly. He was a mulatto, meaning he was descended from blacks and whites, with a light complexion. He had fled on a white horse, with his shoemaker's tools, with which he hoped to gain employment. Such were the details that Jefferson provided about one of his slaves. "Whoever conveys the said slave to me, in Albemarle, shall have 40 [shillings] reward," Jefferson informed the readers of the *Virginia Gazette,* in which he advertised for Sandy's return. Soon Sandy was captured and returned to Jefferson, who kept him for another four years before selling him for £100.[1]

In his lifetime, Jefferson owned some six hundred slaves, about two hundred at any one time, spread across two or three plantations, with the vast majority at Monticello and the adjoining quarter farms. Jefferson wrote that "all men are created equal," that slavery was an abomination, and that slaves should be allowed to resettle elsewhere with funds provided by the government. He backed legislation to stop the importation of slaves. Yet in his lifetime he freed only two slaves, and let but another five go upon his death. (Several others ran away and were not pursued.) The rest were passed on to his descendants or sold to pay debts. They lived in barracks or small cabins, were provided with a cookpot and one blanket every three years, and were forced to labor six days a week. Slaves, Jefferson decreed, would be worked from childhood onward. "From 10 to 16, the boys make nails, the girls spin," he wrote. "At 16, go into the ground or learn new trades." Invalids could shuck corn. He expressed pride that his boy slaves produced enough profit making nails to provide "completely for my own family."[2]

Yet just one month after placing the ad in the *Gazette* for his slave Sandy, Jefferson agreed to appear in Virginia's General Court to argue on behalf of a mixed-race man named Samuel Howell, who had been forced into indentured servitude. The case of *Howell v. Netherland* came to trial in April 1770. There were twelve individuals on the court, including William Byrd III as well as members of other venerable Virginia families: two Nelsons, a Lee, Carter, a Burwell, and a Fairfax. Howell was a twenty-eight-year-old whose great-grandmother was white and whose great-grandfather was black or of mixed racial blood. Howell had been forced into indentured servitude because of the circumstances of his ancestry. The law in Virginia at the time said that the child of a mixed-race woman would be enslaved until the age of thirty-one, and that the grandchild would also be enslaved until reaching thirty-one. Jefferson argued, however, that the law said nothing about descendants in succeeding generations such as Howell. Thus, Jefferson claimed, Howell never should have been subject to the law. While he was not arguing against slavery, Jefferson's argument was still considered radical. He maintained that people such as Howell never should have been forced into servitude, using the outlines of an argument he would make in the Declaration of Independence.

> Under the law of nature, all men are born free. Everyone comes into the world with a right to his own person, which includes the liberty of moving and using it at his own will. This is what is called personal liberty, and is given him by the Author of Nature . . . the reducing of his mother to servitude was a violation of the law of nature.[3]

Jefferson did not address the broader question of why, if "all men are born free," it was legitimate for so many to be enslaved from birth, either through forced indentured servitude or slavery. Implicitly, blacks were not included in his definition of all men. Jefferson may have viewed Howell as being white, or predominantly white, and his argument may have evolved from his view that "children of white women should not be made into temporary slaves," as historian Paul Finkelman has written.[4] The court viewed it as a narrow question on the rules governing indentured servitude, although some of the justices may have worried about larger implications for slavery if they ruled in favor of the idea that all men are born free. After Jefferson finished delivering his argument, the attorney for defense—who happened to be Jefferson's mentor George Wythe—was cut off by the judge just as he began to speak. The presiding judge terminated the case, ruling for Howell's master. Howell was returned to servitude and promptly ran away, wearing nothing more than the "common labouring dress" that clothed him.[5] For his part, Jefferson's ownership of an increasing number of slaves, and their children, made clear that his assertion that "all men are born free" was a selective one, indeed.

JEFFERSON WAS WELL AWARE that his slave ownership would be viewed by some as hypocrisy. Yet, like nearly every other Virginia plantation owner with slaves, he could not conceive of a way to live without them. At the time, Virginia's population was about 447,000, more than 40 percent of whom were slaves. Roughly half of the land and property in Virginia was owned by the wealthiest 10 percent of the white population, and Jefferson was part of this elite group. The vast majority of whites in Virginia did not own land and owned either none or at most one or two slaves.[6] In Jefferson's sparsely settled Albemarle County, a majority of the five thousand residents were black slaves.[7] Without slavery, the financial foundation of Jefferson's life would collapse.

Patrick Henry, similarly, spoke about the horror of slavery even as he also kept slaves. In 1773, a Quaker named Robert Pleasants, one of Virginia's most outspoken abolitionists, sent Henry a book by Quaker abolitionist Anthony Benezet, who had written widely on the subject, including a volume called *Some Historical Account of Guinea, Its Situation, Produce, and the General Disposition of Its Inhabitants; An Inquiry into the Rise and Progress of the Slave Trade, Its Nature and Lamentable Effects*. Benezet's book was a cry for freedom, anticipating the Jeffersonian ideal of equality but insisting it be applied to slaves. Benezet castigated Virginia's lawmakers for passing laws that allowed masters "to kill and destroy" runaway slaves and to be "paid by the public" as a method of reimbursement. "If the innocent and most natural act of 'running away' from intolerable tyranny, deserves such relentless severity, what kind of punishment have these law-makers themselves to expect hereafter, on account of their own enormous offences!" Benezet wrote. "Alas! to look for mercy (without a timely repentance) will only be another instance of their gross injustice! 'Having their consciences seared with a hot iron,' they seem to have lost all apprehensions that their slaves are men."[8]

Henry was clearly moved by such passages, though he took little meaningful action. Instead, he wrote a letter to Pleasants in which he acknowledged the hypocrisy of slaveholding but professed himself too tied to the system to end it.

> DEAR SIR: I take this opportunity to acknowledge the receipt of Anthony Benezet's book against the slave trade. I thank you for it. It is not a little surprising that the professors of Christianity, whose chief excellence consists in softening the human heart, and in cherishing and improving its finer feelings, should encourage a practice so totally repugnant to the first impressions of right and wrong. What adds to the wonder is that this abominable practice has been introduced in the most enlightened ages. . . . Would anyone believe I am the master of slaves of my own purchase! I am drawn along by the general inconvenience of living here without them. I will not, I cannot justify it. . . . I believe a time will come when an opportunity will be offered to abolish this lamentable evil.[9]

Both Jefferson and Henry backed a proposal to impose duties on imported slaves. A resolution was prepared to be sent to the king. This, however, fell far short of banning slavery; indeed, imposing duties on the slave trade would have made the slaves already owned by the burgesses and other Virginians only more valuable. Jefferson believed that slaves locally born and raised were more subservient than those imported from Africa and the West Indies. The burgesses argued that the slave trade was a "great inhumanity" that they feared "will endanger the very Existence of your Majesty's American Dominions."

But the king would not let Governor Dunmore endorse such a measure, and it went nowhere. "Nothing liberal could expect success," Jefferson complained bitterly. "Our minds were circumscribed within narrow limits by an habitual belief that it was our duty to be subordinate to the mother country in all matters of government, to direct all our labors in subservience to her interests, and even to observe a bigoted intolerance for all religions but hers."[10] The rejection of the effort to stop the importation of slaves would rile Jefferson for years to come; in a draft of the Declaration of Independence he would cite the matter as one of the reasons for breaking from Britain.

In any case, Virginians continued to hold slaves. The number of runaways continued to increase, especially when slaves learned about the case of James Somerset. Somerset was a Virginia slave who was taken to England and subsequently escaped. When he was recaptured and put in chains for transport to Jamaica, he sued for his release. In June 1772, just two months after the failed Virginia resolution, the British chief justice ruled that slavery "is so odious, that nothing can be suffered to support it, but positive law." The law in England did not allow it, wrote the justice, Lord Mansfield. "The air of England has long been too pure for a slave, and every man is free who breathes it. Every man who comes into England is entitled to the protection of English law, whatever oppression he may heretofore have suffered, and whatever may be the color of his skin." Concluding his ruling, the justice wrote: "Let the negro be discharged."[11]

While England was deemed "too pure" for slavery, the practice continued in the British colonies, and it was the basis of wealth in some English port cities. Still, the Somerset case led some slaves in Virginia to believe that they would become free if they could escape to England or, more realistically, win the protection of the British in the colonies. Thus, when revolution broke out in the colonies several years later, a number of slave-owning families faced the prospect that their slaves would escape, join the British forces, and fight against their former owners.

ONE OF THOSE INVOLVED in Virginia's slave trade was John Wayles, who had represented the murderer John Chiswell. Over the years, Wayles was an agent for slave traders, as evidenced by advertisements he and his partners placed in the *Virginia Gazette* for the sale of 230 "fine healthy slaves" who had "just arrived" from Africa, and for the sale of 40 "valuable" slaves from a local estate.[12] He also collected debts related to the slave trade from many Virginians. As historian Annette Gordon-Reed has written, Wayles "benefited enormously from every aspect of the institution of slavery."[13] Wayles owned a plantation called The Forest, a few miles west of Westover. In 1771, Jefferson frequently visited The Forest, courting Wayles's daughter, Martha Wayles Skelton, a twenty-three-year-old widow whose husband had died after only two years of marriage. She had a son from this first marriage who died when he was about four years old. Martha was described as beautiful and delicate, with large hazel eyes and fine auburn hair. She excelled in riding a horse, using the traditional woman's sidesaddle, and played the pianoforte well. She was, according to one of Jefferson's earliest biographers, well read, intelligent, impulsive, and a "true daughter" of Virginia's "department of housewifery."[14] Jefferson bought a pianoforte from London for Martha as a wedding present, adding a purchase of stockings for himself, while he hurried up plans to build the main house at Monticello. They were married on New Year's Day, 1772. Jefferson told a friend that he envisioned a life of learning and pleasure, the days spent on music, chess, and the "merriments of our family companions. The heart thus lightened, our pillows would be soft, and health and long life would attend the happy scene."[15]

Jefferson's marriage to Martha would greatly enlarge his estate. He would acquire Elk Hill, a plantation located twenty-nine miles southeast of Monticello, where Martha had lived with her first husband. He also would eventually inherit Poplar Forest, a plantation located eighty miles southeast of Monticello. But the biggest gain in "property" was his wife's slaves. As a result of the marriage and eventual inheritance from Martha's father, Jefferson would go from owning 52 slaves to having 187, making him the second-largest slave owner in Albemarle County.[16] One of the newly acquired slaves was a one-year-old named Sally Hemings, who, it was widely believed, was the product of John Wayles's relationship with one of his slaves, thus making her Martha's half-sister. Years later, a relationship between Jefferson and Hemings would become a scandal, and the massive debt owed on the Wayles land would prove ruinous. But at the time, the Jeffersons had every reason to believe the inheritance of land and slaves would make them among the wealthiest families in Virginia.

Indeed, at the age of twenty-eight, Jefferson was on a path toward assured wealth, aristocratic standing, and extraordinary influence in the colony's affairs. He had traveled a great distance since the day he left his remote village, overcoming the difficulties of being fatherless at fourteen and making the most of his ties to the British colonial rulers. Like any great man of wealth in the colonies, he would have his mansion. His mountain had been cleared for the construction of a villa that would be unlike anything seen in Virginia. All seemed perfectly arranged as the couple left The Forest and headed toward Monticello. A snowstorm dumped two feet on the ground late in the day, forcing the Jeffersons to dismount their carriage at the Blenheim estate of Jefferson's friend Edward Carter. Carter lent the Jeffersons two fresh saddle horses, which they rode for another seven miles on narrow, twisting paths. The fires at Jefferson's home had long since been extinguished as the pair arrived in utter darkness. The couple shuttered themselves into the little pavilion and celebrated their honeymoon with a glass of wine.[17]

Jefferson seemed certain a blissful life lay ahead on the mountaintop as long as Martha was by his side. "In every scheme of happiness she is placed in the fore-ground of the picture, as the principal figure," Jefferson wrote. "Take that away, and it is not a picture for me."[18]

Jefferson once provided a telling piece of advice to a daughter about how he viewed the bonds of matrimony. "The happiness of your life depends upon continuing to please a single person. To this all other objects must be secondary."[19] In the years to come of war and revolution, as Jefferson was torn between duties to his wife and a nascent nation, and as Martha was expected to attend to him from crisis to crisis, few adages would be more severely tested.

Revolution

JEFFERSON NOW BEGAN what he believed would be years of quiet content-ment, fulfilled at an Italianate home at the sublime overlook of Monticello. The great house would reign at a central point in a majestic cordon that stretched around him, seemingly protected from the world below. "Where has nature spread so rich a mantle under the eye?" Jefferson wrote in one of his most evocative letters. "Mountains, forests, rocks, rivers! With what majesty do we ride there above the storms!" In the mornings, the sun rose "as if out of a dis-tant water, just gilding the tops of the mountains, and giving life to all nature!"[1]

Only a small brick pavilion had been constructed by the time the Jeffersons reached Monticello for their honeymoon. Slaves leveled the mountaintop, and slowly Jefferson began to build the main house, forever imagining, never really finishing. The gadgetry would appear later: the clock that told the days of the week by the drop of a weighted ball; the machine that copied letters; the auto-matic closing doors; the dumbwaiters. Jefferson likened life at Monticello to living in a brick kiln, the exposed walls waiting years for the friezes and other ornamentation. The original plan called for eight main rooms, the final version for twenty-one.

Just as Jefferson was forever adjusting designs for Monticello, he also was constructing his own philosophy and politics. He was influenced by the writ-ings of Richard Bland, who argued against taxation without representation in *An Inquiry into the Rights of the British Colonies,* as well as by controversies about British collection of customs fees, and the British transport of Ameri-cans "beyond the seas" for trial. In March 1773, Jefferson wrote a resolution that accused Parliament of depriving Virginians "of their ancient legal and con-stitutional rights" and proposed that a committee be established to coordinate the colony's response.[2] Jefferson, who disliked public speaking, arranged for the resolution to be introduced by his childhood friend Dabney Carr, who had become an even closer companion by marrying Jefferson's sister Martha. Carr spoke eloquently and the measure passed without dissent. Dunmore wrote to London that the measure was a sign of "a little ill humour" but he thought it "insignificant."[3]

Two months later, Dabney Carr was returning home from Williamsburg in an unusual late spring snowstorm when he became ill. He felt chilled. He had no appetite. He went to a doctor in Charlottesville, but there was no treatment for Carr's "bilious fever." Suddenly, at age thirty, Jefferson's brother-in-law and best friend was dead. It took days for the news to reach Jefferson, who apparently was still in Williamsburg. Grief-stricken, Jefferson returned home, disinterred Carr from his fresh gravesite, and had him moved to a spot beneath their favorite oak at Monticello, where they had promised each other as boys that they would one day be buried. He wrote an epitaph for the marble stone resting above Carr: "To his virtue, good sense, learning and friendship this stone is dedicated by Thomas Jefferson who, of all men living, loved him the most."

In the months that followed, Jefferson refined his plans for Monticello, with the two tiers of Palladian porticoes echoing the Capitol in Williamsburg that he had admired. An Italian immigrant completed the picture. Philip Mazzei had met Benjamin Franklin in London and came to Virginia with all the proper letters of introduction. Mention was made of possibly growing wine grapes in the Virginia soil. Jefferson, lover of wine and student of all things Italian, was entranced. Hearing that Mazzei planned to inspect property on the western flank of the Blue Ridge, Jefferson invited him to stop at Monticello along the way.

Mazzei, then forty-three years old, was a worldly man who had studied medicine, languages, agriculture, and law—all subjects of interest to Jefferson. Here was someone who had grown up in the very world Jefferson seemed to want to re-create. Mazzei was born ten miles west of Florence, in Poggio a Caiano, which he described as "a hamlet climbing up the side of a hill on top of which stands a villa built by the Medici." Now Mazzei climbed the hill of Monticello, upon which Jefferson was building his own villa.[4]

Mazzei arrived in the evening, greeted by Jefferson, then thirty, his wife, Martha, twenty-five, and their infant daughter, who was known as Patsy. The next morning, while Martha and the baby slept, Jefferson took Mazzei on a tour of the surrounding lands, walking down the slope of Monticello toward a relatively flat shoulder of the mountain. He stopped at the home of a man who owned four hundred acres adjoining Jefferson's property, about one-eighth of it cleared for cultivation. Jefferson urged Mazzei to buy the property, and offered to give Mazzei another two hundred acres of adjoining land.

Mazzei agreed to buy the land and clear it for a vast farm, to which Mazzei would invite a dozen Italians, including several farmers and a tailor. Jefferson eventually convinced Mazzei to plant a vineyard, an effort that would take years and, Jefferson hoped, would make his little mountain range the first place in America to produce wine. Mazzei picked wild grapes, made some tests, and became convinced that Virginia would produce "the best wines in the world." Mazzei would call the gentle rolling farm Colle, from the Italian for "hill," complementing the adjoining Monticello.[5]

In time, Mazzei became one of Virginia's most ardent revolutionaries. He traveled to Williamsburg to be naturalized by Dunmore and saw firsthand the problems with colonial rule. Attending a dinner at the Governor's Palace, Mazzei found Dunmore to be unattractive and brusque, motivated primarily by concern about being in good stead with the king. "I was able to see clearly the weakness of his mind and the meanness of his heart," Mazzei wrote in his memoirs.[6] Returning to Monticello, Mazzei told Jefferson that the British intended to continue limiting the rights of colonists, and that "if we did not wish becoming its victim, we had to arm ourselves, and that the result would either be complete freedom or the harshest slavery." Mazzei told Jefferson that Virginians must be disabused of their notion that English government was the best possible. Jefferson was "surprised" at the notion, according to Mazzei. Since his boyhood, Jefferson had been told the English had perfected government far beyond what had been done in other European countries, and thus the English form was the best. "You did not even dream it should be changed, you had no incentive to find fault with it," Jefferson explained. While Mazzei would inevitably be accused of exaggerating his role in Jefferson's thinking, Jefferson himself wrote that, at this point, the notion of separating from Great Britain "had never yet entered into any person's mind." But clearly the idea was in Mazzei's mind.[7]

Jefferson and Mazzei together published anonymous letters in the *Virginia Gazette.* One such item, written in French by Mazzei and translated into English by Jefferson, told Virginians, "All men are by nature equally free and independent. Such equality is necessary in order to create a free government. Every man must be the equal of any other in natural rights."[8] Later this would be cited by some as evidence that Mazzei had inspired "All men are created equal."[9] In fact, several years earlier, during the trial of Samuel Howell, Jefferson had said that "all men are born free." At the least, Jefferson seemed to be using Mazzei and the cloak of anonymity to test such thoughts and to gauge the reaction to them.[10]

THROUGHOUT THE EARLY MONTHS OF 1774, powerful forces of nature buffeted the mountain where Jefferson was building his sanctuary. It began in late February, when a temblor rolled westward through Virginia, knocking buildings off their foundations, and leading Jefferson to record a "shock of earthquake at Monticello." Jefferson and his pregnant wife, along with their young daughter and slaves, ran outside the house, while others fled down the mountainside, into the fields and forests. Two weeks later, at the mountain's base, water cascaded over the banks of the Rivanna River, one of the most severe floods Jefferson had ever seen. Then, just as it seemed Virginia had settled into its reverie of spring, with the gardens of Monticello bursting with emerald lanes of vegetables, fringed by blooming peach trees and freshly planted vineyards, Jefferson looked west in early May and beheld the Blue Ridge covered with snow. Within hours, frost coated Jefferson's mountain and destroyed nearly all the crops. Amidst these dark hours came the death of Jefferson's sister, Elizabeth, whose mysterious end variously was said to have come when she fled the earthquake or was washed away while trying to cross the Rivanna. Yet in the course of this devastation, joy and sustenance also could be found. Jefferson's wife, Martha, gave birth to baby Jane, their second child in two and a half years of marriage. Fresh seeds were sown and Mazzei's vines were replanted.[11]

It was during this same summer that another storm could be felt throughout Virginia: the rumble of rebellion. Even the gentry, with their vast lands and slaves, were being radicalized. The debt of plantation owners to British traders continued to spiral out of control due to London's restrictions on currency. The Navigation Act imposed by Parliament required planters to sell exports only to certain countries while requiring the use of various middlemen in Norfolk, which amounted to a de facto tax and a restriction on trade. Britain was still refusing to allow settlement in western lands. There were increasing concerns among colonists that the Somerset case in London would set a precedent for freeing slaves. For all of these reasons, many Virginia gentry, including members of the House of Burgesses, believed their way of life was threatened because of policy makers in London.

Elsewhere in the colonies, anger against London was rising as well. In November 1773, British ships carrying tea had sailed into Boston Harbor. Several months earlier Parliament had imposed the Tea Act, enabling the East India Company to export its tea to America without the usual duties. The act allowed the East India Company to forgo its usual practice of selling tea at auction in America, enabling it to deal only with its favored agents. Thus the company had a near-monopoly on tea in the colonies and cut out American merchants. On December 16, 1773, Boston residents disguised as Mohawk Indians climbed aboard British ships and threw 342 crates of tea into the harbor. The British responded by passing the Boston Port Act, blockading Boston Harbor until colonists paid for the destroyed tea.

Without a follow-up action by Virginia, however, the Boston Tea Party may have become just a historical footnote. The British believed that Virginia was its bulwark against revolution. The colony was dependent on slaves, the export of tobacco to England, and the importation of manufactured goods. Virginia was exporting 70 million pounds of tobacco to Britain—40 percent of all exports from the thirteen colonies.[12] No colony could claim greater riches. The question was whether Virginia would lend its support to Massachusetts. The answer came some months later, in May 1774. Jefferson, Henry, and some other legislators met in the book-lined council chamber of the Capitol. Jefferson wrote later that he and Henry were in agreement "that we must boldly take an unequivocal stand in the line with Massachusetts." They "cooked up" a resolution, as Jefferson put it, and on May 24 the House of Burgesses approved a "Day of Fasting, Humiliation, and Prayer" to be held in solidarity with Massachusetts. The Virginia legislators also said they wanted to avert a "heavy Calamity, which threatens Destruction to our civil Rights, and the Evils of civil War; to give us one Heart and one Mind firmly to oppose, by all just and proper Means, every Injury to *American* Rights."[13]

Yet calamity came almost immediately. The day after the House passed the resolution, George Washington arrived at the Governor's Palace, where he dined with Lord Dunmore. Washington was aligned with the burgesses who supported the day of fasting, but, like many Virginians, he also wanted Dunmore's support for opening up land in the western reaches of the colony. The next morning, May 26, 1774, Washington rode with Dunmore to the governor's farm and had breakfast with him. A few hours later, after both men returned to Williamsburg, Dunmore announced he was dissolving the Assembly due to its passage of the measure for a day of fasting. Washington called the dissolution sudden and unexpected.[14] (Some legislators may have been pleased with the dissolution because it meant that they could not act on legislation to provide court fees, potentially delaying the collection of debts from some Virginians.)[15] The impact of the rebellion and the closure of courts can be seen in an examination of Henry's account books. Henry had collected 132 legal fees for civil cases in 1769; this dropped to seven in 1773 and then to zero in 1774.[16] Like an increasing number of legislators, he realized his fortune would rest either on rapprochement with Britain or on revolution.

In any case, Dunmore's dissolution of the House of Burgesses hardly ended the issue of Virginia's response to the Boston Tea Party. Instead, it prompted eighty-nine burgesses to move to the nearby Raleigh Tavern, the great meeting and dancing hall of Williamsburg, where a sign over the Apollo Room declared: "Jollity, the offspring of wisdom and good living." On May 27, this rump legislature of Raleigh Tavern passed a resolution expressing outrage at Dunmore's dissolution and stating that Great Britain was "reducing the inhabitants of British America to slavery, by subjecting them to the payment of taxes, imposed without the consent of the people or their representatives."[17] It was a defining act of revolution. One by one, the legislators signed the resolution, foreshadowing the signing of the Declaration of Independence, which would occur two years later. Nearly every Virginian who would be involved in leading the rebellion, including Washington, Jefferson, and Henry, put his name on the document.

Yet this act of rebellion did not interfere with the Virginians' plans for a "grand ball and entertainment" to be held in honor of the arrival of Lady Dunmore. While Governor Dunmore was despised, his wife was widely admired, her beauty often noted, and her dancing skills considered among the best in the colony. She was the highest-ranking woman in British America, and the burgesses decided to go through with their plans for a tribute.[18] As the sun set, Lord and Lady Dunmore boarded their carriage at the Palace for the short ride to the Capitol, where legislators in their finest breeches and silk stockings waited upon her. George Washington was among those who attended. Jefferson noted in his account book that he took out 20 shillings and "Pd. Towards a ball for Lady Dunmore," although he didn't say whether he showed up. It must have been an extraordinary but awkward evening, with social graces fulfilled, bows delivered, dances performed, and toasts given, even as the members of the legislature that had just been dissolved by her husband talked discreetly of revolution.[19]

Two days later, word arrived from Boston that a gathering held in Faneuil Hall had produced an agreement to boycott imports and prevent exports to the mother country. The resolution had been given to Paul Revere, who rode to Philadelphia with the message, which was then sent by express to the twenty-five legislators in Williamsburg. They called for a new meeting of the burgesses in August to decide how far to go in breaking from Britain.

THE QUESTION OF HOW FAR TO GO preoccupied Jefferson, though not to the point of leading him to neglect his garden. As he noted the harvest of watermelon, cucumbers, Indian corn, and black-eyed peas, Jefferson worked on his most substantial political statement yet. It was two years before Jefferson would write the Declaration of Independence, but it was this document that first cast Jefferson as among the most revolutionary of Americans. Admonishing the king of England, Jefferson wrote that America's government should be equal to the British Parliament, not ruled by it. "Kings are the servants, not the proprietors of the people," Jefferson wrote. "Let not the name of George the Third be a blot on the page of history."[20]

Jefferson tucked two copies of the document into a saddlebag, bade goodbye to Martha and their daughters Patsy and Jane, and headed down the eastern slope of Monticello on horseback. Traversing the Rivanna River, Jefferson picked up the intersection of the Three Notched Road and began the familiar journey to Williamsburg.

Few in the colony were more accomplished riders than Jefferson. The horse, he believed, was the backbone of Virginia, the physical manifestation of liberty. For much of his life, Jefferson treasured long, solitary rides. Unless he was traveling with others or decorum demanded it, he sometimes forwent his phaeton for a favorite mount. He was especially fond of Arabian horses, admiring "their patience of heat without injury, their superior wind, [which] fit them better in this and the more southern climates."[21]

As he rode along, Jefferson could ponder the events of the previous several months, including the dissolution of the legislature by Dunmore and the colonists' response, the day of fasting, which Jefferson believed had gone through the colony "like a shock of electricity, arousing every man and placing him erect and solidly on his center."[22] Now he was on his way to the first Virginia Convention, a sort of shadow legislature that would meet without Dunmore's permission. Jefferson was not ready to break entirely with Britain. He was willing to cede authority to the king so long as legislatures in the colonies were considered autonomous. So he decided to make a plea to King George to change the way he viewed the American colonies. Parliament "had no right to exercise its authority over us," Jefferson reasoned, because Parliament and the legislatures in the colonies both were "free and independent." The king could retain the loyalty of Americans, but only if he recognized that America could exert its own legislative control. The king, Jefferson had written, "is no more than the chief executive of the people," whom he must serve. A single act of tyranny might be "accidental," he wrote, but a king cannot oversee "a series of oppressions" in a "deliberate, systematic plan of reducing us to slavery." Jefferson intended the document to be a private communication to delegates chosen at the Virginia Convention to attend the Continental Congress in Philadelphia. His friends, however, eventually published it, calling it *A Summary View of the Rights of British America.*[23]

As Jefferson rode toward Williamsburg his thoughts may have strayed to the potential penalty for expressing such views. A proclamation had been issued recently by the British making it treasonous for inhabitants of Massachusetts to form an association to present their grievances, which is exactly what Jefferson and other Virginians were preparing to do. The penalty for high treason in Britain had a particularly horrific history. Those convicted of the offense had been variously hanged, burned at the stake, boiled in a vat of heated liquid, or been drawn and quartered. If this did not concern Jefferson, it doubtless worried some of the legislators who would hear his proposal. But Jefferson believed the time had come to end the lethargy of legislature and state the matter clearly.

Nearing Williamsburg, Jefferson was struck with sharp pain in his abdomen, the sign of an illness that had become too common: dysentery. It had killed kings and philosophers. Jefferson believed that riding could cure many ailments, and he stayed on his horse as long as possible. But the episode was so painful that he finally gave up. He handed the two copies of his resolution to a fellow traveler, probably one of his slaves, and asked that the documents be passed to Peyton Randolph and Patrick Henry. Jefferson's courier reached Williamsburg with the orders, but Jefferson's illness robbed him of the chance to explain why they should be followed. Henry did not read the resolution aloud. Years later, Jefferson wrote bitterly and mockingly of Henry's failure in his autobiography: "Whether Mr. Henry disapproved the ground taken, or was too lazy to read it (for he was the laziest man in reading I ever knew) I never learned: but he communicated it to nobody."[24] As for the copy delivered to Peyton Randolph, it was communicated to the convention, and some said that it was applauded, but Jefferson was not satisfied.

The Virginia Convention approved a watered-down set of instructions to delegates of the Continental Congress, while "avowing our inviolable and unshaken fidelity and attachment to our most gracious Sovereign." When Jefferson received a copy of the weakened document, he angrily wrote his objections at the bottom: the grievances were not defined; the states were not required to act uniformly; imports were allowed to continue for another three months. Jefferson's conclusion was stinging: "Upon the whole we may truly say, We have left undone those things which ought to have been done. And we have done those things which we ought not to have."[25] Jefferson's absence not only doomed his proposal but also meant that he would not be at the center of the debate on revolution. Seven Virginians were to be selected to represent the colony at the Congress: Benjamin Harrison, Peyton Randolph, Richard Henry Lee, George Washington, Patrick Henry, Richard Bland, and Edmund Pendleton. Jefferson himself did not receive enough votes to be selected. Reflecting years later on his failure to win approval for his original proposal, he wrote that it was "thought too bold for the present state of things." He was, it seemed, too radical even for the revolutionaries.[26]

LORD DUNMORE, meanwhile, was preoccupied by his decision to wage war in the western reaches of Virginia. He led troops against Indians who, he said, were denying colonists their rights under treaties to hunt in areas that would later become West Virginia and Kentucky. The Indian tribes believed Virginians were violating treaties by settling in areas the natives claimed as their own. After a series of horrific actions, including a slaughter of Indians and a counterattack, the war escalated until the Virginians defeated the Indians in the Battle of Point Pleasant on October 10, 1774, and Dunmore briefly gained some popularity among Virginians who were anxious to settle in the west. Virginia legislators hoped the war would convince Britain to lift the ban on settling in the western lands ceded to the Indians, but London stuck by its position that the Proclamation Line west of the Appalachians should remain inviolate. The conflict in western Virginia distracted Dunmore at a time when colonists were preparing for their own revolt.

IN OCTOBER the Continental Congress issued its Articles of Association, adhering to the watered-down suggestions sent by Virginia. The Congress nonetheless lamented that Britain seemed to be "enslaving these colonies" with taxes and other measures without representation; it approved a measure that would ban imports, and threatened to ban exports. No East India tea would be imported, nor molasses, syrup, coffee, or pimento. The members also said they would ban the import of slaves, although they said nothing about ending slavery for those already in America.

The articles not only angered Britain but also created factions within the colonies. In Virginia, for example, while many residents supported the measures, merchants in the trade port of Norfolk feared they would lose most of their income and many farmers feared the loss of sales. One of the articles, less remembered over the years, took aim at Americans' love of games, gambling, and the theater. In a scolding tone, the article announced that the Congress would "discountenance and discourage every species of extravagance and dissipation, especially all horse-racing, and all kinds of games, cock fighting, exhibitions of shews, plays, and other expensive diversions and entertainments."[27]

It was a slap at southern grandees such as William Byrd III, who was the very face of extravagance and gambling. Jefferson, who liked the theater so much that he had attended daily plays in Williamsburg, might also have taken offense. The article was, in part, the product of a deal with some northerners. The northerners, meanwhile, agreed to the demand by southerners to allow slavery to continue. Loyalists mocked the arrangement. They ignored the order and wrote new plays, casting Patriots as the villains.

The War Is Actually Begun!

ON MARCH 23, 1775, with leaden skies hinting of a snow that never came, the delegates to the Second Virginia Convention gathered in Richmond at the Henrico Parish Church, on Indian Town Hill. Some of the delegates arrived by boat on the James River, at the base of the hill, while others came by phaeton, gig, or horseback. Henry came from Scotchtown, Washington from Mount Vernon, and Jefferson from Monticello. Reaching the outskirts of Richmond, they ascended the hill to the magnificent prospect where the church was set.

Richmond was still a small river port, with tobacco warehouses, taverns, and mostly modest homes, nearly all of them wooden. Perhaps 600 people lived there, enough for the parish to have expanded the church in recent years to accommodate 130 worshipers, making it the largest place to assemble west of Williamsburg. The church had no steeple or stained glass, and sunlight streamed in unfiltered.

Jefferson had urged that this rump session be held away from Williamsburg, to avoid being shut down by Governor Dunmore. Those who entered the church's double set of heavy wooden doors on this day risked being imprisoned and having their property confiscated. Yet nearly every delegate came, about 120 in all, jamming the pews and allowing room for only a handful of spectators. The meeting served, in effect, as the preamble to the Continental Congress that would soon declare independence. Like many of those in attendance, Jefferson was awaiting the words of Patrick Henry, who had become recognized as the voice of revolution.

Henry rose from his first-row seat, ambled to the aisle, and faced his fellow delegates. The delegates would have been well aware of the tragedy Henry had just endured. Henry's wife, Sarah, had become increasingly ill after the birth of her sixth child, screaming and thrashing in such a horrifying manner that she was laced into a strait-dress and kept in a bed in the cellar. Insanity, it seemed, was becoming ever more common. No one could be sure of the cause, whether it was related to a fever or a plague or some other illness. Two years earlier, the Public Hospital for Persons of Insane and Disordered Minds had opened in Williamsburg, the first such facility in North America. But submitting to the hospital's care could be horrific: patients were confined to one of twenty-four cells, with those considered dangerous shackled to the walls by iron rings. Confinement in the Henry basement seemed humane by comparison. Sometime in late winter, Sarah breathed her last. The local church would not bury an insane person in its graveyard, so Sarah rested in an unmarked plot. As Henry was forming his ideas for his speech, he may indeed have had in mind his wife's suffering, how she desired liberty from her illness or death to end it.

Speaking softly at first, Henry laid out the argument for the formation of "a well-regulated militia" in a posture of defense in anticipation of a clash with the king. There was considerable dissent, as this was bound to be viewed as raising an army for war. Henry said there was no choice. "Our supplications have been disregarded; and we have been spurned with contempt from the foot of the Throne. . . . Gentlemen may cry, peace, peace—but there is no peace. The war is actually begun!" Henry raised his voice and quickened his cadence. He thrust his arms forward, crossed his wrists as if manacled by chains, and assumed the appearance "of a condemned galley slave," one observer noted. "Is life so dear, or peace so sweet, as to be purchased at the price of chains and slavery?" Henry asked the delegates, his voice rising again. "Forbid it, Almighty God! . . . I know not what other course others may take. But as for me—give me liberty, or give me death!" At this, Henry was said to have raised an imaginary dagger with which he impaled his chest, and then he returned to his pew.[1]

Henry's words resonated among those familiar with Joseph Addison's play *Cato,* which includes the lines "It is not now time to talk of aught / But chains or conquest, liberty or death." The words were adopted by the American colonists, and later embroidered on the hunting shirts of the militia from Culpeper. A stream of delegates followed Henry to the pulpit. Some urged patience with the mother country. Was there not time to hear a response from the king? Those who agreed with Henry insisted that the colonies had prostrated themselves before His Majesty, to no avail. The king had ordered his ships to block Boston Harbor; he might next blockade the Capes of Virginia. (The suspicion was well founded. Unbeknownst to the delegates in Richmond, Dunmore had written to his superiors in London suggesting that Virginia's "ports should be blocked up.")[2] Jefferson rose in support of Henry's motion.

Then an important but less-noted speech was delivered by Thomas Nelson Jr., the Yorktown merchant and planter whose family had ties to royal government. Nelson's father and uncle had been members of the Governor's Council, and Nelson himself benefited greatly from British trade. But Nelson "convulsed the moderates" as he threw his verbal "bombshell." If the British landed in York County, he thundered, then he, as county lieutenant of the militia, would defy British orders and "repel the invaders at the water's edge." That, in fact, is precisely what Nelson would do some years later when the British invasion began in earnest.[3]

Henry's motion passed, but narrowly. The support of newly arrived delegates from the westernmost counties, some of whom had not been seated at
the first Virginia Convention eight months earlier, made the difference. They
were exactly the kind of members who would be swayed by Henry, as Jefferson
doubtless understood. Henry was made chairman of the committee to form
the militia, with Jefferson one of the members. They agreed that each infantry
company would have sixty-eight rank-and-file members, twelve officers, and
a drummer; each soldier would be supplied with "a good rifle if to be had or
otherwise a common firelock," as well as a pound of gunpowder, four pounds
of ball, and a tomahawk. Similarly, a troop of light horse was to consist of thirty
men, who were required to make their horses accustomed "to stand the Discharge of Fire Arms." How they would pay for such a force was unclear, given
that Lord Dunmore controlled Virginia's purse strings.[4]

Henry was the leader, Jefferson the backbencher. When delegates voted on
sending seven delegates to the second Continental Congress in Philadelphia,
Henry was near the top of the tally. Peyton Randolph received 107 votes,
George Washington got 106, and Henry received 105. The other top vote-
getters who became delegates were Richard Henry Lee with 103 votes, Edmund
Pendleton with 100, Benjamin Harrison with 94, and Richard Bland with 90.
Jefferson received a mere 18 votes.[5] But his authorship of *A Summary View of
the Rights of British America* was now viewed as prescient and his stature had
risen significantly during the convention at Richmond. It was agreed that if a
replacement delegate was needed in Philadelphia, he would be selected.

Dunmore learned of the action of the Virginia Convention and reacted with
contempt. He had dissolved the legislature, yet the legislators had met anyway.
He had issued an order forbidding the election of delegates to the Continental
Congress, but it came too late. Dunmore wrote to his superior that his proclamation had "no other effect than exciting the further insults of the Enemies of
Government here."[6] Meanwhile, the growing call to arms across the colonies
jolted British authorities into action. In Massachusetts, the British sent troops
to Concord on April 19, 1775, in a disastrous effort to try to destroy a cache of
arms being kept there by the Patriots, setting in motion the famous ride of Paul
Revere and the battles of Lexington and Concord.

The next day, an event took place in Williamsburg that has been less her-
alded by history but was of great significance nonetheless. Near the Governor's
Palace stood the public Magazine, filled with arms and gunpowder. The brick
structure was set upon grounds guarded by a high wall and heavy gate, yet
Dunmore was concerned that revolutionaries would seize the gunpowder and
use it against him. He ordered Lieutenant Henry Colins, who was aboard the

armed schooner *Magdalen,* four miles away at Burwell's Ferry, to bring his men to the capital to seize the gunpowder. Colins and fifteen marines marched into town, unlocked the gate, and loaded fifteen half-barrels of gunpowder onto one of Dunmore's wagons. They whisked the powder back to the *Magdalen,* which they sailed to Norfolk before off-loading the matériel to another ship, the *Fowey.*[7]

As word of the seizure spread through Williamsburg, townspeople gathered, muttering about storming the Palace and demanding the return of the gunpowder. Virginians complained to Dunmore that they felt robbed of a means of protecting themselves with powder that belonged to them and might be necessary for defense amid rumors of a slave revolt. Dunmore replied that this was a reason for moving the powder, lest it fall into the hands of revolting slaves. The powder could be returned quickly if the townspeople needed it, Dunmore insisted. Two days later, Dunmore confided to a Palace guest, Dr. William Pasteur, that if the townspeople should revolt, he would "declare Freedom to the slaves and reduce the City of Williamsburg to ashes." The remarks soon were relayed throughout the capital.[8]

The rumor that Dunmore might free the slaves had been circulating for months. Some slaves had gone to the Palace and offered their services to Dunmore. He turned them away but left open the possibility that he might call them back. A leading Williamsburg resident, Benjamin Waller, told Dunmore that the governor had lost "the confidence of the people not so much for having taken the powder as for the declaration he made of raising and freeing the slaves." Now, with the gunpowder gone, many Virginians feared the slaves would be freed and go to Dunmore's side.[9] A militia company from Fredericksburg marched to Williamsburg but was assured that the matter was resolved, so they returned home. Events were spiraling out of control nonetheless. In its April 29 issue, the *Virginia Gazette* included a letter from Watertown, Massachusetts, which announced that the British had marched to Lexington and "without any provocation" fired their weaponry and killed and wounded members of the local militia and seized ammunition. The *Gazette* reported gravely: "The sword is now drawn, and God knows when it will be sheathed."[10]

Patrick Henry, for one, was ready to keep the sword drawn. Other Virginia delegates to the Continental Congress were making their way to Philadelphia, but Henry, hearing of the tumult in the capital, lingered behind. On May 2, at an encampment in Hanover County on the Pamunkey River, he met with 150 armed volunteers. Henry harangued his followers, inveighing against Dunmore's "plunder" of the Magazine, and insisted on marching to the Governor's

Palace to demand the return of the powder. The captain of the militia unit re-signed, prompting the volunteers to vote Henry their leader.

It was only five weeks since his "liberty or death" speech, and Henry in-tended to follow words with action. He ordered his men to march to Williams-burg, picking up volunteers along the way to share in what he viewed as a glorious moment. They had grown to a sizable army, estimated at five hundred well-armed men. He sent seventeen of them to Laneville, the home of Richard Corbin, a member of the Governor's Council who handled treasury matters. The detachment was to determine whether Corbin would be willing to pay £330, the estimated value of the gunpowder. Corbin's wife informed the men that her husband was in Williamsburg.

In the capital, Dunmore learned that an army was on its way. He arrayed cannons outside the Palace and sent Lady Dunmore and their children to the *Fowey,* which had sailed from Norfolk to Yorktown, then called his councilors together to consider their next step. William Byrd III, of course, was sup-portive; indeed, his son, Otway Byrd, was a British naval officer on board the *Fowey.* Also supportive were Corbin and Ralph Wormeley, a devout supporter of England and Anglicanism. The president of the council, Thomas Nelson Sr., was in an awkward position, given that his nephew, Thomas Nelson Jr., had made clear his commitment to the revolutionary cause when he had vowed to repel invaders. Now the *Fowey* lay in the York River with Dunmore's wife and children aboard, threatening Nelson's home of Yorktown with a cannonade if any townspeople should try to interfere with the ship. The governor and his councilors urged Virginians to obey Royal commands and to "exert themselves in removing the discontents" from their midst.[11]

But there was discontent within Dunmore's own midst. One of his coun-cilors was John Page, Jefferson's close friend and fellow member of the Flat Hat fraternity. As the governor and his councilors met in early May to discuss the gunpowder crisis, Page advised Dunmore "to give up the Powder and arms" that the governor had ordered removed from the Magazine. Dunmore flew into "an outrageous passion," pounding his fist on the table, yelling, "Mr. Page. I am astonished at you."[12] When Page calmly replied that he was just doing his duty, Dunmore barred Page from the council, writing that he was "unworthy."[13] The timing of Page's ouster was crucial. He became one of the most revolu-tionary Virginians and would play a key role in urging Jefferson to break from the British.

Amid the tumult on the Council, the *Gazette* reported that Henry was lead-ing an armed band into Williamsburg. Even some of the revolutionary-minded Virginians were aghast at Henry's actions, fearing they would spin out of control at a time when the rebels were not prepared to take on a well-armed British force. They sent messengers urging him to stop his march, warning that he would face cannons at the Palace. Hearing of these concerns, Henry instructed an ally to go to Williamsburg and convince Corbin to pay the £330 in exchange for the gunpowder; Corbin capitulated. Dunmore, unsure how large a force Henry might march into the capital, likely agreed to the matter, even though he considered it extortion. Henry had won his first battle without firing a shot. But he was a marked man. "Patrick Henry . . . and a number of his deluded followers" had "taken up arms and styling themselves an Independent Company, have marched out of their County, encamped, and put themselves in a posture of war," Dunmore declared in a proclamation on May 6. There was "no longer the least Security for the life or Property of any Man" as long as Henry encouraged "outrageous and rebellious practices to the great terror of all His Majesty's faithful subjects."[14]

Jefferson, though not yet convinced that a complete break from Britain was necessary, began to see it as inevitable. Learning of the recent engagement of British and Patriot forces in Massachusetts, he wrote that the action "has cut off our last hopes of reconciliation, and a phrenzy of revenge seems to have seized all ranks of people. It is a lamentable circumstance." Now Jefferson believed that Dunmore was "blowing up the flames" in Virginia, which might have been "intended to intimidate into acquiescence, but the effect has been most unfortunately otherwise." Nonetheless, he was appalled that Henry had sought to storm the capital. "The utmost efforts of the more intelligent people having been requisite, and exerted, to moderate the almost ungovernable fury of the people," he wrote. But Jefferson had second thoughts about this implicit criticism of Henry—perhaps aware that he had also helped excite such anger—and he deleted the reference about "ungovernable fury" from his letter.[15]

Dunmore girded for action. He wrote to the commander of the *Fowey*, instructing him to bring a detachment into Williamsburg. The commander, Captain George Montagu, led forty-three marines off the *Fowey* at midnight and headed toward the capital. They had few arms; Dunmore apparently hoped to give them the muskets that lined the Palace's entrance hall. The detachment performed a flanking maneuver around Henry's militia that enabled it to approach at the northern edge of town, enter the gardens behind the Governor's Palace, and take up position alongside Dunmore. On May 12, Dunmore thought the situation safe enough to arrange for the return of Lady Dunmore and their family from the *Fowey*. No longer feted by the people of Williamsburg, Lady Dunmore arrived back at an armed base, with royal soldiers encamped on the greensward and cannons arrayed at the gate. She huddled with her family in their bedchambers, fearful that Henry and his troops would arrive at any moment.

Barricaded in the Palace, Governor Dunmore wrote to his superiors that he was under siege and could hear the beating of rebel drums. Newly alarmed, Dunmore sent his wife and children back to the *Fowey*. A group of marines also soon departed, prompting a mocking comment in the *Gazette* that "Capt. Montague's detachment of marines (nicknamed boiled crabs) took their departure from this city and are returned on board the Fowey—*to get fat*."[16] The implication was that the lobsterbacks, as they were also known, might soon be fat enough for the kill. Despite his bellicosity, Dunmore was anxious for compromise. It had been nearly a year since he dissolved the legislature. Now he called them to assemble at the Capitol to consider what was known as Lord Frederick North's "olive branch" resolution. Lord North, the British prime minister, proposed that if the colonies paid for their own administration and defense, Parliament would impose no extra duties except those deemed necessary for the regulation of commerce. The proposal was derided as meaningless, but Dunmore insisted the House of Burgesses return to consider it. Peyton Randolph, who was the president of the Continental Congress in Philadelphia, returned to Williamsburg in order to resume his duties as Speaker of the House of Burgesses. That meant Jefferson would be called upon to replace him as a delegate to Congress.

Randolph was greeted in Williamsburg like a returning hero. This man who ten years earlier had opposed Henry's Stamp Act resolutions had become such a leading voice of the revolution that the British government had put him on a "black list" of rebels and Virginia Patriots hailed him as the "father of your country." Escorted by a throng of militiamen, Randolph went to his usual haunt, the Apollo Room at the Raleigh Tavern, where legislators told him they were in no mood to compromise with British authorities. Randolph appointed Jefferson to a committee that would recommend whether or not to agree to North's olive branch. On the following day, the burgesses filed into the Capitol, some wearing hunting shirts and tomahawks lashed to their belts, emulating the uniform of militiamen. They explained that they were prepared to defend themselves in case Dunmore ordered his marines to storm the Capitol. Dunmore, undeterred, urged the legislators to approve North's proposal, which he assured them would give rights and privileges equal to those living in Britain.[17]

As the burgesses recessed and Jefferson studied the proposal in earnest, another event all but ensured Dunmore's political demise. A group of Virginians had decided to break into the Magazine and arm themselves. Unbeknownst to them, the royal government had positioned weapons with spring-loaded mechanisms designed to fire should a door or window be improperly opened, and three people were injured. Blame was immediately placed on Dunmore. Jefferson's friend Philip Mazzei was among those who believed that Dunmore had hoped to cause "a great slaughter and such confusion that the English troops . . . would suddenly have arrived and made a good haul of members of the Convention." But Mazzei concluded that Dunmore "did not even know how to do evil" effectively. No sooner was an investigation launched than some "persons unknown" absconded with the remaining weaponry from the Magazine. Dunmore decided that he could not remain in the capital. Early in the morning on June 8, he fled the Palace, joining his wife and children on board the *Fowey*. He would never return to Williamsburg.[18]

When the House convened a few days later, the mood was entirely against the absent Dunmore. The "olive branch" had no chance. Jefferson, who ten months earlier had concluded in *A Summary View of the Rights of British America* that Parliament had no authority to impose its will on the colonies, viewed North's proposal as a means to legitimize just such an imposition. "We alone are the judges of the conditions, circumstances and situation of our people, as Parliament are of theirs," Jefferson wrote in his official reply. The colonies, he believed, were in a de facto state of independence, and the House approved Jefferson's resolution. With huzzahs all around, he departed Williamsburg to take a seat in the Continental Congress in Philadelphia, where he would join Henry and others as Virginia's representatives.[19]

Dunmore's flight left Loyalists without any base of political or military support in the capital. Attorney General John Randolph, the last Loyalist to meet with Dunmore, was also a cousin of Jefferson, whose mother was a Randolph. Years earlier, Jefferson and Randolph had made an agreement that they thought would last a lifetime: Jefferson would receive Randolph's violin and music should he outlive Randolph, while Randolph would receive a selection of Jefferson's books should Randolph live longer. But now Randolph decided to flee to London. Jefferson bought the coveted violin for £13, one-third of its value.[20] Randolph left behind his son, Edmund, who would become an aide-de-camp to George Washington.

On June 24, with few vocal Loyalists remaining in Williamsburg, a militia leader named Theodorick Bland Jr. led twenty-four men in removing arms from the grand foyer at the entrance of the Palace. The men pulled down 230 firelocks, 158 broadswords, 134 small swords, and 18 pistols without locks, and placed them in the Magazine, now heavily guarded. Many expected a full-scale invasion by the British.

Officials in London, horrified at how quickly the rebellion had grown, assured Dunmore—who they did not yet know had fled—of their support. "The most vigorous Efforts should be made, both by Sea and Land, to reduce his Rebellious Subjects to Obedience," Lord Dartmouth wrote to Dunmore, promising to send more ships to the Chesapeake. Dartmouth could hardly believe what was happening. "The Madness of the People of Virginia," he wrote, "exceeds all bounds."[21]

The Horrid Disposition of the Times

AFTER A TWELVE-DAY JOURNEY along jarring roads, Jefferson's carriage arrived in Philadelphia on June 20, 1775. In the streets soldiers drilled to a drummer's beat and cavalry troops made their way through the crowds. Jefferson rushed to meetings with revolutionary leaders from other colonies, many of whom had been impressed by his *Summary View of the Rights of British America* and other works. John Adams of Massachusetts, with whom Jefferson famously would have a hot-and-cold relationship for the rest of his life, noted that Jefferson's writings "were handed about, remarkable for their felicity of expression, science and a happy talent for composition." Jefferson proved to be so determined and decisive that Adams said he "soon seized upon my heart."[1] One of the youngest members of the Congress, the thirty-two-year-old Jefferson took his seat alongside the sixty-nine-year-old Benjamin Franklin, the fiery Samuel Adams of Massachusetts, John Dickinson of Pennsylvania, and an array of aristocrats and orators.

It quickly became clear that the delegates would serve as a war council. As Jefferson arrived, they learned the news from Massachusetts about the horrific Battle of Bunker Hill, which the British won after three charges but at great cost, losing 226 men, including many officers, with another 828 wounded. The Americans had 140 killed and 310 wounded but had proven they could stand up to the fiercest British assault. "A few more such victories would have shortly put an end to British dominion in America," wrote the British general Henry Clinton.[2]

Jefferson, attended by several slaves, moved into rented quarters, increasingly convinced that armed conflict would spread throughout the colonies. He was asked to draft a document titled "Declaration of the Causes and Necessity for Taking Up Arms." There was no longer a "prospect of accommodation," Jefferson determined. He rejoiced that his fellow Virginian, Washington, had just marched out of Philadelphia "as Generalissimo of all the Provincial troops in North America." (Washington, upon being given the appointment, turned to Patrick Henry and remarked, "This day will be the commencement of the decline of my reputation.") Jefferson marveled at the "adventurous genius" of New Englanders who were constructing a fleet that would "clear the seas and bays here of everything below the size of a ship of war." Although Jefferson clashed with more conservative members over whether to seek an accommodation with Britain, he believed the course had been set, and he had played a vital role in setting it. "The war," he wrote enthusiastically to his brother-in-law, Francis Eppes, "is now heartily entered into."[3]

Back in Virginia, Dunmore's absence prompted speculation that he would soon be replaced. Rumors began to spread that William Byrd III would become governor. Sitting at his desk at Westover, Byrd wrote a letter offering his services to the king in which he contended that he had turned down an opportunity to lead the rebels. "'Tis now impossible to avoid civil war," he wrote on July 30, 1775, to Sir Jeffrey Amherst, under whom Byrd had served in the French and Indian War. "The violent, who are at present by far the most numerous, are in open rebellion & the moderates are aw'd into silence, & have no opportunity to show their allegiance. For my part I meet with many insults, & have given great offense because I will not offer my service to command the army, which our Convention is now raising to oppose His Majesty's Troops." Byrd asked that "when the Americans are talk'd of as traitors, that you will be pleased to mention me as an exception, for I am ready to serve His Majesty with my life & fortune."[4]

Byrd feared that the British would have reason to suspect his loyalties. He likely worried that it would be revealed that his son, Otway, had pleaded with him for permission to leave the British navy, writing to his father that if he were required to remain in it, "I should be the most unhappy in the world." Byrd had refused his permission, and to try to make the refusal stick, he wrote in his will that he would give Otway only a shilling of inheritance should his son should leave the navy.[5]

Nonetheless, the twenty-year-old Otway resigned from the British navy on July 15, 1775, defecting to the side of the revolutionaries. The members of the Virginia Convention were delighted. In August, Virginia delegates meeting in Richmond saw Otway's defection as a way to embarrass his father and to show growing support for revolution. The convention had been considering payment for seventy men to join the Continental army, but lacked sufficient funds. Instead, they agreed to pay only one new recruit: Otway Byrd. The payment to Otway was duly noted in October in the *Gazette,* which announced that Otway not only had joined the Continental army but also had been appointed aide-de-camp to General Charles Lee, second-in-command of American forces.

William Byrd poured out his emotions to another former member of the Governor's Council, Ralph Wormeley, in a letter that reflected the shocked outlook of many Loyalists. "The horrid disposition of the times & the frantick patriotism of those who have taken the lead greatly disturb my peace of mind," Byrd wrote on October 4, 1775. He belittled the rebels who had made themselves members of the Continental Congress, saying they had assumed "regal powers" and were receiving "handsome pay." Without any note of irony, he wrote that members of Congress find "it is difficult for any set of men to give up power," apparently blind to the idea that he was the one who seemed unwilling to give up power. "As long as this can hold everything must proceed from bad to worse," Byrd continued, "'till either we are reduced to punishment by the force of Great Britain, or 'till the people of America, reduced by their distresses, are brought to search for the cause of their suffering, & take vengeance on those who deluded them."[6]

Byrd had another son in the British military, Thomas Taylor Byrd, who remained loyal to Governor Dunmore. Thomas, however, had no illusions that remaining loyal to the British would bring him a significant inheritance. Rather, Thomas had allegiance to his father. He wrote to British general Thomas Gage in Boston requesting an assignment in Virginia, explaining that "owing to my father's attachment to Britain and his daring acts in according therewith, his estates have become virtually useless. Please employ me in some station near Westover."[7] Gage granted his request.

OTWAY'S DEFECTION CAME JUST IN TIME. Remaining a Loyalist in Virginia now was to risk one's life, liberty, and property. The Patriots of Williamsburg erected a "Liberty Pole," on which a flag was to be flown for the Sons of Liberty to gather around. It also served as a warning to anyone who came to the capital that loyalty to the British would not be tolerated. The pole stood across from the Raleigh Tavern on Duke of Gloucester Street. At the top hung "a large mop & a barrel of feathers." A bucket of tar was placed beneath, readying the dreaded punishment of tarring and feathering. Virginians suspected of loyalty to the crown were called to come before the Liberty Pole and dared to recite allegiance to the British crown. This, then, was the price of liberty for Loyalists: not freedom of speech nor freedom of assembly, but tar, feathers, and the ridicule that would follow. A London publisher mocked the Virginians as nothing more than hypocrites, issuing a mezzotint drawing called *The Alternative of Williams-Burg,* which depicted merchants being forced to sign an oath to the Patriot cause in the shadow of the fearsome Liberty Pole.

Across Virginia, Loyalists were hauled in for the most extraordinary punishment. Loyalist Adam Allan, who owned a stocking factory, was accused of returning Virginia's colonial seal to Dunmore. After fleeing Williamsburg for Fredericksburg, he was captured by the citizenry there, "tarr'd & feather'd," and "carted through Fredericksburg upwards of two hours."[8] In Accomack County,

on Virginia's Eastern Shore, John Sharlock told the county committee of Patriots that they were "an unlawful mob" and that he expected "to be employed
at a future day in hanging them." The committee members responded by marching to Sharlock's house, where they found the Loyalist holed up in an upstairs
room with two loaded guns. Realizing he was outnumbered, Sharlock gave up.
The exultant Patriots dragged him to the local Liberty Pole, with the bucket
of tar and feathers at the ready. Sharlock obediently told the committee that he
had changed his mind. He would "declare my most unfeigned sorrow for what
I have done or said," and conceded that they were "a very respectful body of
men, and, upon the most calm reflection, I declare my opinion to be altered."
Sharlock's recantation was published in the *Virginia Gazette* as a warning to
other would-be British sympathizers.[9]

On the southern side of the James River, in Smithfield, a county committee
threatened to tar and feather anyone suspected of Loyalism or anyone who declined to answer such charges. The case of a suspected Loyalist named Anthony
Warwick came before the citizenry of Smithfield in August. The smugglers and
citizens of the small port town, watered by Pagan Creek, were notable for
switching their loyalties when it was convenient. A redbrick courthouse stood
at the center of town, and across the street were a pillory, whipping post, and
hanging tree. Warwick was accused of sending pork to the British in Boston
and gunpowder to Loyalists in the Carolinas. He defended himself by saying
that he was merely a merchant fulfilling contracts. With little doubt that he
would be punished, Warwick did not appear voluntarily. He was dragged by
the hair of his head by the "rabble" of Smithfield for part of a ten-mile trip to
the whipping post. The charges against Warwick were considered and approved.
Warwick was harnessed in the stocks. Nearby were a bucket of hot, bubbling
tar and a basket of feathers. Then the "respectable inhabitants" of Isle of Wight
County "gave him a fashionable suit of tar and feathers," the *Virginia Gazette*
reported in August 1775. Shrieking in pain from the scalding tar, his body covered and his mouth stuffed with feathers, Warwick was dragged from the
stocks. The mob then "mounted him on his horse, and drove him out of town,
through a shower of eggs, the smell of which . . . seemed to have a material effect upon the delicate constitution of the motleyed gentlemen."[10]

The publication in the *Gazette* of Warwick's punishment almost certainly
did what it was designed to do: send a message to like-minded Loyalists that
they could be next to wear such a "fashionable suit" and alert Patriots that it
was acceptable to inflict harsh punishment for support of King George. Indeed,
anyone in Virginia who uttered a pleasant word about the king or questioned
the motives of the revolutionaries was considered a suspect and an enemy. Re-

vealing even a hint of sympathy was grounds for being called before a county committee or the Virginia-wide Committee of Safety, the former acting as county courts and the latter acting as the state's legislature and governor in the absence of British rule. A power vacuum had been created, and in rushed plenty of Patriots, to be sure, but also more than a few scoundrels who took advantage of the opportunity to settle scores or abscond with property.

The *Virginia Gazette* was filled with the names of Virginians who were deemed Loyalists and thus branded as inimical to liberty. In the eastern coastal area near Norfolk, a hotbed of Loyalism, white males suspected of supporting the crown were told to leave for remote western parts of Virginia. If they refused, their property would be confiscated and delivered to the state treasury. In some cases, the local committees targeted wealthy planters who were not Loyalists but merely accused of urging moderation. This was the revolution being stoked from the ground up: lower-class men who did not own property saw the break from Britain as a chance to gain land and become slaveholders. Some recalcitrant members of the gentry who had been the leaders of their towns now were outcasts, forced to leave their wives and children behind as they headed west, prodded by gun-toting Patriots.

Women could also be subject to censure. The *Virginia Gazette* reported that a committee for the county of Isle of Wight held a meeting to consider the case of Mary Easson, who was suspected of giving intelligence to Lord Dunmore. Easson refused to be sworn in or to answer questions, behaving in a "very insolent, scandalous and indecent manner." The committee ordered that a notice be published in the *Gazette* informing Virginians that Easson "holds principles inimical to the rights and liberties of North America, and ought to be considered as an enemy to her country, and that every person ought to break off all kinds of intercourse with her."[11]

WHILE DUNMORE SURROUNDED HIMSELF with a small flotilla of well-armed ships off Norfolk, Virginia's revolutionaries decided it was time to organize a more formal military force. As the British clashed with Washington's army in the north, it seemed only a matter of time before open conflict occurred in Virginia. Henry's friends believed he wanted the job of Virginia's commander in chief. On August 1, Henry and Jefferson left Philadelphia together, heading for the meeting of the Virginia Convention in Richmond that would pick the state's military commander. Henry confided that he was anxious to leave the dry debates of the Continental Congress. According to Jefferson, however, Henry was unsure whether he wanted to become Virginia's commander in chief if it meant abiding by the orders of politicians. "His mind was not formed for subordination, even to a Committee of Safety, or a Convention," Jefferson wrote years later. Jefferson believed Henry wouldn't remain long as a commander, asserting that Henry intended to "withdraw from his military station, after it had served the purpose of procuring him a decent retreat from his Congressional one."[12] In any case, as Jefferson and Henry headed to Virginia, delegates engaged in heated debate about Henry's qualifications. He had no military experience except briefly leading the militia earlier in the year to a position outside Williamsburg. He had cleverly used the threat of force but had never, so far as was known, fired a shot in battle or led men in an attack against an enemy. One contemporary observer, who was probably a delegate and identified himself only as "Cato," published a letter charging that Henry "was totally unacquainted with the art of war, and had no knowledge of military discipline."[13]

Henry's name was put up against those of three seemingly better-qualified candidates: Thomas Nelson Jr., the militia leader who had vowed five months earlier to take on British invaders, and Colonel Hugh Mercer and Colonel William Woodford, both of whom served with distinction in the French and Indian War. Mercer received the most votes, forty-one, to Henry's forty, too close under the rules for anyone to declare victory. Nelson withdrew from the contest and Woodford backed Mercer. But Mercer was denounced for having been born in Scotland and thus suspected by some of being a Loyalist. This time, Henry won a clear majority.[14] Four days later, Henry and Jefferson arrived in Richmond, hailed with huzzahs. Though he did not say so at the time, Jefferson was dismayed to learn of Henry's selection as military commander. Doubts about the wisdom of the choice, however, would soon emerge.

Jefferson remained at the Virginia Convention for only seven days. Learning that his second child, seventeen-month-old Jane, had become seriously ill, Jefferson returned to Monticello and apparently was there when the child died. As he attended to his grieving family and inspected the ongoing work on his house and fields, Jefferson received regular news of the revolution. His Loyalist cousin, Virginia attorney general John Randolph, was making final plans to leave for England. Jefferson wrote that he was sorry Randolph no longer felt "eligible" to remain, and he hoped Randolph would convince leaders in Britain to "put an end to this unnatural contest." Jefferson, whose work in the public stage had barely begun, told his cousin that he looked forward to spending "the rest of my days in domestic ease and tranquility, banishing every desire of afterwards ever hearing what passes in the world." It was not to be. Less than two months later, Jefferson was called again to the Continental Congress in Philadelphia as the divide deepened between America and Britain.[15]

Henry, meanwhile, triumphantly led militia units to Williamsburg, "escorted to town by the whole body of volunteers, who paid him every mark of respect and distinction in their power."[16] Henry's troops set up their tents in the shadow of the College of William and Mary. Untrained and undisciplined, the fighters nonetheless looked fearsome. One group of volunteers wore bucktail hats and carried tomahawks and knives, their green hunting shirts emblazoned with the words "Liberty or Death." They marched beneath a flag that featured an image of a coiled snake atop the words "Don't Tread on Me."[17]

On August 23, 1775, King George finally acknowledged the obvious: he declared America in a state of "open and avowed rebellion." Dunmore conducted raids along the rivers, attracting the attention of plantation slaves. A number of slaves would reach Dunmore's fleet in the coming months, making their way through the marshes aboard makeshift boats or over land. One plantation owner, John Willoughby, found that all eighty-seven of his slaves had escaped to Dunmore. Landon Carter learned that eleven of his family's slaves had done the same. "Lord Dunmore sails up and down the river and where he finds a defenceless place, he lands, plunders the plantation and carries off the negroes," a Norfolk resident wrote.[18] The *Virginia Gazette* was filled with advertisements for runaway slaves.

Virginians increased their patrols, guarded the waterways, and posted men at the highways. The revolutionaries had tenuous control, and there was still fear everywhere—of a slave revolt, of the still-considerable power of Dunmore's fleet, and of enemies from within.

We Must Be Prepared to Destroy It

WHEN JEFFERSON RETURNED to Philadelphia in the fall of 1775, he ago-nized over one of the greatest problems facing Virginia: what to do about the Loyalist center of Norfolk. While the streets of Williamsburg were patrolled by Henry and his band of revolutionaries, Norfolk was the most populous city in Virginia and its most important port. Whoever controlled Norfolk con-trolled the entryway to Virginia and to much of the South.

Jefferson wrote to his friend John Page about the danger, closing with an ominous phrase: "Delenda est Norfolk."[1] It was an echo of the famous cry by the Roman statesman Cato, who said that Carthage must be *delendam*—destroyed—in order to save the empire. Norfolk was overrun with Loyalists who would join with Dunmore, Jefferson believed, and had become Virginia's Carthage. It must be destroyed.

Page grasped Jefferson's historical and literary allusion, both men having been classmates at the College of William and Mary. "The People at Norfolk are under dreadful Apprehensions of having the Town burnt by this Detach-ment. They know they deserve it . . . many of them deserve to be ruined and hanged," Page wrote. He agreed entirely with Jefferson's declaration about Norfolk: "We must be prepared to destroy it."[2]

Norfolk's founders believed their city would be the glittering jewel of Vir-ginian commerce, a great port on the Elizabeth River just a short sail across Hampton Roads from the Atlantic Ocean. A string of warehouses and docks, serving tall-masted ships and tenders, spread across the riverfront. It was here, where merchants tied their vessels to sprawling piers and sunken pylons, that Norfolk's wealth was made. Just beyond the waterfront was a gilded network of parallel streets, lined with some of the most substantial homes in the colonies, the abodes of sea captains and sailmakers, of merchants and traders, all the at-tendants of the ocean and river trade. Another set of streets ran perpendicular to the river, running inland to a redbrick Norfolk Borough Church. A few small farms and a dairy were mingled among the houses.

Much of Norfolk's wealth stemmed from British navigation laws that pre-vented direct trade between the colonies and ports in countries such as France and Holland. The Norfolk traders were middlemen with a near-monopoly. They were typically Scots who were strongly tied to the mother country. Dunmore, too, was of Scottish ancestry. The Scots were among the most loyal subjects of the British monarchy, and were quite separate from the Scotch-Irish, who were among the most antimonarchical residents of America and tended to be small farmers in the Blue Ridge and Shenandoah Valley country. The leaders of the revolution such as Jefferson found a natural ally in the Scotch-Irish, who had fled Ireland for America in search of freedom from British rule and rallied to the cry for independence. But many Scots were considered inimical to liberty.

The most influential resident of the Norfolk region was a Scot named Andrew Sprowle, "a merchant of great reputation," who made the king's ships at a giant shipyard called Gosport, which was separated from Portsmouth by a creek. The Gosport yard included one of the largest buildings in the American colonies, a five-story warehouse with broad stone stairs imported from Britain "at great expense." A large iron crane with a brass pulley system was employed to lift great white pines, fashioned into tall masts, onto the ships. The same system could also be used to slip a completed vessel into the river. Another three warehouses also buzzed with the hammering and sawing of planks.[3] It would be, for a time, the greatest shipyard in America. The British Empire could point to this thriving seaport and see all its dreams for the colonies coming true: the ceaseless exchange of goods and money, the loyal citizenry, the royal standard rippling atop flagpoles in the ever-present breeze.

Along with the wealthy shipyard owners, sea captains and merchants, and a large number of black slaves, Norfolk was populated by a thriving collection of workers who served the ships and sailors. There was Samuel Bacon, a watchmaker who also ran a small dairy; James Baker, a bricklayer; Thomas Newton, a rope maker, Bartholomew Thompson, a tanner; Alexander Guthry, a mariner; Mary Ross, a tavern keeper; and Talbot Thompson, a free black who was a renowned sailmaker. Across the river in Portsmouth, Robert Tucker operated two large windmills, landmarks to every sailor who made his way up the Elizabeth River.

Norfolk was one of the largest cities in America, after Philadelphia, New York, Boston, Charleston, Newport, and Baltimore. One visitor in 1773 estimated it had seven thousand inhabitants "of all colors and denominations, of which perhaps more than two thousand are whites."[4] While Norfolk had its share of transitory taverns, the city had a stable population and sturdy homes, which were populated by "merchants, ship carpenters and other useful artisans, with sailors enough to manage their navigation."[5]

Contrary to popular belief, however, a considerable number of Norfolk residents were Patriots, from the publisher of the local newspaper to members of a local committee that backed the ban on imports and exports to Britain despite the financial damage it would do to their hub. Indeed, when a debt collector and suspected Loyalist named John Schaw was found to have told Dunmore to watch out for a particular Patriot, the townspeople of Norfolk seized Schaw, "parading him into town to the tune of Yankee Doodle." Schaw escaped the crowd, running into a nearby home. Curses were yelled, more townspeople gathered at the door, and it was found that Schaw was "endeavoring to get up a chimney." Schaw felt compelled to appear before the Norfolk Borough Committee in August to declare "my sincere repentance," and he vowed to be "a zealous advocate for the rights and liberties of America."[6]

Most Loyalists in Norfolk were more discreet than Schaw, at least at this fragile point in the revolution, and the city's reputation was attracting those who had fled from their homes elsewhere in Virginia upon being accused of inimical views. Little wonder, then, that Dunmore eyed Norfolk as a safe harbor when he fled rebellious Williamsburg. Norfolk could supply any need, from vessels to food to manpower. Moreover, by controlling Norfolk, Dunmore held sway over the strategic swath of land and water by which Virginia breathed and prospered, the mouth of the Chesapeake. Norfolk, Dunmore believed, was his salvation.

As the heat of the summer of 1775 descended on Virginia, Dunmore sailed a fleet up the Elizabeth River. Three were warships: the twenty-gun *Mercury,* the sixteen-gun sloop *Kingfisher,* and the fourteen-gun sloop *Otter.* A fourth ship, the *William,* was a merchant vessel taken by Dunmore to serve as the commanding vessel. The fleet landed at Sprowle's shipyard at Gosport, to fit the *William* further to Dunmore's liking. Dunmore eventually seized more ships, including a newly built vessel called the *Eilbeck,* which he rechristened the *Dunmore,* making it the new flagship. Dozens of smaller ships, owned by Loyalists in flight from revolutionary forces, also eventually joined Dunmore's squadron. One boat that could have been useful was missing: Dunmore had put his wife and children aboard the *Magdalen* and sent it to London, a move that upset British naval officers, who believed he had diverted it for personal reasons.[7]

The Patriots of Norfolk watched with disbelief as Dunmore's fleet settled into Sprowle's shipyard. They demanded Sprowle appear before the county committee. In response, the commander of the *Mercury,* Captain John Macartney, offered his protection to Sprowle and threatened to "place His Majesty's Ship abreast the town" and use "the most coercive measures to suppress all unlawful measure."[8] All loyal subjects and their property would be protected, Macartney wrote to Norfolk mayor Paul Loyall. The city leaders responded to Macartney that "notwithstanding the Utterly defenceless state of the Town . . . [Norfolk] will never tamely submit to the invasion of their privileges by the dangerous and untimely interposition of Military Force."[9] This was hardly a response that would be given by a city entirely controlled by Loyalists.

Sprowle was petrified about being labeled a Loyalist. He wrote urgently to city officials that he had no choice but to allow an armed ship land at his yard, and he insisted that he was "as much attached to the American cause as any one (but more moderate than many.)" The sixty-five-year-old Sprowle acknowledged his main interest was "self-preservation." In any event, Sprowle said, the British were back on their ships, and he had no intention of letting them land again at Gosport. Dunmore, who thought he would be welcomed by the Loyalists of Norfolk and Portsmouth, instead found himself stuck between the two, moored in the Elizabeth, short of supplies and lacking the support he had counted on.[10]

Dunmore fired off letters to his superiors, beseeching them for more supplies and support. He drew up a plan to have Indians join in the fight against rebellious Virginians, an audacious proposal given that he was known for having waged war against them. The plan called for the Ohio Indians to "act in Concert with me against His Majesty's Enemies," in return for three hundred acres for every fighter. But one of the men sent by Dunmore to implement the proposal defected to the revolutionary side and the plan went nowhere.[11]

Amid this plotting, Dunmore and his fleet were rocked by one of the worst storms in memory. The winds began softly, approaching from the Caribbean, followed by a low hum and rising waters. The rain grew steadily, then pounded the sandy soil and roiled the rivers. The cry went out: hurricane! All hands on the British fleet scurried to lash down cannons and climb the rigging to reduce the sails. The winds heaved the boats in the water, tossing some twenty vessels onto the shore. Crops were devastated, roofs torn off, and people killed or maimed. The *Mercury* was stuck on a shoal as the three other British craft attempted to get near and protect her. The *William,* carrying his lordship, was awash with water when suddenly Dunmore went overboard, either by slip or push, "and was severely ducked."[12]

Dunmore had barely recovered from this embarrassment when he read the local newspaper and decided he could sit in the harbor no longer. He had suffered from attacks in Williamsburg's newspapers, and he wouldn't stand for the same thing happening at similar publications in Norfolk. Now Dunmore's antagonist was John H. Holt, the publisher of a short-lived newspaper called the *Virginia Gazette, or Norfolk Intelligencer.* Holt likely knew that several items in his newspaper would incite the British governor. One article berated Dunmore's soldiers for plundering the countryside. "Is it not a melancholy reflection that men, who affect on all occasions to stile themselves 'his Majesty's servants,' should think the service of their Sovereign consists in plundering his subjects, and in committing such pitiful acts of rapine as would entitle other people to the characters of robbers." Another article notified citizens of a September 4 meeting of the twenty-three members of the Norfolk Borough committee, which banned the export of goods to Great Britain, Ireland, or the West Indies.[13] The newspaper also published a story about Dunmore's father, who was said to have been involved in treasonous activity in the Scottish rebellion of 1745. Bursting with rage, Dunmore decided to seize control of the newspaper. "The public prints of this little dirty Borough of Norfolk, has for some time past been wholly employed in exciting, in the minds of all Ranks of People the spirit of sedition and Rebellion, by the grossest misrepresentations of facts, both, public & private," Dunmore wrote. He was going to ensure that the scribes "do no further mischief."[14]

So at noon on September 29, Dunmore sent soldiers into Norfolk. Marching through the streets, with a crowd of about three hundred citizens watching, the soldiers arrived at the newspaper office and seized the press, type, paper, and ink. Dunmore was convinced that publishing his own newspaper would turn matters to his favor, writing to a British official that he was going to print a paper from aboard one of his ships.

The city leaders were outraged, especially when the press seizure was followed by the firing of a musket, prompting women and children to flee. The leaders sent a letter to Dunmore beseeching him to stop interfering with their rights. Dunmore responded, predictably, that it was the city leaders who have "totally subverted the laws" by *throwing off all allegiance to that majesty's crown and government* to whom you profess yourselves faithful subjects."[15]

PATRICK HENRY, the man who helped set off the revolution in Virginia, believed that he would be the man to lead the fight against Dunmore. Day after day, he drilled his men in the fields near Williamsburg. To his dismay, Henry now found there was something of a revolt against him. Jefferson had heard Henry was "no soldier" and lacked "personal courage." Jefferson's view of Henry's limitations influenced others to push Henry aside, even though Jefferson would later maintain that he had known "nothing of the facts on which this opinion of Mr. Henry was founded."

Jefferson's friend John Page did have strong views against Henry and, as vice president of the Committee of Safety, was in a good position to block him. Page told Jefferson that Henry had been alerted to a report of an enemy incursion at Burwell's Ferry, near Williamsburg, but that Henry "was so panic struck as to be incapable of giving an order, and the next in command was obliged to array the men, and take the necessary measures for defense." It turned out to be a false alarm. Stories of Henry's incapacity, true or not, gave Virginia's leaders the rationale they needed to prevent him from assuming his military command. Jefferson tended to believe such stories and told Henry's biographer years later that Henry's military efforts should not even be brought "into view" because they raised questions that could overshadow his "unquestioned" value as an orator and statesman.[16]

Whatever Henry's military capabilities, the social strata in Williamsburg remained entrenched. The revolution was, indeed, against authority in London. But education, class, and family background still mattered in Virginia. They were all distinguishing factors even among Patriots fighting on the same field against a common foe. Many legislators had been educated at the College of William and Mary, and quite a few belonged to the Flat Hat Club.[17] A sense of superiority over nonstudents permeated some of the membership, symbolizing the separations that remained in revolutionary Virginia, although Jefferson himself would insist later the club served no useful purpose.[18]

Walker Maury, a member of the Flat Hat Club and the son of the Reverend James Maury, who had been humiliated by Henry in the Parson's Cause case, was among those who doubted that Henry could lead the troops. Henry was "a very improper Person, in my humble opinion, and indeed in that of the Generality of the Gentlemen here," Maury wrote to St. George Tucker.[19] Edmund Pendleton, the president of Virginia's Committee of Safety, believed that men of high standing were refusing to serve under Henry, and he declared himself "anxious and uneasy" about the prospect of Henry's military role.[20] George Washington also thought Henry no military man, writing: "I think my countrymen made a capital mistake, when they took Henry out of the senate to place him in the field; and pity it is, that he does not see this, and remove every difficulty by a voluntary resignation."[21]

So Virginia's leaders decided to send Colonel William Woodford, not Henry, on the march against Dunmore. Henry would have titular control of the force, but he would have to stay—and stew—in Williamsburg. Recognizing Henry's popularity among the citizenry, the leaders flattered Henry by saying he was needed to protect the capital from the British. Henry, unhappy with the turn against him, resigned his commission. Addressing his supporters, some of whom wore black armbands in a sign of mourning, he said, "I leave my service, but I leave my heart with you." The crowd at the Raleigh Tavern included many who swore they would never serve under anyone but Henry. He insisted they remain in military service.[22]

JEFFERSON, STILL IN PHILADELPHIA, was beside himself with worry. He wrote to his brother-in-law, Francis Eppes, on November 7, 1775, agonizing about the failure to hear from anyone in Virginia since late September. In Jefferson's absence from Monticello, his family was staying at The Forest, the Wayles plantation where Martha had grown up. The Forest was near the James River, far more accessible to the enemy than remote Monticello. Tales of depredation, of plundering and pillaging and worse, abounded. Jefferson hoped at least to hear something from a neighbor of the Wayles family, Mary Willing Byrd of Westover, who happened to be visiting Philadelphia, but "she could tell me nothing" about the fate of his wife and children, Jefferson wrote. "I have never received the script of a pen from any mortal in Virginia since I left it, nor been able by any inquiries I could make to hear of my family," he wrote. "The suspense under which I am is too terrible to be endured. If anything has happened, for God's sake let me know it." Jefferson's worry only increased, and he wrote Eppes again two weeks later. Jefferson provided a rare description of a letter he had just written to his wife, saying he had made a "proposition" to Martha "to keep yourselves at a distance from the alarms of Ld. Dunmore."[23] Letters between Jefferson and his wife have not survived, but word of Jefferson's concern apparently got through. Martha and her daughter Patsy returned shortly thereafter to Monticello, where Jefferson would soon rejoin them.

Dunmore, meanwhile, sought to transform the war. For weeks Dunmore had been hoping that reinforcements would arrive. He now concluded that he was on his own. Encouraged by the soldiering capabilities of the slaves who had come to him unsolicited, he tried to open the floodgates. Aboard the *William*, Dunmore composed a document he called a "most disagreeable but absolutely necessary step."

Complaining that rebels had formed an army that intend to "attack His Majesty's Troops and destroy the well-disposed Subjects of this Colony"—a reference to suspicions that Patriots intended to destroy Norfolk—Dunmore declared martial law and ordered Virginians to pledge allegiance to the Crown or be considered traitors. Then he delivered an edict that, while limited, freed slaves belonging to rebels who were willing to fight with him. It was, in effect, the first emancipation proclamation in America, nearly a century before Abraham Lincoln issued his broader edict:

I do require every Person capable of bearing Arms, to resort to His MAJESTY'S STANDARD, or be looked upon as Traitors to His MAJESTY'S Crown and Government, and thereby become liable to the Penalty the Law inflicts upon such Offenses; such as forfeiture of Life, confiscation of Lands, ... And I do hereby further declare all indented Servants, Negroes, or others, (appertaining to Rebels,) free that are able and willing to bear Arms, they joining His MAJESTY'S Troops as soon as may be.

Dunmore held on to the document for one week, and then released it on November 14. The next day two hundred members of the militia of Princess Anne County marched toward Norfolk. (The county at the time covered an area extending from Norfolk to the shores of Virginia Beach, comprising a cape that extended to the North Carolina border.) The militia was too small and ill-equipped to overtake Dunmore, but he feared he was about to come under attack, and decided to strike. At ten o'clock on the night of November 16, Dunmore's combined force of whites and former slaves began an orderly march to intercept the rebels. At a place called Kemp's Landing, gunfire erupted. The stunned militia grabbed their arms but had little time to respond. John Ackiss, a member of the House of Burgesses and a leader of the militia, was "killed on the spot," a correspondent later wrote in the *Virginia Gazette,* making him the first Virginian killed in battle on his home state's soil in the Revolutionary War. Two others were wounded, and seven men were taken prisoner by the British. It was a complete loss for the revolutionary forces. "Not a tenth part of the Militia fired," a disgusted Page wrote to Jefferson, who was still in Philadelphia, attending the Continental Congress. "They fled in the most dastardly manner." The rebels needed better soldiers and a replenishment of the gunpowder and arms that Dunmore had seized. Page wrote to Jefferson, pleading for assistance: "For God's Sake endeavor to procure us Arms and Ammunitions." It would be up to Jefferson to convince the Continental Congress to publish a counterproclamation in response to Dunmore's, and raise a regiment of soldiers.[24]

On the British side, meanwhile, the effectiveness of arming former slaves reinforced Dunmore's determination that the "Ethiopians" could help end the revolt. Dunmore considered the Kemp's Landing battle not a skirmish but a conquest, flying the flag of Britain and widely distributing his proclamation urging slaves to flee and serve as soldiers for the British. He visited the conquering troops and returned triumphantly to Norfolk, where he demanded that the citizenry of the surrounding counties make an oath of loyalty to the king.

Hundreds of people lined up to sign their name into the book of loyalty, after which they were given a red piece of cloth to wear upon their breast. Not everyone signed willingly. "Those who could not conveniently run away went at once and took the oath," wrote one resident.[25] Dunmore claimed that three thousand people signed the book, "relieved to quit the militia and the path to rebellion along which the wealthy planters had forced or beguiled them."[26] But Dunmore also confided to the British military that he was in dire need of more trained men as well as supplies and money.

Newspapers in both Williamsburg and Norfolk urged on the revolution and berated Loyalists and runaway slaves: "The publick, no doubt, will be exceedingly incensed on finding that Lord Dunmore has taken into his service the *very scum* of the country to assist him in his diabolical schemes against the good people of this government."[27] An article announced that eight hundred men under the command of Colonel Woodford, "as brave troops as the world can produce," were on the march to Norfolk. "Should his lordship incline to give them battle, we have not the smallest doubt [they] will give a very satisfactory account of him." Slave-owning Virginians were galvanized. For years, much of Virginia's military budget was dedicated to suppressing slave uprisings, an expenditure that helped explain why the colony was so ill-prepared to defend against invaders. Fearing a mass flight of their slaves, the plantation owners published notices that runaways would be punished by death. "Be not then, ye Negros, tempted by the proclamation to ruin yourselves," said a letter in the *Virginia Gazette*. It urged slaves to cling to their "kind masters." A runaway who returned within ten days would be pardoned. The newspaper also warned that Dunmore had a plan to send slaves to the West Indies.[28]

Henry, who just months earlier had issued his cry of "Give me liberty, or give me death," made clear that liberty did not apply to slaves. On November 20, 1775, three days after Kemp's Landing, he wrote a public letter warning that Dunmore's proclamation was "fatal to publick safety" and urged constant patrols to "counteract this dangerous attempt" to free the slaves. The Virginia Convention, acting in the place of the now-departed royal government, said Dunmore's edict giving freedom to slaves and servants was an assumption of "powers which the king himself cannot exercise . . . arming [slaves] against their masters, and destroying the peace and happiness of his majesty's good and faithful subjects . . . he hath broken the bonds of society."[29]

To the slaves, however, Dunmore's proclamation was a revolution. From the fields where slaves toiled from dawn to dusk to the crowded cabins where they slept on straw beds or stony surfaces, the men, women and children heard that freedom had been promised. The door of liberty had finally been opened, and thousands prepared to take up arms from the British against their masters. Hundreds enlisted in what was called Lord Dunmore's Ethiopian Regiment. They traded in their tattered garments for British uniforms. In a pointed rebuttal to the militiamen who wore badges that bore Henry's slogan of "Liberty or Death," the newly freed blacks were given clothing painted with a new motto: "Liberty to Slaves."

Dunmore learned the militia was on the march and sought to head them off at the Great Bridge, a passage over a broad marsh. Wide enough for six men to walk abreast, the bridge carried travelers on the road to Norfolk, some twelve miles to the north. This was the only way for Woodford's men to approach to the city, given Dunmore's control of the Elizabeth River. Dunmore ordered the hasty construction of a fort on the Norfolk side of the bridge and sent a detachment of British soldiers there, accompanied by the newly established Ethiopian Regiment and a small group of Loyalists, who were given the grand moniker of the "Queen's Own Loyal Virginia Regiment."

Until this point, the fighting between the British and Patriots in the South had been limited to skirmishes. What would follow would be the most significant fight yet in the South, the equivalent of the Battle of Bunker Hill to any Virginian. Although it would receive less notice than what transpired to the north, to those Virginians leading the fight for Independence—Jefferson, Washington, George Mason, James Madison, and a host of others—the Battle of Great Bridge would rank high.

The forces arrayed themselves in early December. Woodford arrived on December 2, 1775, pitching camp in front of a small church at the southern end of the marshy area. The road from the church was lined with a dozen houses, which in turn led to a causeway with another seven houses. At the northern end of the causeway, the hastily constructed British fort was protected by two cannons. The Virginians set up their redoubts in the area between the two sets of houses but had no cannon, making a siege seemingly impossible. The only way to dislodge the British would be a head-on assault over the bridge, which risked making the Patriots easy targets for His Majesty's regiments.

For several days, the British and Virginia sides dug in. Dunmore became alarmed at intelligence—false, it turned out—that the Virginians had obtained cannons. He also heard, correctly, that the Virginians were to be reinforced. He did not know that the Virginians already had assembled some nine hundred men, many of them young and largely untested in battle. The combined British force of regulars, officers, a naval attachment, and the Ethiopian Regiment was estimated at slightly less than seven hundred. Dunmore ordered the attack to begin the following morning.

The fearsome-looking British grenadiers, dressed in their black pants, red jackets, and tall hats made of bearskin, carried long muskets with fixed bayonets and were commanded by a tall, genteel captain named Charles Fordyce. The British wheeled their two cannons into place by dawn of December 9. The light forces prepared to charge. The grenadiers assumed position. Behind them were the Queen's Own Loyal Virginia Regiment and the freed slaves of the Ethiopian Regiment. The planks of the bridge, taken up earlier to prevent an assault by the Virginians, were put back in place.

Across the causeway, the Virginians, stunned at the sudden movement, were called to arms from their tents. Scurrying to take positions, not knowing the size of the British cannons or the depth of the opposing force, the Virginians loaded their muskets. Drummers from both sides strapped on their kits, and soon the rhythmic beating echoed across the marsh, calling the men to battle. Fordyce, acting on orders that presumably came from Dunmore, led the grenadiers across. In a strong, steady march, the first wave of British fired at the Virginians, reloading sharply in time, while the next row of men prepared to level their shot. The Virginians had been instructed to hold their fire until the last possible moment. Now, with British bullets and grapeshot whistling across the divide and the rising sun glistening off the water, the Virginians let loose. Fordyce was hit. Startled, he appeared merely to brush dirt from one of his legs. Reaching for his hat, Fordyce waved it in the air, marched forward, and shouted, "The day is our own!" A Virginia officer ordered his complement of men to train their guns on Fordyce as he strode forward to within fifteen feet of the defenders' breastworks. In the resulting volley of bullets, fourteen were said to have found their way to the target, riddling the British captain's body with such force that he was thrown backward. He died as an officer was told to, leading his men. But he had also led them into disaster. The British, no longer protected by their fort, were exposed in a tight mass. The Virginians behind the breastworks fired at them and could hardly miss. British fell upon the bridge, some to the soil, others into the marsh. The shooting gallery envisioned by the British had been reversed. Some of the British soldiers cried out to the Americans, pleading for their lives.

Lieutenant Colonel Edward Stevens of the Culpeper Minutemen led one hundred men to a spot across from a British battery and ordered them to open fire. When they reached the fort, Stevens found his Loyalist nephew, Lieutenant Peter Leslie, gasping his last breath. Though barely thirty minutes had passed, they were the bloodiest these men had ever seen. The fight was over, the way to Norfolk cleared. It was a stunning victory. A lone Virginian had injured a finger. The British had 102 men killed and wounded, according to an account recorded by a Virginia officer. Dunmore claimed only 17 dead, but he apparently tallied only the deaths of British regulars, not Virginia Loyalists or members of the Ethiopian Regiment; the former slaves were armed poorly and, it seemed, disproportionately sacrificed.[30]

The Virginians captured many of the surviving members of the Ethiopian Regiment and decided to make examples of them, selling thirty-two into slavery in the Caribbean. The Virginia Convention passed a resolution that decreed death to "all Negro or other Slaves, conspiring to rebel or make insurrection."

As for Dunmore, who stayed far from the fight, he was variously described as depressed, livid, or raving like a madman. He blamed his subordinates for the disaster while insisting to superiors that the Virginians had made little progress. But the one-sided nature of the battle helped galvanize opposition to British rule. Some Virginians who had considered joining Dunmore decided to reject the Loyalist banner. At the same time, revolutionary leaders cited the battle as evidence that Dunmore would step up his efforts to encourage slaves to flee their masters and enlist with him. "Lord Dunmore's unparalleled conduct in Virginia has, a few Scotch excepted, united every man in the Colony," Richard Henry Lee wrote.[31]

Washington, who feared that all of Mount Vernon's slaves as well as many indentured servants would escape if they had the chance, was aghast at Dunmore's continued presence. The general had reviewed letters written by Dunmore that had been intercepted by Continental forces. In one of the letters, Dunmore boasted that three hundred slaves had fled their masters to join the Ethiopian Regiment in one fourteen-day period, giving Dunmore confidence that he would soon "reduce this Colony to a proper sense of their duty."[32]

Sitting at his winter headquarters in Cambridge, Washington dashed off a letter on December 26 to Lee. Slaves and servants must be convinced "of the impotency of his designs," Washington wrote of Dunmore. "If my Dear Sir that man is not crushed before spring," Washington wrote, "he will become the most formidable enemy America has; his strength will increase as a snowball by rolling." Forcing Dunmore back to his ship was not sufficient, Washington added. "Nothing less than depriving him life or liberty will secure peace to Virginia."[33]

WASHINGTON'S CONCERNS were well founded. A few days later, Dunmore was aboard the *William,* eyeing the rebels encamped in Norfolk. The city was barren, commerce at a halt, the streets patrolled. Militiamen, taking positions at the second-story windows of the city's grandest houses, steadied their long guns and surveyed the enemy in the harbor. The Virginians could hardly match the firepower of the British vessels, but they had proven the havoc they could wreak.

Dunmore's fleet, accompanied by dozens of private ships captained by British sympathizers, had been the subject of small attacks for days. A sharpshooter harassed the British with terrifying accuracy. The Americans, meanwhile, grew in strength as they came under the command of a Continental officer, Colonel Robert Howe of North Carolina, who combined troops from his state with those from Virginia. Dunmore and the eight hundred or so people on the British vessels were gradually starving, deprived of supplies and unable to go safely on shore. Dunmore issued an ultimatum: let the British gather food or Norfolk would be burned. When city leaders refused, Dunmore vowed to begin the cannonade. The city, with its "costly, elegantly furnished and commodious residences, with fine gardens, and every convenience that wealth could procure," would be set aflame. The British sympathizers who had escaped to Dunmore's ships were aghast. Many owned homes or other property in Norfolk. They told Dunmore that the cannonade should last long enough only to force the rebels from the town.[34]

Inside Norfolk, meanwhile, it was clear to those who had remained that battle seemed inevitable. At around 4:00 p.m., James Nicholson was standing near the riverfront warehouses when British cannon fire erupted. Warehouses stocked with tar, pitch, and molasses burst into flames. The British targets turned out to be buildings once controlled by British sympathizers, setting off a rampage of looting by local revolutionaries, some of them drunk on rum. They stormed houses and came away "loaded with plunder," Nicholson later testified."[35] The British cannonade went on for hours. But the real devastation would come from within.

At 10:00 p.m. John Rogers, a member of the local revolutionary militia, arrived to find several houses on fire. He rushed to investigate. Some Patriots had retaliated for the bombardment by setting fire to various homes, out of either belief that the owner was a British sympathizer or concern that the home would be occupied by the enemy.

"The enemy has set fire to the town," Rogers told a militia comrade as he arrived at one blazing structure.

"That was not the enemy," the fellow militiaman replied. It "was our own people."

Rogers was stunned. Walking down Main Street, he came to watchmaker Samuel Bacon's side business, a small dairy with a pigeon house on top. Rogers saw several militia soldiers "preparing to set fire" to Bacon's house, and he spent many minutes "endeavoring to dissuade them from so doing." One of the soldiers responded that it was "better to destroy the Town" than allow the British sanctuary in Norfolk. Thus, "the house was set on fire and burnt."[36]

Confusion reigned. Robert Smythe, a member of the Virginia brigade, watched some of his fellow soldiers take rum from the houses, proclaiming that officers told them they "were at liberty to plunder the inhabitants."[37] Smythe had heard of no such leeway granted by the officers and it seemed doubtful that such plundering was encouraged. William Chisholm was at his home near Norfolk's distillery when an officer of the Virginia troops knocked on his door. The officer ordered Chisholm to leave his home within forty-eight hours because the soldiers had orders "to burn all of the houses between Kemp's Landing and the Cape [Henry], which were within a mile of the water." Chisholm and his neighbors promptly fled and "encamped in the woods."[38] Women and children could be seen streaming to the countryside, having loaded wagons with valuables even as cannon fire echoed along the river.[39] One resident, William Goodchild, had a small fortune in Spanish coin. He poured the treasure into a chest and buried it by his house, which would soon be set aflame.

Three days later, on January 3, a resident named William Ivey saw several houses being burned. He recognized them as belonging "to persons friendly to the American cause" and raced to find a Virginia officer to declare that a mistake was being made. Ivey "remonstrated with him the impropriety of burning the houses of such persons." The officer harshly responded that "all the houses were to be destroyed." As the argument escalated, Colonel Howe, the American commander, arrived and asked what was happening. Upon being informed that Ivey was questioning the propriety of setting all the houses ablaze, Howe threatened Ivey "with confinement in the Guard House for his giving his opinion." Ivey thus watched in silence as the militia entered the home of Captain George Abyvon, a well-known merchant, and the city's former mayor, who would later be certified by Virginia authorities as a Patriot. Ivey saw the soldiers set a torch to the elegant staircase, which quickly became engulfed in flames, tinder for the fire that soon destroyed Abyvon's house.[40]

In the ensuing days, most of those who had remained in Norfolk streamed out of the smoldering city. British sympathizers rowed to Dunmore's fleet or headed into the countryside, while Patriots either left town or tried to defend their property. Some militia units patrolled the area, occasionally burning dwellings that belonged to sympathizers or might be used by Dunmore. Hundreds of homes had been destroyed, but upward of four hundred were still standing in Norfolk, more than enough to house the British force still stationed just off the riverfront. The Virginians now faced a momentous decision. Should they devote their modest military resources to defending Norfolk, repopulate the city, and try to oust Dunmore's troops? Or should they fulfill Jefferson's prophecy and destroy what remained of the jewel of the Elizabeth River?

In mid-January, Edmund Pendleton, president of Virginia's Committee of Safety, wrote to Colonel Woodford that "it was too shocking to think of our making a conflagration of our own Town." However, given the concern that Dunmore would seek shelter there, Pendleton said legislators were considering a resolution "for demolishing the remaining buildings in Town and suburbs . . . I do not see the propriety of leaving such comfortable lodgings to our enemy." Nonetheless, a resolution to destroy Norfolk failed on January 15.[41] Those wanting the destruction of Norfolk kept pushing. The vice president of the Committee of Safety was none other than Jefferson's friend John Page, who had been urging the destruction of the city for weeks. The revolutionary legislators took the matter up on the following day in a private session. The decision was recorded in a document not published until many years later. It revealed that the legislators not only ordered the destruction of the city but realized the impact it would have on the city's residents. The legislators secretly required that an assessment of the value of every house be undertaken before destruction. In that way, it was theorized, the Patriots of Norfolk would be repaid for losing their homes. "Resolved, that the commanding officer of the troops at Norfolk . . . give notice to the inhabitants to remove with their effects . . . and when the Inhabitants are removed that he cause all such Houses to be demolished as in his judgment may be useful to our enemies."[42]

The Virginia Convention had made their decision: Norfolk, indeed, must be destroyed. Colonel Howe ordered that the units assemble near Norfolk. The soldiers swarmed the city, setting fires as they headed up Bermuda Street, Catherine Street, Church Street. The conflagration could be seen miles across the Tidewater.

When it was over, by some accounts, not a single structure remained fully intact. A portion of the Norfolk Borough Church had survived, but rubble was everywhere—chalky piles of brick from the once-grand houses, smoldering wood from the wharves. During all the years of the Revolutionary War, with the destruction it wreaked on Boston, New York, Philadelphia, and Charleston, the devastation of Norfolk was the most complete. For years afterward, the burning of Norfolk often would be attributed to Dunmore's cannonade. But the story behind the city's destruction was a darker tale, as so many residents later swore in depositions to a Virginia commission. Few felt sorry for British sympathizers whose homes or businesses were destroyed. However, scores of those who sought reimbursement for damages swore that they were Patriots whose homes had been destroyed by Virginia's own soldiers. That number was much larger than anticipated. After some hand-wringing, Virginia's leaders authorized a commission to investigate the claims.

At the end of their investigation, the commissioners produced a report remarkable for its scope, detail, and brutal honesty. They concluded that hundreds of Norfolk residents were indeed Patriots and that most of the destruction was caused by Virginia's soldiers. They produced a chart that showed Dunmore's troops had destroyed 32 houses on November 30, 1775, another 19 houses in the famous fight on January 1, 1776, and 3 more on January 21, 1776. By contrast, the commissioners found that the "troops of the state" had destroyed 863 houses before January 15, 1776, and that the remaining 416 were destroyed in February by secret order of the Virginia Convention. A typical entry described the loss suffered by Samuel Bacon, whose seven buildings were listed as being destroyed by the "troops of the State and orders of the convention."[43]

The report was so potentially politically damaging that it was immediately suppressed. If word leaked out that Americans themselves were responsible for so much of the burning of Norfolk, it might undermine the cause of revolution. At the least, it would have proven deeply embarrassing to those who first failed to defend the city and then ordered its destruction. By one account, the residents of Norfolk eventually were reimbursed by Virginia, but with "depreciated paper money, which was equivalent to a total loss."[44]

The commission's report was not made public until 1836, ten years after Jefferson's death, and even then in the form of a summary buried in an obscure Virginia legislative journal. The detailed depositions about the devastation would be left unpublished and nearly forgotten for decades.

FOR ALL ITS TRAGEDY AND UPHEAVAL, the burning of Norfolk accomplished what Jefferson and Page had hoped. Dunmore's haven was no more. His fleet abandoned Norfolk, sailed up the Elizabeth River, and by the middle of February 1776 was circling the waters off Hampton. For a brief moment, Dunmore believed that a British general, Henry Clinton, would rescue him. But when Clinton entered Chesapeake Bay on a trip to the south, he offered little assistance, instead expressing dismay at Dunmore's seemingly hopeless position.

Dunmore was livid at Clinton's refusal to remain to help him, writing of his "inexpressible mortification" that Clinton was headed to North Carolina, "a Most insignificant Province," while Virginia, "the first Colony on the Continent, both in its riches and power, is totally neglected." Dunmore complained to his superior, Lord Dartmouth, that he had been "imprisoned on board a Ship between eight and Nine Months and now left without a hope of relief either to myself, or the many unhappy friends to government that are now afloat suffering with me."[1]

Dunmore did, however, convince Clinton to leave behind a man whom Dunmore hoped could help him retake Virginia: Thomas Taylor Byrd, the Loyalist son of William Byrd III. The twenty-four-year-old Thomas, descendant of one the greatest slaveholding families in America, was named commander of Dunmore's Ethiopian Regiment of freed slaves. In theory, only the slaves of revolutionaries had been freed by Dunmore, but a number of slaves of Loyalist masters did not make the distinction. Indeed, one of the slaves who joined the Ethiopian Regiment was named William Byrd, indicating that he, or someone in his family, had been owned by the Byrds.

Thomas wrote to his father and vowed to remain loyal to the British, in contrast to his brother, Otway. The irony must have been deeply felt. By following his father's wish to remain loyal, Thomas's job now was to encourage the flight and arming of slaves, something his father could hardly countenance even if it did help the Loyalist cause. "My Lord Dunmore expressed a desire to have me with him," Thomas explained to his father. "His Lordship has done me the honour to appoint me Major to a Corps that he is raising here, which I shall acquit myself to the best of my Abilities for the Confidence his Lordship has been pleased to repose in me." Thomas added that Dunmore "presents his compliments to you" and signed the letter, "your Most Dutiful Son T. T. Byrd."[2]

A month later, on March 30, 1776, Dunmore indicated how heavily he was relying on Thomas Byrd's detachment, writing, "I have been endeavoring to raise two regiments here—one of White People, the other of Black. The former goes on very slowly, but the latter very well."[3]

The risks for slaves were enormous. Three runaway slaves approached a ship, thinking it belonged to the British, and promised to "spend their last drop of blood in Lord Dunmore's service." The ship, however, belonged to the Virginians, and the three were jailed. Two were promptly sentenced to death. They "will be executed in a few days, as an example to others," the *Virginia Gazette* reported. The newspaper derided Dunmore for encouraging slaves to flee and said it was anxiously awaiting the arrival of General Charles Lee, the second-highest ranking man in the Continental army. The newspaper added sarcastically that it hoped Lee would capture Dunmore and thus "provide *our governor* with a more suitable household, agreeable to his *high birth* and *distinguished merit*."[4]

General Lee arrived in Williamsburg shortly thereafter, attended by his aide-de-camp Otway Byrd. Thus, at nearly the same moment, two Byrd sons had arrived in Virginia, serving on opposing sides, headed for what appeared to be a decisive battle on their home soil. Several weeks later, General Lee sailed with Otway on a reconnaissance mission to ascertain Dunmore's strength. During this mission, the two Byrd brothers "came close to shooting at each other," according to a family history.[5] Lee then sailed off with Otway Byrd to the Carolinas. Dunmore sailed with his force, including Thomas Byrd and the Ethiopian Regiment, to Gwynn's Island, at the mouth of the Piankatank River, about thirty miles north of Norfolk, and dug into a defensive position.

THE LEADERS OF THE REVOLUTION saw the destruction of Norfolk as the concluding argument for independence, and used it to their advantage. Believing that the British were almost entirely responsible for the devastation, Samuel Adams wrote that "the cannonading [of] the Town of Norfolk . . . will prevail more than a long train of Reasoning to accomplish a Confederation." In a particularly strident letter George Washington wrote that "the destruction of Norfolk, and threatened devastation of other places, will have no other effect than to unite the whole country in one indissoluble band against a Nation which seems to be lost to every sense of virtue, and those feelings which distinguish a civilized people from the most barbarous savages." The assault on Norfolk,

Washington concluded, was a "flaming argument" that would win over those still wavering on the question of independence.[6] Jefferson, too, justified independence partly on grounds that the British were burning towns at will.

Jefferson himself had been notably absent during much of the fight over Norfolk. For months, he struggled to balance the needs of family and the revolution. He had traveled from Philadelphia to Richmond, went to Monticello at the time that his daughter Jane died, and then returned to Philadelphia. (It was during Jefferson's last visit to the Continental Congress that Martha had gone to her childhood home on the James River, The Forest, prompting Jefferson to worry about her safety. Martha and her daughter Patsy then returned to Monticello.) By late December, Jefferson again left Philadelphia and rejoined his family at Monticello. For the next four months, Jefferson was out of view, writing no known letters. It was a time of great uncertainty: Dunmore was still at large in Virginia, the nascent revolution was in a perilous state, the Jefferson family was still recovering from the death of little Jane, and Martha's frail condition was of increasing concern. Yet some Virginians chided Jefferson for retreating to the comfort of his home and the "pleasures" of his wife, perhaps unaware how frightened Jefferson was about the state of Martha's health. During much of this time, Jefferson was on his mountain, suffering from a nearly incapacitating migraine headache. Then, toward the end of this interregnum came word that Jefferson's mother had died. Jefferson had had a cool relationship with his mother, who was regarded by some as having Loyalist sympathies. He wrote little about her and made only passing reference to her death. One biographer, Fawn M. Brodie, has suggested that Jefferson felt a sense of freedom and independence following his mother's death. At the same time, the defeat of Dunmore in Norfolk gave Jefferson more confidence that the revolution would succeed. Returning to Philadelphia in May 1776, Jefferson was newly energized to begin the work for which he would become best known. He wrote to Page that he had been "so long out of the political world that I am almost a new man in it."[7] Shortly after returning to his seat as a delegate to the Continental Congress, Jefferson received an urgent letter from Page. With Dunmore and his followers still manning heavily armed ships in Chesapeake Bay, Page urged Jefferson to convince the Congress to make the final break with Great Britain. Any further delay, Page wrote to Jefferson, might lead weary Virginians to give up the fight. "For God's sake declare the Colonies independent at once, and save us from ruin," Page wrote, warning that Virginians were weary of war and feared more towns would be destroyed just like Norfolk. He worried that it might not be long until Virginians viewed the revolutionary leaders as "the Authors of their Misfortunes."[8]

Sharing that concern, Henry played a key role in ensuring that the revolution in Virginia not be undone by a counterrevolution. Many who served under Henry, still angry that he had been ousted from his role as a military leader, vowed they would leave their regiments if Henry was not given command. As word of this dissent spread through the capital, dozens of armed men loyal to Henry streamed through the streets, spreading fear that a mutinous force would take over Williamsburg. Henry calmed the men by a spending a night with them in the barracks and fields around Williamsburg and appealing to them to follow the greater patriotic cause of independence.[9]

In mid-May, Page, Henry and other Virginia leaders gathered to formalize their request to Jefferson. The de facto legislature met in the Capitol in Williamsburg to call for independence. Sitting in the seats vacated only months earlier by the colonial burgesses, the 112 members of the Virginia Convention included many of the same gentry who had once worked with Lord Dunmore. The system of government they envisioned was similar to that under which Britain had controlled Virginia, with the difference that Virginians would be in charge. Henry led the way, writing a resolution that called on the colonists to end allegiance to Great Britain and to declare themselves in favor of immediate independence. Only one delegate, treasurer Robert Carter Nicholas, opposed the measure, but he eventually went along with it.

In Philadelphia, Jefferson was concerned that the most important political work was taking place in Williamsburg, and he composed a draft of a Virginia constitution. He feared that in his absence Virginians would produce a weak constitution that would maintain many of the failings of British governance, such as inheritance laws allowing the wealthiest families to maintain their elevated status and preventing the lower and middling classes from being fully represented. Jefferson's recommendation that land and voting rights be extended to more Virginians, for example, was rejected by aristocrats who wanted to maintain their power. But the Virginia constitutional convention did adopt the same reasoning as the Congress for breaking with Britain, following Jefferson's belief that Dunmore's action in Norfolk, as well as his proclamation freeing the slaves, bolstered the rationale for independence. "The king's representative in this colony hath not only withheld all the powers of government from operating for our safety, but, having retired on board an armed ship, is carrying on a piratical and savage war against us tempting our slaves by every artifice to resort to him, and training and employing them against their masters," the Virginians declared. Given this state of "extreme danger," they said they had no alternative but to seek "total separation" from Great Britain.[10]

EVEN AS THEY WERE GATHERED at the Capitol to enact their constitution, the Virginians feared Dunmore would show up at any moment with a convoy of ships and try to retake Williamsburg. At the same time, a stubborn band of Loyalists threatened to undermine the revolution. The Goodrich family, with a father and five adult sons, used five boats to "zealously" raid the rivers, following Dunmore's order to "seize, burn or destroy everything that is waterborne." The Goodriches gave up "their Houses, Negroes, Plantations, Stock and everything else" to serve him and the king, Dunmore wrote. But such raids mostly infuriated the victims and turned them into more zealous Patriots.[11] The elder Goodrich eventually was captured by Patriot forces and put into the Williamsburg jail, where he was soon joined by two of his sons.[12]

The British had hoped to triumph with its Ethiopian Regiment, commanded by Thomas Byrd, but it was being decimated by disease. Dunmore wrote to Lord Germain that illnesses had killed "an incredible Number of our People, especially the Blacks." If it were not "for this horrid disorder, I am Satisfied I should have had two thousand Blacks, with whom I should have had no doubt of penetrating into the heart of this Colony," he wrote. He eventually separated the sick from the well, putting them at opposite sides of Gwynn's Island.[13] Dunmore's last hope was to be reinforced. In June, the British transport *Oxford* headed toward Virginia carrying 217 Scotch Highland Regulars, two hundred mattresses, a hundred tents, three large barrels of rum, and two barrels of gunpowder.[14] As the *Oxford* neared Virginia, it was approached by a small boat manned by three men, who offered assistance in navigating the shallows. The *Oxford* crew accepted the assistance, unaware they had sailed into a trap set by Virginia's modest naval force.[15] James and Richard Barron, the brothers behind the trap, climbed aboard the *Oxford* and found some American prisoners on board. Before the British realized what was happening, the *Oxford* was taken without a shot. "Of what Service would they not have been to me here!" an anguished Dunmore wrote on June 27 upon learning of the capture of the *Oxford* and her men.[16] It was one of the most important, if little-noted, early victories of the Revolutionary War in Virginia. The clever and resourceful Barron brothers, operating a tiny, makeshift force, had outwitted one of the world's great navies in the waters of the Chesapeake Bay.

The news of the *Oxford*'s capture was exuberantly conveyed to Jefferson in Philadelphia, where he was preparing drafts of the Declaration of Independence. Page wrote to Jefferson that the capture of the *Oxford* was "truly providential." Edmund Randolph assured him that efforts were being made to convince the 217 men aboard the *Oxford* to consider becoming Americans, especially the "many valuable Artificers," the craftsmen of the tools of war. "Some of them are violent vs. America, others tolerably moderate, and many from contending Passions curse the Parliament and Congress in the same breath," Randolph wrote.[17]

Jefferson hoped the capture of the *Oxford* would boost the confidence of a nervous citizenry. "I am glad to hear of the Highlanders carried into Virginia," he wrote. "Great efforts should be made to keep up the spirits of the people the succeeding three months, which in the universal opinion will be the only ones in which our trial can be severe."[18] He could hardly imagine the war would continue for another seven years.

Jefferson paid close attention to the plans to oust Dunmore. Being intimately familiar with the topography of Gwynn's Island, where Dunmore remained, Jefferson drew a detailed map of the landscape, including the location of inlets and a pond. He also provided an estimate of the effect of the tides on a channel that separated the island from the mainland.[19]

On July 8, 1776, as Dunmore and his straggling crew huddled on ships or in huts on Gwynn's Island, Virginia's military decided to blast him out. Dunmore's fleet consisted of *Roebuck, Fowey, Otter, Dunmore,* and "60 other vessels of various sorts," most of which were occupied by Loyalists who had sought Dunmore's protection. At 7:00 p.m., the Virginians put in place a line of eighteen-pound cannons, arrayed on the mainland toward the enemy fleet. Early the next morning, the first shot was fired. It passed through the hull of the *Dunmore,* doing considerable damage. A second shot killed the boatswain. Dunmore himself was wounded in the leg by a nine-pound shot. The *Dunmore* was able to return fire for fifteen minutes before lifting her cables and sailing away. Many of the private vessels followed in flight. "Good God, that ever I should have come to this!" Dunmore was heard to say.[20]

For their part, the Virginians were hampered by their lack of a large ship that could follow the fleeing British; they had mostly small boats and canoes. A standoff ensued for the rest of the day, and most of Dunmore's fleet fled during the night. One of the last to leave was Captain Byrd. He was "huddled into a cart, in a very sick and low condition, it is said, and carried down" to one of the last vessels to depart, the *Virginia Gazette* reported. Dunmore had relied upon Byrd to build up his army with runaway slaves. When Byrd left, much of his regiment was dead or dying.[21]

Virginia troops boarded their small craft and landed on the island, where they found an appalling sight. Some thirty members of the Ethiopian Regiment, seriously ill from small pox or other diseases, had been left behind. Many others had died during the weeks that Dunmore occupied the island. One officer counted at least 130 graves, some of which contained more than one body.

"It is supposed they buried 500 Negroes on the island," an officer wrote in his journal, which was published by the *Virginia Gazette* shortly after Dunmore fled. "Many poor Negroes were found on the island dying of a putrid fever . . . a child was found sucking at the breast of her dead mother," the officer wrote. The bodies of a number of British who had been burned alive in huts during the cannonade had been hurriedly buried. "Such a scene of misery, distress and cruelty, my eyes never beheld," the officer wrote.[22]

One grave was "neatly done up." It was said to contain the body of the "Lord of Gosport," Andrew Sprowle, the shipyard owner who once was one of the wealthiest men in Virginia. It was Sprowle whose Gosport shipyard had hosted Dunmore's fleet but who had nevertheless insisted to Norfolk leaders that he was not a Tory. In the end, Sprowle had sailed with Dunmore and died some thirty miles from the shipyard that he had made into one of the greatest in America.

Dunmore spent a few more weeks sailing around Virginia's waters, but his days as governor were over. He finally left the state on August 2, 1776. As Dunmore sailed out of Virginia's waters, never to return, he was concerned enough about Virginia's fledging military force to write to his superiors that it was not safe "to trust one of His Majesty's Sloops alone in the bay."[23]

Life slowly returned to normal in Virginia, meaning Dunmore's emancipation proclamation was void and slaves were once again considered personal property. Shortly after Dunmore's departure, the *Gazette* somewhat gleefully announced the capture of the "black banditti" at Gwynn's Island and published many ads appealing for the capture of runaway slaves. One ad sought the return of a horse and slave; the owner could not recall if the horse was marked, but a "notorious" slave named Jesse, who stood five foot four inches, was "branded with the initials of his Master's name."[24]

Some of the advertisements that sought runaway slaves were published in the same July 20, 1776, issue of the *Gazette* that printed the Declaration of Independence. Jefferson had proposed a paragraph be included in the Declaration that blamed King George III for allowing the importation of slaves to continue, castigating him for vetoing efforts by Virginia "to prohibit or restrain this execrable commerce." He had not, however, proposed that slaves be given their freedom. His view was that there were enough slaves in Virginia, and he envisioned a day when they would be moved to their own colony. He blamed the king for fomenting slave uprisings against white masters. The king "is now exciting those very people to rise in arms among us, and to purchase that liberty of which *he* has deprived them, by murdering the people upon whom *he* also obtruded them; thus paying off former crimes committed against the *lib-*

erties of one people, with crimes which he urges them to commit against the *lives* of another." The words were struck from the draft by other delegates, enabling the importation of slaves to continue.[25]

As he was being chased from Virginia, Dunmore must have been particularly incensed to learn that his archnemesis, Patrick Henry, was being sworn in to take his place, becoming the first revolutionary governor of Virginia. Henry, having previously watched his authority as Virginia's military leader slip away, now warned that the abuses of aristocrats from the prerevolutionary era must not be allowed to continue after independence. "Perhaps I am mistaken, but I fear too great a bias to Aristocracy prevails among the opulent," he had written May 20, 1776, to Richard Henry Lee regarding the proposed constitution for Virginia.[26]

Counterintuitive though it may seem, some Virginia leaders hoped that Henry's return to politics would make him weaker by taking away his military role. But those who pushed Henry back into politics may not have realized he would become governor. Philip Mazzei had written to Henry that his "heart was filled with joy" that Henry had agreed to go from the military back to his political role, adding that "Mr. Jefferson . . . joined me in that opinion." Jefferson "foresaw the calamities, to which we would have been reduced for the want of such a man as you in the Senate at this juncture," Mazzei wrote. "Now I am easy: You are there; I fear nothing." But Henry was not in the Senate. A month after Mazzei wrote the letter, Henry was elected governor.[27]

The prospect of Henry in the Governor's Palace made some leading Virginians uneasy. His election was sealed only after assurances that the governor would have few direct powers and that his actions would need the approval of the House and Senate, having already passed muster with the eight-member Governor's Council, which was larded with conservatives such as Benjamin Harrison.

Animosity toward Henry quickly surfaced. Jefferson's brother-in-law, Francis Eppes, wrote to Jefferson, "You have heard no doubt before this that Patrick Henry is our Governor. What a strange infatuation attends our Convention. At a time when men of known integrity and sound understanding are most necessary they are rejected and men of shallow understanding fill the most important posts in our country. What but inevitable ruin can be the consequence of this?"[28]

Archibald Cary, the Speaker of the Senate and a friend of Jefferson's, was equally appalled. Cary lived at his estate, Ampthill, on the James River just below Richmond. He was hardly a model of liberty or religious freedom. As chief magistrate in Chesterfield County, he had imprisoned Baptist ministers who dared to preach their faith and then blocked them from trying to deliver sermons from the prison window. Jefferson's slave Isaac described Cary as an abusive, callous, and "dry-looking" man who acted as if he was the master of Monticello when visiting Jefferson, applying a horsewhip to Isaac for supposed infractions as minor as failing to open a gate in anticipation of Cary's arrival.[29] Shortly after Henry's election, Cary approached Henry's stepbrother, Colonel John Syme, in the lobby of the House of Delegates. "I am told your brother wishes to be Dictator," Cary told Syme in his characteristically brusque manner. "Tell him that the day of his appointment shall be the day of his death, for he shall feel my dagger in his heart before the sunset of that day." Syme responded that if such a proposal existed, Henry had not had a hand in it.[30]

Jefferson recalled how "our circumstances being much distressed, it was proposed in the house of delegates to create a *dictator*, invested with every power legislative, executive and judiciary, civil and military, of life and of death, over our persons and over our properties." Jefferson opposed the measure, arguing that he had not fought for revolution so that it be placed under "the omnipotent hand of a single despot." The dictatorship plan did not go through. Henry would be governor, but the weakest one possible.[31]

WHILE VIRGINIANS WERE BUSY ousting Dunmore, Jefferson was finishing his work on the Declaration of Independence. The encomiums due Jefferson for this work have filled volumes. The break with the British Empire changed history and inspired a spirit of revolution that continues unabated. But historians have long since demonstrated that the Declaration was, like many products of politics, filled with compromises and conundrums.

Given that it was written by a Virginian, the document can be looked at in the context of what was happening at that moment in Virginia. Slaves, who made up the majority of Jefferson's Albemarle County population, were an integral part of the economy, including at Jefferson's plantations. Purchase of lands in the west had been stalled by British rules protecting ownership. The religion of many settlers in the Piedmont and Blue Ridge was non-Anglican. In other words, many of Jefferson's interests went beyond the oft-cited anger over debts, Parliament-imposed taxes, and trade restrictions. The Declaration's stirring phrase that "all men are created," as aspirational as it may have been intended for the long term, signified at the time that white men in America were equal to white men in Britain. Slaves were not included. This certainly seemed contradictory to many people at the time as well as later, but the denial of equality was, to use Jefferson's phrase, self-evident. Dunmore hoped to forestall a revolution by freeing the slaves, but he may have ensured its arrival by angering slave owners who organized against him. Similarly, the Declaration of Independence meant that Americans were free to ignore the British restriction on acquiring western Indian land. Indeed, to Jefferson, the fight for independence was a war of two fronts—against British control of the colonies as well as against Indian control of western land that Jefferson believed would be part of an independent America. "Nothing will reduce those wretches so soon as pushing the war into the heart of their country," Jefferson wrote from Philadelphia, in reference to reports about attacks by Indians allied with the British. "But I would not stop there. I would never cease pursuing them while one of them remained on this side" of the Mississippi river.[32]

Even as the Declaration of Independence was about to be approved, Jefferson was somber. He had let it be known that he did not want to be reelected as a delegate to the Congress, due in part to concern about his frail wife. Nonetheless, he seemed genuinely shocked that some of Virginia's representatives took him at his word and nearly failed to reappoint him. He wrote to William Fleming, a friend in Williamsburg, expressing concern that Virginians were questioning his patriotism. He revealed that he had been asked to write the Declaration, a role that many Americans did not realize until years later. "It is a painful situation to be 300 miles from one's country, and thereby open to secret assassination without a possibility of self-defence," he wrote. "I am willing to hope nothing of this kind has been done in my case, and yet I cannot be easy. If any doubt has arisen as to me, my country will have my political creed in the form of a 'Declaration &c' which I was lately directed to draw. This will give decisive proof that my own sentiment concurred with the vote they instructed us to give."[33]

Fleming assured Jefferson that there was no reason for concern. Jefferson's near-failure to be reappointed to the Congress was a result of a letter from Jefferson himself "signifying your intention to resign" due to concern about his wife's health. "Make yourself perfectly easy," Fleming wrote to Jefferson. "You are as high in the estimation of your countrymen as ever."[34]

The combination of the Declaration of Independence, the departure of Dunmore, and the election of Henry cleared the way for a new Virginia. But Jefferson's hope that the conflict would last just a few months would prove naive, of course. The British would eventually return to Virginia with a much stronger force. Belatedly, some of the revolutionary leaders worried that the destruction of Norfolk had made the state more vulnerable to invasion. "Norfolk might have been easily Savd," Adam Stephen, a veteran of Virginia's military, wrote to Jefferson on July 29, 1776. "We feel the loss of it daily. Such of the Inhabitants as were our friends would have expedited our armed vessels, fitted our Privateers, and facilitated all of our Naval affairs."[35]

Even Page, who had hectored Jefferson about the need for the destruction of Norfolk, sought to recast his role. He told Jefferson that he had urged the placement of cannons at Norfolk during the prior October, but claimed that his advice had been ignored. If the batteries had been placed "as I advised, Norfolk would not have been burnt," Page wrote. In another letter, he said he had called for cannons to be arrayed in order destroy Dunmore's fleet. If such a plan had been enacted and failed, Page told Jefferson, "I could have agreed to be hanged."

But the fallout from Norfolk was being swept aside in the euphoria over the Declaration. Page added to his letter a postscript that would become one of the most-quoted statements about the Revolutionary War: "I am highly pleased with your Declaration," Page wrote Jefferson. "God preserve the United States. We know the race is not to the swift nor the battle to the strong. Do you not think that an angel rides in the whirlwind and directs this storm." It was little noticed that the stirring phraseology, lifted partly from Ecclesiastes, was created with the fiery whirlwind of Norfolk still fresh in the minds of Page and Jefferson. More destruction was certain now that the race was fully engaged.[36]

ON DECEMBER 13, 1776, the American general Charles Lee was at White's Tavern in Basking Ridge, New Jersey. Lee and a dozen of his soldiers spent the night there, about three miles from his main army of two thousand men. A British patrol intercepted two American guards and learned that Lee was at the tavern. Lee had a reputation as an eccentric but brilliant British commander who had defected to the American cause. While he was in his nightshirt writing a letter that was critical of Washington—"A certain great man is most damnable deficient"—the tavern was encircled by the British patrol, including a cavalry officer named Banastre Tarleton, who later would play a major role in the invasion of Virginia. A fifteen-minute standoff ensued. Finally, Tarleton ordered shots fired into the door of the tavern, prompting Lee to emerge. He was taken prisoner and tied to a horse. Tarleton ordered Lee's pigtails cut off and led him on a twenty-five-mile ride, at the end presenting the prisoner to his superior, General Cornwallis. The capture greatly enhanced the stature of twenty-two-year-old Tarleton, sealing his relationship with Cornwallis. It would be remembered later, when Tarleton would be given the mission of trying to replicate that success by going after Thomas Jefferson.

The capture of Lee dispirited the revolutionaries only briefly, however. Less than two weeks later, on Christmas Day, Washington led American forces across the Delaware River and captured nearly one thousand Hessian soldiers who were allied with the British. Word of the American success quickly reached Virginia, where toasts were made to celebrate the possibility of a quick march to victory.

He Lost Everything

ON NEW YEAR'S DAY, 1777, the Virginia countryside lay frozen and still, the beginning of a most severe winter. At William Byrd's Westover estate, chunks of ice formed along the edges of the James River. With Dunmore vanquished, war seemed distant in these rural lands. Only the echo of the occasional carriage could be heard on the hard-packed roads, the riders huddled under blankets as they passed the great plantation houses, from which unfurled lazy streams of chimney smoke.

Byrd was bankrupt and bereft. The ongoing war left him with little hope that the many people indebted to him would repay. He was not surprised that Jefferson and Henry had led a revolution. But he must have been startled that Benjamin Harrison, his next-door neighbor and a fellow planter, not only had sided with the revolutionaries but also had been asked to read aloud the Declaration of Independence in Philadelphia. Many of his fellow former members of the Governor's Council had either switched to the Patriot side or gone into hiding.

Byrd seemingly could not win no matter which side in the war was victorious. If the British had won, the Patriots who owed him large sums of money would have even less wherewithal to pay their debts, and he feared he would lose title to his remaining slaves. An equally harsh fate awaited Byrd were the Patriots to win. Those Patriot Virginians who owed him money would have felt no compulsion to repay a man they would view as a traitor and Loyalist ally. Moreover, Byrd's trade with the British—the underpinning of his tobacco business—would likely not continue in the event of a Patriot victory.

Writing his will in 1774, Byrd had said that his debts were created "through my own folly and inattention to accounts" and embittered "every moment of my life." At the same time, he blamed his financial problems on the "unjust will of my insane mother," whose sin apparently was to have failed to have provided money for her stepchildren. Byrd was equally harsh to his namesake, his "ungrateful" eldest son, William Byrd IV, who died at age twenty-one in a horse-riding accident in Britain and left nothing for his father in his will. Byrd had, in turn, disinherited Otway, the Patriot. Byrd seemed obsessed with issues of inheritance and likely felt ashamed that he would leave behind mostly debt. He himself had inherited 179,000 acres, hundreds of slaves, and all the accou-

trements of a great fortune. Now he had lost most of the land and had mortgaged most of his slaves. Finally, on September 19, 1776, he sold a Richmond
home he had built after marrying his first wife, Elizabeth. There was now little
else left to sell other than Westover and a home in Williamsburg.

Briefly, Byrd pondered doing what had caused him to disinherit Otway:
switch sides. It was suggested he might lead the 3rd Virginia Regiment, which
had responsibility for the coastal region bordering North Carolina. Archibald
Cary, a nearby James River planter who had become a revolutionary, wrote that
Byrd had "made an offer of his services, and we are well assured his appointment will engage great numbers, officers as well as Soldiers, who served under
him in the [French and Indian] War."[1] But many were suspicious. If Byrd could
so easily offer to switch from one side to the other, what was to stop him from
doing so again? This was the man who disinherited his own son for leaving the
British navy. One of the most suspicious was Landon Carter, who owned the
plantation of Sabine Hall. Carter, who was distantly related to the Byrd family,
had been appalled by Byrd's treatment of Otway. He wrote in his diary that
Byrd was trying "to solicit an appointment to be Majr. Genl. Here. I know
some such Panders to him as to wish him success; but I would never trust him,
and shall always remember his treatment of . . . his son, who left the Navy to
assist his own country even against the threats of being disinherited by his
father."[2]

Byrd's offer was turned down. Jefferson believed Byrd was rejected because
of the view that he was "no soldier." Although he had been the commander of
Virginia's regiment during the French and Indian War, Byrd had accumulated
few distinctive military engagements during his five years as a colonel in that
conflict. Doubt about Byrd's military capabilities, Jefferson wrote, "occasioned
a refusal of command solicited by Colo. Byrd, one of our highest citizens in
rank & wealth."[3]

No one outside Byrd's family had a closer view and understanding of Byrd's
despair than his friend and former fellow member of the Governor's Council,
Ralph Wormeley. It was to Wormeley that Byrd had written about how the
"frantick patriotism" of the revolutionaries "greatly disturb my peace of mind."
After hearing of Byrd's rejection, Wormeley took out the letter he had received
from Byrd and on the back wrote his view as to what happened. Wormeley said
that Byrd "offered his military services to the convention," calling it a "strange
desertion." The reason for Byrd's turnabout, according to Wormeley, was his
anger at Dunmore's proclamation to free the slaves. (While the proclamation
only freed the slaves of Patriots, slaves of Loyalists were also known to have

fled, and many more might be expected to do so once the principle of freedom for some slaves became widely established.) In the end, Byrd's effort to switch sides failed because "he was not trusted," Wormeley wrote. "He lost everything."[4]

On December 26, 1776, Governor Henry issued a proclamation calling on Virginians to join the militia to fight the British "to put a speedy end to the cruel ravages of a haughty and inveterate enemy, and secure our invaluable rights." Significantly, Henry also was considering a resolution that could have forced British sympathizers, presumably including Byrd, to leave Virginia. Both Henry and Jefferson were stepping up their efforts to seize the property of Loyalists. At the same time, Thomas Paine, the author of *Common Sense,* published a diatribe against Loyalists such as Byrd, writing, "I should not be afraid to go with one hundred Whigs against a thousand Tories, were they attempt to get into arms. Every Tory is a coward . . . though he may be cruel, [he] never can be brave."

Byrd could find no way out of the predicament of debt and the perception of disloyalty. Yet there was one last act he could take to help his family. Byrd would have been well aware that were he gone, Mary might be allowed to stay and retain Westover, as long as she kept her sympathies—whatever they were—to herself. He may have seen death as the honorable way out.

The exact circumstances of Byrd's death on New Year's Day, 1777, would never be conclusively known. Some said he had been deathly ill and succumbed to his sickness. But a darker story was told by neighbors and family members over the years, repeated in biographies and not disputed in memoirs written by his grandchildren: Byrd picked out a pistol (likely the dueling weapon that he had failed to use years earlier against Robert Bolling), aimed at his head, and pulled the trigger.

Two days later, the *Virginia Gazette* published a short notice, sandwiched among proclamations by Governor Henry calling for militia to form against the British:

> The Hon. William Byrd, in the county of Charles City, a Gentleman who was much respected and esteemed by all who had the pleasure of his acquaintance.
> His life, his breath, his faculties are gone, Yet virtue keeps him from oblivion.[5]

The estate's enormous debts and responsibilities, however, were not gone. They passed to the pregnant Mary Willing Byrd, who was "now reduced from affluence to want," one of Mary Byrd's granddaughters wrote years later. With little cash on hand and eight children to care for, she scavenged to stay afloat. "She wanted clothes for her children and was glad to use her curtains for dresses and the linings for undergarments," her granddaughter wrote.[6]

Three months after Byrd's death, another notice appeared in the *Gazette*. Much of the estate was for sale, including a redbrick home with four rooms on each floor in Williamsburg. Next, Mary offered to sell the greatest treasure of Westover: the books assembled by generations of Byrds, the collection that Jefferson had counted and coveted, and which had been perused by so many Virginians who visited the estate. A brief advertisement announced the availability of "the very valuable library of the said deceased, consisting of near four thousand volumes."[7] Mary Byrd would do whatever was necessary and sell whatever she could—so long as it helped her keep her beloved Westover.

JEFFERSON'S WORK on the Declaration of Independence did not bring freedom from Britain. Instead, it formalized the escalating war for which the new United States of America was scarcely prepared. To make independence a reality, Jefferson put an extraordinary amount of faith in a man named Benedict Arnold.

Arnold was regarded as one of America's most brilliant but difficult commanders. Born in Connecticut to a wealthy merchant family, the great-grandson of the royal governor of Rhode Island, Arnold grew up with the expectation that he would remain a loyal subject of the crown. But his father went deeply into debt and became alcoholic, leaving no money to pay for Arnold's education. At age fifteen, in 1766, Arnold joined the Connecticut militia, which was trying to halt a French invasion from Canada. The British lost the battle and were supposed to be allowed clear passage to return to Connecticut, but hundreds of men, women, and children were attacked during their retreat by Indian allies of the French. This left Arnold with bitter feelings toward the French, who he believed should have stopped the massacre. Returning home, Arnold became a pharmacist and soon became nearly broke as a result of British taxes, which he vehemently protested. A British sea captain called him a "damned Yankee" and, in the resulting duel, was injured by Arnold. Arnold became captain of a Connecticut military unit in 1775 as it became increasingly apparent that Americans would go to war against the British. Later that year, he helped capture Fort Ticonderoga, which had been a British stronghold on the New York shore of Lake Champlain, and was picked to lead a major expedition against the enemy into Canada. Arnold's mission was to lead 1,100 men through the Maine wilderness and link up with another American force in Quebec, where the British were in winter quarters.

Jefferson was one of Arnold's greatest boosters. He believed the British did not have "any intimation of Arnold's expedition" and predicted that his force would soon be "in possession of Quebec."[1] As the weeks passed and reports of Arnold's progress continued to arrive, Jefferson's confidence in Arnold grew. On November 29, 1775, before Arnold had entered Quebec, Jefferson was so optimistic that he boasted to his cousin, Loyalist John Randolph, that Canada was on the verge of joining what would become the United States. Quebec had likely "open'd its arms to Colo. Arnold," Jefferson wrote. "In a short time we have reason to hope the delegates of Canada will join us in Congress and complete the American Union as far as we wish to have it completed."[2] Two weeks later, Jefferson wrote John Page that Congress was preparing to promote Arnold to brigadier general in anticipation of the capture of Quebec.

In early December, Arnold did reach Quebec and joined up with Montgomery's forces. As the Americans prepared to fire upon the fort at Quebec, however, the British launched round after round of fire at the Americans. Major General Montgomery was killed. The American force retreated and regrouped, staying at a distance from the fort for several months and launching occasional raids through the early spring.

Then, in early May, eighty-two British vessels sailed up the St. Lawrence River, carrying reinforcements. It seemed that the Americans would be overwhelmed. The British split into two forces, planning to push Arnold's men to the northern shore of Lake Champlain, where they might be trapped. But the Americans had prepared for such a move and ordered the construction of lakeworthy vessels. The British, who had no comparable vessels, considered quickly constructing a small fleet in an effort to entrap the Americans on the lake. However, the British command decided it was impractical and let the Americans escape. Though the Americans had survived to fight another day, the battle was viewed at the time as a loss.

Jefferson wrote to Thomas Nelson on May 16, 1776, about the "disagreeable news of a second defeat at Quebec." An American force "could not resist the enemy."[3] In the following two months, as disturbing reports arrived about the conduct of the American military in Quebec, Congress formed an investigative committee to look into the matter, including Arnold's performance. Jefferson, known for his lawyerly precision, was appointed to the committee. It was this little-remembered task that Jefferson performed on what would become the most notable day in American history.

During the same week that Congress prepared to adopt the Declaration of Independence, Jefferson pulled up a chair and attended the nation's first congressional investigation, known formally as the inquiry into the "Canadian campaign." With Jefferson taking careful notes, many of the questions focused on the competence of Arnold.

The first witness, Captain Hector McNeal, testified on July 2 that Arnold was disliked by his men. "The New York troops particularly were dissatisfied with Arnold because he wrote some letter which appeared in the newspapers, reflecting on them," McNeal testified, according to Jefferson's notes. This appeared to be a reference to Arnold's complaint that the men had retreated too quickly during the attack on the Quebec fort.[4]

The testimony also focused on the questionable decisions made by Montgomery, who was killed during the attack on the fort and thus not able to defend himself. The witnesses told how many of the men under Montgomery and Arnold had smallpox, suggesting that it was spread by an infected man sent to them by the British. The attack on the fort occurred with four feet of snow on the ground, with the wind and snow blowing in the faces of the Americans. As soon as Montgomery was killed, his second-in-command ordered a retreat. While some witnesses said this ruined what seemed to be a good chance to capture the effort, others said that the wet conditions ruined the gunpowder and only one in ten guns used by the Americans fired correctly. If that was the case, then a retreat made sense.

On July 4, 1776, General David Wooster appeared before Jefferson and other members of the investigating committee. Wooster testified that Arnold retreated from Quebec due to a lack of gunpowder. "This prevented the place falling into [Arnold's] hands," Wooster testified, again according to Jefferson's nearly verbatim notes.[5]

The testimony continued until July 27, painting a portrait of a sick, poorly clothed, ill-fed, and disgruntled corps of American soldiers, many of them anxious to return home once their time of service had expired. Notwithstanding the testimony that had been presented, Jefferson remained Arnold's defender. On August 9, Jefferson wrote approvingly that Arnold was commanding vessels on the lakes of upstate New York against the British. "General Arnold (a fine sailor) has undertaken to command our fleet on the lakes," Jefferson wrote to his brother-in-law, Francis Eppes.[6]

During the summer of 1776, the British forces in Canada had been busy constructing small boats; they set sail from the northern end of Lake Champlain on October 7. It was an impressive fleet, including several large ships as well as a number of highly maneuverable flat-bottomed boats outfitted with guns. Five days later, the British reached the American fleet under the command of Arnold, lying off Valcour Island. Arnold was vastly outnumbered; he apparently had no idea such a large British fleet would find him. In the ensuing fight, the Americans were ordered by Arnold to flee to the woods. The British captured an American ship, the *Washington,* and Arnold ordered a number of the fleet's boats destroyed in order to avoid their falling into enemy hands. The British seemingly had Arnold cornered, but the overall British commander, Sir Guy Carleton, feared waging a campaign as the season turned to winter and retreated up the lake.

The battle could be viewed either as an embarrassing defeat for Arnold or as a tactical victory, allowing him to save his men and prompting the British to respond with their retreat. Among Arnold's critics was Richard Henry Lee of Virginia, who provided a series of prescient insights about Arnold's failings in a letter to Jefferson. Arnold did not "seem to apprehend any [danger] until he was defeated by an enemy four times as strong as himself," Lee wrote. "This Officer, fiery, hot and impetuous, but without discretion, never thought of informing himself how the enemy went on, and he had no idea of retiring when he saw them coming, tho so much superior to his force!"[7] Those who saw it as a victory believed Arnold, with an inferior force, had prevented the British from advancing.

Congress promoted Arnold and summoned him to Philadelphia. But he soon became disenchanted when he was displaced by a local favorite, prompting him to once again resign his commission. Then came word that the British were readying an attack on Fort Ticonderoga. Washington convinced Arnold that his services were needed. Arnold agreed to head back toward Lake Champlain, anticipating a battle that could determine the outcome of the war.

The battle featured several men who would later play key roles during the invasion of Virginia. Among the British officers preparing to face off against Arnold was the British brigadier general William Phillips. Phillips was the grizzled embodiment of British power, a stout man with a large nose, the father of six children with two women, neither of whom he was married to. He was the kind of general who might appear in a painting of a great battle, not at the front but slightly obscured from view, yet included because it was clear he had played a decisive role. Phillips would be counted on for his military intelligence, boldness, and determination. Alternately charming and brusque, he believed that his men could drag a cannon nearly anywhere, no matter how steep the hill. "Where a goat can go, a man can go, and where a man can go, he can drag a gun," Phillips said. Throughout his military career, he would oversee countless cannonades, issuing the order to fire pulverizing rounds at masses of the anonymous enemy. It was brutal work, physically and psychologically, that was perhaps best mastered if one could somehow think only in terms of mathematical formulations of trajectory, velocity, and wind, rather than the bloody human calculus of the shredding of so many bodies. Phillips decided that the members of the artillery corps needed something to occupy and inspire them, so he created an eight-man unit called the Royal Artillery Band, who were "obliged to wait upon the commanding officer so often as he shall desire to have music." Thus was born a band that would, for generations to come, provide the music to stir the artillery soldiers of Britain.[8]

By 1776, with the revolution under way, Phillips was called upon to lead the Royal Artillery in Canada, where Americans were attempting to oust British forces poised to strike at New York. He was to be accompanied by Baron Frederick Adolphus von Riedesel, the leader of a large auxiliary corps of Hessian troops. Phillips and Riedesel sailed from Britain aboard the eighty-two-vessel convoy for a showdown with Benedict Arnold.

Phillips hoped to regain control of Fort Ticonderoga, on the southern shore of Lake Champlain. His army amounted to about 7,800 men, roughly half of them Hessians. Phillips convinced his men that they could drag their guns up a hill overlooking the fort. The move was detected by the fort's American defenders, who abandoned their station when they realized they were outmanned and outmaneuvered. The British soon experienced a series of disasters: supplies were low, roads were often impassable, and most of a detachment of 1,200 Hessians sent in search of food were killed or captured in the Battle of Bennington. The Americans, meanwhile, eventually collected a force of fifteen thousand, strengthened by local units from throughout New England and New York, as well as riflemen from Virginia. They were also supplied by friendly residents. Washington urged that Benedict Arnold be sent to the scene. "He is active, judicious, and brave, and an officer in whom the militia will repose great confidence," he wrote.[9]

After weeks of encounters, the British and American forces faced each other near the town of Saratoga. The first of two major battles left hundreds dead and wounded on both sides, with the British position seriously weakened. The British commander, John Burgoyne, had thought he would be joined by General Henry Clinton's force, but it did not arrive. In the second and decisive battle, Burgoyne relied heavily on Phillips, who oversaw the artillery bombardment of American positions while Riedesel also launched a series of attacks.

Arnold, meanwhile, had clashed with the overall American commander, Horatio Gates, who relieved Arnold of his command. As the battle continued, however, Arnold impulsively mounted a horse and rode out onto the battlefield to issue orders. At one point, Arnold's horse was shot out from under him, and Arnold reinjured the leg that had been hurt in Quebec. While Arnold was castigated by Gates for reentering the field, he was hailed by many as a decisive figure in the battle. "It was he and no other who beat Burgoyne at Saratoga," British army historian John Fortescue wrote of Arnold, describing him as both "unprincipled and unstable" and possessing a "true magic of leadership." The fight was suspended at darkness and ended the following morning with the vastly outnumbered British and Hessians offering their surrender.[10]

The Battle of Saratoga was a turning point of the war. Within weeks, France announced it recognized the sovereignty of the United States, a move that eventually would result in French ships coming to the aid of American forces in Virginia at a most crucial moment. As word of the victory reached Williamsburg, Governor Henry issued proclamations hailing the achievement. The citizenry lined Duke of Gloucester Street, cheering local militias and shouting huzzahs to Arnold. Cannons were fired, church bells rang, and taverns overflowed with the slosh of celebration.

THE VICTORY ALSO PRESENTED A CHALLENGE: what would the United States do with the British and Hessian prisoners of war? The Americans had initially agreed to a "convention" that the prisoners would be returned to Britain on condition they never fight again in America, but Congress decided that enforcing the measure was impossible. As a result, after 1,100 prisoners were allowed to return to Canada, the remaining 4,100 or so members of what became known as the "convention army" prisoners were to be marched to barracks near Boston. Phillips and Riedesel were named the leaders of their respective force of British and Hessian prisoners. But the barracks proved insufficient and were considered too vulnerable to rescue efforts by the British.

During the Congress's debate over where to send the prisoners, the representatives from Virginia made a proposal: the Congress should pay to send the prisoners to a site near the village of Charlottesville. In a tradition that has been followed by countless members of Congress ever since, the Virginia delegates believed that the federal payment would provide a bonanza for the local economy. Among the leaders of this effort was Jefferson. Although some in Charlottesville feared that bringing thousands of enemy soldiers to their remote area would make Albemarle County a target for an invading British rescue force, Jefferson believed that the prisoners would bring money to buy local goods and that among them were craftsmen who could be put to good use at the area's plantations. Jefferson wrote to John Harvie, a Virginia delegate to the Congress, about the possibility of finding skilled workers. Harvie responded on September 15, 1778, that "it is possible that a number of the Convention prisoners may be sent to Virginia this Fall or Winter."[11] Shortly thereafter, Harvie offered his land near Charlottesville as a location for prisoner barracks, and Congress promptly approved the proposal. The prisoners would be settled a few miles from Monticello.

The prisoners were abruptly informed that they would be marched from Boston to Charlottesville in bitter winter conditions, with scarce rations and thin clothing. Most of their baggage would be left behind. Local residents taunted the prisoners as they marched out of Massachusetts.

Nearly half of the prisoners were Hessians, who would play a crucial role throughout the Revolutionary War. All told, an estimated thirty thousand Hessians would fight during the seven years of the war, accounting for nearly one-third of those who fought on the British side. The soldiers were from six smaller German states and known collectively as "Hessians" because the largest percentage came from the state of Hesse-Cassel. Under the treaty between King George III of England and Landgrave Friedrich II of Hesse-Cassel, for example, the German state agreed to supply England with twelve thousand troops, to be kept together under German command. In return, the English paid more than £100,000 per year plus 30 crowns per man.[12] The treaties between England and five other German states that supplied soldiers were similar. The majority of the German prisoners marching to Charlottesville were from the north German state of Brunswick, serving at the behest of Duke Charles I.

Many of the Hessians had been conscripted into service against their will, facing debts or penalties that forced them into the military. One such soldier, forced into the corps for failing to carry his student papers, described the other "recruits" as including "a runaway poet from Jena, a bankrupt merchant from Vienna, a haberdasher from Hanover, a discharged postal clerk from Gotha, a monk from Wurzburg, a civil servant from Meiningen, a Prussian sergeant of hussars, a cashiered Hessian major from the Fortress and others of a similar stamp."[13] Married men were allowed to bring their wives, who became "camp followers" and helped prepare food. The Hessians were assured that the Americans would be easily defeated and that they would win glory and treasure for their service. Some were stunned upon encountering the tall "fine-looking and sinewy" Americans, as one wrote, expressing wonder that "Dame Nature had created such a handsome race! . . . the men of English America are far ahead of those in the greater portion of Europe both as respects their beauty and stature."[14]

Some of the Hessian forces, particularly those under the command of seasoned officers, were highly skilled and among the most feared forces of the British, put in the forefront of many of the most heated battles. A number were relatively well educated, especially when compared to some English recruits. But others could barely handle a musket and had little education.

As the British and Hessian prisoners marched south from Massachusetts, they left behind, as one wrote, the "quite grand" houses of Cambridge, the "antique Roman" buildings of Harvard College, the "thriving little city" of Worcester, and the "tolerably kind, but damned inquisitive" people of Springfield. On the whole the prisoners were a wretched sight, many having worn the same clothing for several years—aboard ship, marching through the woods, and in the barracks. Desertions became common, particularly among the Hessians. One Hessian soldier wrote of being attracted to young "nymphs" who appeared along the roads, exhibiting their "exceedingly white teeth, pretty lips, and sparkling laughing eyes." One "roguishly offered us an apple, accompanied by a little courtesy," a Hessian soldier wrote, explaining how "the fair sex were the cause of our losing some of our comrades" to desertion.[15] The German settlements in Pennsylvania and the western side of the Blue Ridge in Virginia also encouraged Hessians to consider desertion. Some local German families offered to pay Hessian prisoners. Such Hessians "were persuaded to stay behind, and the girls did their best to keep them for husbands. Even the officers were not safe from such proposals, and I know of some to whom girls were offered with a fortune of $3,000 to $4,000," wrote a Hessian officer, August Wilhelm du Roi.[16] By the time the prisoners reached Charlottesville, their ranks had been thinned by between three hundred and four hundred deserters.[17]

As the prisoners reached the barracks in January 1779, they beheld an appalling site: half-constructed log cabins, few provisions, and a landscape swirling in snow. Many preferred camping in the woods. "Never shall I be able to forget this day, which was terrible in every way," du Roi wrote of the day they arrived in Charlottesville. "Never have I seen men so discouraged and in such despair as ours, when, tired and worn out from the long trip and the hardships, they had to seek shelter in the woods like wild animals."[18] Jefferson was delighted to watch the prisoners arrive, convinced they would spend money on local goods and provide talented craftsman. And there was one other benefit: Jefferson had heard that some of the Hessian officers were excellent musicians. He hoped they would find a suitable house just down the road from Monticello.

Who Would Have Expected All This Here?

FROM THE HILLTOP OF MONTICELLO, Jefferson could see the prisoners' encampment, surrounded by an area six miles in circumference that had been almost entirely denuded of timber. The logs had been cut to build crude cabins, but the slaves and other workers who were supposed to construct the barracks had run out of time and materials, leaving dozens of partially finished structures amid the rolling, snowy landscape northwest of Charlottesville. As the war raged in the North, Virginia continued to be a state of relative tranquility, or so it seemed from the vantage of Monticello. The remote foothills of the Blue Ridge, Jefferson believed, provided the perfect place for a prisoner-of-war camp. There was little chance the prisoners could be rescued by British forces.

By the time all of the nearly four thousand prisoners arrived, the Albemarle Barracks became the most populated environ in all Virginia, nearly twice the population of Williamsburg. It dwarfed Charlottesville, which had perhaps fifteen buildings around the courthouse square. The barracks were set near Ivy Creek, about ten miles away via the main road, or five miles on a footpath. The country was rough and remote, with only one house between the town and the barracks. The hastily constructed barracks were built in four rows of twelve, laid out in closely connected squares. Each barrack housed eighteen men. Rain had "free passage" through the porous roof, windows and chimneys were deemed "superfluous" because of the loose construction, and fires were built in the middle of the floor.[1]

The horrid conditions prompted some to urge Congress to move the prison away from Charlottesville as soon as possible. The barracks were "ill provided [with] very little Water near them," wrote William Finnie, quartermaster of the Continental army's southern department, to Congress on February 7, 1779, three weeks after the prisoners arrived. The wagons hauling provisions for the prisoners had to travel seventy miles along rough and often impassable roads, Finnie said. The nearby Rivanna River was impossible to ford for lengthy periods after even the lightest rains. So bad were the roads around Charlottesville that wagons were frequently sank to their axles. Finnie wrote that "it would be found almost as practicable to Waggon over a new drained Lake, as through these Grounds in the Winter season."[2]

Jefferson was mortified, worried that the Congress would take away the prisoners just as they were starting to pour money into the local economy. He drafted an angry letter to Governor Henry that ran to more than 3,500 words, by far the longest he would ever write to Henry and one of the lengthiest he wrote on any subject. Given his position "in the neighborhood of the present barracks," Jefferson wrote, he believed the troops were contributing $30,000 a week into Albemarle County's economy (much of which was controlled by Jefferson and his friends). Launching an attack upon a commissary who contended there was not enough food in Albemarle County to feed the troops, Jefferson wrote sarcastically, "If the troops could be fed upon long letters, I believe the gentleman at the head of that department in this country, would be the best commissary upon earth." Jefferson painted his effort to keep the prisoners in Albemarle in moral terms, saying it was a matter of honor to treat the prisoners well, which he insisted was being done in Charlottesville. "Is an enemy so execrable that, though in captivity, his wishes and comforts are to be disregarded and even crossed?" Jefferson wrote. "I think not. It is for the benefit of mankind to mitigate the horrors of war as much as possible."

Jefferson portrayed the location as if it were an impregnable fortress, and promoted the citizens of Albemarle County as staunch defenders who would rush to stop British troops in the unlikely event of a rescue effort. The prisoners were far "from the access of an eastern or western enemy." If the British should try to invade Charlottesville, Jefferson continued, "they must pass through a great extent of hostile country; in a neighborhood thickly inhabited by a robust and hardy people zealous in the American cause . . . no place could have been better chosen." In fact, two years later, the British would easily penetrate to Charlottesville in search of Jefferson himself.

Having made his case to keep the prisoners close to Monticello, Jefferson argued that the prison camp must be improved for the rank and file, while the British and German officers must be allowed to rent local houses, with pleasant surroundings and ample food. Jefferson got his way, partly due to the fact that Congress didn't want the difficulty and expense of once again moving the prisoners. "The officers, after considerable hardships, have all procured quarters, comfortable and satisfactory to them," Jefferson assured Henry.[3] The governor allowed the prison to remain.

Conditions at the barracks gradually improved, due in great part to the industry of the prisoners themselves, who were ordered by their officers to improve the buildings, plant gardens, and corral livestock. This spirit of enterprise blossomed throughout the spring. The barracks became a lively center, with its own store, coffeehouse, "large church," and taverns. A local resident named John Hawkins built "four houses of entertainment equipped with billiard tables," at which the prisoners apparently imbibed much peach brandy. A

company of British soldiers erected a "comedy theater," with two plays performed every week, complete with changes of scenery and a sign that read:
"Who would have expected all this here?" The performances attracted Virginians from miles around. As one Hessian officer wrote, "The officers lend the
necessary clothing to the actors; drummers are transformed . . . into queens
and belles!" The plays sometimes included satirical performances that mocked
the Americans, to much laughter among the prisoners.[4]

The small number of guards was unable to stop escapes, which became so
common that the prison population shrank to about three thousand within a
year. Some of those who escaped made it back to British lines, but others, especially the Germans, settled nearby or moved farther west.

Jefferson, meanwhile, went to work arranging for British and Hessian officers to rent some of the grandest homes near Monticello. He saw to it that
General Phillips moved into an estate called Blenheim, the home of Jefferson's
friend, Colonel Edward Carter, seven miles south of Monticello. The "charming mansion" of Blenheim was filled with slaves who tended to Phillips's needs,
a fellow officer wrote.[5] When Phillips was comfortably settled, Jefferson wrote
to him of the importance of being friends in spite of the war. "The great cause
which divides our countries is not to be decided by individual animosities," he
wrote, urging that "we keep up the intercourse which has begun between our
families."[6] Phillips, in turn, invited the Jeffersons to dinner, an invitation Jefferson immediately accepted. Phillips also invited Jefferson to a play being put
on by British prisoners at the Albemarle Barracks despite the likelihood that
the players would mock their Virginia guards as part of the drama. There is no
record of whether Jefferson accompanied Phillips to the makeshift theater. But
whatever play was performed by the prisoners at the Barracks, it could hardly
match the plot twist to come, in which two years later Phillips would command
an invasion that targeted Virginia and Jefferson himself.

Meanwhile, the Hessian commander Baron de Riedesel inquired about
renting Colle, the estate owned by Phillip Mazzei. The vineyards of Colle,
planted with Jefferson's encouragement, were the most ambitious experiment
in viticulture in America. Mazzei was about to depart for Europe, having been
urged by Jefferson and others to seek loans to help pay for the revolution. Thus
his home was available for rent. Riedesel and his family, as well as four lower-
ranked Hessian officers, moved in. One of the German officers was an excellent
violin player, just the accompanist that Jefferson had been seeking. Jefferson
"would have been sorry if I had rented it to other people because of the German officer, who, besides being a very polite young man, played the violin very
well," Mazzei wrote.[7]

The arrival of the German officers at Colle solved a musical problem but proved disastrous to Jefferson's viticulture dreams. As Jefferson recalled it, Mazzei "planted a considerable vineyard, attended to it with great diligence for three years. The war then came on . . . he rented his place to General Riedesel, whose horses in one week destroyed the whole labour of three or four years, and thus ended an experiment, which, from every appearance would in a year or two more have established the practicability of that branch of culture in America."[8] It would be long after Jefferson's death before productive vineyards on Monticello's hillsides would become reality.

Riedesel was soon joined at Colle by his wife, Baroness Frederika Charlotte Luise von Massow Riedesel, and their three daughters, all of whom had taken the unusual step of following the major general across the Atlantic, staying in the rear as battles were fought, and now accompanying him as the most privileged of prisoners. The baroness quickly took charge in Charlottesville, arranging for the construction of an "exceedingly pretty" large house on the Colle property and buying much of Mazzei's livestock.[9] Following Jefferson's example, the Riedesels had local blacks to do their work, and soon they had plenty of meat and vegetables. While the baroness did not object to slavery, she thought Virginia masters treated slaves badly, letting children "run naked" until they were sixteen years old and then dressing them in rags. The slaves "work like beasts or receive beatings."

The Riedesels were "comfortably fixed" at their new home, where they "received every attention from Jefferson," wrote Jefferson's great-granddaughter, Sarah Randolph. The baroness was a woman of "immense stature, who shocked Virginians by eschewing the local tradition that women only rode horses in the side saddle manner" and "mounted a horse" as she rode about the fields of Monticello and Colle.[10]

The baroness was such a regal oddity in Charlottesville that people visited just to stare at her. She, in turn, found many Virginians inexplicable. She described in detail the unusual traits of some of Jefferson's neighbors. "The Virginians are generally inert, a fate which they attribute to their hot climate," the baroness wrote. "But on the slight inducement, in a twinkling, they leap up and dance about; and if a reel—an English or a Scottish national dance—is played for them, immediately the men catch hold of the women who then jump up as if possessed; but as soon as they are led back to their chairs they sit on them like blocks of wood."[11]

Jefferson's family formed a social circle with the Riedesels, bonded by the friendship between Jefferson's daughter Patsy and the Riedesel's three daughters. Baron Riedesel fondly recalled his time at Monticello, with its harpsichord, pianoforte and violins. "The many proofs of [Mrs. Jefferson's] Friendship can never be effaced out of our memory," Riedesel wrote Jefferson, assuring him that after "this unnatural War" is over, he would "render you any Service in my power as a token of my personal regard for you and your Family."[12]

The importance of music in the relationship between Jefferson and the enemy officers could not be overstated. For years, Jefferson had yearned for learned musical companionship. Music, he wrote, was "the favorite passion of my soul, and fortune has cast my lot in a country where it is in a state of deplorable barbarism." Jefferson practiced his violin up to three hours a day for at least a dozen years, scaling back his sessions only when the revolution intruded. Jefferson was described by contemporaries as a talented violinist who embraced a European style that separated him from the local fiddlers. He particularly loved the sonatas of two Italians, Antonio Vivaldi and Arcangelo Corelli. Having failed to implement a plan to bring Italian musicians to Monticello, Jefferson was delighted that one of the German officers, Friedrich Wilhelm von Geismar, was an accomplished violinist who could join him in duets at Monticello. Geismar was a spirited young officer who had served under Lieutenant General John Burgoyne at Saratoga and had his horse shot from under him. He had a reputation for battlefield heroics—and for outdrinking his fellow officers during all-night sessions of carousing. But having surrendered at Saratoga, Geismar called himself a "humble prisoner" and said that he would "take off my hat with deep respect" to the Americans. As Jefferson and Geismar played violin, with Mrs. Jefferson accompanying on her pianoforte, the elegantly dressed Baroness Riedesel led the dances late into the evening.[13] The war must have seemed distant, even with the enemy so close.

Jefferson did not forget Geismar's valued musicianship, writing a letter on April 21, 1779, urging that the Hessian officer be freed in a prisoner swap so that he could be with his ailing father in Germany. "His personal merit, with which I am become intimately acquainted, entitles him to every indulgence," Jefferson wrote.[14] Geismar's release was eventually arranged. In exchange, he gave Jefferson a most valued gift: all of the sheaves of sheet music he had brought with him to America. "Be my friend, do not forget me and persuade Yourself of my Sincerity," Geismar wrote. The two remained friends for the rest of their lives.[15]

Jefferson would leave it to others to note the many ironies of his life at this time—being served by slaves while entertaining his enemies, embracing European tastes and sensibilities while straining to break free of European ties. Yet while Jefferson played duets with officers who once had led brutal assaults against Continental forces, many local residents feared the prisoners in their midst. The barracks of Charlottesville, remote and lightly defended, seemed a tempting target for the British or local bands of Loyalists. Should the prisoners escape, the tide of the war could turn once again. And if the enemy officers entertained by Jefferson were one day exchanged in a prisoner swap, they would be intimately familiar with the rivers and roads of Virginia, including those that led to Monticello.[16]

The Conflagration in the Night

WITH THE BRITISH AND HESSIAN troops imprisoned in Charlottesville and the war in early 1779 taking place far from Virginia, Governor Henry envisioned a peaceful end to his third one-year term in office. He had worked to strengthen the militia and build a navy, hoping this would leave the state well-defended as an American victory appeared all but assured. The British seemed moribund, practically ignoring Virginia and sitting defensively in New York. Unbeknownst to Henry, however, the British command had decided on a dramatic change in strategy. Henry Clinton, who had become commander in chief of British forces after the debacle at Saratoga, named a new naval commander—Sir George Collier, who was stationed in the tranquil British colony of Nova Scotia. Collier was ordered to return to New York and prepare an offensive. Storms nearly doomed the whole mission. One ship, with 175 men, women and children aboard, struck a shoal near New York and began to sink. Everyone perished except 27 people "who climbed up the shrouds and masts" until they were rescued by Patriots, who promptly imprisoned the survivors.

Arriving in the harbor at New York, Collier was horrified to discover that of the fleet of a hundred British men-of-war, only three, in his estimation, were battle-ready. Collier realized he was "invested with almost a nominal command and without power," according to an entry in a journal kept by an officer on Collier's ship. Instead of hunkering down in New York, as his predecessor had done, Collier decided that the best move would be to attack a vulnerable location and capture some ships.[1]

A British spy network reported that two warships and other vessels at the shipyard near Portsmouth were near completion and that the Virginians were stockpiling weapons and ammunition. The state had become a supply center for the South, providing food, men, weapons, and equipment. If the British could destroy the goods and the ships, they would go a long way toward cutting off the South and ending the rebellion. "The way which seemed most feasible to end the rebellion was cutting off the resources by which the enemy carried on the war . . . these resources were principally drawn from *Virginia*," according to the officer's journal. All it would take was one bold strike from the sea. Collier convinced Clinton to go along with the plan and won approval to take seven large ships, twenty-eight smaller transports, and at least 1,800 men. He also took along several privateers, who joined on condition they could keep their plunder.

On May 5, 1779, the British invasion fleet set sail from New York, arriving at the Capes of Virginia three days later and anchoring amidst a severe thunderstorm near Willoughby Point. From their anchorage, they controlled the entry to Virginia and the passage to the James River. The British had long blockaded the capes, halting much of Virginia's export and stifling the state's economy. But since the departure of Lord Dunmore in 1776, the British had remained offshore, content to contain Virginia rather than invade it. Now the British prepared for attack. While Governor Henry had made strides in building a navy, Virginia was hardly prepared to fight such a large British force. The sixty-four-gun ship HMS *Raisonnable* led the British flotilla, but it was too big to navigate the Elizabeth River, so Collier anchored it and ordered the crew to move its pendant to the smaller forty-four-gun *Rainbow*. On May 10, with the *Rainbow*'s sails failing to draw enough wind, troops clambered aboard flat boats, covered by the guns of the *Cornwallis* and two smaller gunboats, and headed farther up the Elizabeth River. "The sight was beautiful, and formed the finest regatta in the world," wrote an officer in Collier's ship journal. The main target was the vital port town of Portsmouth, with its troves of supplies, arms and ships. But the town was guarded by its geography. The British would first have to pass Fort Nelson, ideally situated on a spit of land that jutted into the river just in front of the shipyard. The earthen fort had fourteen-foot parapets, which contained forty-eight enclosures. About one hundred Virginians manned Nelson, under the command of Major Thomas Matthews.

Nearing the fort, the British fired a "warm cannonade," which the Virginians briefly returned. The British left ships to cut off any escape route upriver and landed their troops two miles from the fort. The plan was to launch a combined river-and-land assault the following morning. During the night, however, the Virginians had concluded they were overwhelmed and possibly trapped, and decided to make a nighttime escape. In the view of the officer writing in Collier's ship journal, they abandoned the fort "with great cowardice . . . leaving the thirteen stripes flying." The Virginians also left behind "a great number of cannon" and ammunition, according to Collier's ship journal.[2] With the fort abandoned, Virginia's naval treasure awaited the invaders: the great shipyard that Andrew Sprowle had built at Gosport, with its five-story warehouse and its great cranes and pulleys. The finest naval yard in the colonies, it had been left mostly standing when Norfolk had been destroyed in 1776. Now the works at the Gosport shipyard would be destroyed. There were 137 vessels and "five thousand loads of fine seasoned oak-knees for shipbuilding, and infinite quantity of masts, cordage, and numbers of beautiful ships of war on the stocks."[3]

Had Norfolk been left standing, the city might have defended the vital waterways at the entrance to Virginia. But it was still nearly as desolate as when the last buildings were torched. The workers at Gosport had no time to prepare for a defense, but when they saw how easily Collier had slipped past Fort Nelson, they took one desperate measure. For months, Virginian shipwrights had worked on the twenty-eight-gun *Virginia*. Rather than leave the vessel as a prize for the invaders, they set their namesake ship aflame before fleeing. Two other ships were also burned. Another six, still under construction, were captured.

Collier ordered six ships to head up the South Branch of the Elizabeth in pursuit of the fleeing Virginians. The small but powerful British subfleet captured or destroyed twenty-two more vessels. Only one, a fourteen-gun privateer called the *Black Snake,* put up a significant defense before being taken. Two British were wounded, the only British casualties of the invasion.

Collier sent another arm of the British fleet against the nearby town of Suffolk, where more supplies were stored. The British destroyed many buildings, burned thousands of barrels of tobacco, and took away valuable goods. There were reports that the British, or their privateers, treated the Virginians roughly, stripping rings from the fingers of the local women and murdering several Frenchmen who had been loading tobacco. The Virginia militia raced to hide their military supplies at a farm in nearby Nansemond, owned by one William Pugh. But the British discovered the cache and "destroyed his property, burnt his houses, killed his stock, took away his negroes, and did many other wanton acts of violence," Pugh's family said in a claim for damages. A neighbor said Pugh was targeted by the British because "his zeal caused the enemy to have a particular hatred towards him."[4]

In Williamsburg, meanwhile, Governor Henry remained unaware of the scope of the invasion, failing to order a substantial call-up of the militia until May 13, five days after it had begun. A few hundred soldiers finally began to march into Williamsburg, accompanied by the student corps of College of William and Mary, but they were far from the action. Henry did not have enough men or ships to stop the British. However, the governor did respond sympathetically to a complaint that the British had let some slaves flee to their ships. He sent a letter to Collier asking for "the restitution of four negro slaves, said to be on board some of the British ships." Collier believed the letter carrier was a spy, and so he did not send the slaves back to their master.[5]

The British occupied land that Lord Dunmore had lost nearly three years earlier, including Norfolk, the valuable supply depot at Kemp's Landing, the city of Portsmouth, and the shipyard of Gosport. Hundreds of slaves from local plantations streamed to Collier's fleet and were granted their freedom. By May 28, three weeks after the invasion began, much of Virginia's supply chain to the South had been destroyed. A stunning number of vessels, at least 130, had been burned or captured. "Our success," Collier wrote to Clinton in New York, "infinitely exceed our most sanguine expectations." The populace, thus tamed, would surely "return to obedience to their sovereign."[6]

Collier considered his next move. Thirty miles to the west was Williamsburg, and farther toward the mountains was Charlottesville, where several thousand British and Hessian prisoners were under light guard. If Collier could free the prisoners and add them to his force, he could likely capture much of Virginia. But heading west would have required significant battles with local militias, and he hesitated at the risk. What was paramount, Collier believed, was that Portsmouth remained in British hands. The port city, Collier wrote to Clinton, "appears to me of more real consequence and advantage than any other the crown now possesses in America; for by securing this whole trade of the Chesapeake is at an end, and consequently the sinews of the rebellion destroyed."[7]

Had Collier's advice been followed, the War for Independence might have gone differently. At the very least, Britain might have had enough naval strength at Portsmouth to forestall the subsequent disaster at Yorktown. But Clinton was concerned about the growing threat from American fortifications on the Hudson River. The attack in Virginia was planned as a quick strike, not as an occupation. Collier was told to return to New York.

Collier and his fellow officers were aghast at the order. They were certain that Portsmouth held the key to controlling Virginia and thus the South. Collier tried to point out "in very strong terms" that keeping Portsmouth in possession of the king "would distress the rebels exceedingly" and halt completely their passage on the Chesapeake. The evacuation of Portsmouth would be "a fatal and unfortunate measure, *universally regretted* by all who were acquainted with its great importance, and the advantages which would have resulted to Great Britain," wrote the officer in Collier's ship journal.[8]

Clinton had left Collier with no choice, however. Collier ordered his troops to collect the thousands of pieces of oak, the beautifully crafted masts and planks of the Gosport shipyard. Just as Virginians had destroyed Norfolk to ensure that the British could not occupy it, the British destroyed much of the

Gosport shipyard so the Americans could not use it against the British. Soon the remains of the yard were ablaze. "The conflagration in the night appeared grand beyond description," a British officer wrote, even as he lamented the thought of so many fine masts being turned to ashes.[9]

With the bonfire illuminating the night sky, the fleet set sail in late May for New York. They took with them 17 captured ships, 90 Loyalists, and 518 former slaves who had taken advantage of the invasion to win their freedom. Far more than ships and supplies had been destroyed in Virginia: also shattered had been the sense that Virginia somehow was detached from the war. The feeling of security was replaced by fear that the next attack would reach Williamsburg and beyond.

The British departure coincided nearly to the day with the end of Henry's term, an embarrassing conclusion to his tenure. It all could have been far worse, however. Thanks to Clinton's insistence that he leave Virginia, Collier did not make it as far inland as the Chickahominy River, where the state had built a new shipyard in hopes of making it less vulnerable to British attack.

As Collier departed Virginia, a pair of British privateers brought him a prize: an American ship bound for Europe. Among the passengers on the *Johnston* was Philip Mazzei, who was on board to begin a mission to seek funds in Europe to support the war effort in Virginia. Jefferson had urged the mission, describing Mazzei as a "zealous whig" who had everything necessary to be the state's representative in France and elsewhere. Mazzei had been given a further set of credentials by the Hessian renting his home, General Riedesel. The document, intended as a pass in the event Mazzei was detained by the British, requested that "whoever reads it may shew every possible attention to Mr. Mazzei, his Lady & daughter, & I shall consider such Civilities in the same light as if they were received by myself . . . I consider Mr. Mazzei as worthy of generous treatment as he cannot be looked upon as a public Enemy of Great Britain but merely a Passenger of his own Country." In fact, few had pushed more strongly for revolution than Mazzei. As the ship carrying Mazzei approached the Capes of Virginia, the privateers *Lord North* and *Apollo* obstructed its passage. Rightly fearing that the *Johnston* would be seized, Mazzei threw overboard a satchel containing the most sensitive documents, weighted by a four-pound ball.[10] He told the sailors aboard the privateer that he was merely a farmer who grew grapes in the hills of Virginia.

Nonetheless, Mazzei was brought to New York and presented to Collier, who, Mazzei had been warned, was like a "stingy hard and spiteful old woman." Collier said he knew Mazzei was a revolutionary and an agent for Virginia. He had found among Mazzei's remaining papers several pieces of legislation proposed by Jefferson, including one for religious liberty. One of Mazzei's captors said that Jefferson and Mazzei "were the biggest rebels in the Colonies and deserved to be thrown into the sea with anchors tied to head and feet." Collier asked Mazzei what he had intended to do in Europe. "I pretended I did not know what he meant and answered that I was going to Tuscany, called back by my interests there," Mazzei later wrote. After weeks of imprisonment and with Collier occupied with other matters, Mazzei managed to win his freedom. He found passage to Europe, where he spent several years fruitlessly trying to get loans of gold or silver for the revolution.[11]

In Williamsburg, meanwhile, the legislature prepared to select a new governor. The candidates, put up by various legislators, were Jefferson, Thomas Nelson, and John Page. Nelson was a wealthy and popular merchant and planter and a leader of Virginia's militia in the region near Yorktown. Page had served as president of the Governor's Council and as lieutenant governor, and, when Henry had become seriously ill, he had acted as governor. But Nelson and Page were both from the Tidewater planter class, which was still considered too closely tied to England, the Anglican Church, and the old order of things. Jefferson was a Piedmont politician at a time when that region was ascendant, and he had the backing of some of Henry's allies. In hindsight, it is noteworthy that Jefferson had no military background. After none of the three candidates pulled enough votes to gain a majority on the first ballot, a second ballot gave Jefferson the victory with sixty-seven votes, six more than Page. The contest was a painful one for Jefferson and Page, who had been such close friends for years. Now, having lost the governorship to Jefferson, Page sought to assure his friend that he had no "low dirty feelings" about the matter. Jefferson responded to Page: "It had given me much pain, that the zeal of our respective friends should ever have placed you and me in the situation of competitors."[12] Jefferson insisted to his friends that he had been a reluctant candidate.

Jefferson's acceptance of the governorship was announced in a short notice in the *Gazette,* in which he gave "my most grateful acknowledgement . . . in a virtuous and free state, no rewards can be so pleasing to sensible minds, as those which include the approbation of our fellow citizens." He promised "assiduous attention, and sincere affection to the great American cause." To friends, however, he confessed unease. The appointment as governor "has withdrawn me from the society of my late neighbors," he wrote, and "is not likely to add to my happiness. It would be wrong to refuse the governorship, Jefferson believed, though he feared it would also bring "intense labor and great private loss."[13]

The Enemy Will Commit Great Ravages

ATTIRED IN HIS FINERY and attended by his slaves, Jefferson climbed aboard a phaeton drawn by four horses and took the familiar road to Williamsburg, nearly two decades after arriving in the capital as a student. He passed by his old college quarters at the Wren Building, turned up Duke of Gloucester Street, and came to the familiar intersection from which the emerald green led to the Governor's Palace. Jefferson's arrival coincided with growing concern that another armada of British invaders would sail up the James River at any moment. The capital was up in arms, bustling with fresh-faced student soldiers, roughly dressed militia from the farms and mountains, and a smattering of Continental soldiers. There was "no illumination of the city, no welcoming committee," only a Spartan greeting by legislators who hoped that the quiet genius of Jefferson could lift Virginia from its lethargy and rekindle the spirit of revolution.[1]

Jefferson immediately received dire warnings from his friends about the collapsing state of affairs in Virginia. The economy was in shambles, and a number of counties failed to submit taxes. The state was woefully short of weaponry. Pirates were running up the bays, rivers, and inlets, plundering at will, while British ships sailed up and down the coast. William Fleming, a Virginia delegate to the Continental Congress, wrote Jefferson that the rate of inflation was "almost beyond conception," and fears were growing that "the enemy will commit great ravages." The Continental army, he warned Jefferson, was restless because of the lack of proper payments. "I am persuaded that if something effectual is not speedily done . . . the disbanding of our army must inevitably be the consequence."

The aim of the British, Fleming continued, "seems to be to carry on a kind of piratical war in detached parties, by burning our towns, plundering our sea coasts, and distressing individuals." Meanwhile, Fleming lamented, "the bulk of the people thro'out the states, seem to have lost sight of the great object for which we had recourse to arms, and to have turned their thought solely to accumulating *ideal* wealth, and preying upon the necessities or their fellow citizens. I have heard much, but seen very little, of patriotism and public virtue."[2]

Jefferson had heard rumors of alleged "cruelties" perpetrated by the British during the Collier invasion, but, as he told Fleming, "I am not able yet to decide within myself whether there were such or not." He had heard "testimony" from both sides and had not drawn a conclusion. Jefferson's tone reveals how strongly he believed in a certain civility between enemies. He found it hard to believe their fellow officers could commit depravities elsewhere in Virginia.[3]

Yet Jefferson could see evidence of the depravities of war as he roamed Williamsburg and read the dire news in the *Gazette.* The newspaper offered a harrowing combination of notices about British victories, Continental army failures, military deserters, and runaway slaves. One slave owner, William B. Walker, urged the *Gazette*'s readers to be on the lookout for Precept, "a small fellow," and Toney, who had "several scars about his body" and spoke good French. Walker had "reason to suppose they will try to get on board the British fleet." He offered a reward of $20 each. By contrast, Robert Prentis offered $30 for the return of a brown bay horse.[4]

Rewards were larger—$50 each—for deserters from the militia or Continental army. Around the time that Jefferson became governor, the *Gazette* provided a painfully detailed description of six deserters who until recently had walked the streets of Williamsburg. Stephen Hawk, five feet five inches tall, with dark brown hair, round shoulders, "a down look," and a face "pitted with the smallpox," had been aboard the frigate *Randolph* before it sank. William Thompson, five feet seven inches, his face also pitted by smallpox, was "very talkative when in liquor." John Mitchell, six feet, "pock pitted," who often covered his brown hair with a round hat bound with gold lace, had served three years in the Continental army. William Stone, five feet seven inches, a blacksmith with large eyes and dark hair, favored an old light-colored cloth coat, blue jacket, and leather breeches. James Waters, five feet seven inches, was "pock pitted" and wore a white flannel jacket and leather breeches. The sixth, a Frenchman named Jean who was about five feet eight inches in height, wore a cocked hat and spoke broken English.[5]

As Jefferson read the letter from his friend Fleming and scanned the report of the six deserters from Williamsburg, the reality of being a wartime governor must have weighed heavily upon him. The days of listening to high-flown debates on the floor of the legislature or writing great words of revolution would be replaced by a ceaseless stream of crises. Jefferson's strength had been in conceptualizing liberty, not in making it a reality, as symbolized by his lifelong torment over slavery. Now that torment was writ large in his duties. He could no longer rail against the governor because he was the governor.

He was not even sure whether it was wise to continue the war, given the weakened state of the Continental army and local militias. "It would surely be better to carry on a ten years' war some time hence than to continue the present an unnecessary moment," Jefferson wrote Fleming, alluding to suggestions that a peace treaty be signed with the British.[6] However, he soon became convinced that only military victory would end the war. Defeat would cost Jefferson everything, including his estate and possibly his life. He issued a proclamation calling for British Loyalists to leave Virginia and for British property to be confiscated in an effort to solve the state's financial problems. But such directives were fraught with difficulties, given the divided loyalties within families, and ultimately they failed. Many Virginians, struggling with a poor harvest, suggested that a renewal of trade with Britain would solve the state's problems.

JEFFERSON FOUND THE FAMILIAR HALLS of the Governor's Palace far removed from the elegance of the days of the British governors. As a young man, Jefferson often had visited the palace, dining with the British governor, admiring the rows of muskets and swords lining the walls, and gazing upon the fine china and furniture—an assemblage of wealth that could run to 11,500 pieces. Most of the arms, silver, and furnishings had long since been taken away, either by the departing British governor who owned them, or perhaps by ransacking rebels. Jefferson ordered the taking of an inventory, which found several hundred items, including chairs, tables, lamps, china, glasses, and prints. It was grand enough, but the days of balls and midnight dinners were mostly past. The young state of Virginia was rapidly going broke.[7]

An abundance of opulence also might have been out of place in any case because the position of governor was far less influential than in royal days. Jefferson himself had supported efforts to curtail the governor's power, arguing that the governor should be compelled to heed advice from a council of advisors and have his power checked by the House and Senate. Jefferson's drafts of the Virginia constitution had included a long list of things that a king could do but a governor could not, including declaring war, raising an army, building armed vessels or forts, and even erecting lighthouses. While parts were modified and some of the restrictions never enacted, his proposals underscored how deeply he worried that a governor might turn into a tyrant. While a governor did have authority to conduct routine business if the council could not be assembled in a timely matter, Jefferson was often reluctant to use even that modest power.

One area in which Jefferson was willing to exert power involved vacating Williamsburg. He had never gotten over his disdain for the place, and had been trying since 1776 to move the capital inland, to Richmond, an unincorporated village of 684 people. Such a move would be a reward to the Piedmont and to those western legislators who had ensured his election over the two candidates from the Tidewater. Richmond was closer to Albemarle County and to his political power base, and it would orient Virginia to the west, which Jefferson viewed as the state's future. Moreover, moving the capital to Richmond would create a clean architectural slate, leaving behind the relics of royalism in Williamsburg.

Williamsburg's merchants and landowners objected to the plan, of course. But Collier's invasion reinforced Jefferson's argument that Williamsburg was dangerously exposed and easily could be swamped by a large enemy force. Williamsburg was situated some fifty miles from the Capes of Virginia, approachable by landings from the south on the James River and from the north on the York River. Richmond, by contrast, was about twice as far from the Capes, approachable on the James only after the navigation of the narrowing and serpentine bends of the river, and more easily defended from the hills and the broad stretches of field and forest. In theory at least, the militia would have time to prepare Richmond's defense if word came of an invading force. Jefferson's plan was approved and, notwithstanding Richmond's lack of housing or even a suitable place to put the governor and government, the transfer of power began.

SHORTLY AFTER ASSUMING THE GOVERNORSHIP, Jefferson resumed his cordial relationship with British general William Phillips and the Hessian commander Riedesel. Phillips wrote to Jefferson that he lamented the loss of Jefferson's company, and asked if Jefferson had any objection to him taking a trip with Riedesel to Berkeley Springs, about 134 miles north of Charlottesville, near the Pennsylvania border, in an area that later became West Virginia. The springs, known for curative powers, had been a major attraction since at least the 1760s, when squatters began building cabins in the area. In 1776 the Virginia legislature granted a petition to two hundred people who wanted to create a town called Bath, intended to be a resort similar to the one in England. A year later, seventy leading citizens, including George Washington, purchased lots around the springs. In 1779, when Phillips and Riedesel proposed to visit, an inn had just opened that provided lodging for a mix of guests, including Hessian prisoners, wives and children of Continental officers, and other refugees of war.

Notwithstanding the state of war existing between the United States and Britain at that moment, Jefferson apparently saw no reason to fear that Phillips and Riedesel would use the trip as a scouting mission for a future invasion of interior Virginia. Collier's invasion may have shown the vulnerability of the state's coastal region, but Jefferson still did not believe the British would get near Charlottesville, and he could "foresee no probability" that the British prisoners would have to be removed from Virginia. Jefferson assured Phillips that "no impediment can arise on my part to the excursion proposed . . . to the Berkeley springs for your amusement."[8]

At the moment Jefferson was granting the passes, however, hundreds of prisoners were deserting the Albemarle barracks. One report that crossed Jefferson's desk revealed that four hundred prisoners had escaped, with some heading into the woods and alarming local residents, and others making their way to British forces opposing Washington. Washington was livid. He did not have "the smallest confidence" that the prisoners would abide by their agreement not to rejoin the British army. He urged that the escapees be captured and put under "close confinement . . . to convince them of their errors, and as an example to others."[9] It was a major embarrassment. Under Jefferson's watch and in sight of his home, the poorly guarded barracks had been breached easily. Jefferson reported to Washington that some of the escapees had forged passports or false oaths of loyalty to the United States, possibly obtained "with the connivance of some of their officers."[10]

However, Jefferson did not believe that either Phillips or Riedesel had had anything to do with the escapes. Phillips maintained he had known nothing about the matter, writing the American commander of the barracks, Theodorick Bland Jr., that "I cannot possibly know any thing concerning them after they have left the troops of the convention." He insisted that it did not concern him whether the escapees returned to the British lines or defected to the Americans. Moreover, Phillips wrote, any deserters who gave up Great Britain for America were "miscreants, who will embrace any cause, and change from party to party, from fear of punishment or hope of reward."[11]

Riedesel soon began his journey to Berkeley Springs, bringing his wife and several of the Hessian officers. After taking the baths and complaining that they had actually been a detriment to his health, Riedesel received word that he and Phillips were to be exchanged for American prisoners. Riedesel met with Phillips and the two officers made their way to New York, where the exchange was to take place. Shortly before reaching New York, Phillips received word that the exchange was delayed. Known for his temper, Phillips banged his fist on a table and exclaimed, "This might have been expected of men who are all rascals!" Jefferson apologized to Riedesel but said he was hopeful the delay meant that he would have "a pleasure we should otherwise perhaps never had had; that of seeing you again." Riedesel and his wife and their newborn daughter, whom they named America, eventually were allowed to go to Canada, where Riedesel served the British as a senior military official.[12]

Jefferson looked forward with particular pleasure to the day he could once again socialize with Phillips. "The hour of private retirement to which I am drawn by nature with a propensity almost irresistible, and which would again join me to the same agreeable circle, will be the most welcome of my life," Jefferson wrote Phillips.[13]

Phillips would return to Virginia, but it would not be to pay the kind of social call that Jefferson envisioned. Phillips was now in British-controlled New York, where he eventually was given his freedom to rejoin the British army. One of Phillips's first actions in New York was to visit the mansion of a fellow British general, his old friend Charles Cornwallis. Cornwallis was preparing to sail to South Carolina on a mission that would result in the capture of Charleston. Soon it would be decided that Phillips, too, would lead an invasion to the south.

JEFFERSON BELIEVED that when Virginians faced the imminent threat of invasion, they would quickly close ranks, volunteering for the national army and heeding calls to form units in the local militia. But the system was failing, and Jefferson knew it. Now, at the worst possible moment, it was on the brink of collapse.

During the early stages of the War of Independence, many Virginians had volunteered to confront the British. Indeed, so many people were anxious to take up arms and be rid of Dunmore that Jefferson had worried about "the almost ungovernable fury of the people." Then, after Dunmore fled, many Virginians felt a burst of patriotism and volunteered to serve in the Continental army. For example, in Northumberland County, on Virginia's northern neck, 163 men enlisted, and thousands of men followed their example in other counties.

But as Virginians returned from their Continental army service, many told tales of horrid conditions, lack of pay, lack of arms, and seemingly endless rounds of sickness. Of those 163 men who enlisted from Northumberland County, 61 died from disease and only 5 from combat wounds.[1] A similar toll was experienced by regiments across the state. As war dragged on, it became increasingly difficult to convince Virginians to leave their homes and families and volunteer for service. Commander in Chief Washington, meanwhile, was anxious to create a more professional Continental army and pushed Virginia to send men for three-year terms.

Jefferson saw signs in his own Albemarle County of how quickly the patriotic spirit could be dashed, due in part to clashes of economic and social interests, and in part to valid concerns of men who feared leaving their homes at a time when crops needed tending and families faced threats from slave uprisings and British invaders. Jefferson's friend and personal physician, George Gilmer, decried the lack of volunteers for county service, blaming a system that enabled wealthy men to avoid service. Out of three hundred men who were supposed to turn out for local duty, there were "so few that I am afraid to name them," Gilmer wrote. The rules were "calculated to exempt the gentlemen and to throw the whole burthen on the poor."[2] Such concerns were valid even as the system changed from one that relied on so-called Minuteman units to one that drew upon potential militia members. Every white male between sixteen and fifty years of age was expected to serve in the militia. But many of those who were supposed to serve in the militia were subsistence farmers or manual workers who could not afford to leave their fields and families. Moreover, many of those who owned property or paid taxes on more than three slaves were exempt from militia service. In other words, those least able to afford service were required to serve, while the wealthier could avoid it. Nonetheless, the breadth of the militia system, with hundreds of men expected to be ready in every county on a moment's notice, gave Jefferson hope that it would serve the state well at a time of crisis.

The system frequently broke down, however, because some of the same men who were expected to serve in the militia were also being asked to serve three-year terms in the Continental army. After the initial burst of voluteerism for the national force had resulted in so many Virginians dying of disease or returning home with tales of woe, Virginia began to seriously consider a request from Congress to implement a draft. Despite increasingly hefty bounties for service, Virginia's leaders couldn't even get some of the state's poorest men to volunteer in the Continental army. "I really believe that numbers of our lazy, worthless young Men will not be induced to come forth into the service of their Country unless the States adopt the mode recommended by Congress of ordering Drafts from the Militia," Richard Henry Lee wrote to Jefferson. Jefferson feared that instituting a draft would cause a backlash. He preferred to help raise bounty money to attract new recruits, providing £51 to induce a leading military man in Albemarle County named John (Jack) Jouett Jr. to enlist. It would turn out to be a crucial connection: several years later, Jouett would play a decisive role in saving Jefferson's life. Bounties, however, would not prove a successful enough way to raise recruits. By the time Jefferson became governor, he would conclude that he had no choice but to back a draft, a measure he knew many Virginians would consider the "last of all oppressions."[3]

Throughout the governorships of Henry and Jefferson, Virginia tried a host of measures designed to attract recruits. The state's small population of free blacks was encouraged to enlist, and some black slaves were even allowed to enlist as substitutes for their masters. But none of the measures worked and the state fell increasingly short of its recruitment quota. Henry, who had come to prominence in part because of his ability to attract hundreds of volunteers to his side, was appalled that so few men seemed willing to fight for liberty. Pouring out his frustration to Jefferson after the latter had succeeded him as governor, Henry wrote, "Do you remember any instance where tyranny was destroyed and freedom established on its ruins, among a people possessing so small a share of virtue and public spirit? I recollect none, and this, more than the British arms, makes me fearful of final success without a reform."

Moreover, Henry was worried that the state was being torn apart by conspiracies. There were many people who were thought to be good Patriots who "keep company with the miscreants, wretches, who, I am satisfied, were labouring for our destruction." The "wicked individuals" should be "shunned and execrated," Henry warned Jefferson.[4]

By September 1780, after Jefferson had been governor for fifteen months, Virginia was so desperate to fill its quota of three thousand volunteers for the Continental army that the legislature passed a measure promising recruits who agreed to serve until the end of the war a taxpayer-financed bounty of $12,000 as well as three hundred acres of land. In addition, those who fulfilled the recruitment contract would receive a bonus in human chattel—"a healthy sound negro, between the ages of ten and thirty years," which would be contributed by wealthier Virginians. The state's major slave owners complained that an initial version of the act would force them to give up one of every twenty slaves to army recruits, even if they were to be reimbursed with interest after the war. In the end, the slave bonus was all but ignored because it was enacted during a period of mayhem when British forces were roaming the state. Yet the measure's passage underscored how few Virginians wanted to volunteer for the Continental service. No amount of money or land seemed to be enough.[5]

Indeed, even as the measure made its way slowly through the legislature, Jefferson complained that "a very considerable proportion" of the latest recruits were boys and old men.[6] Jefferson wrote a pleading letter to Washington, informing the commander of American forces that southern troops were in tatters. Jefferson had hoped to send 7,000 men from Virginia "into the southern service," of which he expected only 5,500 to be fit for duty. But he had supplies for only 3,000. "We are still more destitute of Clothing, Tents and Wagons for our troops," Jefferson wrote. He suggested that a fleet of the French navy spend the winter in Chesapeake Bay, providing extra security.[7]

Washington was all sympathy but could not help. "It would be a most desirable thing, if we had Magazines of Arms, Ammunition, Cloathing and Tents formed as Your Excellency mentions, but unhappily this is not the case, nor have we a Store of these essential Articles at any point," Washington wrote on October 10, 1780. "I am sorry to find that the Southern Army suffers for provision. We are at this moment destitute of a drop of Rum for the Soldiery, and cannot obtain some Blankets we have at the Eastward, for want of transportation."[8]

Throughout the coming invasions, the lack of recruits, as well as the difficulty of raising a well-armed militia, would be a recurring crisis. Jefferson would complain on a sometimes daily basis that the militia did not turn out, did not have arms, or did not have proper clothing or even shoes. And every time word came of a British victory, a flurry of Loyalist activity would take place. In one case a band of British sympathizers in Bedford County in southwest Virginia, where Jefferson had his Poplar Forest plantation, seized ammunition that was to be used by the local militia. The action led to panic that the Loyalists would unite with invading British forces to form a second front.

The Bedford County militia was led by Colonel Charles Lynch, who was known for his tough tactics. He once had suspected Loyalists tied to a walnut tree and lashed until they cried out, "Liberty forever!"[9] Jefferson wrote to Lynch to be careful how he meted out punishment. However, he also praised Lynch for seizing the suspected conspirators and expressed astonishment that any Virginian would help the British. "Your activity on this occasion deserves great commendation, and meets it from the Executive," Jefferson wrote. "The method of seizing [the Loyalist conspirators] at once which you have adopted is much the best. You have only to take care that they be regularly tried afterwards."[10]

Lynch, who happened also to be the presiding local justice, sentenced a leader to a year in prison and a fine of £20,000. The charge had been treason. Virginia law stipulated that the state's General Court, not the local circuit court, should pass judgment on such an allegation. Lynch countered that he needed to deal with the matter quickly and locally.

In the wake of protests that Lynch had exceeded his authority, the legislature supported Lynch, arguing that he had done what was necessary and would not be punished. Whatever the merit of the case, the precedent that a local official could take state law into his own hands without fear of recrimination was hotly debated. Someone described the practice as a "Lynch law," occasionally shortened to "lynching," leading some etymologists to conclude years later that it was the source of a word synonymous with racial terror. There are other theories as to the source of the word "lynching," but the belief that Charles Lynch's law spawned the word is laid out in articles going back more than a century.

In the end, the responsibility for defending Virginia would fall most heavily on its militia. The Virginia Declaration of Rights put it succinctly: "That a well regulated militia, composed of the body of the people, trained to arms, is the proper, natural, and safe defense of a free state, that standing armies, in time of peace, should be avoided as dangerous to liberty; and that in all cases the military should be under strict subordination to, and governed by, the civil power."[11]

The problem was that nearly every element of the declaration was at times unfulfilled. The Virginia militia often was poorly regulated, was not truly composed of "the body of the people" (given that many landowners were exempted from service), and was largely untrained or lacking in arms. The requirement that Virginia should have no standing army meant the state had to rely on a system ill-prepared to respond to a major invasion. Jefferson and many other Virginians worried that a standing army would abuse its power and act tyrannically. However, its absence meant vulnerability to attack. Finally, the militia was under the "strict subordination" of civil authorities, but those authorities—namely, the governor and his council—often lacked the will or the power to ensure that the men would turn out, thus undermining the most important element of their authority.

Despite all of this, the Virginia militia consisted of thousands of men who fought against overwhelming odds and far better-equipped and -trained armies and navies. In Jefferson's Albemarle County, where turnout of units was sometimes poor, were men such as Charles Lewis. Early in the revolution, Lewis headed up a company of county volunteers. When that service ended, he volunteered to serve in a militia corps in the west, fighting against the Cherokees. Then, after commanding another regiment, he resigned to take care of a "large family." But he subsequently agreed to command a regiment at the Albemarle Barracks, only to die of unspecified reasons during that service.[12] Meanwhile, several thousand of Virginia's best soldiers were serving in the Continental army outside its borders at a time when the state faced an imminent threat of invasion.

FOR MANY VIRGINIANS, one of the rationales for the rebellion—to end taxation without representation—had backfired. The conflict was so costly that it had caused taxes to go up time and again. Paper money became so depreciated that it was nearly worthless. One of the new taxes required most Virginians to pay with crops such as corn and barley, in addition to tobacco, and at much higher rates than before the war. A Jefferson-backed poll tax was also instituted, requiring that slaveholders pay according to the number of slaves they owned. For militiamen facing a draft into the national army, the tax situation became even more onerous. In order to avoid being drafted, men in various districts paid taxes to raise more bounty money to meet the quota for local recruits. The poor complained that they didn't have enough money to pay for a substitute. The wealthy complained that they were taxed disproportionately. One wealthy Virginian, Theodorick Bland Sr., wrote to his son, Theodorick Bland Jr., that he had paid about £2,560 to help pay for substitutes in the draft for both of them, under a law that "will soon reduce the most opulent fortune to a level with that of the inferior class of people, especially if the assembly continues to put the power of taxation into the hands of the very lowest class."[13]

The lower classes had reason to feel resentful. Under the rules of the state, only well-off white male property owners could vote. As Jefferson later noted, "The majority of the men in the state, who pay and fight for its support, are unrepresented in the legislature." (Jefferson added that the system of representation was unequal. Warwick County had 100 "fighting men" and Loudoun County 1,746, but both had the same number of legislative delegates.) Indeed, one of the inducements to service was that a Virginian who enlisted for the duration of the war would become part of the landed class, and presumably be given the right to a vote.[14]

Some recruits collected large bounties from local citizens only to desert the army and use the money to buy land in remote western areas of the state. This prompted a backlash, with angry Virginians urging that deserters be deprived of all land. A petition from Charlotte County residents to the legislature complained that too many recruits took "large contributions from individuals, and deserted immediately."[15] Yet despite the increased inducements, recruitment went poorly in many counties. Antidraft riots occurred not only in counties where Loyalism persisted, but also where many men felt it was not in their immediate economic or family interest to serve far from Virginia.

The lack of military recruits provided an ironic twist: it played a key role in the enhancement of religious freedom. Jefferson, who was raised an Anglican but decried what he later called Virginia's system of "religious slavery," was surrounded by non-Anglicans in Albemarle County. He estimated that by the onset of the revolution, two-thirds of Virginians were dissenters; likely the guess was too high, but it demonstrated his outlook at the time. The largest groups of dissenters were the Presbyterians, many of whom lived in the shadow of the Blue Ridge Mountains, and the Baptists, who were populous in the Piedmont. A number of Lutherans also lived in the Shenandoah region. All three groups were inclined to support revolution if it meant more freedom for their faith. Methodists, meanwhile, tended to back the British or remain neutral. Quakers and Mennonites cited antiwar beliefs in their effort to stay out of combat, and they usually accomplished this by paying a fee or finding a substitute. Many religious dissenters had fought for years to attain freedom of worship and had objected to paying taxes to support a faith they did not practice. This was not a fight against the British, but rather had become one against the Anglican establishment in Virginia. As Jefferson later wrote, many of the dissenters in Virginia came from families that had fled from religious persecution in England and "cast their eyes on these new countries as asylums of civil and religious freedom" but they "found them free only for the reigning sect." While Virginia's leaders had eased some restrictions at the onset of the revolution, dissenters wanted complete freedom. Jefferson was their champion, writing later that "it does me no injury for my neighbour to say there are twenty gods, or no god."[16]

As Virginia officials struggled to find military recruits, the victims of religious discrimination sought to make a bargain with the state. If their faith was more fully tolerated, they would support the revolutionary cause. "These things granted, we will gladly unite with our Brethren of other denominations, and to the utmost of our ability, promote the common cause of Freedom," the Baptists of Prince William County wrote in a petition. The most extraordinary petition, signed by ten thousand people, demanded the birthright of religious freedom and "Equal Liberty!" With Jefferson playing a key role in what he called "the severest contests," Virginia exempted dissenters from paying the Anglican tax and then lifted the levy altogether. While it is impossible to say how many Virginians fought as a result of the gradual easing of religious restrictions, it helped recruit some of the most fervent fighters in the cause of revolution in Virginia. It would be nearly a decade before Jefferson's statute for religious freedom was formally adopted, providing broader rights to members of all faiths. Jefferson believed it had been essential that the dissenters take advantage of the revolutionary wartime spirit, when the people were "united."[17]

THE BITTER REALITY, however, was that Virginians did not seem all that united. Antidraft protests took place throughout Virginia, both in areas where Loyalism persisted and in Patriot-dominated regions where militiamen were fed up with constant calls to leave their homes and serve the state or Continental army. In Prince William County, where forty-eight men were drafted, nine of them deserted, while two others "cut off their fingers after the draft" in an effort to avoid service.[18] In southwest Virginia, hundreds of men "had actually enlisted to serve his Britannic majesty, had taken oaths of allegiance to him," Jefferson was told. There were insurrections in the counties of Washington, Montgomery, and Henry, the last of which was within seventy miles of the Albemarle barracks. This alarmed Jefferson, who believed the counties "had always been considered as a barrier" to any effort by the British to free their countrymen and the Hessians. "Other counties equally relied on may fail us in the hour of trial," Jefferson wrote, seeking help and advice from Congress.[19]

In Northumberland County, disputes broke out over religion, class, and military service. For example, while Baptists were now officially tolerated by the state, some of Northumberland's Anglicans apparently were not prepared to embrace them. When a charismatic Baptist preacher known as the "Wonder Boy" addressed seven hundred supporters, the event was disrupted by local opponents, led by a pistol-carrying man who ascended the speaker's platform. The Baptists pulled up fence posts and "warmly resisted" the opponents.[20]

In September 1780, with Jefferson seeking more men from the county to be drafted into Continental service, dozens of Northumberland militiamen revolted, protesting that they would refuse to be drafted to serve in the Continental army. The riot escalated when one of the militiamen got into an argument with his captain. The two men aimed their rifles at each other and fired. Captain Edwin Hull, a wealthy landowner and slaveholder, was killed, while the soldier who started the feud, Joseph Pitman, was wounded.[21] Seeking to bring the men under control, Thomas Gaskins, the county lieutenant, arranged for thirty-nine of them to be court-martialed. If the men turned themselves in, the punishment would be precisely what the men had been trying to avoid —an eighteen-month term in the Continental army. When the disobedient men refused to submit, Gaskins asked other militiamen to round up "those that mutinied," he wrote to Jefferson. "But to my great surprise few or none appeared in our favor and the Very men I confided in appeared in arms against us . . . almost the whole county was inflaim'd."[22]

Some of the rioters fled to British vessels, while others remained at large. A group of thirty-two men, mostly officers, responded by trying to subdue almost "a whole county," Gaskins told Jefferson. It was with such incidents in mind that Jefferson struggled with pleas from his military commanders to call up more men. He was reluctant, as he put it, to "harass" the militia by calling them up unless he was convinced the need was urgent. He was fighting one war against the British, worried about another against the British-allied Indians in the west, and, it sometimes seemed, a third against the very men he was counting on to defend the state.

This Dangerous Fire Is Only Smothered

AS JEFFERSON FILED HIS LATEST REPORT to Congress, he knew the state was too weak to stop another British invasion. Nonetheless, he continued to feel confident that such an attack was unlikely. General Clinton, the British commander, "would scarcely consent to spare men from New York," Jefferson assured Congress in September 1780. It "does not seem probable" that the British would try to take possession of Portsmouth, Jefferson wrote.

But then Jefferson continued with an ominous admission. Should the British "go directly contrary to obvious principles of reason" and launch a new invasion, "they would find us in a condition incapable of resistance." After giving arms to three thousand recruits to the Continental army, the state did not have a single usable musket left for the militia. Nor did it have tents. Virginia's defense rested on the hope that the British would somehow not be interested in seizing the largest, wealthiest state, which held vital supply lines to the southern theater of war.[1]

What Jefferson didn't count on was that Clinton once again had his eyes on Virginia. On October 16, 1780, Clinton ordered General Alexander Leslie to invade the state. The goal was to reestablish fortifications along the Elizabeth River, around Norfolk and Portsmouth, the abandonment of which, the British now realized, had been a mistake. With Lord Cornwallis trying to hold down rebels in South and North Carolina, the British were constantly frustrated by the flow of troops, food, and supplies through Virginia. The British wanted to intercept supplies intended for Continental forces in the Carolinas and tie up Virginians who might otherwise be headed south. Eventually, it was hoped, Cornwallis could come north, hook up with Leslie in Virginia, and launch a full-scale assault on Virginia that would win the war for Britain.

Leslie commanded 2,200 men and a fleet of six ships. The largest was the *Romulus,* ringed by forty cannons, followed by the *Blonde,* with thirty-two guns. There were also a twenty-gun ship commanded by John Goodrich; the sloop *Delight,* with sixteen guns; and two smaller craft. The fleet arrived at Portsmouth on October 21, landing near the same position abandoned earlier by Collier. Two days later, most of the fleet moved to Newport News and Hampton. Virginia's small navy and ill-prepared militia were almost entirely ineffectual in their efforts to stop Leslie. The British once again had cut off the main supply route to the South.

Thomas Nelson, the militia commander from Yorktown, sent an urgent letter to Jefferson, informing him there was "no possibility of preventing" Leslie from taking control of the port cities. "The confusion is so great" that it was unlikely an adequate militia could be mustered. He had "a poor prospect" of getting the necessary cavalry. The cattle that had been collected for the militia "have fallen into enemy hands." Worse, many of the armaments that until recently were at Williamsburg had been moved to the new capital. "We have not a single piece of Artillery. They were all carried away to Richmond with the Ammunition."[2]

An even more dire warning came from Jefferson's friend James Innes. While Virginians' belief in the cause of independence was "unanimous and firm," Innes wrote Jefferson, he feared Virginians would cave in to the enemy in short order. "The feelings of the man, may in a fatal moment, swallow up the sentiments of the patriot." Worse, many militia members from the coastal area had felt abandoned after Jefferson moved the seat of government from Williamsburg to Richmond. According to Innes, the only solution was for Jefferson to send militia from upland portions of the state to help defend the coast.[3]

The size of Leslie's invading force was unclear to Virginians. An article in the *Virginia Gazette* put the fleet at fifty-four ships—including twenty-five large vessels, carrying five thousand men—vastly overestimating the size of the six-ship fleet and more than doubling the actual number of men.[4] Jefferson confided to Samuel Huntington of the Continental Congress on October 22 that "the want of Arms prevents every hope of effectual Opposition." Jefferson mistakenly estimated the enemy fleet to be sixty ships, against which Virginia's ragtag assemblage of vessels, few of which were equipped with enough cannons to send into battle, had no chance. "Of the troops we shall be able to collect there is not a single man who ever saw the face of the enemy," Jefferson wrote.[5]

On October 25, four days after Leslie's fleet arrived, one thousand British infantry troops were scattered around Newport News and Hampton, prompting many townspeople to flee. Leslie sent a cavalry force of one hundred horses along the main roads, spreading fear through the countryside that the invasion fleet would soon move toward Richmond. A smattering of armed Virginians "turned out with the greatest alacrity" to oppose the invaders, but they were far too few to stop the cavalry, Jefferson wrote. The state's cartridge paper was "nearly exhausted," and two thousand boxes of ammunition that had been purchased in Baltimore had probably been seized by the enemy.[6] Without such supplies, the state's muskets were "really useless." Jefferson sought help from Washington, but the Continental army could spare nothing.[7]

THE INVASION FORCED JEFFERSON to reconsider whether it had been a good idea to have thousands of loosely monitored captured enemy troops encamped at Charlottesville. A number of the prisoners had easily escaped their captors and began a circuitous march to the sea in an effort to link up with Leslie. After days of indecision, Jefferson finally conceded that it was time to act. The British prisoners at the Albemarle barracks were to be marched northward to Fort Frederick in Maryland. "It will be utterly impracticable as long as they remain with us to prevent the hostile army now in the State from being reinforced by numerous desertions from this corps," Jefferson wrote Thomas Sim Lee, the governor of Maryland, on October 26. Jefferson, however, believed that Hessian prisoners were unlikely to return to the British army and thus allowed them many of them to stay in the Charlottesville area.[8]

Jefferson was also worried about traitors among Virginians. A "very dangerous Insurrection" was planned in Pittsylvania County, 140 miles south of Richmond, and had been uncovered only at the last minute. "The Ring-leaders were seized in their Beds," Jefferson wrote. "This dangerous fire is only smothered: when it will break out seems to depend altogether on events." The insurrection threatened to spread to a swath of the state stretching from the southern Blue Ridge Mountains to the central Piedmont. "Indeed some suspicions have been raised of its having crept as far as Culpeper," referring to the town nearly ninety miles northwest of Richmond.

As for the rest of the state, Jefferson said he was "perfectly happy" with the turnout of militia, but he worried about the small cache of available arms. "Were any disaster to befall these, we have no other resource but a few scattered Squirrel Guns, Rifles, etc. in the Hands of the western People."[9]

Leslie's force, meanwhile, was committing "horrid depredations" in Hampton. The ships were strung out across the mouth of the James River, stoking fears that the fleet was headed toward Williamsburg and Richmond. But the fleet had not moved significantly for several days, leading Jefferson to conclude that it was awaiting orders and was ready for the taking—if only Americans had the means. Jefferson dashed off a letter to Horatio Gates, the commander of the Continental army's southern forces, urging that their allies in the French navy hurry to Virginia and capture the British fleet. "Notify the French Admiral that his enemies are in a net if he has leisure to close the mouth of it," he wrote. Virginia forces would assist in the capture from the land if the French would come by sea. With a bit of bravado, Jefferson added that his decision to remove the British soldiers from the Albemarle barracks in Charlottesville meant that Virginia would have plenty of space to imprison Leslie's men.[10]

But the French fleet was unable to come to the rescue, enabling Leslie to attack at will. The British took control of a swath of land around Suffolk, south of the James River, and seized horses, oxen, and carts. It was a classic maneuver for preparing a full-fledged attack on land and sea, with the ships expected to sail up the James, accompanied by troops and cavalry shadowing them on land. A number of Loyalist families who earlier had fled the area were allowed to accompany Leslie's fleet, and they now started moving into houses and farms occupied by the British. It seemed as though the enemy intended to stay and to expand their reach.

The British had every reason to believe they could easily march inland. So far they had seen little sign of opposition: Loyalist families in the area had greeted them warmly, and hundreds of slaves had fled their masters, believing they would be protected in their newfound freedom by the British. There had been no head-on clash of armies; the only significant encounter was a small fight that resulted in the death of three Virginia militiamen and one British soldier. If the British were planning to rescue those still remaining at the Albemarle barracks, as Jefferson feared, they would find a relatively clear path and perhaps assemble a force large enough to control much of Virginia.[11]

Yet there was something strange about the British preparations. Instead of taking advantage of their surprise invasion and the disarray among Virginians, they continued to stall. A British deserter, Peter Christian, told the Patriots that Leslie's force intended to draw the Virginians to Suffolk, tying up the local militia and preventing them from aiding Continental forces in the South. Then, said Christian, Leslie's forces planned to head to Baltimore. Jefferson, who eagerly digested the defector's statement, found this all a bit confusing. If Leslie's forces planned to head to Baltimore, how did he plan to protect Loyalist families who had moved into houses and farms near Suffolk? "Their movements here have been truly incomprehensible," Jefferson admitted to Maryland governor Lee, warning him of the possible attack on Baltimore. Jefferson, who had downsized his estimate of British strength from 5,000 men to 2,500, conjectured that Leslie had expected to link forces in Virginia with the fleet of Lord Cornwallis, who was still in South Carolina. The failure of Cornwallis to make it to Virginia left Leslie "without an object," Jefferson wrote. Still, he could not be certain of this. "We have not data enough to confide in any opinion."[12]

Jefferson's intuition had been right. Leslie was frozen in place. On November 4, Leslie sat down at his headquarters in Portsmouth and wrote a plaintive message to Cornwallis. "My Lord, I have been here near a Week Establishing a

Post. I wrote to you to Charles Town, and by another Messenger by Land. I cant hear for a certainty where you are. I wait your Orders." A few days later, a British courier on his way from Portsmouth to South Carolina encountered a Virginia patrol. The local troops were used to encountering escaped Convention troop prisoners and deserters, so they were not startled to come across a lone British soldier. As a matter of routine, however, the Virginians asked that he allow himself to be searched. The soldier obliged, nonchalantly putting his hand in his pocket. Then he pulled his hand out and raised it to his mouth, as if putting a quid of tobacco in his cheek or stifling a yawn. The Virginians thought it strange and demanded that the British soldier open his mouth; there was found the secret message from Leslie to Cornwallis. Jefferson later described the prize in detail: a letter "written on silk paper, rolled up in gold beaters skin, and nicely tied at each end, the whole not larger from a goose quill."[13]

A British ship soon arrived with orders from Cornwallis to Leslie: leave Virginia and rush to the South, where Cornwallis needed support. On the night of November 15, Leslie abruptly departed from Virginia, abandoning the defensive works he had begun to establish in Portsmouth. He also left behind hundreds of slaves who had fled their Virginia masters and been promised freedom, but for whom he had little space aboard the ships.

Having watched the departure in darkness from a safe distance, the Virginia militia began to trickle into the town on the morning of November 16. Two days later, General Peter Muhlenberg, a Virginia militia leader, wrote to Jefferson that the British were in full flight. It was hardly a military victory, but it permitted Jefferson a rare moment of exultation. While his forces were not responsible for Leslie's retreat, he could take solace in the thought that Virginians fighting in the Continental army had helped pin down Cornwallis in the South, thus foiling plans for a joint Leslie-Cornwallis assault on the state.

Jefferson's next move, however, left the state even less prepared should another invading force arrive. He ordered the four thousand militia that Muhlenberg had assembled at Portsmouth be marched to Petersburg and "disbanded by the Governor's order." At the same time, in keeping with his obligations to the Continental Congress, he ordered four hundred of the best-equipped Virginians to South Carolina, where federal forces desperately needed men in their battle against the British under Lord Cornwallis. "The moment the enemy leave us I hope a good reinforcement may march from their present encampment to the Southward," Jefferson informed Samuel Huntington, president of the Continental Congress, on November 19.[14] But the officers in this group complained bitterly that they had not been paid or provided with adequate clothing for their men. They signed a resolution that they would not head south until their demands were met. This rebellious threat was quelled only after the officers were promised better treatment.[15]

Jefferson was relieved that he could send home the restless militia and convince the near-mutinous Continental soldiers to head south. The best strategy, he and his advisors believed, was to cut off British forces in South Carolina to ensure they did not try to come to Virginia. However, this significantly diminished Virginia's defense at a time when the state had learned precisely how vulnerable it was to invasion. The question now was whether the British would launch a third invasion or whether the brevity of the raids by Collier and Leslie showed that the enemy had no interest in remaining in the state.

JUST AS VIRGINIANS WERE RIDDING themselves of Leslie, they began to hear an incredible story. Benedict Arnold, the American general who had been hailed years earlier in the streets of Williamsburg as a hero, had defected to the British.

Arnold's defection revolved to a degree around a wealthy Virginia-born Loyalist named Beverley Robinson. Robinson was the brother of the late Speaker of the House of Burgesses, John Robinson, the "pasha" whose loan scheme to Virginia's gentry was one of the early sparks of revolution in the Old Dominion. Robinson's father had been an acting governor of Virginia and president of the Governor's Council. In the incestuous world of Virginia gentry, Beverley Robinson had ties to all of the major families, including one to Jefferson. He also was a childhood friend of Washington's. He had moved to New York, where he married a woman who inherited a massive (sixty-thousand-acre) estate on the Hudson River near West Point.

While many of his Virginia friends became revolutionaries, Robinson remained steadfastly Loyalist and indeed became an advisor to the British governor of New York. When forced to flee from his Hudson River estate and move to Manhattan, he created the Loyal American Regiment, personally leading attacks against the rebel forces. Should the British be defeated, Robinson would be among the biggest losers, forced to leave behind his estate. But should the British win, few men would have been better rewarded. He likely would have been among the most influential men in a reunited British America. He had put his money and his life at stake for the king, and the risks he had taken would be remembered.

Robinson needed powerful allies, and he focused on Arnold, whom he thought the most influential American officer likely to switch to the British side. In May 1779, Robinson wrote to Arnold urging him to defect, playing nimbly upon the general's ego, loyalty, and prejudices. "It is necessary that a decisive advantage should put Britain in a condition to dictate the terms of reconciliation," Robinson wrote to Arnold. "There is no one but General Arnold who can surmount obstacles so great as these. A man of so much courage will never despair of the republic, even when every door to a reconciliation seems sealed."

The letter also played upon one of Arnold's greatest fears: that the French would use their alliance with America to influence its policies. Arnold had detested the French ever since he was a young man and witnessed an Indian massacre that he believed had been condoned by French forces. Robinson knew this and stressed the French role in the war. How soon would American liberty "turn into lewdness, if it not to be under the safeguard of a great European power? Will you rely upon the guarantee of France?" Robinson doubted those who insisted the French would not exact "a slavish obedience" in return for their support. No, Robinson said, it would be far better to be under the protection of Britain, a benevolent giant of commerce, with "so many countries acknowledging our sway." "United in equality," Robinson concluded grandly, "we will rule the universe."[1]

The argument might not have been persuasive on its own merits, but at the moment he received Robinson's letter, Arnold was an angry man, livid at his treatment by Congress and George Washington. Moreover, he had just married a nineteen-year-old Loyalist named Peggy Shippen, who also had ties to Virginia. Her first cousin was Mary Willing Byrd, who had grown up in Philadelphia and moved to Westover after marrying William Byrd III.

Peggy had been the belle of Philadelphia during the occupation of the capital, attending dances with British major John André, who sketched drawings that captured her enigmatic smile. He gave her a lock of his hair in a golden locket. After a lavish party that was occasionally interrupted by the sound of gunfire, André left with thousands of British troops and Loyalists. The city they abandoned had been shattered by months of occupation, the detritus of the departing army littering the streets. Anyone who remained behind and was suspected of Loyalism was branded as inimical by an increasingly radical faction of Philadelphians emboldened by the British retreat to New York. The tea parties of Society Hill had been supplanted by meetings of querulous men who wanted to banish the theater, limit the activities of women who once attended British officers, and generally establish a world that struck some as Puritanism in the name of patriotism. To the revolutionaries, however, the remnants of royalty in Philadelphia were potential traitors.

Into Peggy Shippen's world arrived General Benedict Arnold, the city's new military general, using a cane to support a leg that was two inches shorter than the other. A brusque yet charming man in his dashing Continental uniform, he told tales of naval battles and horseback charges in distant theaters of war. Arnold had been appointed by George Washington to bring order to the unruly capital, and he had been urged to treat all people fairly and equally. Arnold took this order so literally that when he became entranced with the lovely Peggy Shippen, he invited her to accompany him to official government functions.

Arnold's advances were welcomed by Peggy but initially rejected by her father, Judge Edward Shippen, whose qualms diminished over time as Arnold
showed his sympathy for Loyalists and Quakers charged with crimes on grounds
that may have been political. Arnold also purchased the grandest estate in the
region, Mount Pleasant, on the Schuylkill River, and put the deed in Peggy's
name, with her father as a trustee. Word of their engagement inflamed the rad-
icals, who objected to Arnold escorting Peggy to the local playhouse while they
were trying to ban theatrical productions. Arnold was accused of Loyalism and
attacked for profligate spending in the *Pennsylvania Packet,* which published a
subscriber's anonymous broadside: "When I meet your carriage in the streets,
and think of the splendor in which you live and revel . . . and of the decent fru-
gality necessarily used by other officers, it is impossible to avoid the question,
'From whence these riches flowed if you did not plunder Montreal?'"[2]

Arnold's timing was atrocious. As military governor, he was expected to
entertain, but this happened just when a growing number viewed his lavish entertainments as little different from those of the British. Arnold, who received
no salary for several years, was locked in a battle with congressional officials
over his expenses. For some time he had paid many of his military expenses out
of his own pocket, and he was still waiting for reimbursement. Congress was
forever requesting receipts and conducting audits, a review that Arnold believed was engineered by political enemies. He compounded the problem by
taking advantage of his power as military governor to give a local merchant an
exclusive contract to buy goods abandoned by the British and unneeded by the
American military. Arnold insisted he did not profit from the arrangement,
but word of it led to charges of improper conduct. Investigation followed investigation. One committee cleared Arnold of most charges but referred the
matter to a court-martial.

While awaiting the trial and defending himself against "the many abusive misrepresentations and calumnies which are daily circulated by a set of wretches,"
Arnold resigned as military governor and married Peggy on April 8, 1779. The
trial was delayed repeatedly, prompting an exasperated Arnold to write to
Washington on May 5 that if the general "thinks me criminal, for heaven's sake
let me be tried immediately and, if found guilty, executed." Having suffered
wounds that nearly cost him a leg, and legal actions that had put him deeply in
debt, Arnold complained bitterly that he had become "a cripple in service of
my country," which rewarded him with "ungrateful returns."[3]

It was at this moment that Beverley Robinson took up his pen and set
down the rationale for Arnold to defect. Robinson and his allies apparently had
broached the idea earlier, but Robinson's letter of May 1779 was the most direct

proposition, and it was delivered when Arnold was likely to be most responsive. Arnold felt betrayed by the country that he had served heroically for years, he was in debt because of the ingratitude of Congress, and he was politically opposed to the alliance with France that now was at the heart of the American strategy to win independence. He convinced himself he had no alternative. Remaining on the American side could lead to excoriation, expulsion, or even execution. The British were offering him financial rewards, fealty, and a position of command, all things he craved. Nor did the odds seem so long that he would be joining the victorious side. Men such as Beverley Robinson were raising troops of Loyalists who had proven to be good fighters. Americans were tired of the war, and American soldiers were fed up with unpaid service in horrific conditions. There might be as many as fifty thousand Loyalists prepared to serve the king. Combined with the power of the British navy and the English and Hessian soldiers, it was enough to overpower the Patriots. William Franklin, the former royal governor of New Jersey (and the illegitimate son of Benjamin Franklin), was in New York raising thousands of Loyalists for the British service. Arnold believed that were he to defect, thousands would follow him.[4]

Arnold sent a message asking for a proposal that outlined specific monetary and military arrangements. The matter was taken to Sir Henry Clinton, who had recently employed Major John André as his aide-de-camp. André would be the conduit: he knew Peggy, who would be an active participant in the plan, at times keeping it alive. Arnold, meanwhile, proved his bona fides by leaking vital information to the British, telling them about the movements, strengths, and weaknesses of Washington's troops. Negotiations continued for weeks, with the British at one point insisting that Arnold would be useful to them only if he regained a command. What would be most helpful, Clinton suggested, would be to obtain the plans for West Point, the vital fort about fifty miles up the Hudson River.

As negotiations with the British broke down, Arnold finally attended his court-martial, which acquitted him on most counts but found him guilty of violating military order and discipline. Washington said that Arnold's action in the case of the ship *Charming Nancy* was "peculiarly reprehensible." Arnold had given a pass to that ship to take merchandise out of Philadelphia at a time when such shipments were prohibited. The ship was captured by a privateer, prompting Arnold to send government wagons to rescue the cargo, which was then sold in Philadelphia, possibly enabling Arnold to share in the profits. Separately, federal officials quarreled with Arnold over repayment of his expenses and salary, eventually forcing him to take a loss of $9,154, which seemed to leave him with no chance of making a financial recovery.[5]

Washington's reprobation and the court-martial verdict were not severe enough to force Arnold out of the army. Indeed, Washington assured Arnold that he would furnish him "with opportunities of regaining the esteem of your country."[6] The opportunity would soon be presented: Arnold was offered command of the fort at West Point. This led him to revive his discussions with the British, sending an overview of the security at West Point and detailing its weaknesses. He offered to send blueprints that would enable the British to take the fort—actually a string of forts spread across the cliffs and plateaus—with little effort. Clinton offered £20,000 if Arnold's information led to the capture of three thousand men and the artillery of West Point. Arnold countered that he needed insurance that he would be paid if the plot was discovered and he was exposed. With Peggy acting at one point as intermediary, offers were sent back and forth. Arnold finally assumed command of West Point in August, passing more vital information on to Clinton. Washington had given command to Arnold of a fortress that the American commander in chief considered the "key to America." Arnold now prepared to hand that key to the British commander.

As Arnold assumed command of West Point, he decided the perfect spot for his headquarters was not at the fortress itself but at a nearby mansion confiscated from Beverley Robinson. On August 4 Arnold arrived at the large white mansion, which sat a mile from the riverfront and about two miles from West Point. There Arnold wrote out requests to other Continental officers for the names of all their spies in the region. He ordered the withdrawal of some men and cannons from the garrison, making it more vulnerable to attack. He agreed that, for the first time, he would meet in person with André, who needed to verify that he really was dealing with Benedict Arnold and not a double agent.

Arnold, meanwhile, received a letter from Washington informing him that the general planned to stay overnight near West Point during a mission to visit with French commanders. He asked Arnold to prepare food for fifty men and forty horses and to keep the journey a secret.[7] Arnold promptly informed the British of Washington's travel plans. Perhaps Washington could be seized at the same time as the capture of West Point. Arnold wrote to Washington saying he looked forward to seeing him soon in person. He closed the letter, Arnold's last to Washington as an American soldier, "I am, with sentiments of the most profound respect and esteem, your Excellency's most obedient servant, B. Arnold."[8]

A few days later, Washington arrived near West Point, along with the Marquis de Lafayette, the French officer who would soon lead troops into Virginia. Arnold had dinner with Washington, Lafayette, and other officers at a house near King's Ferry. Afterward, crossing the Hudson with Arnold, Washington took out his telescope and saw a British ship, the *Vulture,* in the distance. Arnold assured Washington that there was no danger and that West Point was secure. Indeed, he told Washington that he had just received a letter from the *Vulture,* from Beverley Robinson. Robinson, who had sailed up the river in hopes of meeting with Arnold, said in the letter that he wanted to check on his house. Arnold asked Washington whether Robinson could be granted permission. Washington strongly rejected the idea of Robinson roaming around an American headquarters.[9]

Later that evening, as Arnold bade goodbye to Washington, the commander in chief said he would return in five days to inspect West Point and stay at the Robinson mansion. André, meanwhile, left New York, hoping to finally have his face-to-face meeting with Arnold. Sent off by his fellow officers with a series of toasts and drinking songs, assured that his mission would lead to an elevation in rank, André was urged by Clinton to follow three rules: not to change out of his British uniform, not to enter American lines, and not to carry any communications from the Americans with him.

André, twenty-nine years old and the rising star of the British officer corps, was certain he was about to turn the tide of the war. He rode out of New York, headed along the shore of the Hudson, and then hitched a ride on a British gunboat to the *Vulture.* There he was welcomed by Robinson, who wore the red and green uniform of his Loyal American Regiment. André then switched to a small boat, which took him to a dock at the foot of Long Clove Mountain. André climbed out of the craft, and walked up a road to a stand of fir trees. Benedict Arnold emerged from the wood. The two men talked for several hours, Arnold going over the best mode of attacking West Point and André admitting that the British were not able to meet all of his financial demands but promising that Arnold would eventually be made whole. Arnold's protestations must have been loud and long, but the plot was finalized nonetheless. Both men were convinced that their actions would result in the capture of West Point and its three thousand men, possibly including the visiting Washington and the Marquis de Lafayette, and soon end the war.

As Arnold headed back to his headquarters at the Robinson house, André waited until the following nightfall to begin a winding, tortuous route back to New York City. Finding himself behind American lines, he used a pass provided by Arnold to get through a local guard and eventually was riding alone on horseback when he ran into three men who forced him to stop. Seeing one of the men dressed in the coat of a Hessian soldier, André was convinced they were British allies. "Thank God, I am once more among friends," André said. "I am glad to see you. I am an officer in the British service." The men were actually "skinners" who robbed Loyalist travelers. "Get down, we are Americans," one of the men said. Stunned, André pulled out his pass from Arnold. The Americans were unimpressed. "Damn Arnold's pass! You said you was a British soldier. Where is your money?" Taking André to a nearby wood, they stripped him to his boots and found some Continental dollars. Then, demanding that André remove his white-topped boots, they noticed papers bulging from one of his stockings. Reading the documents from Arnold about West Point, one of the men exclaimed, "This is a spy!"

Arnold was at his headquarters at the Robinson house when he received word that André had been captured. He delivered the news to Peggy, told her to burn his papers and look after their infant, and fled. Arnold leaped onto his horse, galloped downriver, and met up with the *Vulture,* where Beverley Robinson helped him on board. After telling Robinson that André had been captured and the conspiracy exposed, Arnold ordered the ship to head to New York, where he would join the British army.

At 10:30 a.m., shortly after Arnold fled, Washington arrived at the Robinson home along with the Marquis de Lafayette and 160 other officers and soldiers. Not yet aware of the conspiracy, Washington then traveled to West Point, where he expected Arnold to meet the entourage with the usual cannon salute. Instead, Washington found the fort undermanned and no sign of Arnold. The dismayed commander crossed the Hudson and returned to the American headquarters at the Robinson home, where he was handed a sealed document. Unfolding the papers, Washington discovered the truth. The other officers gathered around, sensing something in the general's manner as he sat with a stony, ghastly look on his face. "Arnold has betrayed me," Washington announced angrily. "Whom can we trust now?"[10]

The question would bedevil Washington for months, leaving him uncertain about divulging secrets to fellow officers. Rumors immediately began to cascade through the Continental army about disloyal generals, especially those from foreign nations of whom Washington seemed so fond. Washington had been further fooled by Peggy Arnold. Unaware that the wailing Peggy was part of the conspiracy and only theatrically playing the role of victim, Washington provided passes for Peggy and her infant to go to Philadelphia. She arrived just as residents were parading an effigy of her husband through the streets.

Arnold, meanwhile, sat at a desk on the *Vulture* and composed a letter to Washington. He was now writing as a loyal subject of King George III. "The same principle of love to my country actuates my present conduct, however it may appear inconsistent to the world, who very seldom judge right of any man's actions," Arnold wrote, insisting also that Peggy knew nothing of the scheme and should be set free.[11]

When the missive arrived at the Robinson house, it was passed to Washington, final confirmation that the "hero of Saratoga," whom Washington had alternately praised and pilloried, had "gone to the enemy."[12] Rebuffing suggestions that André be exchanged for Arnold, Washington ordered fourteen generals to sit in a one-day court-martial of André. Several of the generals would soon face Arnold in battle, including the Marquis de Lafayette and the Prussian Baron von Steuben. André had been found behind American lines, wearing a disguise and carrying papers that provided intelligence to the British, all steps that Clinton had urged his aide to avoid when meeting with Arnold. Washington signed the warrant for André's hanging. While several thousand American soldiers watched, André, dressed in a fresh uniform of royal regimentals and boots, tied a white handkerchief around his eyes as he stood on a wagon. He slipped the noose around his neck "without the assistance of the awkward executioner." Asked if he wanted to speak, André uttered a phrase that would endear him to his countrymen and evoke admiration among many of those watching: "I pray you to bear witness that I meet my fate like a brave man." The wagon was jerked away, and André "instantly expired."[13]

Arnold, meanwhile, was in New York, badgering Clinton to pay him the promised fees and angling for a generalship. Arnold was filled with ideas of how to win the war for the British, starting with the seizure of Congress in Philadelphia, where many of Arnold's enemies now felt vindicated for their attacks on him. Arnold told Clinton that the Americans were tired, hungry, and broke, anxious for peace with Britain. In a public letter, Arnold urged soldiers to follow him in defecting. The war, he said, had become illegitimate when France "joined in the combination." It was better, he said, to stay in league with the British than to trust a French monarchy that was "too feeble to establish your independency" and which was "fraudulently avowing an affection for the liberties of mankind while she holds her native sons in vassalage and chains."[14]

To prove his worth, Arnold said he would assemble a corps of Loyalists, cobbling together new recruits and the legions of Robinson's Loyal American Regiment, the Queen's Rangers, and others. His proposal to seize Congress was rejected, but Clinton liked the idea of sending Arnold southward, where the British were in need of help.

Washington, concerned about Arnold's plans, learned that British vessels were being prepared to go to sea, but he did not know their destination. He sent a series of letters to Governor Jefferson, reviewing how Arnold committed treason and warning that "the enemy have not laid aside . . . their preparations for an expedition." The letters were vague, suggesting that a fleet of unspecified size was leaving on an uncertain date for an unknown location in the South.[15] Jefferson received the letters in the aftermath of Leslie's abrupt departure from Virginia. Relieved that the state was rid of the second invasion force in eighteen months, Jefferson had time to attend to family duties, remaining with his frail wife as she gave birth to another daughter, Lucy Elizabeth. Yet as he read over Washington's letters, Jefferson must have wondered if the commander in chief realized how ill-equipped and undermanned Virginia had been during the Leslie invasion. Washington's underlying message seemed clear: if the British were heading again to Virginia, the state must rely on militiamen for defense. The Continental army was occupied with battles elsewhere.

The British "must now mean to make a push in some other more remote quarter," Washington told Jefferson. The commander in chief told the governor that he trusted there were enough men of "abundant virtue" to withstand the "most vigorous and artful efforts" of the British.[16]

Bring Him Alive to Headquarters

IN THE DAYS AFTER ARNOLD'S DEFECTION, Washington was filled with worry. One report suggested that another top officer was in league with Arnold. Washington wondered: how vast was the conspiracy? Washington summoned one of his most trusted officers, General Henry Lee of Virginia, to his tent to discuss the Arnold case. Lee, known as "Light Horse Harry" for his brilliant leadership of the cavalry, doubted the allegation that another American officer was in league with the British. He suggested in response that the accusation had been planted by Sir Henry Clinton "in order to destroy that confidence between a commander and his officers on which the success of military operations depends."[1]

Washington considered the idea, then noted that until a few days earlier it would have seemed equally implausible that Arnold was a traitor. He asked Lee whether he knew of a soldier who could learn whether there were other conspirators and then lead an effort to capture Arnold. "I have sent for you, in the expectation that you have in your corps individuals capable and willing to undertake an indispensable, delicate, and hazardous project," Washington told Lee, giving him documents that spelled out the condition under which the trusted soldier would seize Arnold. Under no circumstances, Washington said, should Arnold be hurt or killed, even if that meant he escaped capture. He wanted to make an example of Arnold, not turn him into a martyr. "Public punishment is the sole object in view. This you cannot too forcibly press upon whomsoever may engage in the enterprise."[2]

Lee replied that the only way to capture Arnold was for an American to pretend to defect to the British, become a close and trusted confidant of Arnold, and then bring him back. Few officers would want to risk their reputation by switching loyalties. The Continental army, meanwhile, would feel obligated to remain silent about the true nature of the defection, not wishing to reveal the secret mission. A spy who failed would both be hanged and go down in ignominy.

Who could perform such a courageous task? He would have to have the qualities of a sailor, soldier, and spy, have brute strength and great intelligence, and possess so fervent a belief in the revolutionary cause that it would outweigh countless risks. Lee said only one man he knew had all of these qualities. He was a sergeant major from Loudoun County, Virginia, named John Champe.

The twenty-four-year-old Champe had enlisted four years earlier and proved himself a gallant fighter. He was a large man, "full of bone and muscle; with a saturnine countenance, grave, thoughtful, and taciturn of tried courage and inflexible perseverance," Lee wrote. But Lee worried Champe would reject the proposal because he might be mistakenly perceived as a traitor if the mission failed.[3]

Washington replied that Champe was "the very man for the business; that he must undertake it; and that going to the enemy by the instigation and at the request of his officer, was not desertion, although it appeared to be so." Champe should take comfort that "the vast good in prospect should be contrasted with the mere semblance of doing wrong."[4]

At eight o'clock that night, Lee returned to his troops and sent for Champe. As the Virginian entered Lee's tent, Lee welcomed him warmly and laid out the mission. "I have watched you ever since you joined the corps," Lee recalled that he told Champe. "I have found you uniformly brave, discreet, orderly, sagacious, full of ambition, yet of ambition of the most legitimate kind, and I know that you feel yourself to be on the high road to promotion." Lee then explained that Champe was to capture Arnold. "I am but a medium of communication between Washington and yourself."[5]

Champe was apparently overwhelmed. He assured Lee that no soldier had greater affection for Washington, for whom Champe said he would "willingly lay down his life." Moreover, he was "charmed" by the plan, which was "powerful and delicious" in the way it would repudiate Arnold's treachery. Champe was not concerned with the danger of the mission, but he was haunted by the idea of deserting the army he so deeply respected, "to be followed by enlisting with the enemy." Lee assured Champe that "his reputation would be protected by those who had induced him to undertake the enterprise, should he be unfortunate."

The appeal to his patriotism and the assurance that Washington believed he was uniquely suited for the job sealed it for Champe. He would undertake the mission.

With the agreement in hand, Lee read the instructions to Champe, who wrote them down in a code only he could decipher. Champe would be allowed to recruit two men to help him, but neither man should know the other's name. Finally, Lee stressed Washington's insistence that Arnold not be killed. "If, therefore, you find that you cannot seize him unhurt, do not seize him at all; and if the choice be between his escape and his slaughter, let him go. To kill him would give the enemy an excuse for alleging all sorts of falsehoods against us."[6]

But how should Champe defect without raising suspicion? Trying to cross enemy lines would entail much risk, possibly ending the mission before it began. The enemy might not realize Champe's intention, and Continental soldiers would be unaware of the mission and might try to pursue him. Indeed, it would strengthen the illusion that Champe were defecting if he was pursued by Continental troops. Lee assured Champe that he would do everything he could to delay the pursuit long enough to enable Champe to flee while leaving the impression that the defection was real.

Lee pressed three guineas into Champe's hands and wished him luck. Champe was to let Lee know as soon as possible that he had arrived in New York City, where Arnold was gathered with his troops. The two men agreed on a time when Champe would race to enemy lines. They synchronized their watches, saluted, and said goodbye. Champe returned quickly to his tent. He put on his cloak, packed his bag and orderly book, and fetched his horse.

A half hour later, the camp's watch officer ran toward Lee's tent. Agitated and emotional, the officer told the general that a member of the army's patrol had come across a soldier on horseback headed away from the camp. Challenged, the horseman struck his spurs into the animal's sides and galloped off. The patrolman could not catch the fleeing horse and rider.

Lee pretended to be too tired to understand the explanation. Was this just some fellow from the country? Lee inquired. No, it was someone from the army, the officer replied. Impossible, Lee said, feigning disgust. His soldiers did not desert.

The chagrined officer skulked away. On a hunch, he headed toward the stable, where he was informed that a horse was missing and that it belonged to Sergeant Major Champe. The officer then went to Champe's tent, only to find that the sergeant major was gone, along with his suitcase and orderly book. The officer raced back to Lee's tent and asked for permission to pursue Champe.

Knowing he must delay the pursuit, Lee hemmed and hawed. He talked about the character of officers. Finally he acceded to the pursuit, but said a different officer should lead it. More time was wasted. After another ten minutes, the new officer arrived, and Lee delivered his order. "Pursue as far as you can with safety Sergeant Champe, who is suspected of deserting to the enemy, and has taken the road leading to Paulus Hook," Lee said. "Bring him alive, that he may suffer in the presence of the army." Then Lee added: "But kill him if he resists, or escapes after being taken."[7]

The pursuit party left around midnight, just as rain began to fall. The moistened ground provided them with an unexpected advantage: Champe's horse wore a particular kind of shoe that left a telltale mark in the mud. Champe had been gone for an hour, but he would have to stop before reaching enemy lines and carefully consider how to cross. Lee worried that during this crucial period of deliberation, the pursuers would capture him. The chase went on for hours, with the pursuers stopping at forks in the road to examine where Champe's horse had made its impression upon the earth. Finally, at dawn, the pursuers could follow the horseshoe prints without stopping, and they galloped at full speed.

Champe had reached a high point of land near the village of Bergen, New Jersey, when to his horror he looked back and realized that a band of pursuers was less than a half mile behind him. Desperate now, Champe raced by Bergen's Three Pigeons Inn and remembered a shortcut. Then he recalled that he had previously taken the same side road with the very men who were now pursuing him; they would know the shortcut too well. So, feigning in the direction of that road, he headed for his destination by another route. A few miles away, at Paulus Hook, were two British galleys.

The pursuers, meanwhile, entered Bergen in the belief that Champe was heading for the shortcut. One soldier waited by a bridge—and waited. The deception worked. The soldiers asked villagers whether they had seen a man on horseback. Indeed they had, but they did not know where he had gone. Finally, a soldier found the telltale print of Champe's horse. The race resumed.

Champe sensed the pursuers at his heels. Stopping momentarily, he lashed the bag to his saddle. He pulled out his sword and tossed its scabbard into the woods. The pursuers were now less than three hundred yards behind him. He plunged his spurs into his horse, waved his sword in the air, and raced on. Now he could see his destination ahead of him—the port of Paulus Hook, one mile across the Hudson River from New York City. Would the British galleys be there, as Champe believed? The sight came into view: two galleys bobbing gently in the Hudson, just off shore. British sentries patrolled the marshy riverfront.

Champe had seconds to deploy his stratagem. He leaped off his horse and dove into the marsh, hoping the British would realize he was trying to defect. Both the enemy and his pursuers could justifiably shoot him now. "Help!" Champe yelled as he flailed in the muddy waters.

The British sentries sized up the situation immediately: a Continental officer was defecting, and his own men were bearing down on him. The British promptly starting shooting at the pursuers, who quickly realized they were no match for the men of two enemy warships.

A small boat was lowered into the river for the rescue, and Sergeant Major John Champe of Loudoun County, Virginia, bedraggled after a night on the run, was welcomed aboard by the finely uniformed representatives of the British navy. Champe was taken across the river to New York City and provided with a letter from a British officer, who attested to the extraordinary and dangerous circumstances of the desertion. Surely this would be of interest to the man now leading the British garrison on the great island at the entrance to the Hudson River.

Champe's deception was complete. He was given a British uniform and billeted near Arnold's headquarters. Four days after his defection, he was brought to a British adjutant general, who debriefed the young Virginian. Champe knew that the British believed disaffection was rampant in the Continental army. The defections of Arnold—and now Champe—were irrefutable proof. So Champe told the British what they wanted to hear. The spirit among American troops was low, and Arnold's defection had encouraged them to follow suit. Soon "Washington's ranks would not only be greatly thinned, but ... some of his best corps would leave him."[8]

Convinced of Champe's sincerity, the adjutant general sent him to see General Clinton. It was Clinton who was chiefly responsible for approving the plans to pay Arnold for his defection and who believed that many more Americans would come to the British side. Clinton quizzed Champe for an hour, then rewarded the American with a couple of guineas and a letter of introduction to Arnold.

Arnold made his headquarters at the King's Arms Tavern, at 9–11 Broadway. It was a two-story wooden structure, with a facade of yellow brick imported from Holland and a steep pitched roof. The extensive garden reached all the way to the Hudson riverbank.

At his meeting with Arnold, Champe said he had been inspired to defect by Arnold's example, and that others would soon follow. Arnold "expressed much satisfaction on hearing from Champe the manner of his escape, and the effect of Arnold's example," according to an account written years later by Lee.[9] Arnold assured Champe that he would have the same rank in the British forces as he had had with the Americans. Champe hesitated—or pretended to hesitate— for days over the offer, prompting Clinton and Arnold to woo him repeatedly.

Through his conversations with the British officers, Champe concluded that Washington's concern about another American officer turning traitor was unfounded. "Great was my satisfaction at being able to report that the [accusation against another officer] had no foundation in truth," Champe said later.

Once established in the British camp, Champe carefully observed Arnold's routine. He could have easily assassinated Arnold had Washington allowed it. Instead, Champe watched his prey making regular visits to a garden, and devised a plan of capture. "I found that every night, before going to bed, Arnold was in the habit of visiting that garden, and I immediately resolved what to do," Champe recalled years later in a conversation with a British officer.[10]

When Champe returned to his quarters that night, he met with one of two fellow spies that Lee had arranged for him to work with. Champe outlined the plan in a message to be couriered to Washington, who was pleased. "The plan proposed for taking A——d (the outlines of which are communicated in your letter, which was this moment put into my hands without date) has every mark of a good one," Washington wrote Lee. Nevertheless, Champe "must be very circumspect," Washington continued. "Too much zeal may create suspicion, and too much precipitancy may defeat the project. The most inviolable secrecy must be observed on all hands."[11]

Once his plans were set, Champe informed Washington, again via the courier, that he expected to capture Arnold three nights hence. On the night of the expected capture, Lee was to go to Hoboken and wait for Champe and his two confederates to arrive with Arnold as prisoner.

Champe proceeded to set the scene for the abduction. The garden Arnold often visited was separated from the lane by a wooden fence. Under cover of darkness, Champe loosened a section of the fence, then replaced it so that it appeared untouched. He instructed one of his accomplices to bring a boat to a nearby landing on the Hudson. Champe would arrange for the other confederate to be admitted into the garden. Then, clutching a cloth that he intended to use as a gag in Arnold's mouth, Champe would sneak into the garden. The two men would grab Arnold, stuff the cloth in his mouth, and carry him to the landing. Should someone stop them, Champe would say that Arnold was a drunken soldier being taken to headquarters.

AFTER WEEKS OF PLEAS FROM ARNOLD that he be allowed to lead a major expedition, Sir Henry Clinton finally granted Arnold's wish. Arnold was given orders to lead 1,600 men to the south. Clinton believed Arnold had been held in "very high estimation" during most of his time as a rebel military leader and now would "exert himself to the utmost to establish an equal fame" with the British. Clinton hoped that giving Arnold such an important command would provide a "strong incitement" to other high-ranking American officers to defect.[12]

The men in Arnold's fleet were told to assemble immediately aboard their vessels, headed toward an undisclosed destination. Such orders on short notice were not unusual, for British naval strategy often shifted abruptly. Sailors constantly changed from one ship to another, heading in and out of port, return-ing briefly to harbor only to be told that new battle plans required immediate departure. One British officer described such a scene around this time, recall-ing how his men had arrived at New York and were given a brief leave that was suddenly canceled. He witnessed the "droll yet distressing scene" of a husband being taken "from the arms of his wife." The sailor and his spouse were in bed. The "frantic partner of his bed, forgetting the delicacy of her sex, pursued us to the doors with shrieks and imprecations, and exposing their naked persons to the rude view of an unfeeling press gang."[13]

Champe, wearing his British uniform, had no choice but to comply with Arnold's orders to go aboard ship. "I was hurried on board the ship without having had time so much as to warn Major Lee that the whole arrangement was blown up," Champe recalled years later.[14]

As a result, at the prearranged time Lee waited on horseback in the woods with several soldiers. Hours passed, but Champe did not show up. Lee finally returned to headquarters to inform Washington of the mission's apparent fail-ure. Washington was "chagrined" and worried that Champe had been "detected in the last scene of his tedious and difficult enterprise."[15]

Champe, meanwhile, had no way of knowing where he was going. Even the captains of some ships had not been told precisely where the fleet was headed. The British hoisted an admiral's flag as they departed, hoping to deceive Amer-icans into thinking that the mission was more significant than it appeared. In a sense, it was.

Only after the ships departed on December 20 and were far at sea did Champe realize he was part of an expedition against his home state. The inva-sion of Virginia was under way.

Invasion

A NORTHWESTERN GALE BLEW FURIOUSLY into Arnold's fleet as it headed south from New York. The winds picked up on Christmas Eve, the sea foaming with whitecaps. Then the skies darkened and the rains came, pounding the British ships for the next two days in a soaking deluge. Visibility diminished almost completely as wafts of mist rose from the sea to meet the clouds.

The sloop-of-war *Swift* and the armed brigantine *Rambler* heaved in the swells, suffering under the weight of cannons and troops. Ships were driven by the winds to shallow water near the coast. Rain pelted the sailors' faces as they climbed the rigging and tied up sails to avoid being swept away. As waves crashed onto the decks, Arnold and the other commanders ordered the men to lighten the ships. Sailors raced to unshackle the heavy cannons, working in small groups to heave many of their most prized armaments into the sea. The *Sally,* bristling with weaponry, was swamped with water and came close to sinking.[1]

To venture on deck was to risk sliding into the abyss. The ropes were sodden, the planks slicked, making it nearly impossible to maintain footing. A sailor tackling a winter gale could quickly find his jacket drenched and then frozen to his back, his hands numb, his eyes perpetually blinking away the moisture. Many of the men had experienced such danger before and knew how quickly frostbite could take hold, leading to the loss of sensation in their hands or feet. But they also knew how men were lost at sea for failing to deal immediately with the threat of a ship overburdened by winter.

The situation was especially desperate on board the ship that carried a hundred of the finest horses that Arnold could assemble. The tightly packed animals were panicked by the howling winds and rain, the lightning and thunder. They could not be contained as the boat rocked in the sea and water swamped the deck. The boat itself was "very bad, infamously provided and totally unfit for service." As the storm raged, the horses' caretakers finally were forced to let more than forty of the animals go overboard, desperate to save weight and prevent the ship's sinking. "The very Skippers were fearful of sailing, and it required every exertion of the Quarter-Masters to oblige them to weigh anchor, and, at sea, the utmost industry and labor could barely keep them from foundering," wrote John Graves Simcoe, the commander of the Queen's Rangers.[2] Four ships, including one with four hundred men, became separated from the main fleet, not to be seen again for a week. For days, it was feared the vessels had sunk to the bottom of the Atlantic. On the day after Christmas, the fleet "was so scattered by a gale" that those aboard a ship carrying a Hessian corps found themselves adrift, with no other vessels in sight. In an effort to keep details of the mission secret, the officers in charge had not been told of their precise destination. Instead, they had been given a sealed letter, to be opened only in the event that the ships were separated. Now, after two days without seeing another ship, the Hessian officer ordered this "letter of rendezvous" to be opened and the destination revealed: the Cape of Henry at the mouth of the Chesapeake.[3]

The storm had one beneficial effect for the British: it hid the fleet from anyone who might have spied them from land. Arnold was determined to push on, believing that the British could win the war if they captured Virginia. He took comfort that many of his men were Loyalists, including a corps of Virginians, underscoring the British view that Virginia was deeply divided about the revolution more than four years after the Declaration of Independence. Arnold was sure that thousands more would defect to the British as he sailed up the James River.

THE VIRGINIA COAST HAD ATTRACTED seafarers, pirates, and plunderers since the earliest days of British exploration. From the Atlantic Ocean, the capes of Virginia seemed like two great gates, inviting vessels to enter the state's network of riverine highways. The settlers of Jamestown went through this opening as if pulled into a vortex; many other ships followed. The Indians living along the riverbanks could do nothing to stop these great British ships, and the settlers began to establish a series of villages and forts along the inland waterways, wary that the Spanish would come through the same waters and take Virginia for themselves.

The waterways were Virginia's strength and weakness. They stretched across the state from the Atlantic to the Appalachians, forming a necklace, with Jamestown, Richmond, Petersburg, and other towns and cities strung like beads across it. During the Revolution, the British often blockaded the Capes with their massive ships, while the Virginians were barely able to construct a handful of poorly equipped vessels.

Before Collier's raid in early 1779, Virginia had as many as sixty-nine armed vessels, although many were poorly equipped and lightly manned. Many were captured, destroyed, or badly damaged during the raid. Later that year, when Jefferson became governor, his administration calculated that the state had only twelve serviceable warships, with a combined eighty-eight guns and 343 naval personnel.[4] The navy received only two vessels in 1779 and 1780, neither of them warships; one was a packet boat that served as a messenger service and the other was intended to carry supplies to the prisoners at Charleston.[5]

Jefferson had been urged by aides to place ships at the Capes to prevent a seaborne invasion. But Jefferson believed this was impossible, given the state of what he called "our miserable navy." Expressing the need for additional ships, Jefferson said that "it has been my uniform opinion that our only practicable defense was naval." His effort to institute such a defense, however, was "unsuccessful beyond all my fears."[6]

Jefferson had been deeply impressed by an unusual ship developed by the Pennsylvania navy, an open, half-deck vessel with one or two triangular sails known as lateens attached to small masts. These ships had been effective during engagements on the Delaware River and later were used by Arnold.[7] Jefferson hoped that Virginia would build such vessels, but the plan was changed repeatedly as it passed through the legislature and state Navy Board. In the end, a frustrated Jefferson wrote, there was "100,000 pounds laid out to not a shilling's benefit." He believed "we should be gainers were we to burn our whole navy."[8]

The British seemed to capture American ships at will, while the Americans rarely caught a British vessel. "A British prize would be a more rare phenomenon than a comet, because the one has been seen but the other has not," Jefferson wrote.[9] In 1779, the Virginia navy vessel *Dolphin* encountered three British ships shortly after passing Cape Henry. Captain John Cowper, who had vowed never to surrender his vessel, unwisely decided to engage the British despite being outmanned, and the *Dolphin* was promptly shredded on all sides by a cannonade. Virginians watched the engagement from the shore, barely making out the sails of the four ships. The thunder and smoke of the cannons could be heard and seen in the distance, but when the battle ended, all that was visible was three British vessels departing. The *Dolphin* sank and her entire crew of seventy-five died. It was the worst loss in the short history of the Virginia navy, emboldening the British and leaving Virginia's sailors hesitant to engage the enemy at sea unless they had clear superiority.[10] Failing to gain help from the state or Congress, Jefferson suggested to a French diplomat that it would be worthwhile for Paris to order a fleet to Virginia "to protect the Commerce of your own state . . . what is best for your nation, is best for us also."[11]

Notwithstanding Jefferson's disillusionment, Virginia's navy occasionally had done wonders even with its limited resources in the early days of the revolution. Through guile and daring, James Barron, whom Jefferson had picked to head the state's navy, had captured several British ships while sailing on

Chesapeake Bay aboard the *Liberty*. But the invasions by Leslie and Collier devastated the navy. Moreover, the destruction of Norfolk had resulted in the loss of shipwrights, sailmakers, rope workers, and countless other experts in the trade. The shipyard at Portsmouth had been mostly destroyed. The newer ship-yard on the Chickahominy River near Williamsburg was still a small operation. Much of the state's navy consisted of privately owned vessels impressed into service; the owners hoped to capture British ships or to seize property owned by Loyalists. Virginians seemed resigned to the fact that if an invasion came by sea, the enemy would have free rein and could not be stopped before they reached land. Some believed it was impossible for Virginia's forces to defend a region larger than some European countries with a minuscule force: less than one militiaman to every square mile, and only one in five militiamen in posses-sion of a serviceable weapon.[12]

At the same time, Jefferson was distracted by fighting on another front. During the days that Arnold was en route to Virginia, Jefferson was more con-cerned about British stirring up the Indians—a faraway threat in the Ohio country—than about the possibility of another seaborne invasion by the British. Just six days before Arnold's invasion, Jefferson wrote about enemies forming in the south and west, while making no mention of a threat from the north that might result in an invasion through Chesapeake Bay. "There seems but one method of preventing the savages from spreading slaughter and desolation over our whole frontier," Jefferson wrote about the Indians to militia leaders in west-ern Hampshire and Berkeley counties on December 24, 1780. "That is by car-rying the war into their own country." On Christmas Day, Jefferson wrote a lengthy letter to his friend and Albemarle County neighbor, Brigadier General George Rogers Clark, filled with explicit instructions about how to attack the Indians. Jefferson proposed sending Clark everything from four cannons and a thousand spades to whatever boats were necessary. Jefferson wrote that he had received intelligence that "a very extensive combination of British and In-dian savages" was planning to invade the state's western frontier. By some esti-mates, Jefferson wanted to devote as many as one thousand valuable Virginia soldiers to his westward aspirations, which would further weaken Virginia's de-fenses in the east.[13]

The legislature had recognized how vulnerable the eastern portion of the state was to an invasion from the sea. A few months earlier, in October 1780, the legislature passed an act that required that "proper attention shall be paid to the defence of the commerce and the shores of Chesapeak bay and its de-pendencies." The measure called for a number of vessels to be fully manned and armed "for the purpose of suppressing the cruizers belonging to the enemy, and affording protection and safety to the good citizens inhabiting the shores of the bay and rivers."[14] The terms of the act were never fulfilled, however. While the invasion was under way, Jefferson acknowledged, "we had three vessels of 16 guns, one of 14, five small gallies, and two or three armed boats. They were generally so badly manned as seldom to be in condition for service."[15]

Jefferson seemed fed up with being governor under such conditions. He urged his old friend John Page to take his place, leaving the impression that he might resign before his term expired the following June, or at least not seek a third term. A horrified Page implored Jefferson to remain at his post. "I know your love of study and retirement must strongly solicit you to leave the hurry, bustle, and nonsense your station daily exposes you to," he wrote Jefferson, but insisted there was no one else in Virginia who had the ability to lead the state at such a moment. Jefferson remained as governor, hoping that reports of a British force headed southward were another false alarm.[16]

If an invasion did come, Virginia had no system to warn its citizens. No riders were posted at lookouts, no drums of tar that could be lit as fire signals were set out, no full-time force manned artillery along the coast. A communication system set up earlier by Jefferson, consisting of some of Virginia's finest horsemen posted at forty-mile intervals, had been shut down due to the expense and the belief that it was no longer needed. The legislature also had failed to approve plans to construct a series of fortified batteries at key points along major rivers.

Such was Virginia's state of affairs as Arnold sailed south: an ineffective navy, no lookouts, a dispersed and poorly armed militia, a recalcitrant legislature, and a coastal citizenry still recovering from the last two invasions.

Few doubted Arnold's ability as a naval commander. Five years earlier, when Arnold was fighting on the American side at Lake Champlain, Jefferson himself had written that Arnold was "a fine sailor."[17] His British superiors hoped Arnold would, at the least, tie up American forces in Virginia, preventing them from coming to the aid of troops battling against Cornwallis in the Carolinas.

Arnold had his own ambitions, as can be seen clearly by a secret deal he struck that he hoped would enrich him. Arnold's 1,600-man force was split between the British army and navy. While Arnold was the lead commander of both services, he had direct control only over the army. The navy was overseen by Thomas Symonds, commander of the forty-four-gun HMS *Charon*. Under the British rules of engagement, Symonds's naval forces were allowed to keep as "prizes" the bounty from captured enemy vessels. It was a major incentive to serve in the highly risky profession of sailor. The army did not typically trade in such prizes. Arnold thought this was unfair. As the ships sailed to Virginia,

Arnold proposed to Symonds that the navy and army split the prizes equally, no matter which branch seized the ships and plunder. Arnold later swore in a deposition that Symonds had readily agreed to the plan.

Sir Henry Clinton, who had of course chosen Arnold for this mission, gave him somewhat limited orders. Arnold was to destroy some arms depots if there is a "favourable opportunity" and only if "it may be done without much risk." Arnold's main mission was to establish a base at Portsmouth, just as Collier had suggested, and gather together as many Loyalists from Norfolk and Princess Anne counties as possible. After establishing the base, Clinton continued, Arnold was not to "make any excursions from thence unless they can be effected without the smallest danger to the safety of the post which is always to be considered as the primary mission."

Arnold promptly stretched these orders to fit his designs. He viewed the instruction to destroy the arms depots as a license to head straight for the interior of Virginia on a two-week raid before setting foot in Portsmouth. From the moment he reached Virginia, Arnold would make clear that he was his own commander. Indeed, Clinton had anticipated Arnold's aggressiveness and made clear that he did not entirely trust him. He told Arnold not to take any major action until checking with two British officers—Simcoe, the aforementioned leader of the Queen's Rangers, and Colonel Thomas Dundas, head of the 80th Regiment of Foot.[18] Clinton gave Simcoe and Dundas the authority "to execute the duties of the command which is entrusted to his direction" in case of Arnold's death or incapacity. "Incapacity" was loosely defined. If Dundas or Simcoe thought Arnold was taking an improper action, they could assume command. The order was to be kept secret from Arnold. "You are upon no Account to make known that You are possessed of such a Commission," Clinton told the officers.[19]

Arnold assembled a nimble corps, including specialists in *la petite guerre*, or "little war," in which small units engaged in ambushes and raids. These included the Queen's Rangers, an expeditionary force of Loyalists who specialized in unorthodox tactics and wore green jackets—instead of the traditional British red coats—that kept them better hidden in forests from spring through fall. The Queen's Rangers were accompanied by an independent attachment, the Bucks County Volunteers, Loyalists serving under Captain William Thomas. Another group, the Loyal American Regiment, was under the command of Lieutenant Colonel Beverley Robinson Jr. It was Robinson's father who had played a key role in convincing Arnold to defect to the British and who had also arranged for his son's commission in the regiment. While many British officers would chafe under Arnold's command, Robinson reveled in it, delighted to be serving on the mission to restore Virginia to the control of the crown.

An elite group of Hessian soldiers completed the convoy. It was led by Johann von Ewald, one of the most revered Hessians to serve the British. Unlike British officers, many of whom received their commissions as a result of family connections and financial payments, Ewald's position was based purely on his knowledge of the art of war. He would go on to play one of the most important roles in the invasion of Virginia, ably performing his duty but also clashing with Arnold at key moments.

On December 29, the fleet assembled at Cape Henry, passing the Chesapeake Bay estuary at 4:00 p.m. and anchoring that evening at Lynnhaven Bay. At nine o'clock the next morning the fleet set sail and reached Hampton Roads, at the mouth of the James River, and proceeded to Newport News, where Arnold anchored in the evening. Despite a howling wind, Arnold gave a pre-arranged signal for commanding officers to leave their ships and row aboard small craft to the sloop-of-war *Charon*. There Arnold laid out the battle plan: a swift strike against an unwitting enemy. The larger ships, carrying the artillery and cavalry corps, would provide an armed escort. Most of the men were transferred to open sloops and boats, where they huddled on crowded decks, bundled up against the wind. Each man was given five days' rations: salted meat, biscuits, and plenty of rum. The food and drink were expected to last until they had reached the capital, Richmond.

A Fatal Inattention

JAMES BARRON OF THE VIRGINIA NAVY was aboard the *Liberty* in Chesapeake Bay on the evening of December 30 when he saw a stunning sight. A fleet of twenty-seven ships had slipped through the Capes of Virginia, heading straight for Willoughby Point near Norfolk. Neither Barron, though the ablest sailor in Virginia, nor the *Liberty* was any match for what now loomed before them.

Barron could not be sure of the fleet's origin, but he thought it unsafe to venture too close to inspect the ships. Instead, he came about and headed for Hampton, where he met one of that town's prominent merchants, Jacob Wray. Wray quickly jotted down Barron's discovery.

> This moment Commodore Barron [has] come in the Liberty out of the Bay & his report to me was that a fleet of 27 Sail is just below Willoughbay point 18 of them Square Rigged Vessels. This is all at present he turned his boat about & gone to make further discoveries.[1]

The message wound its way through the tortuous relay system of the time: Wray raced to the Yorktown home of the regional militia commander, Thomas Nelson Jr., who read the note and immediately summoned a messenger. Horsemen galloped through the night to get the precious document into the hands of Governor Jefferson in Richmond.

Finally, at dawn on New Year's Day, a weary rider ascended Shockoe Hill, reaching the governor's townhouse at 8:00 a.m. He found Jefferson strolling in the garden, and gave him the message, which the governor digested in his usual calm way.

The news should have set off alarms across Virginia. But, frustratingly, the origin of the vessels was unclear.[2] Was this the British invasion Jefferson feared? Or was it the French reinforcements he had been expecting? He could not be certain, and so he did not order military action. False alarms were a regular occurrence; calling up the militia at every possible threat would result in waste and recriminations. William Tatham, a friend and soldier who visited him at the time, wrote that "as other intelligence led [Jefferson] to suppose they were nothing more than a foraging Party, unless he had farther information to justify the measure, he should not disturb the Country by calling out the Militia." Two days would pass before a general call for the militia went out.[3]

Jefferson asked Tatham to mount his horse and gather information about the fleet, then went about the business of his day, including the payment of £30 to the midwife who had recently delivered his daughter Lucy Elizabeth. The following morning, sitting in his chambers, Jefferson wrote letters to military and political leaders, enclosing the news about the fleet in a rather mundane tone. "I have this moment received information that 27 sail of vessels" arrived in Virginia, Jefferson wrote a military commander. With "no other circumstances being given to conjecture their force or destination," he was dispatching militia leaders to the coast to gather further information.[4] Then Jefferson wrote to the Speaker of the House, Benjamin Harrison, that the size of the fleet "has given suspicions that it may be hostile, more especially as we have been lately informed that an embarkation was taking place at New York." Jefferson said he "thought it my duty to communicate it to the General assembly" because he hoped they would provide "some advice to the Executive on this subject."

WITHIN HOURS OF REACHING the Virginia shoreline, Arnold ventured to Newport News, where he discovered a fleet of unarmed boats loaded with tobacco. The Virginia sea merchants, bobbing in the water, were no doubt awestruck at the tremendous fleet in their midst. Arnold, anxious to grab the first prizes, ordered them to be seized. The British had soon captured six brigs and schooners "and burnt and destroyed as many more," according to the account of Bartholomew James, a British officer aboard the HMS *Charon* who participated in the attack.

Arnold's appetite was whetted. He believed that the Virginians had sailed more boats up Hampton Creek. Having already come close to losing ships in shallow waters, Arnold wanted to find some "intelligent pilots"—local men who could be coerced to serve as navigators for the invaders. At 8:00 p.m. on New Year's Eve, he ordered three hundred men to land at Newport News, and commenced a march inland. Striding through the dense woods in utter darkness, the British found a house "from which we took a rebel prisoner as our guide," as James wrote. The Virginian was hauled off by the invaders "amidst the deep lamentations and cries of his disconsolate wife and children." As the prisoner led the way to the small settlement of Hampton, the British became concerned that anyone who saw them would notify the militia. The solution was to take prisoner every Virginian they encountered. "We continued during our march to examine all the houses, and take into custody all those we found therein, to prevent their alarming the country, which, though absolutely necessary and unavoidable, was distressing beyond measure to those unfortunate inhabitants," who were "too much alarmed even to speak," James recalled.[5]

At midnight precisely on New Year's Eve, the British arrived at Hampton, where they walked down the streets for two hours and went door to door, "taking out of their bed the principal inhabitants." The soldiers then marched away from Hampton "without committing any other outrages than those that are ever unavoidable with such a body of men, in an enemy's town in the dead of night." What these further outrages might have been, Bartholomew James did not divulge.

Arnold was convinced that the only Virginians aware of what was happening had been taken prisoner. In fact, while Jefferson and other state leaders remained unaware of what was happening, local militia leaders had learned of the approaching fleet and had ordered their men to gather arms and prepare to confront the invaders.

One British squadron, composed of five boats, was dispatched up the Nansemond River on a reconnaissance mission. The river was wide at some points, about a half mile across, but at others it narrowed to fifty yards, putting the British in danger of being attacked if the militia gathered. Rowing as silently as possible, the British searched for homes where people might provide intelligence about the region. The men were unsuccessful until several hours later, when a group led by James reached a "house of some consequence" and went ashore. Expecting to find a large family, James instead came upon on "a most lovely young lady alone, sitting by the fire, weeping immoderately." James earnestly believed he had come to relieve inhabitants from the rebel yoke. He tried to calm the young lady, assuring her that the local populace was not even aware the British had landed. "You are much mistaken," the lady responded, "if you think your being in this river is a secret, for know, sir, it has been discovered ever since you entered it, and the country some hours alarmed. My father, who is a colonel in the militia, is gone with several detachments down the river to cut off your retreat." The lady said that several hundred militia were gathered nearby, waiting to attack the British. James was aghast, ordering a full retreat.

The darkness protected the British as they passed the militia, which engaged them in a brief assault that left one man wounded.[6] Meeting with his superiors, James relayed what he had learned: unless the British controlled both shores of the river, it would not be safe to pass through the Nansemond in daylight. But he reported that Hampton had some reliable Loyalists. He was "loaded with presents" from one family and had been able to collect enough forage, including fifty-seven cattle and forty-two sheep, to feed part of the army. He marched away with the livestock, which were guarded by "six butchers with their professional instruments" and driven by thirty slaves the British had freed from local plantations. That evening, gathered on their vessels, the British enjoyed their first Virginia-style feast.

On the northern shore of the James River, meanwhile, some 250 members of the Virginia militia heard about the approaching British and gathered a few miles northeast from Newport News. This was a remarkable, little-noted feat. Jefferson, writing twenty-seven years later, would insist that it was "well remembered there was no militia ready in the field to oppose the invaders."[7] What he apparently meant was that he and other leaders did not immediately issue a call for the militia. But two separate journals, written by a British officer and a Hessian officer, provide nearly identical accounts that demonstrate the local militia quickly appeared on the scene on their own.

With the state's top military leaders unaware of what was happening and nowhere near the action, it was left to local commanders to take control. They were Virginia's first line of defense, but they had no major armaments; most of the militia felt lucky if they had a rifle or musket, or at least a sword or hatchet. In the distance, the militia could see the approach of a flotilla, but apparently not well enough to realize that the ships were bristling with cannons and crowded with British troops.

Arnold received word of the gathering militia and ordered Johann von Ewald, the leader of his Hessian troops, to attack. Arnold could not have made a more effective choice. Throughout the invasion of Virginia, Ewald would prove the most reliable officer. Indeed, Ewald may have been the most talented Hessian officer of the Revolutionary War. He was a student of the art of military engagement, and would go on to write celebrated texts on the tactics of field battles. He was also an astute observer, composing a battlefield diary that would provide one of the most vivid accounts of the war.

Ewald was born in 1744 in Kassel, Germany, the son of a post office bookkeeper. When Ewald was fourteen, an elderly uncle took him to a battlefield, where the youngster is reported to have exclaimed, "Oh, how happy are they who die for their country in such a way!" He joined the infantry at age sixteen and was promptly wounded by a musket ball to the right leg, but rejoined his post in time to be on duty when the Seven Years' War ended. When he was twenty-six, while dining at an inn called Hof von England, he and a friend became drunk on "excellent wine," which encouraged an argument that escalated into a duel. A slender man of medium height, Ewald drew his sword against his friend but could not see well in the darkness. Swords clashed until finally the friend saw his opening, driving his sword into Ewald's left eye. Ewald was near death for eleven days as surgeons performed three "extremely painful operations" to try to save him. "Only after thirteen months had passed could I leave my room," Ewald wrote later. His face partially disfigured, his left eye socket now filled with a glass ball, Ewald worried that he would never serve again. But there was no keeping Ewald away. As he convalesced, he studied the military arts and published his first treatise, "Thoughts of a Hessian officer About What He Has to Do When Leading a Detachment in the Field."[8] That battlefield, he decided, would be America. In May 1776, as revolution roiled the colonies, Ewald volunteered to lead a company of Hessians. Many had no ideological or political care about the revolution; they were soldiers and would fight on the side that paid them. Others believed in loyalty to a sovereign. Ewald's force was considered the elite of all the Hessians, consisting of sharpshooters who were trained to roam the large battlefields and make small but deadly raids at night and in forests.

Arriving in October 1776, Ewald and his foot soldiers, known as the Jägers —literally, "hunters"—participated in numerous battles in New York and, in 1780, helped lead the successful siege of Charleston, South Carolina. Yet unlike some of his British colleagues, Ewald had a healthy respect for his foe. Americans were "the best light infantry-men of the world because every one of them is an experienced hunter and knows all the cunning that is as much part of war as it is of hunting," Ewald wrote. The Americans "stalk away like a cat from the pigeon house."[9] Ewald approached the fight against Americans in the same stealthy manner, planning attacks at night and in small groups, relying on surprise and battlefield psychology as well as shooting skills. Now Ewald was in command of a battle that he had every reason to think could be the beginning of a decisive series of engagements that could end the war.

With Arnold's larger vessels anchored in the James, Ewald led a group of four open boats, loaded with his Jägers, a number of sharpshooters, and several Queen's Rangers. A small number of Americans could be seen on a high bank. Just beyond the shore were more than two hundred Virginians behind a series of fences. Ewald wrote that he was ordered "to land at my discretion and attack them, and in particular I should try to capture several prisoners and catch a few natives." The Jägers would lead, followed by the Queen's Rangers. The British rowed to "within rifle shot" of the Americans and then halted to survey the scene.

Testing the American defense, Ewald ordered several shots fired at the Americans. The ploy revealed Ewald's position, but he believed it worth the risk. The Americans responded with a meager volley of small-arms fire. Ewald now felt sure that the Virginians had no cannons. He drew closer and ordered his men to prepare arms. The soldiers pulled their rifles to eye level, trying to steady their aim in the bobbing sloops. All was ready.

This time Ewald's men fired a full volley of bullets across the water. The startled Virginians returned fire at the boats, wounding three British soldiers. Ewald's force plunged into the frigid waters, swords drawn, heading toward the shore. The Virginians, despite holding the high ground, quickly retreated to a nearby plantation.

Ewald climbed up the steep shore, established a base, and took fifty men to pursue the Virginians. Taking a couple of wounded men as prisoners, he learned that he was facing 230 members of the militia. Failing to find the Virginians, Ewald's force camped overnight at Warwick, although he complained that he was "alarmed three times by the enemy" during the night.

The attack was nominally a success, but it was clear to Ewald that a better-prepared Virginia force could have slaughtered his men. "That the enemy lost his nerve and left—that was luck! But had they taken a stand, and thrown themselves upon the jägers and sharpshooters when I climbed up the steep bank with my men, which could not be done in the best order, all would have been lost." Arnold believed it all to be a grand success, and came ashore to congratulate the men for their bravery. Ewald, however, was furious, making it clear he believed Arnold had put his Jägers at unnecessary risk. "Arnold looked at me and remained silent," Ewald wrote. "I turned around and went to my men."[10] Whatever their differences, they both knew that the real significance of the skirmish between Ewald's forces and the militia was not its success in scattering a small, lightly armed force. It was, instead, that it had made an announcement to all Virginia: the British had landed.

The following morning, January 1, 1781, was unusually warm. As the British prepared to leave Warwick, a small Virginia force appeared in the distance, taking some shots at Ewald's men before quickly departing. The river was at ebb tide; thus, the boats had to be kept far out in the broad James. It took the British fifteen minutes to trudge through the water to reach their vessels, where they huddled together in a drenched, crowded mass.

Arnold, meanwhile, saw a chance to make a quick profit. Manning the deck of the *Charlestown,* he came across five Virginia ships, four brigantines and a schooner, mostly engaged in transporting hogsheads of tobacco. These were valuable prizes. The men aboard the brigantines—the *Charity, Langslee, Jenny,* and *Rattlesnake,* and a schooner called the *Fly* or *Betsy & Peggy*—must have been shocked at the armada that suddenly descended upon them. Quickly Arnold's men forced the ships ashore and confiscated the huge supply of tobacco. Then they commandeered the ships, but they could not get one of the brigantines off the shore. Rather than leave the boat behind, Arnold ordered his men ashore to push it off, "but they were fired upon and beat away by the Rebels on shore," he later recounted.

The newly appointed brigadier general of the British army was appalled that some poorly armed rebels were keeping him from seizing the fifth boat. He sat at his desk on the *Charlestown* and angrily composed a stark warning to the rebels on shore:

ON BOARD THE CHARLES TOWN
Jan. 1st, 1781

Sir

His Majesty's Ship Charles Town having drove a Brigt. on Shore, and having Her Boats fired upon by a Party on Shore in Attempting to get her of[f], I have to [tell] you that however disagreeable It may be to me, unless you immediately desist firing, and suffer the Prize to be taken away with all Her Materials, I shall be under the Necessity of landing and burning the Village, which I wish to avoid.

I am
Sir
Your humble Servt.
B. Arnold B Genl[11]

With His Majesty's cannons aimed at the townspeople, the rebels quickly complied, no doubt astonished that the traitor Arnold himself was commanding the attack.

In Richmond, meanwhile, Jefferson was unaware of the building conflict. He still thought the fleet might be French or foragers. Meeting with five member of the Governor's Council, Jefferson reported receiving the note about the twenty-seven ships that had been spotted entering the Capes of Virginia. Curiously, the council minutes summarized the letter as warning of "a British Fleet of 27 Sail arriving in our bay."[12] In fact, the letter didn't mention that it was a British fleet, and Jefferson's actions indicate that he remained unsure whether it was an enemy. In his diary, the governor recorded that he had learned nothing new on this day, writing: "No intelligence."[13]

The next day, Arnold sailed farther up the James, nearing Burwell's Ferry, a landing on the northern bank about five miles from Williamsburg. There the British seized two Virginia ships and several rebels. As word spread of the approaching force, Williamsburg was "in confusion, and the inhabitants alarmed by the expectation of an immediate engagement at Kings Mill," wrote William Tatham, who had been sent by Jefferson to gather intelligence. Tatham headed toward Kings Mill, at Burwell's Ferry, and found Arnold's troops preparing to disembark and attack a militia force variously estimated at between fifty-five and two hundred men, many of them ill-equipped and wearing an assortment of hunting shirts and other clothing. The militia force seemed no match for the more than one thousand well-armed assortment of British solders, Hessian Jägers, Queen's Rangers, and sharpshooters. "On my arrival I found . . . [the militia] waiting to give the Enemy battle as they land; and most of the Enemy's ships were come to anchor off the Place, a small boat taking the Sounding toward the Shore, and larger boats filled with men were maneuvering towards the land in readiness for debarkation," Tatham wrote.[14]

Nathaniel Burwell, whose ferry landing was at the center of the action, reported to Jefferson that twenty-three of Arnold's ships, "full of men," had arrived at 10:00 a.m. on January 2 and were met by two hundred militia, "a number very insufficient for the present purpose." But Burwell vowed that "nothing shall be wanting as we're able to oppose the Enemy if they attempt to land."[15]

Arnold, having persuaded a group of rebels a day earlier to acquiesce to his demands after sending a threatening message, tried the tactic again. Now commanding the HMS *Hope,* Arnold sent a naval officer ashore with a white flag and a message warning the Americans "to lay down their arms and obey their King."[16]

ON BOARD HIS MAJESTY'S SHIP HOPE
2nd Jan. 1781

Sir

Having the honor to command a Body of His Majesty's Troops, sent for the protection of his Loyal Subjects in this country, I am surprised to observe the hostile appearances of the Inhabitants under Arms on the Shore. I have therefore sent Lieut White, with a Flagg of Truce, to be informed of their intentions. If they are to offer a vain opposition to the Troops under my command, in their landing, they must be answerable for the consequences.

At the same time I think it is my Duty to declare I have not the least intention to injure the peaceable Inhabitants in their persons of property, but that every thing supplied the Troops by them, shall be punctually paid for.

I am Sir
Your most Hble Servant
B. Arnold Br. Genl.[17]

This time, however, the commanding officer on shore did not acquiesce. He was Thomas Nelson Jr., whose family had built much of Yorktown and who owned a large brick home in the center of town. His uncle had been on the Governor's Council and loyal to Lord Dunmore at the time of the revolution, but Thomas had sided with the revolutionaries, signed the Declaration of Independence, and loaned money to Virginia to help fund the war.

A portly man who was frequently ill, Nelson was nonetheless named a brigadier general of the state militia due to his wealth and rank in society (he owned several plantations, twenty thousand acres in five counties, four hundred slaves, five hundred cattle, and one hundred horses and mules).[18] He had confessed to Washington that his military rank was "unmerited" and that he had a "want of military knowledge," and he added, "I am sure that there never was a People worse prepared for Defense than we are." Still, he vowed "to make myself a soldier," and his zeal for the revolution overcame his obvious shortcomings.[19] It was Nelson who, after Patrick Henry gave his "Give me liberty, or give me death" speech, vowed to repel British invaders from the water's edge. Now Nelson had a chance to keep his promise.

Nelson read the message from Arnold carefully. He then asked the English officer whether the author "was the traitor Arnold." If so, Nelson said, then he would like to speak to whoever ranked below Arnold, because he "would not and could not give up to a traitor." Indeed, Nelson continued, "if he were to get hold of Arnold, he would hang him up by the heels, according to the orders of Congress." The English officer returned to the *Hope* and dutifully recounted Nelson's message word for word, to which "Arnold was obliged to make a very wry face," according to Ewald.[20] Nelson's refusal to surrender to Arnold had the aura of bravado, but it sent a message that the Virginians would not retreat as hastily as the Warwick forces had. Luck also played a role. George Wythe, who had taught Jefferson at the College of William and Mary and was a signer of the Declaration of Independence, was out hunting partridges with two companions when he saw Arnold's fleet and realized what was happening. The hunters "took a pop" at Arnold's force, leading the British to worry that a much larger Virginia force lay in the woods, backing up Nelson's refusal to surrender. Arnold walked his ship's deck, eyed the sails, and gauged the wind. He judged the breeze strong enough to carry the force farther upriver, closer to Richmond. He decided that an attack on the former capital of Williamsburg was not worth the risk of losing both men and favorable winds. He ordered his men to prepare to sail farther up the James, in the direction of Richmond.

At 10:00 a.m. on January 2, Jefferson finally received confirmation that a British invasion was under way. It was two days after Arnold's arrival. Yet Jefferson was still wary of calling out the full militia. Instead, he called for a quarter to a half of the militia from nearby counties to assemble. He hoped to muster 4,600 men, nearly three times Arnold's number. Unfortunately, the orders were sent to the counties not by messengers but by local legislators, whose speed varied greatly, depending on age and constitution.

Jefferson's letters now had the proper air of alarm. "I have this moment received confirmation of the arrival of a hostile fleet consisting of 19 ships, and two brigs and two sloops and schooners, the advance of a fleet were yesterday morning in Warrasqueak and just getting into motion up the river with a favorable wind and tide," Jefferson informed Benjamin Harrison, urging the Speaker of the House to turn out militiamen. He told Harrison that Arnold's destination appeared to be "up James River." The phrase must have chilled Harrison, whose plantation, Berkeley, was located twenty-five miles east of Richmond, directly on Arnold's route to the capital.[21]

Jefferson did not blame himself for failing to prepare for invasion. The failure, he wrote, lay with others in not warning him. "From a fatal inattention to the giving us due notice of the arrival of a hostile force, two days were completely lost in calling together the Militia," Jefferson complained, without any hint that he was at least partially responsible for the lack of preparation.[22]

James Fairlee, a militiaman near Williamsburg, watched Arnold's fleet weigh anchor and head up the James River. Fairlee counted the ships, marveling at the vessels "very full of Troops" and a ship that seemed filled with horses. There were nine ships at the front, followed by perhaps another twenty. Nelson's militia force, by comparison, was poorly equipped and had only 176 men, including officers, he wrote. Then Fairlee hastily added a postscript. It would be helpful "to procure a Spy-Glass," he wrote, "as we have not one in all our Army."[23]

The Most Wretched Situation That Can Be Conceived

AS BRIGADIER GENERAL ARNOLD ORDERED his fleet up the James River, Governor Jefferson turned over the military leadership to a fiery-tempered fifty-one-year-old Prussian officer who had first set foot in the state only two months earlier. Major General Frederick William von Steuben was a most unlikely choice to become the de facto leader of Virginia's Continental and militia soldiers at the darkest hour. Years later a biographer aptly described Baron von Steuben as both "a systematic, circumstantial and deliberate liar" and the most influential American officer during the Revolutionary War after Washington.[1] Steuben's tenure in Virginia would prove so controversial that within months of taking command he would declare his "disgust" with Jefferson's lack of military preparedness, while some Virginians believed Steuben so incompetent that he deserved to be hanged. At the outset of the invasion, however, Jefferson viewed Steuben as a savior.

Born in Magdeburg in the Prussian Empire, Steuben became a military officer at seventeen and served in the Seven Years' War, during which he was wounded. He called himself a baron, though he acquired the title by falsifying his lineage. His military service had been so outstanding that Frederick the Great named him among those destined for high rank. His career in the Prussian elite seemed ensured. Shortly after gaining this honor, however, Steuben abruptly resigned, for reasons never fully understood. Some maintain that Steuben had a feud or even a duel with another officer, or that it was related to the discovery that he was not descended from nobility. A friend of Steuben wrote to a German prince that Steuben had been unjustly "accused of having taken familiarities with young boys which the law forbids and punishes severely." The friend asked for the allegations to be shown to be false and Steuben's "innocence" to be "attested." Some believe the allegations were a slander prompted by religious bigotry, noting that Steuben was a Protestant from a Catholic-dominated region. Steuben himself said he quit the Prussian army because of "an inconsiderate step and an implacable personal enemy."[2]

After Steuben left Prussia he sought to sell his military services in France, where he wound up out of work and was often broke. With encouragement from French officials who believed he could help the American cause, Steuben went to Paris to meet Benjamin Franklin. Franklin was so impressed with Steuben's knowledge of military drills and tactics that he agreed to exaggerate

Steuben's credentials to convince Congress to hire him. Franklin authored papers that introduced Steuben to Washington as having been "Lieut. Genl. in the King of Prussia's service," a much more significant rank than the captain Steuben had been.[3] Another benefactor, Silas Deane, sent a letter to Congress in which he claimed (falsely) to have seen Steuben's "certificates of his services" and said it would waste too much time for Steuben to retrieve them.[4]

It was arranged that Steuben would travel to America on a ship that was covertly carrying gunpowder from France. Dressed in the resplendent scarlet and blue uniform of a lieutenant general, Steuben carried Franklin's letter in his pocket. Years later, an aide recalled Steuben climbing aboard the ship, describing "an old German baron, with a large brilliant star on his breast, three French aides-de-camp and a large spirited Italian dog."[5] Steuben endured a sixty-six-day trip, which featured two fierce storms and an attempted mutiny, before arriving in Portsmouth, New Hampshire, where the gunpowder was unloaded. He was one of small number of Prussians to fight on the Patriot side, compared to the thirty thousand Hessians who fought for the British.

Steuben arrived in America in 1777 to seek the glory denied him in Europe. One American official, observing the distinguished-looking man in his elegant uniform and array of medals, described him as appearing like "the ancient fabled God of War."[6] For all his colorful attributes and fake titles, Steuben had in fact mastered light infantry drills in Frederick the Great's army, a skill much needed in Washington's army. Washington was convinced enough of Steuben's qualifications to make him his inspector general. The job made him one of the highest-ranking officers in the Continental army. Steuben became renowned for instilling discipline in the troops, beloved among the men for his colorful trilingual cursing when he could not find the English to convey his orders, and famous for writing a field training manual known as the *Blue Book* that became a standard reference for the American military.

Writing a close friend, Baron de Frank, Steuben boasted that if "the first field-marshal of Europe had arrived in my place he could not have been received with more marks of distinction than I was." Steuben delighted in "what a beautiful, what a happy country this is! Without kings, without prelates, without blood-sucking farmer-generals and without idle barons! Here everybody is prosperous." He wrote, with an exaggerated sense of self-importance, that he was one of the most powerful men in all of North America. "Now, is Canada my hunting-lodge; Georgia my country-seat; and this strip of land the eighth of the world. At each of these extreme ends an order signed by me will be executed. This is somewhat flattering to an ambitious man; and you can, therefore, recognize your friend!"[7]

Steuben became a dedicated Patriot and later an American citizen. He was at the fortress of West Point when Arnold defected to the British and nearly captured the valuable fort and Washington himself. When Major André was captured, Steuben served as one of the court-martial judges and voted for André's execution. Shortly afterward, Steuben was inspecting some soldiers when he learned one of them was named Jonathan Arnold. Steuben asked the soldier how he could live with the traitor's surname. The young soldier agreed it was shameful and asked what name he should take instead. "Steuben," Steuben suggested. The soldier agreed not only to change his name to Jonathan Steuben but also to pay the baron $2 per month for the remainder of the war for the privilege.[8]

Now Steuben had been given responsibility for defending Virginia against invasion by the very man he so detested. He had little time to prepare. He had arrived in Virginia in November when the new southern commander of the Continental army, Major General Nathanael Greene, left him in Richmond with orders to find troops and supplies for the army in South Carolina. Steuben quickly determined that Virginia was bereft of guns, clothing, supplies, and qualified soldiers, making it impossible for him to fulfill Greene's needs for the Continental army. Steuben wrote letters urging that stronger measures be taken to turn out Continental army recruits and lamenting the poor shape of militiamen, whose three-month terms afforded little time to instill discipline in them. In Virginia, unlike his days with Washington, when he could issue an order and expect to have it followed, Steuben did not have the power to call out the state militia. Governor Jefferson, meanwhile, often seemed unable to have his orders obeyed. Steuben was, understandably, immensely frustrated by what he viewed as a weak governor and recalcitrant citizenry. When the militia did turn out, they were technically under his command, but they were under the immediate command of local militia leaders whom Steuben barely knew and often did not trust.

Worse, when the militia did show up, they often were ill-equipped and poorly dressed. Steuben considered many of Virginia's soldiers to be "utterly naked" and "in the most wretched situation that can be conceived," he wrote in a letter to Jefferson. It was an act of "inhumanity" to enlist such men and let them "die by inches."[9] He urged a new draft system that would ensure a full turnout of qualified men, stressing that all social classes should be equally represented, a proposal that he said would "prevent the abuses that now exist [of] children and Infirm Men put into the Field, nor men receiving enormous bounties and immediately deserting." It was an insightful analysis, but the letter was sent only two weeks before Arnold's invasion, and Steuben struggled for months to get it implemented.[10]

The militiamen, meanwhile, were just as understandably frustrated by the system in which most of the burden of fighting fell to the lower classes. Many worried that their families and property would be at the mercy of the British invaders, complaining that the state did not have the means or equipment for a proper defense. They were paid in depreciated money. While thousands of patriotic men risked their lives, there were also those who were poor and hungry, anxious to return home at the end of their term of service, which typically lasted three months at this point in the war. Thomas Nelson Jr., the militia commander in lower Virginia, wrote Jefferson that the state's defense "must not rest on the Militia under its present Establishment" because so many men were distressed "at leaving their Plantations and Families." If Nelson released the militia from service on schedule, he said, he would not have one-third of the needed number.[11]

Steuben became Virginia's military leader by default; he happened to be the highest ranking Continental officer in the state when Arnold invaded. While Jefferson and the council and legislature still retained their authority over militia, Steuben was expected to direct military movements. Jefferson told Steuben to "consider the militia of every place as under your command from the moment of their being embodied, and to direct their motions and stations as you please."[12]

In the first days of the invasion, Steuben was far from the action, having set up headquarters near Richmond at an estate called Wilton. Steuben, with reason, was concerned about protecting the entry to the capital. One of his most urgent recommendations in the weeks before the invasion had been to establish a major fort at a place called Hood's Point, but the legislature had stalled and done little. As it turned out, this was precisely the place where Arnold was headed on the evening of January 3. Had the Virginians mounted a better defense, it is the place where the invasion could have been stopped.

Hood's Point jutted from the southern shore of the James River at about the halfway point between Jamestown and Richmond. It is one of the most serene and strategic places on the James. A series of steep cliffs rise from the shoreline at the precise point where the James funnels into a relatively narrow channel. Inlets are scattered along both sides of the point, Ward's Creek to the east, and Flowerdew Hundred Creek to the west. Standing atop the bluff, one sees a wide stretch of the James in the distance. On either side of the river were a series of great plantations, including those owned by such prominent families as the Tylers, Byrds, Harrisons, and Carters. Tobacco fields tended by slaves reached nearly to the shoreline. From aboard ship, one could see mansions, barns, stables, and docks. A vessel approaching from the Atlantic entered the James as if going into a funnel, beginning at the widest end and then threading through a narrowed channel with a series of twists, shoals, and sandbars that required careful navigation. The height of the point was a perfect place from which to rain cannon fire on enemy ships. A shooting gallery could not have been better constructed. It should have been the West Point of Virginia.

Jefferson recognized the strategic value of the spot, believing a well-fortified encampment could stop the British from approaching Richmond. He had written a year earlier that such batteries were of "great importance to the security and quiet of the country above them" and two months earlier had requested that the legislature approve construction.[13] A month before the invasion, Jefferson pleaded with the legislature to strengthen the battery at Hood's. But the legislature failed to act and Hood's was only a shadow of what Jefferson and his advisors had envisioned. Steuben was dumbfounded. He was used to an executive's orders being followed. Yet the legislature was rebuking the governor's desire to repair an obvious deficiency in the state's defense. "I could wish the Assembly might come to some determination on this subject," Steuben wrote Jefferson two weeks before the invasion.[14] A fifty-man gang could have completed the fort in two weeks, Steuben reported.

The existing fortification at Hood's Point was therefore woefully inadequate. It lacked most of the necessary cannons, and its breastworks were made only in anticipation of an assault coming up from the river. The fort's rear was exposed, as the Virginians expected that a series of swamps would forestall any attack from the rear. So it was that a band of Virginia militia estimated at no more than ninety soldiers was entrusted with the defense of Virginia's interior. They had, by the British account, three twenty-four-pound cannons and two howitzers, or, by the Virginia account, two ten-pound cannons and one howitzer. Either way, the manpower and weaponry were hardly equal to the task of stopping a great British fleet, no matter how advantageous their defensive position atop Hood's Point.

The British, however, did not know this as they approached a bend in the river that revealed the promontory of Hood's Point. From the river, it was difficult to tell whether Hood's held a heavily fortified army or an ill-equipped militia unit. The land was thick with oak, ash, sycamore, and cypress. Arnold had been warned to expect a fierce assault. "Toward evening General Arnold received intelligence that an American corps had fortified the heights of Hood's Point, and had stationed infantry and cannon there to bombard us in the narrow winding channel," the Hessian officer Ewald noted in his journal. Arnold ordered his fleet to anchor just before the bend in the river, hoping to give his men time to prepare for a bombardment. But one ship inadvertently went by Hood's Point and promptly received fire. The skipper and his sailors raced to sail the ship around the bend, avoiding injury.

The battle cry was given. Arnold ordered the twenty-four-gun sloop *Hope* and the twelve-gun privateer *Cornwallis* to attack the Virginia batteries. The cannons from the *Hope* and *Cornwallis* fired in strict order, round after round splitting through the trees, the thunderous blasts echoing off the river.

The British now split their forces. A detachment that included Hessians and Queen's Rangers stealthily headed up Ward's Creek, on the eastern side of Hood's Point, protected by the bombardment from the British vessels. Some 130 members of the British force crept closer to the Virginia batteries. The landing was "effected silently and apparently with secrecy about a mile from the battery," wrote Simcoe, the commander of the Queen's Rangers.[15] The plan was to make a circuitous route on land and attack the garrison from the rear. As Arnold's ships continued their onslaught, the Virginians fired a few shots at the British ships, killing one sailor.

Then, abruptly, the ships' cannons went silent.

The Virginians sensed entrapment, and then suddenly became aware that a land force was approaching their rear. Facing either slaughter or capture, with no hope of beating a vastly superior foe, the small band of Virginians wisely retreated, racing through woods and tobacco fields until they reached the road to Petersburg. Moments later, the British forces crept into the garrison, finding it abandoned. They seized the three cannons and two howitzers, but their biggest prize was the possession of the heights of Hood's Point.

The British marveled at the lack of preparation at the little fort. They could not understand why the Virginians had left open a gorge that enabled the British to approach the heights, nor comprehend why the breastworks failed to fully enclose the defenders. "Had they been in a better state of defense, and the garrison commanded by an enterprising officer, they could have easily delayed us until the militia had assembled and strengthened the position," Ewald wrote. "Since the channel in the river lay within small-arms range, this could very easily have prevented us from further undertakings."[16] The "undertaking," as Ewald's understatement had it, was the full-scale invasion of Virginia. Now it could go forward with seeming impunity.

Arnold had remained at a distance during the battle. Now he strode ashore, triumphantly surveying the abandoned fort. Virginia's defense system had proven to be without spine and its soldiers without the means to put up a fight.

There was little reason to think that anything but some ragtag forces stood between Arnold and the home of Governor Jefferson in Richmond, just twenty-five miles up the James River.

At homes and plantations along the James River, alarmed Virginians began to meet at the ordinaries and courthouses, trading rumors and worries about the invasion fleet. Urgent letters were sent to Jefferson. James Maxwell, an officer at the state shipyard on the Chickahominy River, told Jefferson that he was hurriedly trying to reassemble a ship that had just been "totally dismantled" for repairs and was one of the few capable of bearing sizable cannons. At the same time, he said, the militia assigned to the ship were trying to head home because their term of service had expired on January 1. Not a single one of the ship's sailors would agree to remain on duty even though their service was desperately needed, so Maxwell informed the governor that he "shall therefore be under the disagreeable Necessity of detaining them Against their Will." Such was the state of the Virginia navy: few vessels capable of bearing arms, and few sailors willing to serve.[17]

Nelson, who had rebuffed Arnold a day earlier at Burwell's Ferry, wrote that Arnold's next target could be Richmond. "They will make a bold push . . . if not check'd on their landing," he wrote. "If they discover a determination in the Inhabitants to oppose them, they will move with caution, and perhaps return to Hampton with disgrace." But Nelson admitted that his militia force was "very weak" due to lack of arms and reinforcements.[18]

Speaker of the House Harrison, whose vast Berkeley plantation was located on the opposite side of the river from Hood's Point, assured Jefferson that he was assembling the militia. However, Harrison said many militiamen had no arms and that he must "add to this dismal account" that "we have no ammunition of any kind, or so small a quantity that it is scarcely worth mentioning."[19]

A nearly complete lack of intelligence about Arnold's intentions kept Virginians along the James River on constant edge. Arnold would have to put down anchor somewhere. Having been at sea for two weeks and in the James for six days, the fleet was badly in need of a supply base, someplace to marshal its forces, feed the men and horses, and prepare for the next step of the invasion.

JEFFERSON HEARD THE BANGING on his door at 5:00 a.m. on January 4, 1781. A messenger told the governor that Arnold's fleet had overtaken the militia at Hood's Point and was anchored nearby. Five days after the invasion began, Jefferson recorded in his diary that he was now ordering the "whole militia from adjacent counties." He awakened his wife and three daughters and sent them hurriedly to Tuckahoe, fourteen miles up the James River, and ordered that important state documents be moved from Richmond to Westham, six miles up the river. Then, mounting his horse, Jefferson roamed throughout Richmond, trying to raise the militia while overseeing the removal of important papers from the temporary state offices.

Arnold, however, was not heading immediately to Richmond. Instead, he sailed to a plantation on the northern shore of the James, around a long bend in the river from Hood's Point. During the desperate weeks to come, the plantation would become a British garrison, a sanctuary within Virginia from which Arnold and other generals could operate with impunity. Indeed, Arnold had been cordially welcomed by the plantation's owner: his wife's cousin, the widow Mary Willing Byrd.

IT HAD BEEN FOUR YEARS since Mary Byrd's husband had died in despair, having witnessed the loss of his financial empire and the signing of the Declaration of Independence. Mary had kept the plantation going, using dozens of slaves to maintain a thousand acres of fields, forest, and swamp. She had enough to support herself and her family at Westover. Given her deceased husband's British ties, Mary's loyalties had long been a matter of debate. But the men who ran Virginia did not much fear the machinations of a woman, especially a widow preoccupied with keeping a bankrupt estate afloat and caring for her children. A German visitor to Virginia provided a description that matched Byrd's situation. "The free men in Virginia are a lazy lot, who expect their slaves to do all the work for them. . . . A Virginia gentleman is a sociable, courteous, good creature, who has only the one fault, that he is too fond of gambling," wrote August Wilhelm du Roi. "The women are a great deal more industrious."[20]

William Byrd had been a sociable but luckless gambler. Mary Byrd, sophisticated and raised in a well-educated household Philadelphia, was nothing if not industrious. One of her friends, David Meade, who lived across the James River from Westover, remembered her as a woman who "possessed a mind of powers superior to the generality of her sex, and a most generous benevolent and charitable heart."[21] Still, she was a great enigma to most Virginians. She harbored resentment against revolutionaries, whom she blamed for her husband's suicide, and yet was also a subject of sympathy because of the vast obligations she was left on the day Byrd died. She had done nothing to demonstrate that she would support or oppose the revolution herself, and so she was mostly left alone—until early January 1781, when Benedict Arnold sailed up the James River.

Mary Byrd not only had a direct connection to Arnold's wife, Peggy Shippen, but also to Mary's brother, Thomas Willing, a former mayor of Philadelphia who, as a member of the Continental Congress in 1776, voted against the Declaration of Independence. He remained in Philadelphia when it was occupied by the British but did not swear allegiance to the crown. He wound up selling arms to the Continental army—although at a price that made him much detested. He went on to become president of America's first national bank and amass a fortune.

Mary had similarly divided loyalties and honed survivalist instincts. She communicated regularly with Loyalists. When later she was asked about her leanings, she wrote ambiguously to Jefferson, "I wish well to all mankind, to America in particular. What am I but an American? All my friends and connexions are in America; my whole property is here—could I wish ill to everything I have an interest in?"[22]

On the evening of January 3 Mary Byrd was awakened by the sudden burst of cannon fire coming from Hood's Point. Hours later, Arnold gave the orders to set sail, pointing the fleet westward. As Arnold steered around the bend, Westover came into view. The slaves, learning the British were near, streamed from their small dwellings. Liberation was at hand.

Mary Byrd would have seen the enormous ships and smaller tenders of His Majesty's navy and had little doubt they were headed to her home. She decided that she would stay at her home but that her children had to leave immediately. She packed them into a coach and instructed one of her servants to take them "to a place of safety among her friends higher up the country." After the coachman gathered the reins in his hand and set off for the west, however, he may have heard the rumble of troop movements in the distance. He was only halfway to his destination when he "proved untrue" and suddenly leaped from his seat, leaving the Byrd children in "great dismay." The Byrd children, accompanied by a young boy named Jack Hopper, did not know what to do. They apparently were not capable of steering the coach or finding their way along the remote roads. Nearby, American and British troops were gathering for the inevitable clash. Then, in what Mary Byrd always considered an act of Providence, a friend named D. M. Randolph happened by the road. He sized up the situation, "mounted the coach and drove them to the place they wished to go."[23] The children were safe.

Back at Westover, Mary Byrd waited for the British. Despite the hardship of the years since her husband committed suicide, she had insisted upon everything being presentable and in place. While the estate's fields were greatly diminished, the crop had been good, and prospects for the coming season were excellent. Wheat for the animals was plentiful. "The place looked most lovely," her granddaughter wrote. "Everything in beautiful order."[24]

According to family lore, Arnold galloped up the riverfront lawn on his horse and urged his steed up the steps and into the hallway, where he pulled out his sword and slashed two large gashes in the mahogany banister. The story left subsequent owners of Westover to wonder whether Arnold slashed the banister to scare Mary Willing Byrd into submission or to provide her with a cover story—"evidence" to try to convince authorities that he took the house by force. By midafternoon, many British ships were moored near the shoreline, disgorging hundreds of men, horses, cannons, and equipment. Soldiers roamed freely about Westover, with its "forty fine buildings, which because of their style of construction, resembled a small town," Ewald wrote. The Byrd estate was now a British encampment. Arnold's men set up tents, gathered food for the horses, and established a command center for Arnold himself. Around fifty slaves left Westover to accompany the British, either because of the promise of liberation or because they were forced into service.

The British commandeered food, forage, and supplies. "To her great dismay she saw from the Windows their horses" eating the wheat and "all enclosures broken down," Mary Byrd's granddaughter wrote. The British knocked her cows "in the head and butchered [them] before her eyes." British soldiers were put at the foot of the stairs "with a promise of protection."[25]

Mary Byrd cordially welcomed Arnold and his men. "When the officers landed, I received them according to my idea, with propriety," she wrote later to Jefferson. "I consulted my heart and my head, and acted to the best of my judgment, agreeable to all laws, human and divine. If I have acted erroneously, it was an error in judgment and not of the Heart."[26]

Byrd and Arnold spoke at length about the terms of the occupation of her home. Arnold assured her that she would be compensated for the loss of livestock and crop, as well as two ferry boats, three horses, and forty-nine slaves. At Arnold's request, she provided a detailed accounting of her losses to his officers. Arnold assured her that "not one single Vessel shall be allowed to depart this river" until they had been searched for her "people," by which she meant her slaves.[27]

It would later be noteworthy that whatever damage the British did to Byrd's estate, it was nothing compared to what they did to that of her neighbor, Benjamin Harrison, signer of the Declaration of Independence and now Virginia's Speaker of the House. Days earlier Harrison had sent his family away and fled to Richmond just ahead of the invading force, leaving behind his estate, Berkeley. Arnold's troops stormed the mansion, expecting gunfire, and instead were

greeted by slaves, who were invited to join the British force. Viewing Harrison
—not himself—as the traitor, Arnold had his men pile Harrison's family paintings in a heap and torch them. They destroyed furniture and crops and freed
some forty slaves, about one-third of those owned by Harrison. It would be
several years before the Harrisons could live again at Berkeley. Years later, when
a British visitor asked why so many Virginia mansions lacked great portraits,
Harrison replied acidly: "I can account for my paintings and decorations, sir—
your soldiers burned them in my backyard."[28] If Mary Byrd had not originally
planned to conspire with the British, then perhaps her shock at the destruction
next door led her to believe she had no choice. In any event, the portraits at
Westover were undisturbed.

Delegates to the Congress were shocked by the attack at Berkeley, viewing
it as a warning that they could be the next target. "We hear they have done
great injury to the houses of Colonel Harrison of Berkeley, and carried away all
his valuable negros," Joseph Jones, a Virginia delegate to the Congress, wrote
to his nephew James Madison shortly afterward. However, Jones insisted it
would only strengthen the resolve of Virginia forces. "If they attempt to visit
Fredericksburg," he wrote, referring to the city about fifty-five miles north of
Richmond, "I believe they will have reason to repent the enterprise, as there
now is there and in the neighbourhood a considerable force, and a further reinforcement expected to-day."[29]

Here, finally, was some good news. The gentlemen—"and even the Ladys"—
of Fredericksburg were at the gunnery, producing thousands of cartridges, bullets and more than "100 Good Guns" to be sent to local militias. A local official, Charles Dick, wrote to Jefferson that this was "pretty difficult to do with
Money and Provisions," hinting that he was anxious to hear when Virginia's
government would "begin to do Business."

For all the delays, enough men had now assembled to outnumber the British
nearly two to one—there were some 2,250 militia, compared to no more than
1,200 British (with 400 others still at sea). But the Virginians were scattered
and poorly equipped. Moreover, it was believed that the British would turn
south to attack an arms depot near Petersburg, so many militia had gathered
there. Arnold, however, was preparing to march to Richmond.

A LIGHTLY DEFENDED ROAD of thirty miles separated the Byrd estate from the governor's house. Benedict Arnold gathered his officers at Byrd's mansion and discussed his options: remain at Westover and await reinforcements, launch exploratory patrols to determine the strength of the militia, or immediately make an assault on Richmond.

Arnold's second in command, Colonel Simcoe, pushed for a quick strike. "Arnold hesitated whether he should proceed thither or not, his positive injunctions being not to undertake any enterprise that had much risk in it," Simcoe wrote later. But Simcoe was convinced that one day's march to Richmond "might be made with perfect security" and he offered to take some of his troops on an advance patrol, to be followed by Arnold's forces. Simcoe's opinion was respected; even one of his past opponents, Henry Lee, said Simcoe was known for "seizing every advantage" against an enemy. Lee said Simcoe was a man of letters, resembling "the Romans and Grecians." He recalled how Simcoe had led a daring raid in New Jersey in darkness to destroy some vessels and then pretended to be American in order to get forage for his horses.[1]

Arnold, who was familiar with Simcoe's effective strategies, swiftly agreed to Simcoe's new plan, hoping to surprise the Virginians, who likely expected the sea-weary troops to rest for several days at Westover before launching an attack. Not even one full night's respite would be allowed. Arnold declared that they would leave that evening, in a driving rainstorm, with the hope of capturing a vast store of ammunition. A quick rout could turn Virginia over to the British, and the tide of war could be turned as well.

Bracing themselves against the chilly downpour, Arnold and nine hundred of his strongest troops dragged artillery pieces across a muddied landscape in search of the governor of Virginia. "No time was to be lost," Arnold wrote a British commander. "The troops were therefore immediately put in motion."[2]

At the head of Arnold's army were Ewald's Jägers, carefully pushing forward, concerned that at any turn they might be easy prey for Virginians hiding in the woods. He instructed the Jägers that if an attack was necessary, they were to be as quiet as possible and use only their hunting swords. They passed over a narrow bridge at Turkey Island Creek and across two steep heights. Ewald marveled that they had been left unprotected by the Virginians. "A half a dozen men could have easily defended this pass," he wrote.[3]

They were followed by Simcoe and his Queen's Rangers, then the sharp-shooters and other troops, and finally a small corps of rangers on horseback. The British rested at Four Mile Creek, about twelve miles from Richmond, and resumed their march early on the morning of January 5. The militia, meanwhile, gathered nearby, hoping to ambush the invaders. They removed the planks of a bridge, took their positions, and waited for the opportunity to punish the British forces.

The Virginians made a crucial mistake. Simcoe's Queen's Rangers, wearing their green jackets, looked at night to be clothed in the same colors as the Virginia militia. The Virginia troops may have expected the British to wear the bright red coats for which they were famous. So, as some militiamen waited by the bridge for the enemy, they saw at a distance green-jacketed men whom they assumed to be part of another militia unit. Some of the approaching soldiers could be heard talking in a familiar accent, furthering the impression that they were fellow militiamen. But the accent was familiar because many were Loyalists from Virginia, not soldiers from Britain. Convinced the approaching soldiers were friendly, the militia approached Simcoe, who quickly grasped the depth of the militia's misunderstanding. Simcoe, who liked nothing better than using a ruse in combat, casually engaged the militia in conversation and even "reprimanded them for not coming sooner." Then, having won their trust, he informed them they were his prisoners. The stunned and embarrassed Virginians were stripped of their arms and sent to the rear of Arnold's invasion force.[4]

Marching along the Darbytown road, Arnold's forces were nearing Richmond when another militia patrol appeared. Rather than engage them, the militia fled to warn Governor Jefferson and the residents of Richmond that the British were coming.

The British forces reached a clearing in the woods near Richmond. If they remained on the main road, it was possible that Virginians could ambush them. Simcoe told Arnold that by entering the clearing, they would come upon a cart trail that was unlikely to be defended and would lead "through the thickets to the rear of the heights on which the town of Richmond was placed." It appeared to provide an ideal route by which to launch an attack. Arnold, however, insisted on sticking to the main road. He wanted the townspeople to believe that a massive British invasion was under way, with forces emerging confidently from the main road, ready to take over the capital.

Richmond, though the capital of the largest state in America, was still little more than a rough-hewn riverfront trading post of some six hundred people, nearly half of them slaves, living mostly in modest wood-frame houses scattered across two hills. The first, Church Hill, included the grounds of Henrico

Parish Church and a number of residences. At the front of it was Shockoe Creek, and on the opposite side of the creek stood Shockoe Hill, where the main part of town, with both government offices and Jefferson's home, was located. The main street on Shockoe Hill featured a courthouse, jail, market, and craftworks, along with Galt's Tavern and Tankard's Ordinary. Legislators and other visitors crowded into the taverns, sharing a large room that was filled at night with bedding. Richmond had been the capital for only nine months and there had been little improvement since the transfer of government from Williamsburg other than an influx of people desperate for decent housing. It "may at some future period be a great city, but at present it will scarce afford one comfort in life," wrote Eliza "Betsy" Ambler, the state treasurer's daughter, who arrived shortly after Richmond became the capital.[5] There were few carriages to be seen, but during a legislative session everyone seemed to have a horse. "One could almost fancy it was an Arabian village," a visitor wrote, recounting the "swarming of riders in the few and muddy streets."[6] In future years, Richmond would have a state capital inspired by a Roman temple, designed by Jefferson, perched on a hill overlooking the James. A governor's mansion would be built nearby. But at the time Arnold invaded Richmond, Jefferson lived in a modest wood-frame building. From the top floor, the governor scanned the James for invaders, the river being the most likely way to transport thousands of men, horses, and armaments. "Old master kept the spyglass and git up by the sky-light window to the top of the palace looking towards Williamsburg," one of Jefferson's slaves, Isaac, recalled later.[7]

Whether or not Jefferson saw the British in the distance, he had been warned by militia scouts about Arnold's advance. He decided to ride quickly six miles up the James River to Westham, the site of an arms factory. He had earlier ordered the transfer of important state papers to Westham; now he feared the place would be attacked, and he intended to supervise the movement of arms and documents across the James. Once there, he ordered Daniel Hylton, one of the wealthiest men in Richmond, to take charge of the operation. Seven wagons were filled with arms and gunpowder and driven to a courthouse and church far from Richmond. At 11:00 p.m., finally satisfied that the arms and papers would be saved, Jefferson mounted his horse and rode another eight miles to the estate called Tuckahoe, where the governor had sent his family for safety. Jefferson knew the house well, having spent part of his childhood there.

Tuckahoe, set on a bluff overlooking the James, was owned by Jefferson's cousin Thomas Mann Randolph. Exhausted from his day on the run from the British, Jefferson arrived at 1:00 a.m. and checked on Martha and their three daughters: Patsy, eight years old; Maria, two years old; and Lucy, the five-week-old infant. Jefferson was on the defensive in every possible way. He was taking refuge in his boyhood home, having fled from the city that he had insisted be made the capital by arguing that it would be safer from a British attack than Williamsburg. A force of perhaps three hundred militiamen turned out in Richmond but had no chance of stopping a well-armed British force that was three times larger.

Years later, Jefferson would admit to his shortcomings while also still defending his actions at this crucial moment:

> I was never off my horse but to take food or rest, and was everywhere my presence could be of any service. I may with confidence challenge any one to put his finger on the point of time when I was in a state of remissness from any duty of my station. But I was not with the army! true; for first, where was it? Second, I was engaged in the more important function of taking measures to collect an army; and, without military education myself, instead of jeopardizing the public safety by pretending to take its command, of which I knew nothing, I had committed it to persons of the art, men who knew how to make the best use of it, To Steuben for instance, to Nelson and others, possessing that military skill and experience, of which I had none. Let our condition, too, at that time be duly considered. Without arms, without money of effect, without a regular soldier in the State, or a regular officer, except Steuben, a militia scattered over the country, and called at a moment's warning to leave their families and firesides, in the dead of winter, to meet an enemy ready marshaled, and prepared at all points to receive them.[8]

Jefferson's explanation left out several crucial facts. While it was true that Jefferson had ordered Steuben to take command of the militia, he had done this as Arnold approached Richmond, giving Steuben no time to prepare. At the same time, despite admitting that he did not possess "military skill and experience," Jefferson did play a crucial role at a time when many Virginians were on the run. He directed militia operations and delivered prescient orders to safeguard stores and arms. Finally, Jefferson only alluded vaguely to a factor that was weighing heavily on his mind and influencing his decisions: worry about his wife and his young daughters. Over the years, Martha would frequently remain at Monticello or at her childhood home, The Forest, while Jefferson traveled or served in government. He often would write friends and family to express concern that Martha was in danger. Now she was recovering from another difficult birth, caring for her three daughters (including a sickly infant), and racing in rickety carriages on rough winter roads from one hideout to the next.

When Jefferson awoke from a short night's rest at Tuckahoe, his first action centered upon his family. He worried that the British would head to Tuckahoe as soon as they received intelligence about his whereabouts. Just after dawn, he took his wife and their daughters across the James and sent them eight miles farther up, to a place called Fine Creek, where the Jefferson family owned property.

Returning to Tuckahoe, Jefferson met with the commander of the local militia, John Nicholas. Jefferson had ordered Nicholas's men to follow the British, "not with any view to face them directly with so small a force, but to hang on their skirts, and to check their march as much as could be done, to give time for the more distant militia to assemble." Nicholas acknowledged that his men were unable to slow the enemy's advance. Jefferson then went with Nicholas to check on whether his orders to remove arms and papers from Westham had been followed. Arriving at the scene, Jefferson was horrified to see that many arms had simply been piled by the riverbank, exposed to enemy fire. He ordered them to buried and then galloped to Manchester, across the river from Richmond.[9]

At one o'clock in the afternoon Jefferson stood on a hill and watched the British swarm into the capital city. He was "always within observing distance of the enemy," he wrote.[10] Looking across the river at this moment, loosening the draws on his spyglass, he would have seen Arnold leading the English soldiers and their Hessian auxiliaries into the capital. A few cannons had been placed by Virginians at heights around the town, while the main force of the militia gathered on a hill, observing the approach of the British.

The long, meandering train of British and Hessian soldiers, horses, artillery, and supplies emerged from a densely wooded road—an impressive sight, with just the effect that Arnold had suggested. As Arnold reached the town, the British general saw a militia force of nearly three hundred men gathered on a hill in the shadow of Henrico Parish Church, where six years earlier Patrick Henry had famously declared, "Give me liberty, or give me death." Arnold decided that this would be the perfect place to put Henry's challenge to the test, and he called on Ewald to take his Jägers up the steep hill toward the church.

As Ewald's soldiers stormed the heights, they faced a single volley from the militia that wounded one of their men. Three other Jägers "who had gone too far to the right were captured," Ewald wrote. But after firing the volley and hitting only one Hessian, the militia were suddenly facing a charge from several angles. They did not have time to reload and aim at the dozens of enemy soldiers on horseback and on foot. As some Virginians retreated to a ravine, Ewald chased them until he found his force suddenly exposed. As the Jägers stood on "barren, level ground," the Virginians in the wood were so close that they "could count my men," Ewald recounted. It was a "crucial moment for me."[11] To Ewald's astonishment, he discovered that the remaining Virginia force "had no riflemen, but infantry equipped with bayonets." The Jägers easily pushed back the Virginians, who fled farther into the woods.[12]

The rest of Arnold's force, meanwhile, had climbed Church Hill, toward what they believed would be another battle on Shockoe Hill. Simcoe's cavalry found the ascent of Church Hill so steep that many men had to walk their horses up the heights. They feared being shredded by the fire of the Virginia militia at this point, but found that Ewald's Jägers had dispersed them so effectively that the Virginians "made no resistance, nor did they fire," Simcoe wrote. The militia had "retreated to the woods in great confusion."[13]

The British then headed to Shockoe Hill. At first, a group of Virginia horsemen in the lower part of town stood in their way. Simcoe prepared to attack them, but just as he neared the force, he came to an impassable creek, which he said "gave the enemy time to escape to the top of another hill beyond the town." Next, Simcoe planned to ascend Shockoe Hill, uniting with another group of British who had gone around the base of the hill to trap the Virginians in a pincer. The British expected a major battle, especially since it appeared the Virginians were "greatly superior in numbers." But many were without arms and a number of them were merely spectators, believing they would see a good fight.

Some residents did not realize what was happening. They were used to seeing Virginia soldiers come up every few days to the governor's house, "drumming & fifing." So when a group of soldiers arrived with three cannons, some of the spectators thought a Virginia force was taking its position near Jefferson's home. Suddenly, three cannons were fired simultaneously and "everybody knew it was the British." One of the cannonballs "knocked off the top of a butcher's house" near Jefferson's home, prompting the butcher's wife and children to flee. Another group of British soon marched into the main part of town, first the cavalry led by Simcoe and then the artillery corps. "They formed in line and marched . . . with drums beating. It was an awful sight," recalled Jefferson's slave Isaac. "Seemed like the day of judgment was come."[14]

Richmond was now firmly in the control of General Benedict Arnold. The invasion had succeeded "without opposition," he wrote later. "The militia who had collected fled at our approach." As Isaac put it: "In ten minutes not a white man was to be seen in Richmond. They ran as hard as they could." The British cavalry was ordered to race after them, but most of the Englishmen were on horses wearied from the sea journey and the march to Richmond and thus lacked the strength to pursue the Virginians, many of whom were on Arabians.

Arnold and his men swarmed through the town, searching for stragglers. A British officer—possibly Arnold himself—rode up to Jefferson's townhouse.

"Where is the governor?" the officer demanded, according to Isaac's account. The officer insisted he didn't want to hurt Jefferson, but intended to take the governor as a prisoner, displaying a pair of silver-colored handcuffs he had brought for the occasion.

"He's gone to the mountains," responded one of Jefferson's slaves.

"Where is the keys of the house?" the officer asked.

"Mr. Jefferson left with them," the slave replied.

"Where is the silver?"

"It was all sent up to the mountain," the slave responded. In fact, he had hidden the silver throughout the house, including in the ticking of a bed and in the kitchen.[15]

Convinced that Jefferson had escaped, the soldiers began the business of plundering. They went into Jefferson's cellar, broke off the necks from the bottles of the best wine and Antigua rum, and poured their contents into large barrels. The British then took corn from the corncrib and meat from the meat house, laying the food out in parcels for soldiers to put in their packs.

Next, they took away Isaac, making the child wear a cocked hat and a "monstrous" British red coat with sleeves dangling to the ground. The sight sent his mother "crying and hollering" at the fear of separation, Isaac said years later. The British rounded up Jefferson's slaves, from seven to ten by various counts, and continued their raid on Richmond. Isaac, whom the British insisted on calling "Sambo," was ordered to beat a drum as the entourage marched through town. The British then went up the James River, raiding several large houses and plantations, taking slaves along the way. They entered an estate called Mount Comfort, owned by Samuel DuVal, one of Richmond's wealthiest residents, where the floor was left "flowing with the Liquors spilt by the British soldiers."[16] Eventually, the British reached Tuckahoe, where Jefferson and his family had been lodging only hours earlier. The British searched the house, took away thirty people, mostly slaves, and returned to Richmond.[17]

Arnold and his men, meanwhile, continued to interrogate the remaining residents in an effort to find Jefferson. Arnold announced to the citizens of Richmond that he considered the items stored in warehouses to be his "prize goods," meaning that he and his men would take the merchandise—"Tobacco, Rum, Wine, Sugar, Molasses, Sail Cloth and Coffee"—for their personal use and profit. First he offered the citizenry a deal. He would pay half the cost of the goods he intended to seize in exchange for their safe delivery to ships that he intended to confiscate on the James River. As a precondition of the deal, "the owners of the Goods" were required "to put Hostages into the hands of General Arnold."[18]

Arnold did not specify who would become hostage, leaving some to believe that he was suggesting the citizens should seize Jefferson and deliver him up. In any case, the proposal was sent via messenger to Jefferson, who promptly rejected it. He could hardly make a deal with the traitor. Jefferson was well aware that Arnold, in his original plan to let West Point be taken by the British, had intended that Washington be captured as well.

His deal rejected, Arnold seized the goods. Soldiers marched into several warehouses and stores and removed everything they could find. Then, in a scene that preceded the better-known destruction of Richmond during the Civil War nearly a century later, Arnold's troops set about plundering and destroying. By the British account, Arnold's troops destroyed 2 warehouses, 503 hogsheads of rum, stores of grain, 21 carriages, 2,200 small arms, 4,000 French musket locks, and 50 bolts of canvas. Others, including Ewald, declared that the destruction was far greater. Many houses were burned. Shops and even some churches were robbed, the goods laid out for soldiers' prizes. So much wine and whiskey was poured into the streets that it was said even the hogs got drunk.

Arnold then sent Simcoe and Ewald to Westham, the site of the foundry that was the major source of Virginia's weaponry. Simcoe's forces carried caches of gunpowder down the nearby cliffs and dumped them into the James River. Ewald captured all the foundry workers, including a fellow countryman, Lieutenant Colonel Frederick Warneck, a German noble who had served during the Seven Years' War. Then the British blew up the powder magazine and its seven hundred barrels of powder, destroyed the machinery and two mills, and set the works ablaze. Pockets of gunpowder were stored throughout the building, causing explosions to rocket through the foundry. Virginia's most vital weapons factory, essential for winning the war, was heavily damaged. "Many explosions happened in different parts of the buildings . . . and the foundry, which was a very complete one, was totally destroyed," Simcoe wrote. Isaac said the explosion at the foundry felt "like an earthquake."[19] Jefferson wrote that the boring mill and magazine were burned and the foundry roof destroyed but believed that some equipment inside the foundry was not damaged.[20]

As the buildings at Westham smoldered, Simcoe's weary force returned to Richmond. With many townspeople having fled the capital, some of the British soldiers occupied local houses and, as Simcoe put it, "there obtained rum." Ewald, as usual, was blunter in his diary, writing that two-thirds of his men "were drunk because large stores of wine and beer had been found in the houses. They were so noisy that one could hear us two hours away." Ewald joined with Simcoe and Arnold, whose men "were cantoned in sweet repose," as Ewald described their state of stupor.[21]

The Richmond expedition, Ewald wrote in his diary, "resembled those of the freebooters, who sometimes at sea, sometimes ashore, ravaged and laid waste everything. Terrible things happened on this excursion; churches and holy places were plundered." With "half the place in flames," forty-two ships "were loaded with all kinds of merchandise for the corps' booty," Ewald wrote.[22] The vessels, some of which apparently were seized from local residents, stretched for miles along the James River from Richmond to Westover. Explaining his actions to superiors in New York, Arnold wrote that the burning of buildings in Richmond and the taking of tobacco was Jefferson's fault. The "nominal governor," as Arnold belittled his former ally, had failed to respond to his proposal for half payment for the merchandise. Nor had Jefferson, whom Arnold noted was hiding "in the neighborhood," agreed to provide hostages. "As Mr. Jefferson was so inattentive to the preservation of private property, I found myself under the disagreeable necessity of a large quantity of rum to be stove, several warehouses of salt to be destroyed; several public storehouses and smith's shops with their contents were consumed by the flames," Arnold wrote. He also blamed his own soldiers. "Private property was burnt without my order by an officer who was informed it was public property."[23]

Yet the greatest prize—Jefferson—had escaped. Arnold and his men searched everywhere and quizzed anyone they could find. Still, they could not find the governor of Virginia.

Jefferson was constantly on the move. After witnessing the arrival of British troops from the vantage of Manchester, across the river from Richmond, Jefferson rode a few miles away to a place called Chetwood's, where he expected to rendezvous with Baron von Steuben. But Steuben was nowhere to be found. Jefferson was told Steuben was at a home some twelve miles up the James River from Richmond. The governor once more got on his horse and set off to find the Baron, again to no avail. During this ride, he passed near Westham and likely heard the same earth-shaking explosion that so impressed his young slave Isaac, and certainly deduced that the foundry had been hit. He watched Arnold's forces depart Richmond but could not be sure how far outside the capital they were encamped. In fact, most of the British were just a few miles away.

That evening, Jefferson rode along the banks of the James River, heading northeast to Fine Creek, where Martha and their three daughters were hiding.

He assured them that they were now safe and spent the night with them. Then, on the morning of January 7, he went off again in search of Steuben, riding hard through a downpour. Approaching Westham, he saw the destroyed foundry and went across the river to check on the arms that he had ordered buried. So much rain had fallen that the dirt cover had been washed away and the arms were once again exposed. After so much riding, Jefferson's horse was "exhausted at length by fatigue" and "sunk under me in a public road, where I had to leave him," Jefferson recalled later. Carrying his saddle and bridle on his shoulders, he walked to a nearby farm, where he borrowed "an unbroken colt" and then headed to Manchester.

For two days, Jefferson raced throughout the area near Richmond, galloping for hours through nearly ceaseless rainstorms. "During this crisis of trial I was left alone, unassisted by the co-operation of a single public functionary," Jefferson wrote in a letter years later. The members of the legislature and Governor's Council had fled to their families, Jefferson recalled, but he stayed in the area and tried to manage the state at its darkest moment so far in the war.[24]

At 2:00 p.m., Jefferson was back in Manchester, still anxious to get in touch with Steuben. Steuben finally received a communiqué from Jefferson and expressed dismay at how minimal the state's defense had been against Arnold. "I have not heard of a Single Gun being fired at them either on their March from Westover or during their Stay at Richmond," Steuben wrote Jefferson. Steuben, who had received a report that many militiamen had no weapons, urgently requested that Jefferson send a thousand arms.[25]

But as their letters to each other arrived via messenger, Jefferson and Steuben still could not find each other. Jefferson wrote to Steuben that he felt "very unfortunate" to have missed Steuben even though he had spent "two days . . . riding over the same ground on which you were on." Now, "having rode thirty miles thro' the rain," Jefferson was too exhausted to set out on another potentially fruitless mission to try to find him. Instead, Jefferson replied to Steuben's request for a thousand arms by saying it was "impossible" to fulfill. "Are there no Continental arms which can be used on the present occasion?" Jefferson asked. Steuben had in fact been holding five hundred arms for the use of the Continental army, which he reluctantly released to the militia after Jefferson pressed him.[26]

Jefferson's callout of the militia was slowly reaching the counties, but the returns were not good. Colonel George Gibson wrote from Petersburg that only ninety men had showed up, prompting him to write. "What can occasion this total Departure from Virtue on the Part of the People?"[27] Just a day later,

Gibson painted a different picture, saying, "The Gloomy prospect of Yesterday begins to be dispell'd." The militia corps had grown from ninety to one thousand men, and "many more men may be expected." Jefferson's faith in the militia finally was being rewarded, though only after the British had left Richmond.

Having failed to find Jefferson, Arnold returned to the Byrd plantation on the morning after the Richmond assault. Simcoe objected to leaving Richmond so soon, saying his men were too weary and ill-fed. He suggested a half day's march, followed by food and rest. Arnold "was sensible to the reasonableness of the request" but rejected it; he said he was reminded of what had happened in 1777 during a clash known as the Danbury Raid. Arnold, who had been on the side of the Continental army at that time, faced a large British force. The fight was a standoff, but as Arnold told the story to Simcoe on this cold morning four years later in Richmond, a delay of just a couple of hours by the British forces in Danbury would have been devastating to them. The lesson was clear, he argued. The men immediately would be forced to march back to the safety of Byrd's plantation.

Arnold's haste was costly. Rains had turned the roads into a muddy wash. Horses moved slowly and some simply stopped. Artillery was dragged along, constantly needing to be pulled from the muck. The path became so narrow, snarled by trees, that the men were forced to march single file, making it impossible for officers to see dangers ahead. Sixty British soldiers, "too fatigued to keep up," were captured by Virginians, according to Ewald.[28]

Another group of British was south of Richmond when a group of militia gathered at a nearby riverfront plantation began firing at the enemy. This prompted a British officer named H. J. Evans to send a letter to the militia leader, warning that he would burn "every House on that side of the River if my ships or Boats are molested from your side of the Water." Evans added the usual British line that he was merely trying to protect Loyalists. A Continental army officer on shore, General William Smallwood, was infuriated. He belittled "the absurdity and Effrontery" of the British contention that he was protecting Loyalists. "Your Boats and Crews under that specious Sanction are plundering and robbing them of their Property," Smallwood wrote. A standoff ensued.[29]

Arnold had accomplished a nearly complete victory at Richmond, but the edges of his conquest were already frayed. As word spread that the invasion was being headed by the despised traitor, the militia was inspired to turn out in large numbers. The very name Arnold did more to galvanize Virginians than the state's leaders could otherwise have hoped to accomplish.

JEFFERSON AWOKE BEFORE DAWN on January 8 at his lodgings in Manchester. Across the river, smoke still rose from the ruined warehouses and other buildings destroyed by Arnold's men. The city otherwise seemed eerily calm. Jefferson received intelligence that the last of the British had long since departed, while reports came in that the militia was gathering in stronger numbers. There were three hundred men under John Nicholas at The Forest, Martha Jefferson's childhood home, six miles west of the Byrd plantation of Westover. Nelson had gathered his two hundred men at Charles City Courthouse, to the east of Westover. Across from Westover, on the south bank of the river, George Gibson commanded his suddenly formidable force of one thousand men, which joined with Steuben's eight hundred. If the forces could be coordinated and somehow find enough cannons, they might be able to take on Arnold's men in a harassing action, if not outright battle.

Richmond, meanwhile, was "in the utmost confusion," a military aide informed Jefferson. Some local residents returned shortly after Arnold departed and had been "very mischievous," plundering from vacant houses and stores, "perhaps more so than the enemy." The aide, George Muter, urged Jefferson to cross the river back to Richmond as soon as possible. "Perhaps your Excellency's presence here, will be of signal service if in your power to come."[30] After surveying the situation from Manchester, Jefferson decided that it was safe to return, ending his three days on the run and crossing the James at 7:30 a.m.

Many parts of the capital were in ruin. The streets were littered with broken "pipes" of wine and whiskey, the remains of the liquid congealing in the muddy streets, mixing with shattered glass and broken tree limbs. The detritus of Arnold's raid could be seen everywhere. Balls of grapeshot littered the ground. Fires smoldered, having been doused by the heavy rains that fortuitously saved some of the buildings from complete destruction. Stepping across the wreckage that littered nearly every street, Jefferson entered the wood-frame governor's home. The townhouse had been scarred by some British volleys but stood with little damage. Inside, all was quiet. The slaves had been taken by the British. Descending to the wine cellar, Jefferson discovered that his favorite bottles had been emptied or stolen. For several hours, Jefferson rode through Richmond, assessing the damage, until a "good gale" came in from the east, drenching the city once again.[31]

As bleak as things looked, Jefferson felt fortunate. He had narrowly escaped capture, as had his wife and children. Many armaments had been saved and few men had been captured, injured, or killed. Jefferson told Washington that Steuben deserved much of the credit for agreeing at the last moment "to direct our smallest movements." Writing to a militia leader named George Weedon, Jefferson confessed: "In truth we have escaped to a miracle."[32]

But much remained uncertain. Jefferson did not know that Arnold's ultimate mission was to establish a permanent British base at Portsmouth or that thousands more British soldiers would soon arrive. In truth, the invasion was just beginning.

The Enemy Mean to Overrun Us

ON THE MORNING that Jefferson returned to Richmond, Arnold's men awakened at Westover, where they had rested "quite spaciously" in the buildings of the Byrd plantation. For most of the British and Hessian soldiers, it had been their first full night of sleep on land in weeks. They had departed New York in mid-December, sailed stormy seas to Virginia, and then rapidly advanced to Richmond in an invasion that was now in its ninth day. Arnold's effort could have hardly have gone more smoothly. Virginians had barely put up a fight.[1]

As he gathered his officers in his quarters at Westover, however, Arnold learned that hundreds of militiamen were collecting either at the Charles City Courthouse tavern, about six miles away, or at a nearby encampment. The militia was hardly prepared to attack the larger British force; many of the men had raced from their homes, ill-prepared for battle, and were waiting for direction. They also made a crucial mistake. John Tyler Sr., a member of the Virginia legislature who lived at Greenway Plantation, located near the tavern, warned the county militia leader, Colonel John Dudley, "to place his men in a position for defense" because the British were so near at Westover. Tyler advised the militia leader "to remove his party from the tavern, for, if left there for drinking and carousing as usual, they would surely be surprised." But the "haughty" militia leader "would not heed" Tyler's warning.[2]

Arnold ordered Simcoe and Ewald to prepare for a surprise nighttime attack. Late in the day, leading a troop of mounted rangers, they left Westover and ran into a pair of Virginia soldiers guarding the road to the courthouse. Asked to identify themselves, a British soldier gave what he understood to be the password. The ruse worked and the British were allowed to pass the first guard, who was seized. A second guard raced off when his gun misfired.

It was around midnight on a frigid evening, and about 140 militiamen huddled inside the one-and-a-half-story tavern, many eating and drinking by the fireplace. Suddenly, buglers appeared inside the tavern, and British riflemen outside began firing. Amid this noise and confusion, a throng of British stormed in, firing at close range at the stunned Virginians. A "great deal of blood" splattered the walls amid the wails of the wounded. One of the Virginia soldiers raced up the stairs to evade the attackers. A British ranger aimed his musket and killed the man as he ascended the steps. "They took us by surprise, dispersed the whole corps of horse [and] killed six of our men," William Seth Stubblefield, the militia's orderly sergeant, testified later.[3] Others put the death toll differently. Jefferson claimed only one was killed; Ewald said the British had shot some thirty men, while Arnold said twenty were dead. Another dozen or so militiamen were taken captive, including a captain.

Those who did escape jumped on their horses and galloped to the nearby encampment, where the main body of militiamen, under the overall command of Thomas Nelson, was stationed. Many of the men at the camp heard about the attack and fled twenty-three miles to the east, to Williamsburg. The militia was "completely frightened and dispersed," Simcoe wrote. The lone British casualty, Sergeant James Adams of the Queen's Rangers, was shot during the raid and heard to say, "I do not mind dying, but for God's sake do not leave me in the hands of the rebels." He was taken back to Westover, where he died the following day. The funeral took place on the grounds of the plantation, with the British corps in attendance. A flag that had flown at Hood's Point was placed with Adams as the casket was lowered. As the funeral at Westover came to a close, four British vessels, which had gotten lost during the voyage to Virginia, sailed up the James River. The invasion force now was stronger by four hundred men and a wealth of additional supplies.[4]

Meanwhile, Nelson, who had so effectively prevented Arnold from attacking days earlier at Burwell's Ferry, apologized to Governor Jefferson for not stopping Arnold's corps. He was, he wrote Jefferson, "pained to the very Soul that we have not been able to prevent the Return of the Enemy." Nelson had hoped to stop the British on their way from Richmond to Westover but was slowed by a storm. "I intended a Blow at their Rear, when the Gates of Heaven were opened, and such a Flood of Rain poured down as rendered my Plan abortive by almost drowning the Troops, who were in Bush Tents, and by injuring their Arms and Ammunition so much that they were quite unfit for Service."[5]

While the militia on the north side of the James River never came close to attacking Arnold, another group of militia gathered on the opposite side. For the first time during the invasion, Baron Steuben was going on the offensive, bringing a force to the southern shore in hopes of recapturing and strengthening the battery at Hood's Point. Having failed to use Hood's Point to stop the invaders from sailing up the James River, Steuben now hoped to mount cannons at the promontory to fire on Arnold as he departed.

Arnold, however, learned of the plan, having received intelligence that the militia were gathered at nearby Bland's Mills and "he intended to surprise them." Despite a raging gale and thunderstorm, he ordered Ewald on a lead boat with fifty Jägers, as well as six hundred men on several following vessels. The British crossed the James, landing just to the east of Hood's Point. At 10:00 p.m., the storm subsided, revealing a clear, moonlit sky. Following their strategy of ruses, the British noisily acted as if they were aiming cannons at the Virginians, who were heard to scurry away. Ewald went ashore first, taking six men. Two men preceded fifty paces in front, while Ewald and the others followed. They walked on a wide, sandy road, sodden from the fresh rainfall. Ewald had traveled only a short distance when he heard hooves splashing down the road. This was to be expected. The British presumed the Virginians would flee, as they had done previously at Hood's Point. But as Ewald kneeled and put his ear to the ground, he detected that the horses were getting nearer. Steuben knew how to play the ruse as well. He wanted to turn the Jägers—the hunters—into the hunted.

Ewald was wary. He knew the opposing force was overseen by Steuben, a fellow Prussian who was one of the few who had gone to the American side. Still, he hoped to turn the situation to his advantage. Believing that only a few Virginians were approaching, he ordered his men to hide behind some trees. Suddenly, a cavalry of twenty or thirty horses appeared. Ewald hoped they would pass without realizing the British were hiding among the trees, but a Virginian saw Ewald in the moonlight. "Who's there?" he called.

Silence.

"Who's there?" the Virginian demanded.

"Friend of the watch!" Ewald cried out, briefly confusing the cavalry. Then he yelled: "Attack and fire!" The Jägers fired at once from behind the trees. Not knowing how many men were facing them, the Virginians fled. Ewald returned to the fleet and reported the incident to Arnold. One of the best officers in the British service had nearly lost his life acting on Arnold's order to go ashore with only six men. Arnold looked at it differently. He brusquely informed Ewald that he was sorry no prisoners were taken.[6]

Arnold ordered a new assault, but this time he did not choose Ewald as the leader. Instead, he insisted that it be led by a less qualified officer, twenty-seven-year-old Beverley Robinson Jr. Robinson's lack of qualification for a dangerous night mission was so obvious that Simcoe came to Ewald and "begged me not to take offense that Major Robinson and his provincials, rather than myself, would have the advance guard." Ewald wrote that he was well aware that Robinson's father "was a friend of General Arnold." He surmised that the younger Robinson was given the lead of the reconstituted landing party because Arnold "probably wanted to give him an opportunity to get his name in the *Gazette*."[7]

This landing party was much larger than Ewald's. Robinson led a corps of Loyalists, followed by Ewald with fifty Jägers and then several hundred other soldiers. After a half-hour march, the British were startled by a fusillade of twenty musket shots, which sailed over their heads. The British returned fire and kept marching. Then, after another half hour, two Virginians shouted in unison: "Who is there?" Robinson ordered his men forward. Suddenly, a single volley from one hundred Virginians came from the woods, killing many of the Loyalists, while others lay wounded. Forty were killed or seriously wounded. Arnold, who had been in the rear, came to the front to examine the disaster. Ewald was livid, believing that Arnold had violated a cardinal rule by not having an experienced officer lead an advance guard at night. "So it goes when a person wants to do something that he doesn't understand!" Ewald yelled at Arnold. The general did not argue. Instead, he responded "courteously" that Ewald should take command of the advanced guard.[8] Having marched without wagons, the British dragged their dead back to the ships.

Steuben's Virginians had won their first victory, but it only briefly delayed the British. Arnold's men sailed east, past the still-undefended bluffs at Hood's Point, on their way to fulfilling Sir Henry Clinton's order to establish a base at Portsmouth.

JEFFERSON, MEANWHILE, was coming under assault of a different kind. An array of onetime allies and other observers sent letters across Virginia and up and down the coast of the United States, questioning his conduct during the invasion. If the British could capture Virginia, ensnaring thousands of troops and cutting off supply lines to the South, what would happen to the revolution? Even Jefferson's close friend John Page was appalled at the state's lack of readiness. Page was a colonel of the militia in Gloucester, on the north side of the York River. "Arnold the traitor . . . has disgraced our country, my dear friend, so much that I am ashamed & ever shall be so to call myself a Virginian," Page wrote to another militia leader, Colonel Theodorick Bland Jr. "He landed at Westover; but let someone else tell that shameful tale!" It was Page who had written Jefferson five years earlier urging the destruction of Norfolk. Now he lamented that Virginia had established no force at the entry to the James River to prevent such an invasion. It was Page who, in 1779, lost the election for governor to Jefferson but insisted he harbored no ill feelings to his friend. Yet now, deeply critical of the lack of military preparedness during Jefferson's governorship, Page wrote that Virginia was "to our eternal disgrace so unarmed and

undisciplined" after five years of war. While Page said some militia had turned
out, including the Gloucester militia's effort to reinforce the men under Thomas
Nelson, those "gallant few" were not enough to stop Arnold.[9]

Edmund Pendleton, the former president of Virginia's Committee of Safety,
wrote a scathing criticism of Jefferson's action to Washington, telling of "our
disgrace in having Our Metropolis, at 100 miles distance from the Sea Coast,
Surprized and taken without resistance by a handful of Banditti." Pendleton
wrote that Jefferson delayed calling out militia until "it was too late." While
Pendleton was sure Jefferson's "intentions are the very best," he believed the
governor had been "incredulous and not sufficiently attentive." Pendleton told
Washington that "it is only to you Sir, that I speak thus freely" and urged that
the general make "good use" of the information.[10]

Equally harsh criticism came from the pen of Reverend James Madison,
who wrote to his cousin, Virginia congressional delegate James Madison, that
anger at the action of the state government threatened to overwhelm the revolutionary impulse. "Iniquitous Laws produce Disgust, Languor and Indifference," the reverend wrote. "Thus many care not whether Arnold or Steuben are
victorious."[11]

Steuben, having been in the state for barely two months, also portrayed Virginia as being in disarray, writing to Washington that weapons and men were
scattered, while the troops did not have tents or even kettles. "It is impossible
to describe the situation I am in—in want of everything; and nothing can be
got from the state," he told Washington.[12]

Steuben, meanwhile, received a letter from the southern Continental army
commander, General Nathanael Greene, who urged him to stay in Virginia. "I
fear when you leave it nothing will be done," Greene told Steuben. "The state
is lifeless and inactive unless they are often electriced."[13]

"Electriced," or electrified, indeed. It took days for Virginians to realize that
Arnold did not plan to leave the state as quickly as Collier and Leslie. As word
spread that Lord Cornwallis might soon arrive with a vast army, Steuben again
demanded that work begin on the fortifications at Hood's Point. Exasperated,
Steuben dispensed with formalities: "This I insist on in the Name of the United
States."[14]

Jefferson initially agreed, responding, "This shall be done." But it was not
done, and three weeks later Steuben lost his patience. He told Jefferson that he
felt responsible for the "shameful" lack of opposition, as it was he who had been
given the responsibility of military commander. Yet he was powerless to order
the work at Hood's Point. "My wish is to prevent a Repetition of the Disgrace,
but . . . I can do nothing without the assistance of the Governor," Steuben

wrote to Jefferson.[15] Jefferson explained to the former Prussian officer that under the laws of Virginia, a governor "had no power to call out the militia to do fatigue duty." There was no money to pay common laborers. The problem, Jefferson told Steuben, was that he could not call upon "a freeman to labor without his consent, nor have a slave without that of his master."[16]

Steuben reacted with disbelief. It made no sense to him that the militiamen could be ordered to risk their lives by fighting behind a woeful defense system but could not be ordered to build a strong defense. Nor did it make sense that Jefferson would not order slaves to do the work. There were tens of thousands of them across Virginia tending to tobacco fields and doing other labor. Jefferson himself owned some two hundred slaves at his three plantations. Yet Jefferson and the other slave-owning leaders of Virginia could not find the necessary few dozen men to work a couple of weeks to fortify Hood's Point and prevent Arnold from penetrating deeper into the interior of Virginia? Steuben angrily picked up his quill and wrote to Washington. "The Executive Power is so confined that the Governor has not in his power to procure me 40 Negros to work at Hood's," Steuben wrote. "In fact, My Dear General, I fear that without some speedy assistance, our affairs in this Quarter will go very badly."[17]

For the remainder of Jefferson's term, this would be the constant theme of the former Prussian officer. Jefferson and other Virginia leaders feared a standing army and a tyrannical governor, and they had limited a governor's powers.

In fairness, Jefferson's hands were also restrained, if not shackled, by the legislative restrictions and the will of the people he governed. He had weathered draft riots, tax protests, and other citizen unrest in response to efforts to recruit soldiers and raise militia. Steuben was not elected by anyone or directly accountable to militiamen who resented being repeatedly called to duty. Still, over the years, Jefferson himself would eventually concede much of Steuben's point and conclude that more forceful power by an executive was necessary during an invasion. He eventually came up with a plan that would enable militiamen to skip some of their service if they volunteered to help build the fort at Hood's Point. The idea was sound, but the effort would come too late.

Like any governor facing an outsized crisis, Jefferson turned to the federal government for help. He ordered Benjamin Harrison to complete the mission that was supposed to have begun two weeks earlier: to go to Philadelphia and plead for reinforcements. The revolution was at stake.

Harrison left for Philadelphia at the very moment that many of Arnold's troops were encamped on the lawn of his beloved Berkeley estate. He arrived in Philadelphia on January 11 and must have wondered whether he would ever be able to return home. He knew that Jefferson and the Virginia delegates were in flight from Arnold, and that the defense of his state now depended on his mission. But as Harrison met with the Board of War, the response left him even more distressed. There was "not a shilling in the Continental Treasury," Harrison wrote to Jefferson. Congress "cannot command men" and was unable "to furnish them for the field."

Harrison put it even more bluntly to Washington: "The enemy mean to over-run us."[18]

AFTER A WEEK OF RAIDING TOWNS and plantations along the James River, Arnold and his fleet entered the Chesapeake crossroad known as Hampton Roads and sailed just short of the Atlantic, turning south to the Elizabeth River and passing by the desolate remains of Norfolk. Ewald marveled that even five years after the city was destroyed, "the blackened, burned ruins presented a dismal prospect to the eye."[1] On the opposite side of the river lay Portsmouth, still largely intact, the breastworks of the abandoned Fort Nelson still visible. The broad avenues of Portsmouth were mostly quiet, with many residents having fled the periodic raids, but the city still had about 150 buildings, mostly wooden homes surrounding the sturdy Trinity Episcopal Church, which would be turned into a British garrison.

This was the same region where Lord Dunmore had headed in search of Loyalists, only to flee when the haven of Norfolk was destroyed. Collier and Leslie had also come, establishing a base at Portsmouth but then leaving in haste. Finally, after five years of staking claims to this vital area and then leaving, the British intended to stay. It was Arnold's job to build a fort and assure Loyalists in the area that this time they would not be abandoned. Anchoring their ships in the Elizabeth, the soldiers and sailors landed in their smaller transports and once again planted the British flag in the city named for a great English port. The men set about building six redoubts, connected by rows of broken branches that were intended to slow an enemy's advance.

To control Portsmouth was to control the Atlantic entrance of Virginia and the mouth of the James River. But it was an isolated spot, no longer the citadel of commerce, as a result of the destruction of Norfolk and near-abandonment of Portsmouth. Still, thousands of Virginians lived in the hinter regions along the James and the Elizabeth, fishing and farming as they tried to navigate amid the clashes of British and Virginians. While the region was no longer filled with Loyalists, it had plenty of inhabitants who were watching the war's progress carefully in an effort to stay with the winning side.

Arnold, however, was convinced that thousands of Loyalists were just waiting for his force to arrive to declare their allegiance to the king. He wrote to his superiors in New York that on the day of his arrival, "the whole army to the great joy of the inhabitants marched into Portsmouth in good health and high spirits." Then, as the fort was being built, Arnold met with four hundred people near Portsmouth. He assured them that "the King was firmly resolved to protect them" and that he himself would "sacrifice his blood and life for them."[2] Those assembled took the oath of loyalty to the king, much to Arnold's satisfaction. He had written an open letter to Americans urging them to follow his example and vow their loyalty, and here was proof of his influence.

But Ewald, traveling with Arnold, saw a different image, created by the power of such a massive armed force. As the Virginians promised loyalty, some made "wry faces, as though they would choke on it," Ewald noted in his diary. He was unconvinced by the "good show" that the local residents actually intended to support Arnold's forces.[3] Later, Ewald put it even more bluntly, saying that "the inhabitants of the city as well as the people of the whole area were rebels, and those few who could be called royalist were so frightened off by the enemy that they did not dare to give the least bit of information."[4]

Indeed, any openly Loyalist resident of Virginia risked the loss of his property, expulsion, or prison. Given the difficulty of escaping to British-held areas such as New York, many who sympathized with the British still felt it most prudent to sign oaths to Virginia. The most ardent Loyalists had fled or joined the British army. Still, a handful did provide assistance, including James Tait of Cabin Point, who served as a guide and scout for Arnold, and William Peter Matthews of Hampton, who provided maps and supplies. When the war seemed to be going heavily in favor of the British, a small surge in Loyalist activity occurred, only to die out as the Patriots gained ground.[5]

The lack of Loyalists in Virginia mystified Ewald, who had traveled from Prussia to help the British and had been assured he was fighting for people who, like him, believed in the role of a sovereign leader. One morning, Ewald left Portsmouth and breakfasted with one of the wealthiest men of coastal Virginia, Thomas Reynolds Walker, a county lieutenant and owner of an estate valued at £50,000. Ewald made clear his exasperation, fuming that wealthy Virginians who declared loyalty to the crown were doing little to help the British forces, while many of the poorer residents were risking everything for independence. "Why don't you raise a battalion for the defense of this area?" he asked Walker. "You as the first citizen of the county, can accomplish whatever you want by setting an example for your neighbors. Everyone will follow you. Uniforms and weapons will be furnished readily for the war, and these people would be very well paid."

Walker, however, remembered the way Collier and Leslie had invaded the state, only to leave quickly, exposing Loyalists to attack. "I must first see if it is true that your people really intend to remain with us," Walker told Ewald. "You have already been in this area twice. General Leslie gave me the same assurances in the past autumn, and where is he now? In Carolina! Who knows where you will be this autumn?"

Ewald's anger only grew. "How can you be called friends of the king if you won't venture anything for the right cause?" He marveled that the rebellious Virginians were willing to "abandon wife, child, house and home, and let us lay waste to everything. They fight without shoes and clothing [yet do so] with all passion, suffer hunger, and gladly all the hardships of war. But you loyalists won't do anything! You only want to be protected, to live in peace in your houses."[6]

Later, however, Ewald reflected on Walker's motivation and decided he could not blame him. Walker had no desire to be a soldier and indeed "would have been a fool if he had acted as I had advised him." He had one of Virginia's great fortunes, as well as a wife who was "one of the most charming blondes that I have ever seen in all my life!" Had Walker openly fought for the Loyalists, he would be risking everything, just as William Byrd had done, and could hardly be sure of the outcome. Such was the state of war in Virginia that the British could rely more on Hessian soldiers than on those local residents who professed loyalty to King George III.

With so few Loyalists coming to Arnold's aid, many Virginians believed he was building a trap for himself by putting nearly every British soldier and sailor in the cramped environs of Portsmouth. Yes, he had a force of 1,600 men, but he was surrounded by a half million Virginians, from which 50,000 militia were supposed to be available. It would take only a small French fleet to bottle Arnold up in the Elizabeth River while militia forces swarmed the redoubts. For much of Arnold's stay in Portsmouth, hundreds of militiamen skirted the edges of his compound, constantly harassing his forces.

Indeed, months before the British dug in at Yorktown, Virginia's military leaders hoped Portsmouth would be the place where they surrounded and defeated the British. Arnold, aware of the danger of a siege, sent an expeditionary force to Great Bridge, the crucial causeway where Lord Dunmore's army had been defeated by militia forces five years earlier. As the British neared Great Bridge, they met a Loyalist—which Ewald regarded as something of a miracle —and learned that a large militia force was heading toward them.

With hopes of capturing Arnold in a bold strike, Steuben had ordered the available militia to head toward Great Bridge. The British arrived there first, finding its twenty-five houses abandoned by people who "left us their good Madeira" and provisions. With the help of three hundred slaves who had fled their masters for the freedom promised by the British, a star-shaped fort was quickly built, capable of holding one hundred men and two cannons. The

Virginia militia, however, had one thousand men massed at a nearby plantation. Arnold learned about the assemblage and sent his men through "pathless woods" in hopes of making a surprise attack. The British, seeing campfires aglow at the plantation, were preparing to storm the grounds when they realized they had been tricked. No militia remained at the plantation; the Americans had diverted the British to an empty field while they headed elsewhere.[7]

Steuben's strategy of trapping Arnold was unlikely to succeed unless the French provided naval support. At the urging of Virginia emissaries, the French sent the sixty-four-gun ship *Eveillé* and two smaller transports from Rhode Island. The ships were expected to arrive off the Virginia coast in mid-February. While the fleet was smaller than desired, it still might bombard Arnold's forces from the Elizabeth River, softening up the British entrenchments and enabling the militia to storm the redoubts. But a British spy learned of the plan, and Arnold's superiors in New York sent a ship southward to warn him that the French were headed to Virginia.

The British mission to warn Arnold was headed by Captain Josias Rogers, who sailed so swiftly that he beat the French by several days. Rogers was paying a return visit to the Old Dominion, one that he must have relished. Five years earlier, as the revolution was gaining hold in Virginia, he commanded a ship sent to the colony as part of an effort to quell the rebellion. Instead, his own men rebelled against him in a mutiny. He was eventually left alone aboard his moribund ship, made his way to the mainland, and was imprisoned in Williamsburg "in a vile jail among prisoners of all denominations." In the hot, stinking "vault" that was "covered with vermin," Rogers had many hours in which to ponder his revenge against the Virginians should he ever escape. After two months in confinement, Rogers and other prisoners were marched under guard toward Richmond, and then farther into the dense, wooded interior of Virginia. Finally they arrived in the little village of Charlottesville, in which Rogers counted some fifteen houses, "situated under the blue mountains, and surrounded by rocks and precipices." Rogers expected an even rougher treatment in this wild setting but instead was "treated with the greatest humanity . . . entirely left to themselves" and boarded at a public lodging house. Each prisoner was given 1 0 pence per day. For eight months, the men lived what they described as a respite from the war and the unruliness of Williamsburg, regularly heading into the mountains to gather wild fruits and greens, which they ate on the banks of a shaded riverbank. Rogers was freed as part of a prisoner exchange and returned to duty as a British commander. Now Rogers was again headed to Virginia, at the helm of the eighteen-gun *General Monk,* with a warning to Arnold that the French were on their way.[8]

The British officer Bartholomew James wrote in his journal that the *Monk* "arrived from New York with an account of the French ship of the line and two frigates [headed] to the Chesapeake Bay."[9] With the warning in hand, Arnold sent some ships off the coast, hoping to trap the French, but failed to find them. Then he ordered some of his ships up the Elizabeth River, believing they would be safe from the largest French vessel.

When the French arrived in mid-February, however, they seemed more interested in capturing prizes than trapping Arnold. They stumbled upon and captured one of Britain's mightiest ships in Virginia, the forty-four-gun *Romulus*. The commander of the small French force, Commodore Le Gardeur de Tilly, had few men with him and, unsurprisingly, he was not anxious to remain stationary in a tributary and subject to constant bombardment from the British. The Frenchman was further distressed when he learned that the Virginia militia was poorly armed and possessed only a few cannons. He would not take the largest vessel up the Elizabeth, just as Arnold had figured. Instead, Tilly sailed away from Virginia, taking with him the *Romulus*.

General Peter Muhlenberg, the Virginia militia leader on the scene, was livid. He believed Arnold could have been trapped by the combination of the militia forces and the French vessels. Muhlenberg was mortified "at seeing the glorious prize, on which he had counted with so much certainty . . . snatched from his very grasp."[10] The most lasting impact of Tilly's mission, however, was that it so alarmed the British commanders in New York that they decided to send thousands of reinforcements southward to join Arnold.

Honor Is Like an Island

THE BRITISH COMMAND IN NEW YORK was astonished by the breadth of Arnold's success in Virginia. They had expected Arnold's invasion to be a diversionary tactic. Instead, he seemed able to control any part of the state he entered. British officers reported that Arnold was "bold, daring," and "enterprising & determined upon every occasion."[1] The invasion interrupted the flow of supplies to more southern states, and all but halted the effort to draft men for the Continental army who were needed in the Carolinas.[2] Frederick Mackenzie, the deputy adjutant general under Clinton, marveled in his diary that Arnold had managed to reach Richmond and destroy valuable rebel supplies, succeeding where prior British efforts had failed. Mackenzie wrote that he was "almost sorry" to admit "that such a man as Arnold should have executed with an inferior force, what a British General did not even attempt with a superior one."

Still, in his diary Mackenzie expressed surprise that Arnold did not completely destroy the American supplies. "Arnold's reasons for not destroying the great quantities of Tobacco, and Merchandize at Richmond and on board vessels in James River, do not appear to me, to be good and sufficient."[3] The reason would soon become apparent: Arnold preserved the tobacco and other goods because he wanted to keep some of the spoils for himself.

Behind the scenes, Arnold was locked in a furious struggle with British naval officers in Virginia. He had fallen out with Thomas Symonds, the commodore of the British navy in Virginia. According to Arnold's secret deal with Symonds, the army and navy were to split the prizes from their invasion—the captured ships, tobacco, rum, and other spoils—equally. But the agreement ruptured. On January 24, Arnold ordered one of his officers, Bartholomew James, to return to New York with some of the prizes, along with dispatches to the British commander in chief about how well the invasion was going. James dutifully collected Arnold's letters, put them in a trunk for safekeeping, and went to collect similar dispatches from Symonds.

Symonds flew into a rage. He countermanded the order from Arnold, insisting James remain in Virginia. James was stunned, writing later that "some unaccountable difference and disagreement [had] taken place between the two commanding officers." Symonds "directed me to return immediately to Portsmouth" and he returned the dispatches to Arnold.[4]

Unbeknownst to James, the dispute was about money. Arnold and Symonds were angrily writing each other at the time about whether Arnold deserved any of the prizes of war. "I am not a little Surprised to be informed that some Gentlemen of the Navy should say 'that the Army are not entitled to any Prize money,'" an indignant Arnold wrote to Symonds on February 4. He warned Symonds that he was going to proceed as if the agreement to split the prizes was in effect, writing that he was planning to take "the Army's half of prize goods," including a hundred hogsheads of tobacco that had recently been confiscated. Arnold warned that "the World will Judge" how Symonds was seeking to "evade the Agreement made between us" and vowed to put the matter before their commanders in New York.[5]

This dispute, mostly overlooked in historical accounts of the invasion of Virginia, demonstrates how the British force was being torn apart from the inside. Arnold was increasingly distrusted and despised by his fellow officers, who began to share the view that Americans had formed of Arnold—that he was more interested in prizes and money than in fighting for his country.

Eight British deserters from Symonds's ship, the *Charon,* walked into Williamsburg on March 2 and provided an account of the dissension, which in turn was forwarded to Jefferson. The deserters said "that a Quarrell had happen'd between Arnold and Commodore Symonds relative to the Division of Tobacco and other articles taken by the navy while the army was embarked." The deserters also revealed that "Arnold was not on speaking terms with the officers of the Navy, and much detested and suspected by the officers of the army."[6]

Arnold escalated the dispute a few days later, suggesting that Symonds was either cowardly or disloyal. He had urged Symonds to send some ships up Chesapeake Bay after an intelligence report indicated that an American force was sailing south on those waters. But Symonds refused, according to Arnold, by "alleging that he has orders to keep the ships in shoal water, which I believe he is heartily inclined to do, whenever he thinks there is danger."[7] Eventually, even Frederick Mackenzie, who earlier had written so rapturously about Arnold's talents, came to a dark conclusion about Arnold's motivation, writing: "The love of money, his ruling passion, has been very conspicuous in Virginia."[8]

EACH MORNING ARNOLD AWOKE IN VIRGINIA, he slipped two small pistols into his pockets. He was surrounded by some of the greatest armaments of the British navy and protected by handpicked soldiers and sailors, yet he feared the possibility of capture at every turn. Congress had condemned him to death. Anyone lucky enough to seize Arnold would be ensured a handsome reward and heroic standing. Arnold was arrogant to a fault, endlessly bragging of his exploits and proud of having duped the Americans at West Point. But he had one fear, or so he said: being captured alive. When the risk of capture arose, he would become "very restless." Were he to fall into American hands, he wanted the means to control his destiny. Ewald wrote that Arnold would use the pistols as "a last recourse to escape being hanged." Arnold remembered that one of the final requests of his co-conspirator, John André, was to be executed by a firing squad instead of the traditional hanging for treason. Washington had refused the request.

Ewald readily acknowledged that had Arnold's plan to control West Point succeeded, "it would have put an end to the war, preserved the thirteen great and beautiful provinces for the Crown of England." But he, like most in the British service, was aghast that Arnold's plot not only had failed but had led to the death of a beloved British officer.[9] Seven years earlier, in 1774, André had visited Ewald in Kassel, helping to convince Ewald to serve with the British forces. "He was my friend, and had shown much friendship for me and the Jäger Corps," Ewald wrote. When André was hanged for colluding with Arnold, he was mourned by American and British officers alike. "All the American officers had attended the funeral procession," Ewald wrote. "The enemy pitied him and his friends deplored and lamented his fate." The British officers wore black crepe bands around their arms for eight days.[10]

Arnold, by comparison, was despised by officers on both sides. Americans wanted him hanged, while the British, even while making him a brigadier general in command, did not entirely trust him. He had, after all, proven that he would switch sides. Many believed he could be bought.

Ewald, himself a well-paid Hessian auxiliary officer, wrote that he would have gladly paid with his life "for England's success in this war." But Ewald viewed Arnold as serving the British for "self-gain alone."[11] Just as bad, Ewald believed, Arnold was not respected by either officers or the men beneath him. Ewald had a host of reasons for disliking Arnold: the manner of Arnold's defection, the resulting death of André, the condescension to others, and his questionable military strategy. Ewald kept a poem with him through the war that provided a window on his feelings:

> *Honor is like an island*
> *Steep and without shore:*
> *They who once leave,*
> *Can never return.*[12]

Arnold had left the island of honor when he rowed to the British ship *Vulture* in the Hudson River, and no victory could be great enough to redeem him in the eyes of Ewald or many other officers in the British service. "This man remained so detestable to me that I had to use every effort not to let him perceive, or even feel, the indignation of my soul," Ewald wrote.[13]

At one point during the invasion, Arnold struck up a conversation with a captured American captain. "What should be my fate, if *I* should be taken prisoner?" Arnold asked. Looking at the leg that was wounded during Arnold's heroic service as an American general, the prisoner responded, "They will cut off that shortened leg of yours wounded at Quebec and Saratoga, and bury it with all the honors of war, and then hang the rest of you on a gibbet."[14]

For his part, Jefferson referred to Arnold as a "parricide." Literally, a parricide was one who murdered a parent; this was what Arnold had tried to do to the country that had nurtured him. Once it became clear that Arnold had no intention of leaving Virginia as quickly as the prior invaders, Leslie and Collier, Jefferson became desperate to remove him. If he could capture Arnold, Jefferson believed, the British invasion would fail. So Jefferson came up with a plan to pay 5,000 guineas for the capture of Arnold. He outlined the idea in a January 31, 1781, letter to General Peter Muhlenberg, the second-ranking military official in Virginia after Steuben, urging the proposal be a matter of "profound secrecy."[15]

Muhlenberg was one of Virginia's most experienced military leaders, having commanded the state's Continental forces at Valley Forge in Pennsylvania as well as leading those forces in Virginia. As a resident of Woodstock, located on the western flank of the Blue Ridge, Muhlenberg shared Jefferson's affinity for westward expansion. Moreover, he was the very embodiment of a fighter for religious freedom. The son of a German immigrant to Pennsylvania, Muhlenberg had served as the cleric of a Lutheran church in Woodstock. According to tradition, Muhlenberg told his congregation in 1776, paraphrasing a verse from Ecclesiastes, that there is a time to preach and a time to fight for one's country. He then supposedly took off his robe to reveal his army uniform.

While the story may have been embellished over the years for dramatic effect, there was no question that Muhlenberg switched from being a preacher to an army officer. He raised what became known as the "German Regiment," and he became one of Washington's favorite generals. Jefferson valued Muhlenberg's close ties to the mountain soldiers from the area around Woodstock who fought so effectively due to years of practice with their hunting rifles. Muhlenberg was celebrating Christmas at his isolated home beyond the mountains when Arnold invaded, and it took several days for him to hear news. When he finally realized what was happening, he headed to Fredericksburg, about fifty-eight miles north of Richmond, to collect a militia force.[16]

Now Jefferson was asking Muhlenberg to play a potentially decisive role in ending the invasion. Jefferson made clear his doubts about the reliability of local militia, urging Muhlenberg to hire frontiersmen for the mission because he had "peculiar confidence in the men from the Western side of the Mountains." Jefferson gave Muhlenberg the authority to hire as many men as necessary, "reveal to them our desire, and engage them [to] undertake to seize and bring off this greatest of all traitors."

If the men were caught, Jefferson warned, the British would be justified to give them "the most rigorous sentence." But were they successful "in bringing him off alive," they would receive 5,000 guineas between them and, more importantly, "their names will be recorded with glory in history."[17] Muhlenberg and his men never even got close, however. Arnold had become paranoid about plots to kill him, and kept a "trusty guard surrounding him day and night."[18]

With the kidnapping plan foiled, Jefferson turned to an even more desperate measure, proposed by a Virginia navy captain named Beesly Edgar Joel. Joel suggested turning an old navy vessel into a "fire ship" filled with explosives. It would be crashed into Arnold's vessel, either killing Arnold or forcing him to abandon his craft and be captured by waiting Virginians. It was a common strategy at the time, sometimes resulting in the spectacular destruction of an enemy vessel. Jefferson enthusiastically embraced the plan. He wrote to Thomas Nelson Jr., the militia commander, saying that Joel required a "worthless" vessel, adding, "I think the object will justify the risk." Jefferson then laid off the details to Nelson, ordering him to "have everything provided which he may think necessary to ensure Success."[19]

Jefferson apparently did not realize that Joel had a questionable background. A year earlier, Joel had deserted from the British army, winding up in the care of Washington's forces. In an effort to prove his worth, he told them that an American general was in the employ of the British. This information was conveyed shortly before it was discovered that Arnold had committed treason. However, Joel told the Board of War that he was referring to another general, Robert Howe. Washington was convinced that Joel was a spy and not to be trusted. He wrote the Board of War that he suspected Joel of "the worst intentions" and that he was an example of the British "practicing the arts of corruption."[20] Washington agreed to let Joel go free on condition that he was "not to come near the Army."[21] Joel then headed south, where he apparently had no problem volunteering to serve in the woefully undermanned Virginia navy.

Upon receiving Jefferson's order, Nelson gave Joel permission to proceed with the fire ship plan. The plot promptly spun out of control. Joel went to the Virginia shipyard on the Chickahominy River, near Williamsburg, with an order to be supplied with an unneeded ship. The only available vessel was the *Dragon,* which had lain under water for months and was, according to Joel, "totally unfit for service." But it seemed perfect for the singular service that Joel intended—sailing it into Arnold's ship and setting it afire. After five days of work, Joel and his crew managed to raise her and put her in condition to sail into the James River. He also hired an incompetent pilot who managed to get the *Dragon* stuck on a bar in the river for three days.

When Joel and his crew managed to get the *Dragon* back to the shipyard, Nelson ordered that Joel end the enterprise. Joel was aghast. He wrote to Jefferson that Nelson was stopping the plot just as Joel believed he was "ensured of success . . . to be thus stop't is surely strange! And must cast a shade on me." He told Jefferson that he anxiously awaited his order to continue the plot. "Allow me to observe that if successful she will be of more service than the whole fleet have hither to been," noting correctly that much of Virginia's navy "now lays [out of service], and I fear will remain so totally unprepared, and useless."[22]

Nelson, meanwhile, told Jefferson the Virginia navy was so badly in need of ships that even a derelict vessel was a prize worth keeping. While the *Dragon* was admittedly in poor shape, Nelson had thought that Joel would take "some old Hulk that would not have been any loss to the State should the enterprise fail." Moreover, Nelson wrote to Jefferson, "Between friends, there is almost a certainty [the plot would fail], it being known to all the lower County and probably to the British before this day."[23] At the same time, Joel was being derided by others in the Virginia navy who considered him an "impudent" defector who couldn't be trusted.

Jefferson, who had hoped the entire matter would be handled discreetly, gave in, writing Joel that the element of surprise had been lost but that he was grateful to Joel for proposing such a brave enterprise. "The risk to which you had meant to expose yourself has furnished full sentiments of gratitude in every breast which it merits."[24] To the dismay of his detractors, Joel was subsequently given command of a ship, the *Louis,* sailing on missions to stop the flight of slaves to the British, a task that he performed so successfully that he was promptly promoted to major.

Jefferson, meanwhile, was worried not just about the traitor leading the British forces but also treasonous activity by Virginians. Having received a

February 15 report that Lord Cornwallis planned to head to Virginia to link with Arnold, he worried that the militia in southern and western Virginia counties through which Cornwallis would travel were failing to turn out men. Militia leader James Innes had only a poorly equipped force with which to protect Williamsburg. The militia was "totally destitute" and had no winter coats." They were "lousy dirty and ragged [and] every day more sickly." Many men were so dispirited that Innes said he was worried about mutiny, pleading with Jefferson to send supplies and support.[25]

The report from Virginia's portion of the Delmarva Peninsula was, if anything, more dire. The peninsula was vital to Virginia's defense, bounded on the east by the Atlantic Ocean, on the west by the Chesapeake Bay and sharing a border with Maryland. From every direction, it was vulnerable to British attack. One of the Virginia counties on the peninsula was Accomack, where county lieutenant George Corbin wrote Jefferson that it was impossible to enforce his request for the gathering of arms from the citizenry for the state's defense. Had this request been made six months earlier, Corbin boldly admonished the governor, an armed militia would have gathered and Arnold's invasion might have been halted. But now there was so much disaffection in the county, due to complaints about the Continental army draft, that Corbin had "neither Power or Inclination" to collect arms. "Pray consider our Situation, surrounded on every side by enemies, the British on our Sea and Bay coasts, and the most disaffected part of Maryland compleats our bounds," Corbin said, stressing that nothing would make the citizenry more angry than taking their guns from them. Jefferson had no choice other than to rescind the order.[26]

Searching for a way out of the crisis, Jefferson urged militia leaders in other parts of the state to come to his aid. He wrote to commanders in the southern and western regions to contemplate the dire impact of Cornwallis and Arnold marching without opposition to face a diluted corps in the Tidewater country. "We are all embarked in one bottom," Jefferson wrote in a pleading tone, "the Western end of which cannot swim while the Eastern sinks."[27]

Writing to another militia leader, Jefferson urged a quick turnout of men to make "a sudden and effectual opposition" to Cornwallis.[28] Then, revealing the vastness of the poor militia turnout, Jefferson wrote Brigadier General George Rogers Clark, who was on the western frontier, that it was "mortifying" that militias were coming up short and even threatening open disobedience if the call-up was repeated. Jefferson was aghast that there would be such anti-government fervor at the very moment Cornwallis might be heading north.[29] The destitute state of the militia had "produced murmurings almost amounting to mutinies," a disconsolate Jefferson wrote to Steuben. "There is no hope of being able longer to keep them in service."[30]

THE MORE SUCCESSFUL ARNOLD BECAME, the more some Virginians focused their ire at Mary Willing Byrd, in part because she was a cousin of Arnold's wife, in part because many believed that she was, like her much-despised late husband, a Loyalist. As a result, even during this crucial time of invasion, Jefferson and other Virginia leaders spent many hours handling the growing concerns about Byrd's relationship with the British.

Byrd was obsessed with getting back the forty-nine slaves who had taken their liberty when Arnold landed at Westover. She hoped that a relative among the British troops who had camped at Westover could help her. The relative was Lieutenant Charles Hare, a twenty-five-year-old officer of the HMS *Swift*. He was the brother of Robert Hare, who was married to Mary's sister, Margaret. Thus began a tangled affair that only increased suspicions that Byrd had a deeper relationship with Arnold and the British than she was willing to admit.

Byrd requested that Hare be allowed to travel to Westover on what was called a "flag" ship, an enemy vessel allowed passage under a flag of truce. The practice of allowing such enemy ships to roam the rivers of Virginia was being abused, with suspicions that the truce was regularly broken by spy missions. The Governor's Council had issued a February 3 order specifically urging caution in the use of flag ships. But Byrd had convinced Steuben she was merely a widow who wanted a flag ship to bring back her slaves.

On February 10, Hare sailed from Portsmouth toward Westover, flying the flag of truce. He did not bring any slaves with him, but he did have the horse of one of Byrd's daughters as well as some goods such as cloth. As Hare neared Westover, however, he was stopped by a Virginia force led by Major George Lee Turberville. After several days of holding Hare in custody, the Virginians let the British officer advance to Westover.

Settled in at Westover, entertained by Byrd and her daughters, Hare was discussing his travails of the last several days when a messenger galloped up the long drive with orders for Hare to return to Turberville. Taken back into custody, Hare exploded in anger. He threatened that Britain would "lay waste the whole Virginia countryside" and began making wild accusations that Jefferson was being paid off in gold by the British in order to allow the invasion to proceed. Jefferson, Hare declared, would soon defect just as Arnold had.[31]

A witness to this tirade was Colonel James Innes. In the early days of the revolution, Innes had publicly criticized William Byrd III, and was believed to be the author of an anonymous letter to the *Virginia Gazette* that said Byrd's life had been "remarkable for every kind of immorality."[32] Innes surely now had his suspicions about Byrd's widow, too. He was the last person in the Virginia military that Hare should have offended. Writing to Jefferson, Innes penned an ominous phrase: "I imagine . . . you have heard of the black affair at Westover."[33]

The affair was getting blacker still. Innes demanded that Hare's ship be inspected for illicit goods. Hare refused and was arrested. A militia officer went on board and found that Hare had set packages of papers on fire. A number of letters from Mary Byrd were found. In addition, the ship contained goods such as cloth and brandy. Some believed the goods were payment to Byrd for the use of her property and loss of her slaves, a clear violation of the purpose of the flag of truce.

A militia official, John Nicholas, wrote urgently to Jefferson, informing the governor that the letters "tend to the injury of America." Concerned that Byrd was part of a conspiracy with Arnold, Nicholas ordered Turberville to Westover to search the house. Nicholas informed Jefferson that he felt compelled to "put off all female respect" and urged "the whole correspondence between that lady and the Enemy fairly investigated."[34]

As a result, Virginia's government began to turn against Mary Byrd, just as it had done against her late husband. On February 22, Jefferson and the Governor's Council sent a letter to Steuben, informing him that they "disapprove of Mrs. Byrd's receiving Goods from the enemy in compensation for property taken from her by them."[35]

Byrd and two of her daughters were asleep when militiamen burst into Westover. They ordered the Byrds out of their rooms and began searching the home. When she descended the wide, elegant stairs, Byrd found "two Gentlemen at the foot of them with drawn swords. I desired them to sheath their swords, and preserve them for better purposes than to attack a defenceless Woman, who could not injure her country." She sent an angry letter to Steuben, whom she had met weeks earlier. "Good God what a situation I am in," she wrote. "I have paid taxes during a tedious war; and now am not protected by my Countrymen. The British are suffered to land on my Territory, to use, and destroy, my property, for which I am condemned by my countrymen." She then alleged that some angry Virginians, convinced she was a traitor, had attempted to burn down her house. The effort was unsuccessful, but now she was "condemned to a harder fate."

She enclosed some lines from *Othello,* which read in part: "He that steals my purse, steals trash ... but he that filches from me, my good name, robs me of that, which not enriches him, and make me poor indeed." Finally, in an appeal flush with flattery, she told Steuben: "I have tired your patience, tho I am not tired of conversing with you, with what pleasure could I unbosom myself to you, who see every thing through a proper medium."[36]

Steuben was won over by Mary Byrd's entreaties. He angrily wrote Innes that he had heard that armed men had entered Westover. "This I cannot but disapprove," Steuben wrote. Mrs. Byrd had the right to request a guard be posted at her home.[37]

Innes defended his action, telling Steuben how Hare accused Jefferson of being paid off with gold from the British. "Mr. Hare's conduct was characterized by every mark of impropriety." Moreover, Innes wrote, Hare had headed to Westover with the intent of "securing any suspicious papers." Thus it was appropriate for Turberville to rush to Westover and find the papers before they could be removed or destroyed.

Jefferson was torn. He was sympathetic to Mary Byrd, whom he had known for years. Jefferson had of course represented her husband as a lawyer and visited Westover, counting the books in its great library. Mary was friendly with Jefferson's wife, Martha, who had grown up at a nearby plantation. But he could not condone her conduct. He told Steuben that Byrd seemed to be "more effectually working for our Enemies than if she had pursued their original purpose."[38]

Jefferson and the Governor's Council met again to discuss Byrd's case. They passed a resolution saying that "there appears cause to suspect that Mrs. Mary Byrd hath, during the present invasion, committed an offence" in violation of the law on treason. A trial was set for March 15. The chief witness in the case would be Turberville.[39]

Turberville was, at this moment, facing Steuben's wrath for having interfered with Hare's visit to Westover. Turberville believed his name had been tarred merely for doing his duty. Pulling up a chair at the Raleigh Tavern in Williamsburg, he wrote with disbelief to Steuben. "I have been represented to the Governor in a light which I by no mean deserve, which your own conscience must tell you is wrong."[40] Turberville could not believe what was happening to him. Here he was, a twenty-year-old officer, a former aide-de-camp to Washington, who believed he should be honored for preventing a conspiracy involving Hare and Mary Byrd. Yet instead his honor was questioned. So he challenged the fifty-one-year-old Steuben to a duel. "I must as a man, a freeman, a VIRGINIAN, demand categorically your Answer and your Motives for

denying me that justice which I have an undoubted right to demand," Turberville wrote to Steuben.[41] The duel, however, never took place. Instead, Steuben
ordered Turberville arrested, taking him out of military duty and sending him
to his home.

Byrd, to her disbelief, was facing charges of treason. She sent a letter to Jefferson in which she sought his advice about whether she might be liable. In
reply, Jefferson adopted a friendly, lawyerly tone. He said that she could be liable, but suggested it might only be misdemeanor. "The situation in which you
were placed by the landing of the enemy at Westover was undoubtedly difficult." But he added: "Whether you may have been able to steer with Precision
between the will of those in whose Power you were & the Laws of your country is a question on which the laws have not made me the judge." Jefferson told
Byrd that although he was supposed to be impartial as governor, he hoped "this
troublesome Business" was resolved "perfectly to your satisfaction."[42]

Byrd protested to friends that she had done nothing wrong. "I would die before I would betray my country," she wrote a friend. She would give up her
property and her life, she wrote, "but not my honor." Byrd felt trapped by a
pincer in which the British and Americans were applying equal pressure to her.
She was "suspected by both parties and in the power of one party," her granddaughter wrote.[43]

As the trial date approached, Byrd prepared her own defense. She would
maintain that she was being persecuted because she had been courteous to
British officers and tended to the wounded. "No doubt there were men ready
to make my [great] Aunt's courtesy & humanity a pretense for confiscation,"
her nephew, Joshua Francis Fisher, later wrote. "But in those days, she knew she
would appeal to *gentlemen* in power."[44]

Byrd drove her carriage from Westover to Richmond to present her case to
the court. Just as she was prepared to face her accusers, the court was informed
that the key witness was unavailable. No explanation was given. The failure of
the witness to show up may have saved her from jail, the loss of her property,
even execution. It was never completely explained, but a well-connected Virginian, Arthur Lee, wrote at the time that "I have reason to think she [Mrs.
Byrd] will not be tried at all, because care having been taken to keep the witnesses out of the way."[45]

Steuben appeared to have played a role. It was Steuben's order to arrest
Turberville that kept the fiery young officer far from Richmond at the time of
the trial. Indeed, Jefferson wrote that the chief witness in the case was to have
been Turberville. With Turberville unavailable, the case was dropped. Jeffer-

son, for his part, did not try to revive the case and seemed satisfied with the outcome.

Mary Byrd was allowed to return home and to keep control of her estate. It was a decision that Virginia officials soon would have reason to regret. In the following weeks, thousands more British troops would find Westover the perfect place to encamp in preparation for yet another attack.

We Must Give It Up

WITH ARNOLD ENTRENCHED IN PORTSMOUTH, Jefferson called on legislators to return to the partly destroyed capital of Richmond to attend an emergency session of the General Assembly. Apologizing profusely for the inconvenience of asking lawmakers to leave their homes and make the dangerous journey, Jefferson said he had little choice given that that Arnold's force was "lodged within" Virginia. The army of Lord Cornwallis was also on the march, yet there was not "a shilling in the public coffers" to ensure the state's safety.[1]

Jefferson's primary objective was to win passage of a measure that would compel men to turn out for militia duty in order to prevent "Invasions and Insurrections." Jefferson told the legislators that a considerable number of militiamen were refusing to report for duty, while others had left "in defiance with their arms." In the deferential way of a gentleman speaking to his peers, he suggested that this crisis "may perhaps suggest to them some amendments of the invasion law" in order to defend the state.[2]

The legislators, well aware of the protests against military service taking place in many districts, rejected the proposal by a vote of 32–27. Instead, they took the somewhat meaningless step of requiring that county militia leaders provide a list of the men in their units to the governor within ten weeks, and then spent days arguing over how much should be paid for supplies seized from the citizenry for the state's defense. They also rejected a proposal requiring that a record be published of how each member of the House had voted. Instead, only the numerical tally would be revealed, potentially enabling legislators to avoid accountability for decisions that turned out badly.[3]

It was easier for the legislators to go about the time-honored political tradition of assigning blame for the failures during the invasion. The House of Delegates heard a report that Commissioner of War George Muter had failed miserably in almost every way: weapons had been issued but few had been returned, cannons were either unserviceable or without carriage, muskets were in need of repair, cartridges were unaccounted for, and gunpowder and other supplies were in short supply or unavailable. This series of disasters was the responsibility of many people, including the legislators themselves, but they found the hapless Muter to have run an "entirely deranged" War Office and fired him. Patrick Henry and other legislators, meanwhile, called for a special new legion to protect the state. But funds were short, and the leader of a proposed four-hundred-man battalion "spent more time designing showy uniforms and planning an eight-man band" than he did preparing for battle, a military historian wrote later.[4]

Steuben, incensed over the lack of legislative action, told the Assembly that a significant number of recruits were so poorly suited for service that he refused to enroll them. Across the state, many continued to insist it was more important to protect their families—from both the British and the increasingly likely scenario of slave uprisings—than to serve in the militia. A call for 104 men in New Kent County drew only a dozen, all of whom were unarmed.[5] Many people in Cumberland County objected to a new tax that would pay bounties for Continental army recruits, saying the levy would "destruct the minds of the People, and weaken their Zeal for the public service." Meanwhile, the legislators learned that militia leader Thomas Nelson was so ill that he was confined to his bed, where he would remain for a month.

Feeling isolated and abandoned, Virginia's legislators turned their ire against the other states. A House committee that included Patrick Henry drafted "A Remonstrance of the General Assembly of Virginia," which blasted northern states for failing to come to the aid of Virginia despite having received much aid earlier in the war from soldiers of the Old Dominion. The document threatened to tear apart the nascent and fragile coalition of the United States. "We accompanied our Northern allies during almost every progressive stride it made, where danger seemed to solicit our ardor," the document said, listing battles from Boston to Brandywine. "But when we look for our Northern allies . . . they were not to be found."

Virginia's legislators asked "in the most solemn manner" for other states to supply them with men, money, and munitions. If such aid was not provided, the other states would bear the blame for disaster. They called on "the world and future generations to witness that they have done their duty, that they have prosecuted the war with earnestness, and they are still ready so to act, in conjunction with the other States, as to prosecute it to a happy and glorious period."[6]

However, this overstated broadside was never adopted by the Assembly. There was no doubt that many legislators agreed with its content, and they made sure Congress knew about the complaint. But just as the committee was prepared to urge its adoption, legislators received reports that Congress was at last heeding some of Virginia's demands. Perhaps equally important, they received new warnings that the British forces were once again preparing to close in on Richmond. Three weeks after arriving for the emergency session, the legislators fled the capital, leaving much of Jefferson's agenda undone. A full session of the Assembly would not be held again for two months.

Jefferson's feud with Steuben, meanwhile, worsened daily. Having spent two months fighting over the need for more men, the two now argued over what kind of horses could be borrowed from Virginians. Under the rules of impressment, Jefferson had authorized the military to seize horses from local citizens when needed for battle, but he applied certain restrictions, such as requiring horses only be taken along routes likely to be traveled by the enemy. Many residents detested the rule, which they viewed as an abuse of government authority, and hid their horses. They were especially protective of their stud horses and broodmares, some of which had been imported at great expense or were the valuable offspring of such imports. A growing number of Virginians kept horses mainly for breeding. As the owner of some of Virginia's finest horses, including the extraordinarily fleet Caractacus, Jefferson felt sympathy for those concerned about giving one up in return for a state-issued certificate that might prove worthless. Nonetheless, restrictions on impressing horses caused endless problems for Virginia's military leaders. One militia commander managed to impress thirty-two horses, only to be informed that Jefferson had ordered the return of stud horses or mares "kept for breeding." The order "obliged me to give up some of my most Serviceable Nags," the militia official complained to Steuben.[7] Even when Virginia's military was able to acquire horses, they often could not get men to mount them. A military aide named Benjamin Greene met with Jefferson to try to fulfill a request for twenty such men. Greene reported that Jefferson responded by saying "he thought the men could not possibly be had, for that it was with the greatest difficulty he could procure three today to Guard some powder down the River a little way." Indeed, Jefferson said to Greene that horses "might be procured easier than the men."[8]

Steuben was infuriated. "If the powers of the State are inadequate to furnishing what is indispensably necessary, the Expedition must fail," he wrote Jefferson in a scolding letter, the latest in a series of doomed efforts to get needed supplies. He informed the governor that he would "suspend giving any orders till I receive your Excellency's answer to this."[9] Jefferson, as usual, pleaded a lack of executive authority. He tried to explain that he was balancing his limited powers as governor against the wishes of many Virginians who objected to impressment of property and enforcement of the draft and militia calls. "We can only be answerable for the orders we give and not for their execution," Jefferson wrote to Steuben. "If they are disobeyed from obstinacy of spirit or coercion in the laws, it is not our fault."[10]

Then, just as it appeared Virginia's military command would suffer a complete meltdown, Jefferson received the news he had been anticipating for weeks: a large fleet was on its way to Portsmouth, prepared to bottle up

Arnold. Jefferson and Steuben worked feverishly, hoping to send 4,000 militia against Arnold's 1,600 troops in a final blow. It was all to be arranged by a twenty-four-year-old noble from France, the "boy general," the Marquis de Lafayette.

"OUR MARQUIS," as Americans called Lafayette, would become the most important foreign-born leader in the Continental army. A scion of one of France's wealthiest and most noble families, Lafayette was orphaned at two years old when his father died at the Battle of Minden by the fire of British cannons overseen by artillery officer William Phillips. Heir to feudal lands that stretched across central France, Lafayette dreamed of becoming as great a warrior for France as his father, and exacting revenge against the English.

He was sent to Paris for his education, living at the Palais du Luxembourg and attending the Collège du Plessis, where he was put on the road to royal service. An arranged marriage coupled the fourteen-year-old Lafayette with the twelve-year-old daughter of a French brigadier general, the Marquis de Noailles, whose family was among the most powerful in Paris. With the promise of an ample dowry, and his station among the most elevated in all of Europe, Lafayette moved into the Noailles mansion in Versailles and pursued his calling of military leadership at the Académie de Versailles. Married at seventeen, feted by aristocrats from across Europe, Lafayette was frequently invited to lavish parties with royalty. One night, after Lafayette joined in an obligatory dance with Marie Antoinette, the queen laughed at his lack of grace and what Lafayette called his "awkward country manners," which convinced him that he would never "adapt entirely to the required graces of the court." He felt more comfortable in his military world. Lafayette's commanding officer invited him to join the Masons, an elite and secretive society that at the time in France was critical of monarchies and supportive of America's war for independence. Lafayette was spellbound by speakers at the Masonic Lodge in Paris who called for liberty and the sovereignty of the people. Thus, at eighteen years old, this young man who was the very embodiment of aristocracy determined that he would use his personal fortune and noble title to fight for American independence. It was a confluence of interests: support the Americans, defeat the British, leave Versailles behind, and earn the glory he felt destined to achieve. But the young king forbade Lafayette from leaving Paris, fearing involvement in the American war would upset the tenuous peace between England and France. Lafayette ignored the restriction, escaped the king's men who pursued him, and sailed to America.

Arriving in South Carolina, Lafayette attended some grand dinners and promptly wrote to his wife that America was a country in which "all citizens are brothers. There are no poor people in America, not even what may be called peasants." The young Lafayette apparently saw no reason to mention the society's deep class divisions or the slaves. He traveled to Philadelphia, seeking a military commission, but Congress rejected his candidacy, in part because the use of foreign soldiers was coming increasingly under scrutiny. Washington, who joined the Masons in 1752 and believed strongly in the bond between "true brothers" of "the craft," heard about Lafayette's travails and intervened on his behalf. Taking Lafayette under his wing, Washington made him an unpaid major general and shared his residence with the marquis. Lafayette promptly proved his worth, gallantly commanding forces even as he received a foot wound during the Battle of Brandywine. "I do not know a nobler, finer soul, and I love him as my own son," Washington said of Lafayette.[11]

Returning to France, Lafayette was greeted as a hero. He pleaded the cause of Americans to the royal court and was rewarded with a six-thousand-man fleet, which was placed under the command of Comte de Rochambeau but owed its existence to Lafayette's popularity and ties to the crown. He arrived back in America to find Continental army troops demoralized by a series of British victories during the harsh winter of 1780. As his ship sailed into Boston, church bells rang, cannons were fired, and crowds of people cheered as he was escorted to the house of Governor John Hancock on Beacon Hill, where a lavish banquet was held, followed by a display of fireworks sent skyward from the nearby Common.

Nearly two weeks later, Lafayette held an emotional reunion in New Jersey with Washington, who revealed to him the woeful state of the army. Washington was overjoyed at the news that a French fleet would soon arrive. In the darkest days of that winter, it had seemed the war was lost. Now, thanks to Lafayette, it seemed as if it could be won. Washington implored the states to supply more recruits for the Continental army. "The court of France has done so much for us, that we must make a decisive effort on our part," Washington wrote.[12]

When Washington learned that Arnold had invaded Virginia—prompting countless pleas from Jefferson for assistance—he ordered Lafayette to help the besieged state. Lafayette had been "astounded" by the defection of Arnold, having known him as a man "of Patriotism, and, especially, of the most brilliant courage."[13] Washington no longer seemed worried about Arnold becoming a martyr. If Arnold "should fall into your hands," Washington wrote, Lafayette was to deliver the punishment "in the most summary way."[14]

Thomas Jefferson by Charles Willson Peale, from life, 1791–92. *Courtesy of Independence National Historical Park*

Thomas Jefferson by John Trumbull, from life, 1787–88. *Courtesy of Thomas Jefferson Foundation/Monticello*

View from Monticello, looking toward Charlottesville, 1827, by Jane Pitford Braddick Peticolas. *Courtesy of Thomas Jefferson Foundation/Monticello*

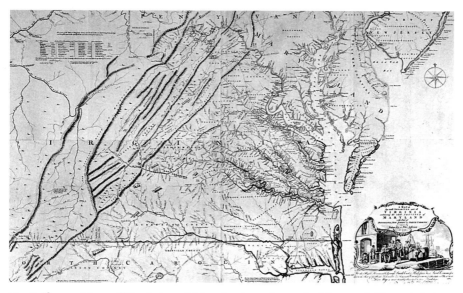

Fry-Jefferson Map, of Virginia and Maryland, co-drawn by Thomas Jefferson's father, Peter Jefferson. *Courtesy of Thomas Jefferson Foundation/Monticello*

ENCAMPMENT of the CONVENTION ARMY

At Charlotte-Ville in Virginia after they had surrendered to the Americans

Encampment of the Convention Army. The Albemarle Barracks near Monticello held several thousand British and Hessian prisoners. Jefferson treated the enemy officers with great kindness and could not imagine that a British invasion force would later enter the valley where the barracks were constructed. *Courtesy of Library of Congress*

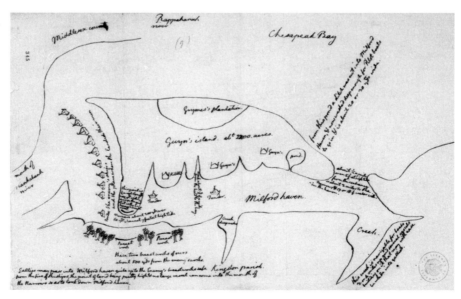

Thomas Jefferson's drawing of Gwynn's Island, where British Governor Lord Dunmore made one of his last stands in Virginia. *Courtesy of Library of Congress*

Patrick Henry, by Thomas Sully. Jefferson credited Henry with setting the spark of revolution but also bitterly blamed Henry for being behind an investigation into his war conduct. *Courtesy of Virginia Historical Society*

William Byrd III, by John Hesselius. Byrd, once one of the wealthiest men in Virginia, gambled away his fortune, hired Jefferson to help solve his financial problems, and was a Loyalist. *Courtesy of Virginia Historical Society*

Mary Willing Byrd, by John Wollaston. Mrs. Byrd, one of Jefferson's friends, was accused of being a Loyalist who helped the invasion forces. *Courtesy of Virginia Historical Society*

John Murray, Fourth Earl of Dunmore, British governor of Virginia, by Charles X. Harris. Dunmore was widely despised by Virginians. *Courtesy of Virginia Historical Society*

RUN away from the subscriber in *Albemarle*, a Mulatto slave called *Sandy*, about 35 years of age, his stature is rather low, inclining to corpulence, and his complexion light; he is a shoemaker by trade, in which he uses his left hand principally, can do coarse carpenters work, and is something of a horse jockey; he is greatly addicted to drink, and when drunk is infolent and diforderly, in his converfation he fwears much, and in his behaviour is artful and knavifh. He took with him a white horfe, much fcarred with traces, of which it is expected he will endeavour to difpofe; he also carried his fhoemakers tools, and will probably endeavour to get employment that way. Whoever conveys the faid flave to me, in *Albemarle*, fhall have 40 s. reward, if taken up within the county, 4 l. if elfewhere within the colony, and 10 l. if in any other colony, from
THOMAS JEFFERSON.

Thomas Jefferson's ad for a runaway slave, *Virginia Gazette*, September 14, 1769. Jefferson's ownership of hundreds of slaves over his lifetime was at odds with his most famous declaration: that "all men are created equal." *Courtesy of Virginia Historical Society*

Thomas Jefferson's sketch of the first version of Monticello. Jefferson was in the midst of building this early iteration of his mansion when the British invaded. *Courtesy of Thomas Jefferson Foundation/Monticello*

Baron von Steuben on horseback, by Johnson, Fry & Company. Steuben, put in charge of
forces in Virginia, was appalled
by Virginia's lack of defensive
preparations. *Courtesy of Virginia Historical Society*

Johann von Ewald, the Hessian
officer who helped lead the
British invasion of Virginia.
Ewald served alongside Benedict Arnold but came to detest
him. *Courtesy of Bloomsburg
University, Joseph P. Tustin Papers, Special Collections, Harvey
A. Andruss Library*

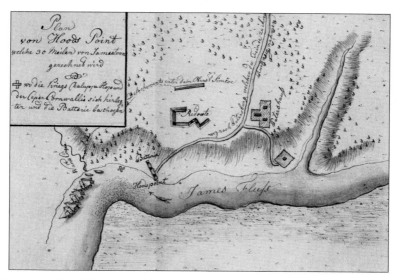

Johann von Ewald's sketch of the Battle of Hood's Point. The battle was a quick victory for Benedict Arnold, enabling the enemy to penetrate closer to Richmond, where Jefferson was living. Translation of Ewald's German inscriptions is as follows. Boats: "Where the sloop of war *Hope* and the privateer *Cornwallis* lay to and bombarded the battery." Ward's Creek: "March of the detachments under Colonel Simcoe." At road: "Road to Petersburg which the enemy took for their retreat." *Courtesy of Bloomsburg University, Ewald Diary, Joseph P. Tustin Papers, Special Collections, Harvey A. Andruss Library*

Jefferson's diary entry for June 4, the day that he fled Monticello just before the enemy arrived, says, "British horse came to Monticello." *Courtesy of Library of Congress*

Banastre Tarleton, the British officer who ordered some of his troops to Monticello in search of Jefferson. *Courtesy of Virginia Historical Society*

LE GENERAL ARNOLD un des Chefs
de l'Armée Anglo Americaine.

E.G. 1894.

Benedict Arnold, the former American general who became a traitor, led British forces
into Virginia during Jefferson's governorship. *Courtesy of Virginia Historical Society*

Thomas Jefferson's hand telescope. The engraving of Jefferson's name may have been made later by his family. He used a telescope to see whether British troops had gathered in Charlottesville before he fled Monticello. *Courtesy of Thomas Jefferson Foundation/Monticello*

THE ALTERNATIVE OF WILLIAMS·BURG.

The Alternative of Williamsburg. This English mezzotint depicts Virginians in Williamsburg signing a loyalty oath, in opposition to British rule, with the suggestion being that the "alternative" was to be coated in the tar and feathers that hung from a nearby pole. *Courtesy of Library of Congress*

CONCLUSION DE LA CAMPAGNE LIBERTE DE L'81 EN VIRGINIE

To his Excellency General Washington this Likeness of his friend, the Marquess de la Fayette, is humbly dedicated.

By le Mere

The Marquis de Lafayette, with James Armistead holding his horse, depicted at the conclusion of the battle at Yorktown, by Jean Baptiste Le Paon, 1738–85. *Courtesy of Library of Congress*

In late February 1781, Lafayette was leading a force of 1,200 men to Virginia. They were an impressive sight in their French-made uniforms, donated by Lafayette, marching in their new shoes from the Continental army, dragging wagonloads of food donated by grateful citizens encountered along the way. A French fleet would set sail simultaneously from Rhode Island to Virginia. The two forces were to meet in Portsmouth, where they would be joined by perhaps four thousand members of the Virginia militia.

Jefferson was ebullient. After months of difficulty in raising the militia, he confidently informed Lafayette that the arms requested by Steuben would be provided. It was the most optimistic letter Jefferson had written since the invasion began. Still, two days later, Jefferson felt obliged to present a blunt assessment to Lafayette of the quality of Virginia's soldiers. "Mild laws, a People not used to war and prompt obedience, a want of the provisions of War & means of procuring them render our efforts often ineffectual." Nonetheless he assured Lafayette that "when we cannot accomplish an object in one way we attempt it in another."[15]

Lafayette was encountering difficulties of his own. As his fleet left Baltimore, intending to head down the Chesapeake Bay to Virginia, it was forced to shore by a band of marauding British privateers. Lafayette trudged ahead by land with a few dozen men on a reconnaissance mission to Virginia, hoping to coordinate plans with Virginia's military leaders and French naval commanders. Arriving in Yorktown on March 13, he was greeted by Steuben and his militia forces. Although Lafayette was twenty-four years old and Steuben fifty-one, the Frenchman outranked the Prussian, a position that Steuben found "mortifying." Nonetheless, Steuben promised that his "zeal" remained high and he expected that "the Marquis will find everything prepared for his arrival."[16]

Indeed, arrangements seemed to be going well in preparation to defeat the British and bring the hated Arnold to justice. Even Steuben had to admit to Washington that Virginia's leaders had met his requests for "every possible preparation."[17]

Everything seemed aligned for an American rout at Portsmouth. Arnold's defenses were poorly prepared. He had left New York with only 300 entrenching tools for 1,600 men, even though he had been told his primary mission was to establish an impregnable base at Portsmouth. As word spread that a large French fleet was headed toward Virginia, British soldiers became increasingly anxious about the security of the fort. Arnold stayed on horseback day and night as he frantically ordered his men to make the miserable works of the fort strong enough to resist the French cannons. The British soldiers piled into the poorly constructed fort, where they huddled in anxiety for twenty-four hours.

At daybreak, a captured Virginian was brought into camp and, after Ewald threatened to hang him, said a force of five thousand French and Americans was marching toward Portsmouth and planned to lay siege to the fort. Ewald and his Jägers were out reinforcing a picket when the Hessian saw an astonishing sight. "The entire opposite bank of the creek was occupied by the enemy," which began firing at Ewald and his men. Ewald was hit in the knee and fell to the ground, but he ordered his small force to continue firing at the Virginians and to prevent them from crossing a bridge. As Ewald was carried away for treatment of his wounds, he ran into Arnold. The general asked the Hessian officer if he believed the post would be lost. "No! As long as one Jäger lives, no damned American will come across the causeway!" Ewald responded. But with thirty-two Jägers facing perhaps five hundred Virginians across the creek, the boast seemed pure bravado. The French fleet was expected at any minute.[18]

The French fleet of eight large ships and three smaller vessels was near the Capes of Virginia when a string of British vessels, alerted to their mission, raced toward them. The French naval commander, Chevalier Destouches, had expected an easy victory against Arnold. Instead, he faced the prospect of destruction at sea just miles from his intended prey.

At 6:00 a.m. on March 16, with a thick haze draped over the Atlantic, a lookout on a British frigate spotted the French fleet.[19] The haze lifted to reveal two forces a few miles apart, each bearing eight ships of the line, ready for a classic confrontation at sea. The British had a slight advantage in cannons. The British ships lined up in a perpendicular fashion at the mouth of the bay, blocking the French from entering Virginia's waters. The French fleet was just to the north, lined up in two parallel columns, prepared to confront the British and make a run for the bay.

The action began not with bursts of cannon fire but with gusts of wind. The British heeded the winds and headed slightly east, away from the bay, so that they could attack the French from a windward position. The French immediately responded, moving to the east as well. Now the French tacked in the wind, making a run for the bay entrance. The British followed the move with an unexpected suddenness. Fire filled the sky as cannonballs hurtled through the air. Officers shouted instructions as sailors raced to their positions.

As the French fleet turned toward the sea to avoid the fusillade, they briefly massed in front of the British and let loose their firepower. The French cannonballs caused considerable damage on three British ships, while the return fire seriously damaged only two French vessels. Still, the French realized they were outgunned. Destouches decided that he could not get past the British blockade of the bay without risking all of his ships and men. He let his fleet drift to the north, out of range.

The British let the French go without further molestation, prompting Bartholomew James, the British officer who kept a journal of his experience of the invasion of Virginia, to write that it was a battle "which will ever stain the annals of this country." While historians would argue over who had won the battle, the result was clear: the French survived to fight another day, but they did so by fleeing from Virginia.[20]

The Marquis de Lafayette, expecting the arrival of a fleet filled with his fellow Frenchmen at any moment, was stunned to learn that a British fleet was bounding through the choppy waters of Hampton Roads. The confusion of the moment increased when a British ship flew a French flag in an effort to trick the Virginians into meeting them in the bay. Captain William Bucker of the Virginia navy sailed toward the fleet but found to his "great mortification" that the ship was a British vessel. Bucker was taken prisoner and shipped to England, where he remained for a year.[21]

In Portsmouth, meanwhile, American commanders learned that British vessels were entering the bay and quickly called off their plans for the siege. The hundreds of Virginians whom Ewald had seen massed on the other side of the creek were abruptly ordered to retreat. Arnold and his men were safe. Most of the British vessels soon sailed away, assured that Portsmouth was fortified.

Ten days later, the news worsened for the Virginians. A new British fleet, carrying 2,200 men, suddenly appeared at the Capes of Virginia. Lafayette was dismayed. It was "a circumstance that destroys every prospect of an operation against Arnold," he wrote Washington. "Never has an operation been more ready (on our Side) nor Conquest more certain." But with the departure of the French and the arrival of this new British fleet, "we must give it up."[22] Lafayette backed a plan proposed by Steuben to send two thousand Virginia militiamen to the Carolinas to try to capture Cornwallis. But the plan was shelved amid objections from militia who didn't want to leave Virginia under any circumstances, and from state officials who did not want such a valuable force of armed men to leave the state at a time when it was so vulnerable to attack. The grim prospects prompted Lafayette to head back to Maryland to reunite with his troops, unsure whether he would return to Virginia.

Aboard the new British fleet, meanwhile, a highly decorated commander walked the deck as his ships bounded across the waters of Chesapeake Bay and headed toward Arnold's fort at Portsmouth. General William Phillips, who less than two years earlier had been one of Jefferson's favorite guests at Monticello, was now in charge of the invasion of Virginia.

Burnt All Their Houses

WILLIAM PHILLIPS WAS EVERYTHING that Benedict Arnold was not: British-born, respected by his men, sure of his command, and, thanks to his time as a loosely regulated prisoner of war in Charlottesville, very knowledgeable about Virginia. Four years earlier, Phillips had surrendered at Saratoga to an American force that included Arnold. Now Phillips was Arnold's commanding officer. The two former enemies had a combined force of 4,500 men. The size of the Virginia militia, on the other hand, was shrinking. Within days of Phillips's arrival, the terms of the state's three-month militia expired, prompting hundreds of men to leave their regiments. They could not have chosen a worse moment. In five years of war, there had never been a larger British force in Virginia. But from the perspective of a militiaman, the presence of so many British presented a new threat to their farms and families. Many stacked their arms and left their units to go home, ignoring the pleas of their commanders.

Anchoring at Portsmouth, Phillips went ashore to inspect the fortifications built by Arnold. He was astonished at the poor quality of the work. It was, he told Clinton, "a bad post, its locality not calculated for defense."[1] Phillips concluded that it was not worth having 3,500 men remain at Portsmouth. Then he boarded Arnold's ship, the *Guadeloupe,* and greeted the man who had defeated him at Saratoga. Phillips was conflicted about Arnold. He had often expressed his disgust for defectors in general, but he respected Arnold's accomplishments on the battlefield. In the eyes of Phillips, Arnold had burnished his image with his extraordinary raids on Richmond and his easy control of Virginia.

Many in the British force were overjoyed that Phillips would replace Arnold as their commanding officer, including the navy men who had feuded with Arnold over the division of prizes; the Hessian officers who detested Arnold's manner and strategy; and others who simply did not like serving under a defector. Phillips had been part of the British military since before some of these soldiers and sailors were born, earning his reputation at the Battle of Minden and other contests. Arnold, by contrast, was performing his first British command. Phillips "drove everyone zealously to duty, which the majority of the men who had served under Arnold up to now did not feel, because everything had been done in the American fashion," wrote Ewald. While overseeing the drilling of the troops in exacting fashion, Phillips also took time to visit "all the wounded and sick, addressing the one with encouraging words and favoring the other with money or good food from his own kitchen."[2]

After consulting aboard the *Guadeloupe,* Arnold and Phillips agreed that a raiding party should be sent up the Potomac River. The primary purpose was to ensure that Lafayette, who had returned to his men in Maryland, did not sail down the Potomac with his reconstituted force. The party also had permission to seize property and goods that could be used against British forces and to destroy what they could not take. This was a fine line: an individual who might have supplied food to Virginia troops could easily be cited as abetting rebels and thus have his property plundered and destroyed by the British. A number of rebel leaders had houses on the Potomac, the most prominent being Washington's estate, Mount Vernon.

The Potomac River mission was given to Captain Thomas Graves, whose cousin, Admiral Thomas Graves, at one point was the commander in chief of British naval forces in the Revolutionary War. Captain Graves was a tough and much-admired Irishman, having traveled on a daring expedition to the Arctic in 1773. His hostility toward Americans was solidified when he was attacked in 1775 while sailing up the Charles River in Boston, fleeing as his ship was run aground and burned.

Graves loosened the topsails and set sail from Hampton on April 3, a fair day with fresh breezes. The thirty-four-year-old captain led a flotilla up the Potomac, terrorizing riverfront residents. John Skinker, a local militia leader in King George County, saw three large schooners and some smaller boats land at a nearby plantation, plunder the home, liberate four slaves, and destroy what they could not take away. Heading farther upriver, the British plundered the house of a Catholic priest, set aflame the home of a person who had fired upon them, and destroyed a linen factory. After reaching the port of Alexandria, the British found that few militiamen had turned out to oppose them, and they saw no sign of Lafayette's troops. The fleet headed back south on the Potomac and, on April 12, assembled a quarter mile from Mount Vernon. The home of General Washington was left in the hands of his cousin, Lund Washington, who believed that slaves and servants would flee at any opportunity.

The British first struck across the river from Mount Vernon. About 100 militia had gathered on the Maryland shore, perhaps not realizing that the British force had about 475 men on ships that carried several dozen cannons. The British sent a representative ashore, demanding vegetables and other provisions and ordering the militia to lay down their arms. The British would pay for the supplies, but if the militia refused to provide the goods and fired on the fleet, the Virginians would be attacked and their property destroyed. The militia commander, Major Henry Lyles, was a crusty former officer in the Continental army. He had spent three years as a prisoner of the British on Staten Island and had won his freedom just four months earlier in an exchange of men. He refused to supply the British and informed them that the militia were armed and would defend themselves.

Under cover of a heavy cannonade from the fleet, two hundred sailors went ashore on nine barges. They set Lyles's home aflame, burned surrounding residences, and routed the militia. Graves made a stark notation in his log: "Burnt all their houses."[3]An American report said two British sailors were killed; Graves reported only that one sailor was wounded during the landing. Thirteen slaves were given refuge aboard the British ships.

On the following day, with smoke still drifting skyward from the smoldering ruins across the river, Graves turned his attention to Mount Vernon. The red and white mansion, set on a rise above the river, was among the grandest homes in America, with its colonnades, jutting cupola, and long piazza. While Washington was away from home, he would spend many hours envisioning the improvements he would make to the estate once the war was over. The estate's riches came not just from the river teeming with herring or the fields planted with crops, but also from the slaves. On this day, seventeen of those slaves fled to the British, who promptly freed them. They included Sambo Anderson, about twenty years old. Regal in appearance, "stout and healthy," he was a carpenter who had been born in western Africa. His skin was a "bright, mahogany color, with high cheek bones . . . his face was tattooed and he wore ear rings which . . . were made of real guinea gold," a neighbor later recalled. Each side of his face had two or three scars, apparently indicating his ethnic group in Africa. He told people that he was the son of an African king, and he may well have been.[4] Other slaves who went to the British fleet included Frederick, forty-five, a "valuable" overseer; Harry, forty, a "horseler"; Stephan, twenty, a cooper; Wally, twenty, a weaver; Thomas, a house servant; and three women, twenty-year-old Lucy, eighteen-year-old Esther, and sixteen-year-old Deborah.[5]

Washington had worried from the first days of the revolution that his unguarded home would be attacked by the British. His greatest fear was that the British would take his wife, Martha, hostage. Washington had left Mount Vernon on May 4, 1775, leaving her behind, and had not been back as the war dragged into its sixth year. Shortly after leaving, he worried that Virginia's then-governor, Lord Dunmore, would sail to Mount Vernon. "I can hardly think that Lord Dunmore can act so low, & unmanly a part, as to think of seizing Mrs Washington by way of revenge upon me," the general wrote to his cousin.

Washington told Lund that if he had any reason to suspect Martha was in danger, he was to take her to Alexandria, along with the general's papers. Luckily, Martha Washington was not at Mount Vernon when Captain Graves arrived with his band of plunderers.[6]

At first, Lund Washington was defiant. He told Graves that General Washington "was well aware of the exposed situation of his house and property." Lund had been told that he was "by no means to comply with any such demands" to save Mount Vernon if threatened by the British. Washington "would make no unworthy compromise with the enemy, and was ready to meet the fate of his neighbors."[7]

In response, Graves ordered his ship to prepare for a cannonade. With British guns trained upon the great estate, Lund Washington gave in. He supplied the invaders with sheep, hogs, and a variety of goods. He did not interfere with the slaves who sought their freedom. On board the British ships, the sailors celebrated their victory with refreshments delivered from Mount Vernon's kitchen.

The bargain at Mount Vernon would become one of the bitterest episodes of the war for Washington. Shortly after Graves sailed south, the Marquis de Lafayette learned what had happened. He promptly wrote Washington, chastising Lund's behavior. "You cannot conceive how unhappy I have been to hear that Mr. Lund Washington went on board the enemy's vessels, and consented to give them provisions," Lafayette wrote. "This being done by the gentleman who, in some measure, represents you at your house, will certainly have a bad effect, and contrasts with spirited answers from some neighbours that have had their houses burnt accordingly."[8]

Washington was furious. He wrote to his cousin, picking up Lafayette's complaint completely and condemning any bargaining with the "plundering scoundrels."

> I am very sorry to hear of your loss; I am a little sorry to hear of my own. But that which gives me most concern, is, that you should go on board the enemy's Vessels, and furnish them with refreshments. It would have been a less painful circumstance to me, to have heard, that in consequence of your non-compliance with their request, they had burnt my House, and laid the Plantation in ruins.[9]

There may, however, have been one positive effect for the Americans of the raid on Mount Vernon. The British had brought the war to Washington's doorstep. For years, Washington had fought the war in the north. Now he was seriously considering bringing his troops south to take on the British in his home state. The months ahead, Washington wrote to his cousin, would bring a trial by fire. Jefferson, hearing of the raids up the Potomac, wrote to local militia leaders that he was "exceedingly sorry" to hear about the "cruel depredations," but he believed there might be positive impact. "It may tend to produce irremovable hatred against so detestable a nation [as Britain] and thereby strengthen our Union," Jefferson wrote.[10]

In the wake of the plundering campaign, however, the militia turnout suffered. As expected, men were reluctant to defend distant areas when they were worried that their own homes and villages were endangered. Jefferson's request for the King George County militia, for example, met with severe opposition from John Skinker, who had witnessed the British attacks up the Potomac. He wrote apologetically to Jefferson that the county militia was poorly equipped—not more than one-third with arms—and said he had no power to secure the requested 150 guns. In any case, Skinker told Jefferson, he had thirty miles "to protect from the depredation of these Pirates." He begged Jefferson to countermand the order for his county's militia until the "great danger" had passed.[11]

In Northumberland County, privateers who were attached to the same fleet that threatened Mount Vernon went ashore and torched the home of the county lieutenant, Thomas Gaskins. It was Gaskins who, eight months earlier, had overseen the court-martial of thirty-nine of his county's militiamen for failing to respond to the Continental army draft. Some of those militiamen had rioted and fled to British vessels. Now, men from British vessels—possibly including some of those who had rioted in opposition to Gaskin's orders—had destroyed Gaskins's estate on Mill Creek. Gaskins wrote to Jefferson, telling of the "great Destruction . . . By the cruel Pirating Vessells By Stealing our Negroes . . . I had my Dwelling house Burnt to ashes." The dire note also included the distressing news that only three men in the county had enlisted in the Continental army, requiring the draft of forty more men, which in turn risked the possibility of yet another riot.[12]

Meanwhile, two counties on Virginia's eastern shore were roiling with rioters angry about the demands for draftees to the Continental army and war-related taxes. After reports spread that protesters in Northampton County had managed to put down the draft, armed men in nearby Accomack County stormed the local courthouse. Posting a sentry at the courthouse door, the men told the county militia lieutenant, George Corbin, that "they all unanimously declared they were determined to oppose the Draft at the hazard of their lives." The riots threw the county "into the greatest confusion imaginable," county officials wrote to Jefferson. Tax collectors solicited funds to pay for the state's defense at their peril. The county was so isolated that an effort to court-martial the mutineers seemed futile. Corbin wrote Jefferson that he had no choice but to "adopt mildness rather than force" because he was surrounded by rioters within the county and hemmed in by British ships patrolling the county's coastline.[13]

Perhaps the worst riot occurred in the western part of the state, in mountainous Hampshire County. Garret Van Meter, the county militia leader, wrote a series of letters to Jefferson with an increasingly panicked tone. The Hampshire militiamen were furious for two main reasons: they didn't like the conditions under which local men would be drafted to serve in the Continental army, and they objected to paying a tax to comply with Jefferson's orders for supplying the state with clothes, wagons, and other militia provisions. They considered the tax unfair, partly because it was levied on western counties relatively unthreatened by the British in order to protect Tidewater constituents who had rarely bothered with western concerns.

At first, Van Meter was able to gather seventy men, who turned back the fifty or so rioters. But the clash only strengthened sympathy for the protesters, who vowed allegiance to each other, not to the state. Some of the men were drinking to the health of King George III and "Damnation to Congress." The next day, 150 men, many of them drunk, gathered to protest the orders of Jefferson and the Assembly, vastly outnumbering Van Meter's men. It was largest uprising yet, spreading fears of a full-scale civil war within Virginia. "I am sorry to inform your Excellency, that a dangerous insurrection has lately arisen in this County," Van Meter wrote Jefferson. Van Meter took every measure possible to suppress the rioters, but the effort had "proved ineffectual by reason of their having a superior force."

Another week passed, and hundreds more rioters roamed throughout the county. Their principal objective, Van Meter wrote Jefferson in yet another panicked letter, was to be clear of taxes and the Continental army draft. The men were trying to persuade everyone in the area "to join them in their Treasonable and destructive measures. For this purpose (as I am told) they swear fidelity to each other."[14]

Throughout Virginia large numbers of militiamen insisted on leaving on the day that their three-month term expired, no matter how precarious the condition of the state's defense. General Peter Muhlenberg felt compelled to approve the discharges. "I tried every method in my power to prevail on them to continue until I could be reinforced from other quarter, but in vain," Muhlenberg told Steuben.[15] Across Virginia, militiamen stacked their arms and marched off. Steuben's mood, often dark-tempered, grew even darker. "Everything is gloomy, very little in our favour, and appearance entirely against us," Steuben wrote to a fellow officer.[16] It was left to Jefferson's friend in Albemarle County, George Gilmer, to buck up the governor, urging that he remain in the job "so long as your country shall have virtue enough to continue you. The envious only hate that excellence they can not reach."[17]

Amidst this series of crises, Thomas and Martha Jefferson faced their own trial. Their youngest daughter, Lucy Elizabeth, had become increasingly sick as the Jeffersons were on the move. They surely feared for the baby's health. Of their five children, two had died very young: Jane Randolph at eighteen months old in 1775, and an unnamed son—the Jeffersons' only son—at less than three weeks old in 1777. Now Lucy Elizabeth, just four and a half months old, was becoming sicker by the day. On April 15, she breathed her last. With everyone's life so threatened by the invasion, the helplessness of a baby's death seemed especially cruel. Jefferson took up his pen and jotted a brief note in his account book: "Our daughter Lucy Elizabeth died about 10 o'clock a.m. this day." It is the only surviving confirmation of the death.[18]

The following morning, an ice storm layered the trees in a crystalline coating, and fierce winds blew across Shockoe Hill in Richmond. The Jeffersons huddled in their townhouse. Jefferson would not be attending the usual meeting of the Governor's Council. There was no pressing need for the session, he explained. But the sadness of it all was evident in a note to one of the councilors. "Mrs. Jefferson," the governor explained, was "in a situation in which I would not wish to leave her."[19]

Uncommon Dangers Require Uncommon Remedies

A BITTER FROST GRIPPED VIRGINIA as the Jeffersons buried Lucy Eliza-beth. Spring seemed to have come to a standstill, overtaken by days of freezing rain and gale-force winds. Apple and pear trees dropped their early buds, and forests again became bare as the cold blasted leaves from the trees. Dr. Robert Honyman, staying at a tavern north of Richmond that was frequently passed by both British and American troops, noted in his diary that the skies were filled with "rain & hail & sleet & snow; frequently cloudy, but always cold, raw, piercing winds."

Like many people in eastern Virginia, Honyman felt increasingly hemmed in by the British. For weeks, Honyman reported, British troops had been storming up Virginia's rivers, "destroying vessels . . . burning houses & taking off Negroes and other property."[1] Some buried their valuables in the woods. They stayed away from the main roads, fearful of being swept up by the enemy. The latest reports reaching Honyman warned that the British were preparing to move from Portsmouth and head west on the James River. The British were "very quiet, but are preparing for some stroke," wrote Honyman. The Virginia militia force led by General Muhlenberg that had shadowed the British was being decimated from within: hundreds of Virginians returned home because their term of service had expired. The loss of "800 rifle men from the back country" was particularly acute, depriving the state of its best marksmen.[2]

While Muhlenberg's depleted force retreated to Smithfield on the southern side of the James River, the British prepared to launch attacks on the northern side around Williamsburg. They believed it would be an easy matter to take Williamsburg and head to the nearby naval yard on the Chickahominy River. Only the storms stalled the attack. Torrents of rain fell on Williamsburg, slic-ing streams of muddy rivulets into the broad thoroughfare of Duke of Glouces-ter Street.

With the government moved to Richmond and many townspeople having fled, the former capital was a quieter place, protected by a militia force of about six hundred men commanded by James Innes. Many soldiers talked of going home. Crops needed planting, slaves were running away, and wives and children needed protection. The militiamen knew that somewhere nearby, thousands of well-equipped, well-armed, and well-prepared British soldiers were aiming their massive cannons at the Virginia shoreline.

General Phillips surveyed the storm from his ship. He had endured three years of inaction, including his time at Charlottesville with the British and Hessian prisoners. Now, sitting at a table with his fellow officers, Phillips unfurled maps of Virginia and plotted his attack. Phillips could be as violent as the storm outside, his temper leading one of his men to call him a "very hard fellow." But he could also be as calm as a storm's aftermath, consoling the wounded—"the most pleasant, unselfish, and courteous man in the world," Ewald called him. He shared his elegant dining quarters with twenty officers at a time, feasting at a table set with damask cloths, silver candlesticks and white china, sipping his Irish claret.[3]

Phillips outlined the mission: destroy Virginia's military capabilities and finish off its will to fight. Arnold had spent weeks softening up the defenses, plundering the storehouses, and panicking the populace. Now the combined force of Arnold and Phillips would root out the remaining defenders, burn the supply depots, and capture what little remained of the state's navy. As the storm finally abated, Phillips ordered 2,500 men aboard their ships at Portsmouth. Only a few hundred men would be left behind to guard the garrison. After sailing up the James River, the British landed at Burwell's Ferry and marched toward Williamsburg, with Arnold and Phillips jointly in command. A detachment of five hundred infantry men and fifty cavalry, heavily armed and well rested, approached the capital.

The militia force assigned to protect Williamsburg was too weak to stand and fight, having been on patrol for fifty hours with "no Sustenance" and suffering "extremely for want of provision," Innes wrote Jefferson. At midnight, Innes ordered his force to retreat. Leaving behind fifteen men who were too ill to march, as well as some supplies, his men marched about six miles to the northwest, to a crossroads known as Allen's Ordinary, named after a local tavern. It was "the nearest position to the Town that can be taken with safety while the Enemy are masters of the water," Innes wrote.[4]

Jefferson, desperate to help his old friend, responded that he was "astonished" at Innes's lack of supplies. The governor called out the militia "within an hour" of being told that the enemy was in pursuit but held out little hope that the call would be heeded. "Tho' our Orders for calling the Militia went out Thursday morning not a Man is yet assembled here," he wrote. It was the same kind of "fatal Tardiness" that had caused Jefferson to abandon Richmond. Jefferson declined to give Innes the power to seize horses, however, saying such impressments had caused "such Disgust as to induce me to avoid it."[5] The British, however, felt no such compunction and took whatever animals they wanted as the spoils of war.

Innes retreated again, marching to Hickory Neck Church, fourteen miles above Williamsburg. At 3:00 p.m. on April 21, as Innes sat down to write his latest report to Jefferson, he learned that the British had sent a fleet of thirty vessels up the nearby Chickahominy River to destroy the shipyard. There was no way to stop such a force, Innes told Jefferson.[6] It was the lowest point yet of the British invasion of Virginia. Richmond was in ruins and partly abandoned. Jefferson and the Council were constantly on the run. Williamsburg was controlled by Jefferson's former ally, Benedict Arnold, and Jefferson's former dinner companion, William Phillips.

For Arnold, it was his greatest moment of triumph since his defection. Having failed to deliver West Point to the British, he instead was serving up Virginia. Four years earlier, the citizenry of Williamsburg had celebrated Arnold's victory at Saratoga and the capture of five thousand British troops. Huzzahs had been shouted and Arnold's name venerated. Now he was a British commander, capturing Virginians and seizing key territory. He strutted on his horse up and down Duke of Gloucester Street, assuring the townspeople they would be well treated. All they had to do was follow his example and switch to the British side.

The British set up a guard at a key intersection of Williamsburg, across the road from a tavern that featured a handsome piazza. The road was bordered by an earthen berm, which stood above a ditch near the gardens of the College of William and Mary. The British placed tree branches in the road in order to stop travelers for questioning. While several soldiers stood guard, another group of sentinels rested by a blazing fire. A gentle rain began to fall, then came more steadily; the burning logs hissed and smoked. A British commander ordered the men to walk with their arms to the nearby piazza to take shelter from the storm.

Suddenly, a burst of gunfire erupted from the nearby wooded area. A company of university students hiding in a thicket brazenly tried to ambush the better-armed British. The king's men leaped across the road, took cover at the berm, and fired in the direction of the students. The would-be attackers quickly fled.

Shortly thereafter, a British column marching into Williamsburg came across two carriages, each drawn by four horses. Inside one of the carriages, a well-dressed gentleman suddenly panicked. The man jumped out of the lead carriage and, mounting an outrider's horse, galloped into the wood. The British shot at the man, but he escaped, according to the account written later by one of the British officers, Lieutenant General Samuel Graham.[7] The British ordered the remaining riders to stay in the carriages while they investigated. As the soldiers peered inside the carriage of the escaped man, they were startled to find a lady who was "seemingly much agitated." She soon convinced the soldiers that she was a woman of some importance. The soldiers decided to take her to General Phillips.

Phillips recognized the lady as one he had met when he lived in the Charlottesville area with the Convention troops. Remembering how kindly he had been treated by Jefferson during that time, he treated the lady in like fashion. Who was the man who escaped from the carriage? Phillips asked. The woman replied that he was her husband, and that they had just married. Phillips said it was foolish of him to run the risk of trying to escape, and said he would likely be captured.

"And if you get him what will be done to him?" the woman asked.

"Madam," Phillips replied, "he shall be sent immediately back to you, that you may enjoy the honeymoon."

The carriages were allowed to pass with their eight sturdy horses, a gesture that surprised some of the British, given that their own horses were still "had not recovered from the effects of the sea voyage."[8]

Several miles away, the second British force, with more than one thousand men, reached the naval yard on the Chickahominy River. The voyage was made possible by the same kind of flat-bottomed boats that Arnold had used so effectively at Lake Champlain when he was in the service of the Continental army. Each of the boats held up to one hundred soldiers and several sailors, who maneuvered it with a small sail and oars. Swivel guns and light cannons were mounted on board.

As the British arrived at the shipyard, they found fewer vessels than expected. Fortuitously, Jefferson had recognized that the ships at the Chickahominy site could easily be taken by the British and destroyed, and had ordered that the ships be anchored farther up the James River, where they could more easily either attack the British or flee from a superior force. Workers had been unable to remove all of the ships, however, and, as Jefferson feared, the British easily captured the shipyard, setting it aflame, destroying a twenty-gun ship that was under construction as well as several armed vessels and a warehouse.

Having captured Williamsburg and destroyed the state shipyard, the British headed up the James, again passing Hood's Point without being challenged. Unlike the January invasion, when Arnold had moved in and out of Richmond quickly, it now appeared that the British wanted to occupy the area around the capital, closing the net on Jefferson and any remaining legislators.

In January, Virginia's militia had outnumbered Arnold's forces by more than two to one, though they were too dispersed to stop his assaults. Now, the combined forces of Arnold and Phillips outnumbered the active militia. Virginia would be lost if the long-promised French support did not arrive soon. Where, Jefferson wondered, was the Marquis de Lafayette? At this desperate moment, a letter from the Frenchman finally arrived. Lafayette was with his troops in Baltimore, preparing to head back to Virginia. "I Apprehend that the State of Virginia Must Need An immediate support," Lafayette wrote in halting English. In order to advance as quickly as possible, Lafayette said he would need to seize many horses, exactly the measure that Jefferson had been reluctant to adopt for fear of alienating the citizenry. But Lafayette said there was no choice if he was to march to the rescue. "Uncommon dangers require uncommon remedies," he wrote.[9]

Four days later, on April 21, Lafayette reached Alexandria and learned the situation in Virginia was worse than he had feared. Phillips was on his way to Richmond, with no likelihood that he could be stopped. Jefferson was running from one place to the next. Lafayette, understanding that he was in a race against the British to save Richmond, again tried to get horses in order to speed his journey. Surely, he wrote to Jefferson, the people of Virginia would help him by providing the needed horses and wagons. He understood that taking the horses and wagons was "Bigg with difficulties." Nonetheless, given the risk of losing Virginia to the British, Lafayette reasoned, "Her inhabitants Could not deny us the Means of advancing to their defense."[10] But as Lafayette advanced into Virginia, he found that Virginians were sending their horses and wagons "out of the way" to avoid having them seized. Needing three hundred horses and thirty wagons, Lafayette wrote angrily to Jefferson that his race to the rescue was being delayed by the very people he was trying to help.

No Wagons, No Intelligence, Not One Spy

JEFFERSON AWOKE IN RICHMOND early on the morning of April 24 amid fresh concerns that Arnold and Phillips were headed to the capital, intent on seizing the governor and the city. The British had spent the prior evening anchored by the familiar environs of Westover, alarming the citizenry and prompting messengers to gallop toward Richmond with warnings that the city might once again come under siege. By 7:30 a.m., Jefferson was aware that the British were on the move, with only twenty-five miles separating Richmond and Westover, and could overwhelm the capital before sunset.

The city was largely undefended. Militia forces were scattered throughout the region, with Innes and his six hundred men north of the capital and Steuben and Muhlenberg with one thousand men to the south. Given such a small, dispersed force, the militia was unsure where to gather. The only reasonable action was to shadow the British and try to determine where they were headed.

As the British sailed farther up the James River, they reached a bend called City Point, near the entrance of the Appomattox River, about twenty miles south of Richmond. It was just a few miles short of Osborne's Landing, where the remnants of Virginia's navy were anchored, prepared to blockade the James if the British tried to ascend the river toward the capital. But the British would wait before attacking the navy or heading to Richmond. Instead, they landed by the Appomattox and marched south, intending to seize Petersburg. As Virginia scouts realized their intentions, messengers galloped to alert the troops of Steuben and Muhlenberg and urge them to gather in Petersburg and protect the city.

Petersburg was an obvious target for the British. Its stores of ammunition, weapons, and supplies made it a key transit point for Virginia's soldiers joining the Continental army in the Carolinas. Steuben and Muhlenberg gathered one thousand men on the outskirts of the town, blocking the entrance. In case of retreat, the militia would cross the nearby Appomattox River at the Pocahontas Bridge. Indeed, retreat was inevitable, given that Phillips and Arnold commanded 2,300 men.

Some of the militiamen from the mountain regions were anxious to prove their mettle. "The backwoods Rifle men had been Grumbling and scolding about so much Retreating and no shooting," one of those backwoods men, Daniel Trabue, wrote years later. "They would rather fight than run so much."

The militia captains picked up the call, but some of the top leaders were wary of putting an untested militia force against the well-armed and highly efficient British and Hessian troops, remembering how Virginia's militia had fled in disarray during some battles in South Carolina.[1]

The restlessness of the militia meshed with Steuben's view that it was essential to delay the British force. A battle of a few hours, even if followed by the inevitable retreat, could demonstrate to the local citizenry that Virginia's men could stand and fight. Moreover, it would satisfy the fighting spirit of the men. "To retire without some shew of Resistance, would have intimidated the Inhabitants and have encouraged the Enemy to further invasions," Steuben reasoned.[2] Steuben was best qualified to oversee a traditional, large-scale battle rather than the small-scale hit-and-run efforts that had frustrated him for weeks. So, after much consultation among the officers, it was agreed the militia would fight. Each regiment was given a hogshead of rum. "Now, boys, drink and fill your canteens," an officer instructed. "But don't drink too much. We are going to fight today."[3]

The long columns of British, Loyalist, and Hessian soldiers arrived at 3:00 p.m. The Virginia militia stood fast in their front lines, firing heavy volleys at the approaching troops. Phillips ordered the cannons to be placed on high land, where they pounded the militia forces and forced them back. The retreat was done in an orderly fashion, the result of Steuben's expertise in drilling the men. He ordered artillery placed on the heights on the opposite side of the Appomattox. Phillips responded in kind, putting his guns in position to fire upon Petersburg.

"Shot!" an American officer yelled each time a British cannonball was launched at them, sending the militiamen flying to the ground for protection. Then the militia jumped up and fired again at the British, until the next round of cannonballs whistled through the air, followed again by the cry, "Shot!"[4]

Soon the British fire was constant and heavy, forcing the militia to lie prone as balls split the earth and dirt flew up in every direction. A militia commander ordered the Virginians to sweep back across the Pocahontas Bridge. As hundreds of militia crowded over the narrow bridge, the British lunged forward with their bayonets, killing a number, until some Virginia artillerymen on the heights slowed the enemy with well-aimed cannon shots. But the British superiority was too great. Trabue watched with horror as the enemy "took off about 40 or 50 of our men before our faces."

The orderly retreat turned into a race for the heights, which in turn were abandoned amid the incessant pounding of British artillery. Trabue had gotten the fight he requested. During the battle, he repeatedly fired at the British and believed he killed a number of them. His rifle "was so hot that I could hardly hold it. If I would spit on it, it would fize. Our Militia that day was very brave." When the battle was over, Trabue realized that he had drunk every bit of rum in his quart-sized canteen, more than he had ever downed in a day, yet "I was Duly sober. Most of the men Did about the same."[5]

Phillips set up his headquarters at Bollingbrook, the home of Mary Bolling, whose nineteen-year-old son, Robert, was a captain of a militia unit that fought heroically in the Petersburg battle. Mary and her four daughters were made prisoners in their own home, with armed sentinels guarding their rooms. She pleaded with Phillips not to burn her tobacco warehouses, prompting the British general to have the tobacco removed to the streets and burned. One of her warehouses, as well as the fencing around her home, was torched by over-eager soldiers. As Bolling complained about her treatment, Arnold warned her not to irritate Phillips, asserting that "he was a man of ungovernable temper."[6]

While the British had won a decisive victory, the militia had proved that it could stand and fight, mounting an orderly defense of unquestioned bravery. The Virginians suffered about one hundred killed, wounded, and captured, while the British reported that their losses were considerably lighter. Steuben sarcastically explained the retreat to Major General Nathanael Greene in South Carolina, writing, "I must confess I have not yet learnt how to beat regular troops with one third their number of militia." He asked to join Greene "as soon as possible, for never was a man more disgusted than I am at the conduct and proceedings in this quarter."[7]

The British occupied Petersburg for a day and then marched north. Phillips took a force to Chesterfield Court House, where he burned 160 log cabins that had served as militia barracks. Arnold headed back to the James River, intent on destroying the remnants of the Virginia navy.

THE SAILORS OF THE VIRGINIA NAVY gathered their ships in a semi-circle near the shoreline at Osborne's Landing, determined to stop a British fleet from heading up the James River to Richmond. Commodore James Maxwell went aboard the ships to count hands. He was appalled by what he found. The largest ships should have had a combined total of 590 sailors, but Maxwell counted only 78. The sixteen-gun *Tempest,* for example, had only 6 men; it was supposed to have 120. Other ships were in a similarly woeful state. Maxwell dashed off a letter to Jefferson, providing him with a list of the deficient man-power and warning that the fleet needed cartridge paper for its guns. A militia force occupied the opposite side of the river. It was hoped that together the Virginia fleet and the militia would halt the British advance to Richmond.[8]

Arnold learned about the location of the fleet with guidance from a Loyalist informant and marched to within sight of the remains of Virginia's navy— 9 large vessels and at least 11 smaller craft, with a combined 126 cannons. Hoping to capture some of the ships as prizes, he sent the Virginians a message in which he urged their surrender. Maxwell responded that he was "determined to defend it to the last Extremity" and would sink with his ships rather than surrender.[9] But the Virginians were in no position for such bravado. They were proceeding on the assumption that they could interrupt the enemy as they tried to sail upriver. Arnold, however, knew the contour of the river and its banks and intended to surprise the navy from the shore.

Arnold ordered four brass cannons taken to the riverbank, within a hundred feet of the Virginia ships. At first it appeared the Virginia ships had the upper hand, as the twenty-six-gun *Renown,* the twenty-gun *Tempest,* and the fourteen-gun brigantine *Jefferson* began firing at the British forces. The militiamen on the opposite shore tried to join in the battle, but they were too far out of range. Arnold's men had the advantage of position. Wheeling artillery to a bluff overlooking the river, the British easily rained shots at the Virginia vessels. The Virginia sailors could not adjust their cannons at a sharp enough angle to return fire effectively. Meanwhile, British soldiers crept through the woods and set up sniper positions, firing at Virginia sailors as they scrambled to defend their vessels. The decisive blow of the battle came when a shot from a British cannon struck a cable on the *Tempest,* turning the ship about and exposing it to attack. The small crew of the *Tempest* had no choice but to abandon the ship. As Arnold's men took over the *Tempest,* using it as a platform to attack other vessels, crews on the other Virginia ships fled amid the hail of cannon and rifle gunfire.

On one ship, the *Jefferson,* crew members valiantly worked to prevent Virginia's best remaining vessels from falling into the hands of the British. As cannonballs hit the decks and bullets whistled through the air, First Lieutenant Richard O'Brien ordered his crew to set fire to as many ships in the fleet as possible. A young sailor, Andrew Monroe, was sent to torch the vessels. With the men on the *Jefferson* protecting his movements with covering fire, Monroe went aboard several of the abandoned ships and lit fuses that exploded caches of gunpowder. As the ships of Virginia's navy went up in flames, Monroe raced back to perform his final, sad task: the destruction of his brig, the *Jefferson.* The ship named for the author of the Declaration of Independence and governor of Virginia was blown up in a spectacular fire, gunpowder exploding, masts crashing into the river, as Monroe scrambled overboard and escaped to the opposite shore.[10]

The battle turned quickly into a rout. In the end, the British seized twelve ships loaded with tobacco, flour, and other goods, while at least nine other vessels were sunk or burnt. The entire Virginia fleet had been captured or destroyed without the loss of a single British soldier. Ironically, one of the Virginia vessels, the *Louis,* had been captained by Beesly Edgar Joel, who had proposed the plot to capture or kill Arnold by setting the British general's ship on fire.[11] Now Joel watched as Virginia's sailors sent their own ships up in flames as a result of Arnold's devastating attack.

JEFFERSON WAS TWENTY MILES up the river in Richmond, dealing with yet another crisis. A series of riots had taken place in western Hampshire County, where the men were refusing to submit to a draft or pay taxes for militia supplies. Riots against drafts and taxes had been taking place for months, but this one had grown to hundreds of protesters. It was the sort of crisis that, some weeks earlier, Jefferson would have responded to by saying that he couldn't force the execution of orders if men refused to obey them. The events of recent days—from the death of his daughter to the knowledge that Phillips and Arnold had a combined force that could overwhelm Virginia—had hardened the governor. He could not rely on his councilors or the legislators, most of whom had long since fled. Jefferson seemed to have an epiphany, a new understanding of his executive role. Whether motivated by fear of attack on Richmond or by the encouragement of Steuben, the governor had been simultaneously emboldened and outraged. The mutineers of Hampshire County, Jefferson wrote, "must be subdued. Laws made by common consent must not be trampled on by Individuals." Jefferson, the revolutionary leader, would no longer tolerate rebellion among the men who were supposed to be fighting for Virginia and the greater cause of freedom.

Jefferson advised the county militia leader, Garret Van Meter, to avoid going against the mutineers all at once in daylight and risk "an open Rebellion or bloodshed." Instead, the governor provided a rather chilling order: "Go and take them out of their Beds, singly and without Noise." If they were not found the first time, Jefferson continued, "go again and again so that they may never be able to remain in quiet at home."[12]

Meanwhile, as Jefferson tried to prepare Richmond for another British attack, a series of letters demonstrated how far he had come since he and Phillips had assured each other that they would never let the war injure their personal friendship. Phillips had alleged that Virginians aboard a ship bearing a truce flag had fired on his men. If it continued, he warned, he would exact the "severest punishment" on the "towns and villages [that] lay at the mercy of the king's troops" and could be "reduced to ashes." Moreover, if any Loyalist was executed by Virginians, Phillips would "make the shores of James River an example of terror to the rest of Virginia."[13] Jefferson learned about the threat, which he called "intolerably insolent and haughty," and insisted the truce flag had never been violated. At the same time, Jefferson was upset that Phillips addressed him in a letter as the "American Governor of Virginia," suggesting that Virginia was still a colony. In response, Jefferson addressed his former dining companion as the commander of "the British forces in the Commonwealth of Virginia," emphasizing that Virginia was a commonwealth, not a colony. "Personally knowing him to be the proudest man of the proudest nation on earth, I well knew he would not open this letter," Jefferson explained to Virginia's delegates in Congress. He then sent a letter to one of Phillips's subordinates informing him that no provisions would be allowed for the British prisoners until Phillips opened the first letter. Jefferson believed that would force Phillips to swallow "this pill of retaliation" or make "an apology for his rudeness."[14] If Phillips's rudeness continued, Jefferson said, "all Intercourse shall be discontinued."

PHILLIPS AND ARNOLD LINKED THEIR FORCES near Osborne's Landing and marched them up the southern bank of the James River toward Richmond. They expected the capital to be undefended and hoped to seize the capital before the Continental army arrived. The British did not realize that Lafayette and his 1,200 men had just completed a swift march from Alexandria, barely in time to meet the advance of the British. Unable to obtain enough horses, Lafayette had decided that he had no choice other than to leave behind his artillery and wagons. The decision would prove crucial. Had he waited for horses, Richmond would have been lost, he wrote.[15]

As the British arrived from the south and entered Manchester, across the James from Richmond, Lafayette came from the north and set up camp in the capital. For a short time on the evening of April 29, the leaders of the opposing forces faced each other from across the river.

James Johnston, a Continental soldier from Pennsylvania, was invited to join Lafayette for dinner at a small log house just below the falls at Richmond, at a ferry landing. Johnston's place at the table gave him a view across the James. As the party began its meal, Johnston "called attention to the fact that Generals

Phillips and Arnold had advanced along the beach and were making an examination with the spyglass whilst their servants held their horses," he recalled. At
that moment, five Virginia militiamen, wearing hunting shirts and moccasins,
approached Lafayette. They, too, had seen the British generals. They asked
Lafayette for permission to go down to the shoreline. With their steady aim,
they "felt sure they could pick off these officers."

This was the kind of opportunity that Jefferson had been hoping for. Here
was a group of frontiersmen, who could shoot a squirrel off a branch in a dense
forest, asking for permission to take a shot at the greatest traitor of the war
and his British commander. While all Americans had more than ample reason
to want Arnold killed, Lafayette had his own reasons for wanting to go after
Phillips: twenty-two years earlier, Lafayette's father had been killed at Minden
in northern Germany in a battle overseen by Phillips. Now Lafayette was presented with a chance to take out Arnold and Phillips in a stroke that could
change the war in Virginia.

But the Frenchman believed that certain rules of war must be followed. "The
marquis refused his sanction, declaring that he would meet the enemy openly
in the field but would authorize nothing like assassination," Johnston said years
later, while making his pension application. "This refusal excited great dissatisfaction" among Lafayette's dining companions. Lafayette's decision was final,
nonetheless.[16]

On the following morning, as Phillips once again surveyed Richmond
through his spyglass, he was surprised to see enemy forces taking up positions
on the heights. A probing charge by six hundred British soldiers across the
James River was pushed back by a small band of mounted militia, who forced
the enemy "into their boats with precipitation."[17] Phillips was nonetheless preparing to give the signal for a full-scale attack when he looked with "astonishment" at what appeared to be an enormous gathering of American forces.
Lafayette had spread Continental soldiers and militiamen along Shockoe Hill,
making them seem like a larger force. Phillips "flew into a violent passion and
swore vengeance" against Lafayette. Unsure of the size of Lafayette's force,
Phillips felt he could not risk an attack so far from his base. Instead, he set fire
to the tobacco warehouses in Manchester as he ordered his troops to head
south, back to Petersburg.[18]

Jefferson's fortunes had changed in the course of these few hours. Lafayette's
men were arrayed along the heights on which the governor's townhouse was
situated, giving him a sense of security that he had lacked for four months. The
governor sent a triumphant letter to legislators, telling them that Lafayette's
Continental troops and the militia had "put these cowardly plunderers under

way down the River." He hoped that legislators could soon meet again in Richmond, assuring them that the capital was "perfectly secure."[19]

Shortly after the British departed, Lafayette and Steuben held a grand review of their troops, which marched in parade on a plain near the capital. The smartly uniformed soldiers of the Continental army stood shoulder to shoulder with the rugged militia, some wearing the traditional hunting shirts, while the marquis and the baron performed the inspection. Having secured Jefferson's confidence, Lafayette then took command of forces in the state. Steuben, knowing his relations with Virginia's leaders were beyond repair, hoped to join General Nathanael Greene in the Carolinas.

The reality, however, was that the British had retreated because they were unaware of the weaknesses of the American forces. Phillips "had every advantage over me," Lafayette confided days later to Washington. The Frenchman was disgusted by the poor shape of Virginia's militia, on which he put "little dependence." He had "no boat, no wagons, no intelligence, not one spy." He had of course left most of his artillery behind in order to arrive speedily at Richmond. Lafayette was successful because he appeared at the most propitious moment on the Richmond side of the river and placed his troops on the heights, intimidating the British from crossing the James. Had Lafayette arrived on the Manchester side of the river, he acknowledged, Phillips would have "given me the slip, and taken Richmond, leaving to me nothing but the reputation of a rash, inexperienced young man."[20]

Phillips, meanwhile, believed he needed reinforcements in order to retain control of Virginia. The question was whether Lord Cornwallis was fed up with fighting in South Carolina and would unite with Phillips and Arnold to create an unstoppable force in Virginia.

Bring Our Whole Force into Virginia

AS JEFFERSON URGED LEGISLATORS to return to the "perfectly secure" capital of Richmond, the British fleet headed east on the James River, carrying a very ill passenger back to the fort at Portsmouth. General Phillips had a "teazing indisposition," which first surfaced two days after he had left Richmond. Four days later, the commander of British forces in Virginia was so unwell that he could not take up his own pen. Then a messenger arrived with an urgent plea from Lord Cornwallis, who had encountered a series of setbacks in South Carolina. After weeks of suggesting that the war could be won in Virginia, Cornwallis was acting upon his impulse and heading north. He wrote that he hoped to join with Phillips in Petersburg. Their combined force of seven thousand would overwhelm Virginia, even with the added forces of Lafayette and the expected reinforcements of another Continental unit.

Phillips read the letter from Cornwallis as he lay in the hospital quarters of his flagship, the *Maria*. With the vessel anchored off Burwell's Ferry, near Williamsburg, Phillips dictated an enthusiastic response on the morning of May 6. He would reverse course and head immediately west to Petersburg, where it would give him "infinite satisfaction" to join with Cornwallis.[1]

Along the shoreline, Virginia scouts who had been tracking the movement of the British fleet dashed back to Richmond, warning that Phillips and Arnold might return. Around this time, two members of the Governor's Council resigned and a third declined to accept an appointment, prompting Jefferson to plead with other councilors to remain in their posts to provide a quorum. Then, at the very moment that Jefferson desperately needed help from the Assembly, the legislators failed him. He had written a lengthy letter to the Assembly in which he laid out the losses incurred during the invasion and proposed some suggestions for forestalling another attack. However, he had emphasized that the question of how more "insults and losses" could be prevented was "fit for the wise Discussion of the General Assembly." But there was to be no such discussion, wise or otherwise. Most legislators were afraid even to come to Richmond.[2]

There was plenty to distract them. For starters, their constituents were being hit anew by economic problems. Virginia, which produced 70 percent of America's tobacco exports, went from shipping 100 million pounds of the crop to Britain in 1775 to about 2 million pounds per year during the main years of the war. Many farmers, from the largest plantation owner to the small tenant, switched to other crops, such as corn, wheat, and cotton, and sold the surplus to the state, which needed the goods to supply soldiers. In York County, for example, 230 property owners or planters—perhaps two-thirds of those in the county—submitted claims for the sale of goods to the state. Given that twenty thousand soldiers would eventually descend on the county, the army's need for food from local farmers was exceptionally high. But farmers often were paid for goods with state certificates that could take years to redeem.[3]

Meanwhile, legislators learned about escalating protests against serving in the Continental army. A number of legislators reported that local men—some of whom had no objection to serving in the local militia—were once again refusing to submit to the draft for the national forces. In western Augusta County, a band of armed men told local officials that they were "cheerfully willing to Spend their hearts blood" in defense of Virginia but would "Suffer Death before they would be Drafted 18 months from their families and made Regular Soldiers of," an Augusta official, George Moffett, wrote to Jefferson. Another official wrote that the protests could not be stopped unless some men were hanged as "examples to the rest."[4] In nearby Rockbridge County, in southwestern Virginia, a hundred men stormed the courthouse and seized the table on which draft papers had lain, swearing that they would serve in the militia but not in the Continental army. A Rockbridge official, Samuel McDowell, wrote to Jefferson that if such acts were allowed to continue, "Government is destroyed and we are [entirely] ruined."[5]

Jefferson's immediate priority, however, was to get militia to turn out and halt the approach of Cornwallis, who was believed to be marching toward Richmond. Jefferson wrote to the militia leader of Prince Edward County, seventy-two miles southwest of the capital, beseeching him to "call every man into the field for whom arms can be procured."[6] With the acute need for militia, the effort to simultaneously draft men for the Continental army was allowed to flounder in many counties, which meant that Virginia provided only one-fourth of the 3,250 men the state had pledged to provide to the federal forces.[7] In many cases, local officials reluctantly decided they had no choice but to treat the protesters leniently, given the need for militia turnout.

Despite Virginia's failure to provide enough draftees to the national army, Jefferson now pleaded with Washington about the importance of sending Continental army forces to Virginia, writing that there were not enough armed militia to face the enemy armies that he feared were heading toward the capital.

Desperate to stop the approaching British, Jefferson suspended the Continental army draft in some counties in order to bring out more militia. The orders did not reach some areas amidst the mayhem of the invasion.

There was an obvious solution to Jefferson's shortage of manpower. A number of state officials and military leaders suggested that more black Virginians, free and enslaved, serve in the militia and Continental army. While the British were enticing slaves to rebel against their masters, either by joining the king's army or simply by fleeing to freedom, only a small number of blacks served on the side of the revolutionaries in Virginia.

By one estimate, about half of the one thousand free blacks in Virginia during the Revolutionary War went into military service, along with perhaps one hundred slaves, most of whom served as substitutes for their masters. Free blacks could be armed, but Virginia law forbade the arming of slaves, although this restriction was sometimes overlooked. Virginia's navy, which had a hard time recruiting whites, allowed blacks to constitute up to one-third of seamen and valued them as being particularly knowledgeable about the state's waterways. In one case, a master named William Hinton sent his slave, Lewis Hinton, to serve as his substitute in the navy. Lewis Hinton served for four years on the *Dragon,* including heroic duty in at least two battles with British warships, and he was later awarded a pension for his service.[8]

The most famous black to serve in Virginia during the revolution was James Armistead, who was employed by Lafayette, for whom he worked as a spy. At great personal risk, Armistead fled to the British force of Lord Cornwallis, saying that he had escaped his master, and brought back vital intelligence to Lafayette. For his service, Armistead was emancipated by the Virginia legislature, but it took nearly forty years for him to receive a pension.[9]

Among those who proposed that slaves be allowed to serve in Virginia's military was James Madison, Jefferson's close friend and a Virginia delegate to Congress. Learning of legislation that would give a slave to whites willing to serve in the Continental army for the duration of the war, Madison asked, "Would it not be as well to liberate and make soldiers at once of the blacks themselves as to make them instruments for enlisting white Soldiers?" Madison pointedly added that such a policy "would certainly be more consonant to the principles of liberty which ought never be lost sight of in a contest for liberty."[10]

Madison's proposal was rejected in late 1780, shortly before Arnold's invasion. But by May 1781, with thousands of British forces roaming the state and Jefferson facing a woeful shortage of Virginians turning out in defense, a courageous militia commander revived Madison's idea. Major Alexander Dick, who saw little chance of filling his units with whites, urged that slaves be required to serve, with the state giving compensation to their masters. "The men will be equal to any," Dick wrote.[11]

Dick's proposal went nowhere in a government that was dominated by slaveholders, including Jefferson, who had no interest in letting go of valuable slaves whom they had trained for a lifetime of forced labor on their plantations. Thus was lost one of the great opportunities of the revolution; had Virginia led the way on setting a path toward freedom for slaves, the rest of the South might have fallen in line. Instead, the revolution in Virginia would solidify the sanctioning of slavery.

At the same time that the proposal to put slaves into military service was rejected, Jefferson was asked to intervene in the case of a slave named William, who had been sentenced to death for conspiring with the British. William was a slave of one of the wealthiest men in Virginia, John Tayloe, whose family owned a great estate called Mount Airy, located about fifty miles northeast of Richmond. William, described as standing nearly six feet tall, with "a remarkable swing in his walk," had escaped from the Tayloe family in 1774, when he was twenty years old. Now, seven years later, he was caught in early April on a ship carrying British forces in Virginia. Recognized as the former slave of the Tayloe family, he was brought to trial, accused of traitorously waging war against Virginia.

A panel of six judges heard William swear that he was not guilty of treason. He explained he had been on shore near Alexandria when a British vessel trying to escape an attack by Virginians took him into service. He was, he swore, "forced on board against his will and that he never took up Arms against the Country . . . of his own free will." A majority of the judges dismissed William's defense, convicted him of treason, and sentenced him to hang. Moreover, the court said, the execution should be used as example to other slaves who dared to fight for their liberty. William's head was to be "severed from his body and stuck up at some public cross road on a pole." The Tayloe estate was to be reimbursed for William's value, which the court determined to be £27,000.

But two of the six judges issued a remarkable dissent. William could not be convicted of treason, they argued, because a slave was not a citizen. "A slave in our opinion Cannot Commit Treason against the State" because he had not been "Admitted to the Privileges of a Citizen [and thus] owes the State No Allegiance," judges Henry Lee and William Carr wrote.[12]

The case laid bare the inconsistencies in the laws regarding slavery. Having refused to grant a slave the rights of citizenship, how could the state expect him to follow the rules imposed on citizens? The case landed on Jefferson's desk when the governor received an appeal from the Tayloe family to prevent

William's execution. Jefferson granted William a reprieve until the end of June in order to give the legislature time to consider the case.[13] A legislative committee then found that the proceedings against William were "illegal" and that it would be "reasonable" to pardon him, a view adopted by a joint resolution of the Assembly. William's life was spared. The record leaves unclear whether William was returned to the Tayloe family to resume his life as a slave, though that may well have been the outcome.[14]

Sixteen years earlier, Jefferson had been in Williamsburg—on his way to hear Patrick Henry deliver a speech at the Capitol—on the day that the bodies of three slaves hung from a gallows for the alleged crime of a minor theft. Such hangings had troubled Jefferson, who believed that a slave might be excused from taking some from a master who had taken so much from him. While Jefferson supported the hanging of a person convicted of treason, William's case may have troubled him. Weeks after playing a role in sparing William's life, Jefferson wrote that he was proud that not a single execution for treason had taken place during seven years of war in Virginia. He attributed the lack of such executions to the state's "lenity" and, ignoring the various insurrections, what he called the "unanimity of its inhabitants" against the British.[15]

WITH SO MANY LEGISLATORS afraid to travel to Richmond, Jefferson decided the Assembly would meet elsewhere. Even that sensible measure could not be immediately adopted. The clerk of the House of Delegates recorded that a session was to be held on May 7 for the purpose of discussing whether to leave Richmond for a safer location. Therein lay a conundrum: so few members dared go to Richmond that the required quorum could not be reached to vote to abandon Richmond. The same happened on May 8 and 9, as House records noted: "The number not being sufficient to proceed to business, the House adjourned."

Finally, on May 10, as Virginia's leaders became increasingly concerned that Phillips and Arnold would join with Cornwallis and attack the capital at any moment, formality was tossed aside. The House clerk hurriedly wrote: "Information being given to the House, of the approach of an hostile army of the enemy towards this place . . . *It is resolved,* That this House be adjourned until Thursday the 24th instant, then to meet at the town of Charlottesville, in the county of Albemarle."[16]

Jefferson, who later would be accused by enemies of cowardice during the invasion, in fact remained in Richmond even as many other government leaders refused to show up. He rode back and forth from Richmond to the Tuckahoe estate where his wife and children were staying. Responding to a letter from Lafayette, who complained about the turnout of Virginia troops, Jefferson argued that his hands were tied due to the absence of the legislature. "I shall candidly acknowledge that it is not in my power to do anything more than to represent to the General Assembly that unless they can provide more effectually for the execution of the laws it will be vain to call on militia," Jefferson wrote, falling back once again on his insistence that he lacked the executive power to force Virginians to show up for duty.[17] His striking phrase "not in my power to do anything" would be cited by those who believed that Jefferson had been wrong to demand that Virginia have weak executive power. Whether the complaint had merit or not, the failure in Virginia went beyond Jefferson's lack of authority; legislators, councilors, and thousands of draft resisters shared the blame. Despite the failures, Jefferson remained convinced that the Continental army and the militia would combine to save Virginia, even if he had to flee Richmond for the relative safety of Charlottesville. The capital, it turned out, was spared for the moment by British strategy. Phillips and Arnold were headed not to Richmond but south to Petersburg to join Lord Cornwallis.

CORNWALLIS HAD ARRIVED the year before in South Carolina, accompanied by his favorite young officer, Lieutenant Colonel Banastre Tarleton. Both were convinced they could turn the tide of the war there. Cornwallis, forty-two years old, a veteran of numerous battles and one of the most respected men in Britain, was the very embodiment of nobility. Born in London's Grosvenor Square, he was the son of an earl, the brother of an admiral, and the nephew of the Archbishop of Canterbury. As a member of the House of Lords, he had opposed such measures as the Stamp Act, which precipitated the American rebellion, but had dutifully accepted several top military positions after it had erupted into war, finally becoming the southern commander in 1780.

Tarleton, twenty-six, had a reputation for being charming with women and ruthless with enemies. Born in Liverpool, the son of a wealthy merchant, he was educated at Oxford. At nineteen he inherited a sizable fortune upon his father's death, but lost most of it within a year due to gambling. His mother purchased a commission for him in the British cavalry and in 1776 he went to America. He rose quickly and captured General Charles Lee in Basking Ridge, New Jersey. Cornwallis and Tarleton had a relationship that seemed akin to that of father and son. Referring to one of Tarleton's strategic decisions, Cornwallis said that it "was too brilliant to need any comment of mine." Tarleton was similarly effusive about Cornwallis.[18]

In May 1780, Cornwallis had been a leader of the British siege of Charleston that led to the surrender of 5,500 American soldiers, including 1,400 from Virginia. He had ordered Tarleton to go after a nearby force of 350 Virginians led by Colonel Abraham Buford. Catching up to the Virginians at Waxhaws, near the border of North Carolina, Tarleton sent a message urging Buford to surrender or "the blood be upon your head." Buford responded that he would defend himself "to the last extremity." But after firing commenced, the Virginians hoisted the flag of truce.

At this point, according to Tarleton's account, his horse was shot from under him, pinning him. His troops believed Tarleton had been targeted during the truce, so they launched an attack against the Virginians. "Slaughter was commenced" before Tarleton could remount, he wrote later in his defense of the action. Tarleton estimated British losses at 5 men, compared to at least 113 American dead; Cornwallis later said 172 of the Virginians were killed.[19] As word of the slaughter spread, Tarleton gained a reputation for being the most savage officer in the British army, earning the epithet nickname "Bloody Ban" and prompting Americans to charge that he gave no quarter to cries for mercy. But in British eyes, a fear of Tarleton was helpful if it prompted Americans to flee. Cornwallis said the British victories had caused "inhabitants from every quarter" to "declare their allegiance to the King."[20] In any event, the surrender of 1,400 Virginians at Charleston and the defeat of Buford's force deprived the Old Dominion of some of its best soldiers at a time when the war was heading inexorably toward Virginia.

Three months later, the Americans suffered another defeat as Cornwallis and Tarleton played leading roles in a battle at Camden, South Carolina. The American force, led by Horatio Gates and including a regiment of 700 Virginia militia, had 3,700 men, compared to Cornwallis's force of 2,100. The British won a decisive victory because Tarleton's veteran cavalry corps cut through the ill-equipped and inexperienced American units. Gates took flight along with some militia units and the battle turned into a catastrophe, with 1,000 killed or wounded Americans, compared to 68 British dead and 245 wounded. "There never was a more complete victory," Cornwallis wrote, while ordering that anyone who switched from being a Loyalist to joining the rebels "should be immediately hanged."[21]

When an "extremely mortified" Jefferson learned that a Virginia militia unit had been among those that fled, he wrote a letter to the unit's commanding officer, General Edward Stevens, expressing his sadness "at our late misfortune, which sits the heavier on my mind as being produced by my own countrymen." Then, in classic Jeffersonian style, he said he preferred to "look forward" and promised to send Virginia militiamen to South Carolina. Despite protest from some who argued was that the militia was being misused as a federal force due to the failure of Virginia to draft enough men for the Continental army, the General Assembly approved sending 2,500 men to join Continental forces in South Carolina. Jefferson justified the action by arguing that Virginians who were sent to South Carolina would keep the battle from being fought in Virginia.[22] His confidence in the militia was challenged when four hundred members of the Virginia unit who had survived Camden deserted and attempted to return home. Jefferson ordered local officials to seize anyone who tried to leave the service, as well as to strengthen efforts to call up more militia. Both moves would spark insurrections across parts of Virginia just as British invasion forces were gathering.

Cornwallis next prepared to meet with a detachment of Loyalist troops led by a British officer named Patrick Ferguson. Before the two commanders could link up, a force of local militiamen surrounded Ferguson's Loyalists at Kings Mountain. When some of the Loyalists offered to surrender, the militia charged forward with the cry that no prisoners should be taken, yelling, "Tarleton's quarter! . . . Remember Waxhaws! . . . . Give 'em Tarleton's quarter!" The 900 militia troops overwhelmed the 1,100 Loyalists, but the shooting continued. When the battle was over, at least 157 members of the Loyalist force were dead, including Captain Ferguson, 163 were wounded, and 698 were captured. The local militia had twenty-eight killed and sixty-four wounded. The militia leaders hung nine Loyalists from oak trees, forcing other Loyalists to watch the grisly scene by the light of flaming pine branches.[23] The defeat of the Loyalists at Kings Mountain on October 7, 1780, prompted Cornwallis to retreat to South Carolina. Four months later, Tarleton was routed in a battle at Cowpens, South Carolina, where the English dead were estimated at six hundred, compared to fewer than one hundred for the Americans. It was Tarleton's worst defeat, and the young cavalry leader probably survived in his post only because Cornwallis staunchly defended him. Then, on March 15, 1781, Cornwallis led an army of 1,900 against an American force of 4,500 at Guilford Courthouse in North Carolina. While Cornwallis forced the American general Nathanael Greene to retreat, the British had one-quarter of their men killed or wounded, making it only a Pyrrhic victory.[24]

The battles demoralized the British, especially the American rout at Kings Mountain, which had been dominated by militiamen. Jefferson later said the "joyful annunciation" of the victory was "the turn of the tide of success which terminated the Revolutionary War with the seal of our Independence." Jefferson's newfound confidence in the militia was soon to be tested.[25]

Cornwallis, deeply frustrated in the Carolinas, decided that the key to win-ning the war was to control Virginia. "I cannot help expressing my wishes that the Chesapeake may become the seat of war, even (if necessary) at the expense of abandoning New York," Cornwallis wrote to Henry Clinton, the British commander in New York. "Until Virginia is in a manner subdued, our hold of the Carolinas must be difficult, if not precarious."[26]

Cornwallis dashed off a letter about his plans to General Phillips. Corn-wallis and Phillips had served together for more than two decades. Cornwallis once helped Phillips with a personal problem as well. Phillips had had a rela-tionship with a married woman named Lady Elizabeth Browne Braithewaite. This relationship produced at least four "bastard" children, at least one of whom was conceived while Lady Elizabeth was married and the three others after she was divorced. Cornwallis used his influence to ensure that the four children were given legal status as Phillips's legitimate offspring and heirs, and Corn-wallis helped at least two of the children attain high positions in the British military.[27] When Cornwallis wrote to Phillips, he therefore did so with the greatest confidence in the security of their relationship.

"Now, my dear Friend, what is our Plan?" Cornwallis wrote. "Without one we cannot succeed & I assure you that I am quite tired of marching about the Country in quest of adventure." He went on to argue that bringing "our whole force into Virginia" could lead to a battle that "may give us America."[28]

"I perfectly agree with you," Phillips replied, although he worried about the impact such a move would have on British defenses elsewhere in the colonies. But Cornwallis had decided. After years of promises that American Loyalists would join with the British, he was convinced that the numbers of such men "are not so great as has been represented" and that their allegiance was only passive. The "most solid plan," Cornwallis wrote to Lord George Germain on April 18, was "a serious attempt upon Virginia." It was notable that Virginia was supplying reinforcements to the Carolinas even "whilst General Arnold was in the Chesapeake." That was proof, Cornwallis continued, that "small expedi-tions do not frighten that powerful province."[29]

So Cornwallis and Tarleton headed to Virginia, planning to hook up with Phillips and Arnold and form an unstoppable force. To Cornwallis, it was the perfect opportunity: Virginia was the most populous and powerful state, yet its governor and many of its citizens were on the run. Cutting off Virginia would stop the supply of arms, food, and men to American forces in the South. Were Virginia brought under British domination, Cornwallis believed, the rest of the colonies would submit.

BANASTRE TARLETON'S TROOPS of horseback dragoons had crossed the Roanoke River, heading toward the meeting of the British forces at Petersburg, when Lord Cornwallis caught up with him. Cornwallis arrived on horseback with six mounted troops serving as his guard and called a halt to Tarleton's march. Some local "country people" were then brought forward. Cornwallis ordered Tarleton's soldiers to dismount and form rank. The local people walked down the line of soldiers and picked out two, a sergeant and a private. The pair was accused of rape and robbery, crimes allegedly committed the previous night. The soldiers were removed from the ranks and in short order sentenced to death. The sentence, Tarleton wrote, "exhibited to the army and manifested to the country the discipline and justice of the British general."[30] The British force resumed its march to Petersburg.

As Cornwallis headed north, he wondered why he had not received any response to his latest coded messages to Phillips. Unbeknownst to Cornwallis, Phillips was going in and out of consciousness as he was being carried in a horse-drawn wagon to Petersburg. Once again, the British established headquarters at Bollingbrook, and yet again Mary Bolling and her four daughters were sequestered. Lafayette, learning of the British movements, marched near Petersburg and ordered his artillery men to fire into the town. Accounts vary about the next three days of Phillips's life. He was described in one report as being comatose. But another report said that when one of Lafayette's cannonballs struck Bollingbrook, killing a slave woman, the general was alert enough to protest, "Won't they let me die in peace?" On May 13, Phillips succumbed to his illness. The disease variously was described as a fever, typhus, or inflammation of the ear. Some speculated that he had died of hard drinking; others that he was poisoned by a jealous Arnold. In any case, the renowned artillery officer of the Battle of Minden, a man who was both a friend and enemy to Jefferson, was buried in a hastily constructed wooden coffin in an unmarked grave in enemy territory on the hillside cemetery at Blandford Church. The slave woman killed in the cannonade of Bollingbrook was said to have been put on top of Phillips's coffin to throw off any effort to unearth his body. Johann von Ewald spoke for many in the British service when he wrote in his diary that "every honest officer must grieve in his heart for the loss of this excellent man." Ewald seemed equally distraught that the death of one of Britain's most respected generals meant that Benedict Arnold would again assume command, at least until Cornwallis arrived.[31]

Cornwallis learned of his friend's death shortly before reaching Petersburg. "You will easily conceive how sensible an affliction it was to me, on entering this province, to receive an account of the death of my friend, General Phillips, whose loss I cannot sufficiently lament," Cornwallis wrote to Clinton. Nonetheless, Cornwallis assured Clinton that he would move ahead, even as he said he was "in the utmost distress for want of arms, clothing, boots, and indeed, appointments of all kind."[32]

Cornwallis was concerned that Lafayette would rush to attack the forces that had been under Phillips's command, but in fact Lafayette believed that he would be "cut to pieces" if he engaged them in a major battle, so he kept at a distance while Cornwallis and Tarleton entered Petersburg.[33] There was now a massive British presence in Virginia—seven thousand men, as well as many freed slaves and camp followers who attended to the troops. The forces included those of Cornwallis and Tarleton, of course, and those that had been under the command of Phillips and Arnold. Cornwallis had "brilliant hopes of a glorious campaign," Tarleton wrote.[34]

On May 24, this massive army crossed the James River and headed for a familiar refuge: the estate of Mary Willing Byrd. The British loaded wagons, cannons, and supplies on flatboats, while many of the horses swam the river, harnessed with ropes and guided by skilled sailors in accompanying vessels. The British army stretched across the James for more than a mile, working against a high wind, to make the journey to Westover. "The swimming went very well," Cornwallis wrote, referring to the difficult task of shepherding the horses across the river.[35]

IT WAS DURING THIS MASSIVE TRANSFER of men, horses, and ships that a soldier managed to walk away from the British force. John Champe, the Virginian whom Washington had sent on the mission to capture Benedict Arnold, had spent five months waiting for the chance to escape. Now, as thousands of British soldiers converged around Petersburg, Champe slipped away. He headed to the western mountains to avoid British patrols, then turned south, into the Carolinas, eventually returning to his unit commanded by Harry Lee. Champe's story soon became known to Lee's corps, which showed their "love and respect" for Champe's "daring" adventure, Lee wrote years later in his memoir. Champe was eventually sent up the chain of command, first to General Nathanael Greene, the southern commander, and then to George Washington himself, according to later accounts by Champe and Lee. Washington congratulated Champe for his efforts and paid him a reward but insisted on discharging him from service. Washington was concerned that if Champe were to be captured by the British and recognized as a spy, "he was sure to die on a gibbet," Lee wrote. Washington's discharge may have saved Champe's life, but it also ended his ability to serve in the military. Champe's story would not become publicly well known until the publication of Lee's memoir twenty-eight years later.[36]

CORNWALLIS QUARTERED HIS HORSES at Westover and gave his troops two days of much-needed rest. After establishing his headquarters at the great mansion, Cornwallis drew up battle plans against the Virginia militia and the Continental Army leader, Lafayette. Mary Byrd was told to remain upstairs at Westover, where she looked through a window at Cornwallis's army encamped in her fields and ruining her crops. Upon meeting with Cornwallis, Byrd complained that she had failed to gain the return of her forty-nine slaves. Cornwallis gave his solemn assurance that she would soon be compensated.

Eventually, Mary Byrd was allowed to return downstairs and tend to some wounded British officers. She was known for her medical abilities; one traveler noted that it was she who treated her slaves when they were ill. "Wounded officers of the British army were brought to her house & were nursed with humanity & kindness," one of Mary's relatives wrote in a family history, contending that these "acts of charity" were later misrepresented as conspiring with the enemy.[37]

Around the same time that Cornwallis was encamped at the Byrd estate, Benedict Arnold sailed back to New York. Various reasons were given for his departure, sickness among them. "I have consented to the request of Brigadier-general Arnold to go to New York," Cornwallis wrote to Clinton. "He conceives that your Excellency wishes him to attend you there, and his present indisposition renders him unequal to the fatigue of service." Cornwallis then alluded to a controversy over the aggressive actions of British privateers, some of whom had viewed the invasion of Virginia as an open opportunity to steal from any Virginian, regardless of loyalty. Arnold, wrote Cornwallis, would provide a report about "the horrid enormities which are committed by our privateers" and said that he wished that the acts of the privateers could be stopped because they were "very prejudicial to his Majesty's service."[38]

Tarleton also wrote about Arnold's departure, though without any mention of illness. He wrote merely that Arnold "obtained leave to return to New York, where business of consequence demanded his attention." One such matter was a proposal by Arnold to take command of an expedition to seize Philadelphia. In addition, given the dispute over Arnold's demand for half of the prizes, there were questions to be answered about plundering and his share of the profits.

The dispute would lead to months of accusations and depositions, with Arnold eventually being awarded a portion of the prizes. Even Clinton, Arnold's chief benefactor, commented to an associate that Arnold "sought to make money."[39]

With Phillips dead and Arnold departed, Cornwallis was now the undisputed British leader of about seven thousand troops. The active Virginia force was far smaller, perhaps a couple of thousand militia along with Lafayette's 1,200 Continentals. Lafayette faced an additional challenge, as he found that many Virginians were suspicious of foreigners. There had been animosity toward Steuben. Now Lafayette was in danger of being similarly rejected, a militia officer wrote, because "the people do not love Frenchmen." Lafayette nonetheless avoided a serious fracture in relations by being diplomatic and solicitous in a way that Steuben had not mastered.[40]

The Continental army promised to send help, ordering an eight-hundred-man Pennsylvania force led by General "Mad Anthony" Wayne to Virginia. But the force was constantly delayed, and Virginians began to hear rumors that northern forces were refusing to help because they felt Virginians had failed to send even half of the required men to the Continental army. Edmund Pendleton, a leading Virginian, became livid after hearing a report that the Pennsylvanians were not marching with all due speed. Instead, Pendleton heard that the Pennsylvanians were making disparaging remarks about the state, such as "Virginia was too grand" and "Let her be humbled by the Enemy."[41]

There was no doubt that some Pennsylvanians, like some Virginians, did not want to leave their home state to defend a place where some of the local people did not want to fight or even allow their horses and livestock to be used by defenders. However, the main reason for the delay was that some in Wayne's force had complained about a lack of pay, leading to a mutiny. Wayne's approach to mutiny was uncompromising. A dozen of its leaders were court-martialed and sentenced to death. Six were killed by firing squad, one was bayoneted, and the five others were hanged. The men were buried and Wayne's army resumed its march south to link up with Lafayette, the soldiers hastening forward in fear and silence.[42] The "prompt and exemplary punishment was a powerful" measure needed to restore harmony and discipline among the troops, Wayne explained to Pennsylvania officials.[43] Lafayette, unaware of the reason for the delay, anxiously awaited the arrival of Wayne's force, writing caustically, "On their arrival we shall be in a position to be beaten more decently, but at present we can only run away."[44]

Cornwallis sensed Lafayette's weakness and was anxious to engage him before Wayne's men arrived. "The boy cannot escape me," Cornwallis reportedly said of the twenty-four-year-old Frenchman. Cornwallis wrote to Clinton that he intended to dislodge Lafayette from Richmond and destroy any military supplies in the surrounding area. After that, Cornwallis said, he was investigating where to settle his troops. With Phillips's death on his mind, Cornwallis was unenthusiastic about returning to Portsmouth, which he viewed as a humid, sandy swamp that was "remarkably unhealthy." He was also considering a village on the York River, which he could fortify and defend with a large fleet. "At present I am inclined to think well of York," Cornwallis wrote of the place also known as Yorktown.[45]

JEFFERSON WAS NOW AT HIS PERCH at Monticello in preparation for the meeting of the Assembly in Charlottesville. Pouring out his fears to Washington, Jefferson urged the commander in chief himself to come to Virginia with a large force of the Continental army. Many Virginians viewed Washington as the "dernier resort"—the last hope—and "your appearance among them I say would restore full confidence of salvation." If Washington showed up and declared that the defense of Virginia was vital, Jefferson believed, any reluctance among Virginians to report for duty would change overnight, and "the difficulty would then be how to keep men out of the field." As for himself, Jefferson made clear that he had no intention of serving a third year as governor when his annual term expired in a few days. He intended to keep his "long declared resolution of relinquishing" the governorship to "abler hands" and retire "to a private station." Washington, fearing that the British forces might leave Virginia and converge on New York, replied that he could not head south.[46]

The British, meanwhile, had decided to remain in Virginia. Any Patriot who could leave the British-infested Tidewater area was on the move. Lafayette retreated from Richmond when Cornwallis's greatly superior force threatened, leaving the capital nearly deserted. As Cornwallis pushed north and west, Virginians fled ahead of him. "People are moving their Negroes, Cattle, Horse &c. from the neighbourhood of the Enemy & from the route which it is supposed they will take. The Hardships, distress & damage at this time is unspeakable," Dr. Robert Honyman wrote in his diary. The British were "very strong in horse & we are very weak."[47]

The next morning, Honyman had breakfast with Thomas Nelson Jr. Nelson confided in Honyman that he would soon lead a brigade against the British but that he was sending his own family to the western mountains. With opposing forces ready to merge near the little crossroads of Louisa, the local farmers and townspeople continued to evacuate. Honyman, while sending his best horse to safety in the mountains, resolved to remain in Hanover County, north of

Richmond. Many of his neighbors, meanwhile, followed the legislature to the presumed safety of Albemarle County.

Briefly, the spirits of the remaining locals were boosted by the best show of force that the Continental and militia forces could muster. Nelson's brigade of militia marched through Louisa around eleven in the morning, followed by the forces of General Muhlenberg, dragging some cannons with them. They were followed by Lafayette and three splendidly uniformed regiments marching with fife and drum. One local woman, inspired with patriotism, acquired a uniform and shoes for her sixteen-year-old son, dressed and buckled him, and told her child to join the American forces, reportedly saying, "Return to me with honor, or return no more!"[48]

Vastly outmanned by Cornwallis and in full retreat, Lafayette headed toward Fredericksburg, where he hoped to link up with the Pennsylvania force. The citizenry was now in full panic, realizing that even the well-armed Continentals were on the run. Honyman was appalled that the Americans had no more than sixty properly mounted horses, while the British had hundreds. He watched as the British army marched in pursuit, sending their cavalry "scouring the country in every direction for miles around." It was, the diarist concluded, "A fearful state of expectation indeed!!!"

The next morning, Lieutenant Colonel Tarleton passed by with as many as four hundred mounted troops, riding "very fast" before they stopped and "enquired the road the Marquis with his army had taken." Honyman emerged from his home long enough to ask Tarleton "to restrain his men & protect us from injury." Tarleton promised to respect private property before riding off with his force.[49]

But Tarleton soon received new orders. The British had intercepted messages that indicated that Jefferson and the legislature had headed to Charlottesville, where they planned to call out thousands of new militia. It would be Tarleton's job to stop the legislature and the governor before they could act. Cornwallis gave Tarleton a succinct order: go to Charlottesville and "disturb the assembly."[50]

Flight from Monticello

A Terrible Clatter of Horses

MONTICELLO WAS A CROWDED EIGHT-ROOM HOUSE in the midst of yet another reconstruction project when Jefferson and several senior legislators arrived in late May, in flight from the latest British takeover of Richmond. The governor, his wife, and their two daughters, along with servants and guests, crowded into rooms with unfinished, exposed brick walls and discussed the gloomy state of the revolution. Jefferson and his guests had known each other for years. They once had worked closely with the British, then turned into revolutionaries and ousted Lord Dunmore. They had all risked much to join the rebellion, and now, as they met in Jefferson's home on the mountain, they wondered if five years of war were about to end in disaster.

Speaker of the House Benjamin Harrison had fled his Berkeley estate on the James River shortly before it was ransacked by Benedict Arnold. Hundreds of British troops had been encamped at Berkeley and the neighboring estate of Westover just a week earlier. Similarly, Speaker of the Senate Archibald Cary, whom Jefferson had convinced to help finance the war, had recently learned that his James River mills had been burned to the ground by Arnold. Another guest, Thomas Nelson Jr., whose family owned a vast plantation in Yorktown, and who was also using his own depleted finances to help fund the revolution, knew that the British had briefly occupied his hometown and likely was concerned they might soon return. These men must have envied Jefferson for having what appeared to be such an isolated mountaintop home.

Many other legislators likely stopped by Monticello as well, including Patrick Henry, who had been targeted by the British for his leadership in the revolution. A number of legislators stayed within a few miles, either at one of the plantation homes in the neighborhood or at a boardinghouse in the village of Charlottesville. As the British swept from the Tidewater to the Piedmont, more legislators fled from their homes and came to Charlottesville, believing that they would be protected by the Blue Ridge's cordon of mountains. One delegate, John Breckenridge of Botetourt County, wrote to his mother: "We all fixed ourselves very comfortably, in full Assurance of being unmolested by the Enemy."[1] The legislators met in Charlottesville's small wooden courthouse and in Swan Tavern, where Jefferson sometimes dined. A number of other buildings were arrayed around the courthouse square, including a row of residences, stores, and boardinghouses.

In sessions that moved back and forth from the courthouse to the tavern, the delegates feverishly debated measures intended to strengthen the state's defenses. Speaker Harrison criticized the legislators for failing to meet for nearly two months at a time when action was desperately needed, declaring that Virginians expected "decisive measures will be taken to rid them of an implacable enemy that are now roaming at large in the very bowels of our country."[2] The legislators had hoped that the force led by Lafayette would stop the British advance toward Charlottesville. But the Frenchman had retreated from Richmond, ceding the capital region to Cornwallis, and now was about fifty miles east of Charlottesville, waiting for the arrival of "Mad Anthony" Wayne and his eight hundred men.

The British domination of Virginia was due to three factors: they had complete control of the rivers and the entrance to the Atlantic Ocean; their seven-thousand-man army was well equipped and nearly twice as large as Virginia's force; and they had a vast superiority in cavalry. These could be overcome, but it would require the arrival of the long-promised French fleet to win back the waters, the addition of Continental army reinforcements and more militiamen, and a willingness by local residents to give up their horses to Virginia forces.

While many Virginians continued to object to providing their best horses to Lafayette's army, the British had stolen "some of the most valuable Horses in the Commonwealth" and were assembling a "very formidable" cavalry, Jefferson told the Assembly. The result was that one of Virginia's great strengths had turned into an advantage for the British.[3]

William Constable, an aide to Lafayette, told the Assembly his force had sixty cavalry horses, while the British had five hundred. Worse, the mounted militia had all gone home, taking with them much-needed saddles, bridles, and other equipment.[4] The legislators, many of whom had considerable wealth tied up in expensive horses, were well aware that their policy on horse impressments was hurting Lafayette. So they inched forward, agreeing that Lafayette should be authorized to impress some horses. But there was the usual catch. "Stud horses and brood mares will always be excepted, because to take them would be to rip up the hen which laid the golden eggs," Jefferson wrote to Lafayette.[5] Jefferson tried to mollify Lafayette by ordering that stud horses and broodmares could be seized if they were not hidden from the enemy. That policy, however, in effect legitimized the already widespread practice of hiding horses. While it prevented thefts by the British, it also impeded efforts by Virginia and federal military authorities to form an effective cavalry.

As the legislators met in Charlottesville, they heard reports of new dissension in Augusta, Rockbridge, and Rockingham counties, located on the far side of the Blue Ridge Mountains. "Those mutinyous rascals in Augusta and Rock-bridge amount to a majority," a militia leader warned. Virginians were "panic struck and have lost much of their military ardor," another wrote.[6] The threat was never greater: the British were approaching from the east, and mutinies among Virginia's militias were spreading to the west.

So now, two months after rejecting Jefferson's request that tougher measures be enacted to compel militiamen to serve, the legislature finally began to act. Laying out the dire circumstances, it declared that "a powerful army of the enemy" was approaching and a defensive force "cannot now be assembled." The legislature then gave Jefferson carte blanche to call out as many militiamen as he deemed necessary "to oppose the enemy with effect," though once again it put off the difficult decision about the extent of punishment for failing to show up for duty.[7]

Even as he and the legislators held increasingly desperate deliberations about battling the British, Jefferson was devoting considerable attention to the second front—his war against Indians who were allied with the British in the west. The governor asked that legislators take time out from their session to attend a ceremony honoring an Indian who supported the Americans, Jean Baptiste Ducoigne, chief of the Kaskaskia tribe. It was a little-noticed event that, in retrospect, revealed much about Jefferson's thinking at a crucial moment.

Jefferson had diverted hundreds of militiamen to the fight against the western Indians, angering some military officials. General Nathanael Greene, the American commander in the South, believed that Jefferson's obsession with fighting Indians had left Virginia unprepared to take on the British. "History affords no instance of a nation being so engaged in conquest abroad as Virginia is at a time when all her powers were necessary to secure herself from ruin at home," Green wrote.[8] By "conquest abroad," Greene meant the territory that the British had agreed to leave to the Indians, but which Jefferson insisted was part of the United States.

Jefferson believed that the two battles were connected. If the Americans beat the British, they would win independence for the colonies as well as take over vast lands in the west claimed by Indians. Many of the revolutionary leaders, including Jefferson, Washington, and Henry, would benefit financially from the ability to fulfill their claims on Indian lands. Jefferson at one point stood to gain seventeen thousand acres. However, his ambition for the region went far beyond accumulating more land for himself.[9] He foresaw a country that expanded inexorably westward. His view toward Indians was paternalistic; he would remove them from their territories, teach them how to farm, educate them, and open up their former lands to settlement by the white man. While

Jefferson viewed the Indians as "equal to the white man" in body and mind, he was not ready to offer them citizenship. In the end, his policies would lead to the appropriation of vast lands and the decimation of many tribes, though he insisted his approach was enlightened and in the best interest of Indians.[10]

Jefferson felt deeply indebted to Ducoigne because the Kaskaskia leader was a model of his Indian policy and one of the few in the Illinois Territory allied with the United States. The mixed-blood chief had helped Jefferson's commander in the Indian wars, George Rogers Clark, by serving as an emissary to the Wabash tribe and helping to rescue Americans trapped at a fort. Ducoigne had provided men, food, and supplies to troops in fights against other tribes. For this, he was paid by the Americans, who wanted to prevent him from switching loyalty to the British. Ducoigne's "well-proved friendship of the United States earned him the hatred of all the other chiefs," observed Speaker Harrison's son, William Henry Harrison, who dealt frequently with Ducoigne.[11]

Thus, even though Ducoigne arrived in Charlottesville at the very moment that Virginia's government feared it would be overtaken by the British, Jefferson believed that Ducoigne's "rank, services, disposition and proposals are such as require attention from us and great respect." On June 1, Jefferson and the legislative leaders held an elaborate ceremony with Ducoigne. In a sign of his admiration for Virginia's governor, Ducoigne had named his son Jefferson and brought the child to the ceremony. Jefferson, in turn, brought his daughter Patsy.[12]

After smoking a peace pipe and pledging solidarity, Jefferson presented the chief with a medal imprinted with the words "Rebellion to Tyrants Is Obedience to God." Under the word "Virginia," an armor-clad woman holds a sword in her right hand and a spear in her left, while pushing her right foot into a man whose crown has dropped to the ground. On the reverse side, under the words "Happy While United," an Indian and a white officer sit together under a tree.[13] Ducoigne, in return, gave Jefferson some buffalo skins with drawings of Indian figures. Jefferson studied the drawings and promised that he would "always keep them hanging on the walls in remembrance of you and your nation." The skins may have been among those that Jefferson later displayed in his "Indian Hall" at the entrance to Monticello, part of a collection that later included works from tribes of the far west.

Then Jefferson got to the business at hand. He assured Ducoigne that Americans would remain allies with the Kaskaskia so long as the tribe did not help the British. "We, like you, are Americans, born in the same land, and having the same interests," Jefferson said. At a moment when Jefferson and the legislators themselves had fled the British, the governor assured the chief that Virginia was as strong as ever, while the enemy had become weak.

> You find us, brother, engaged in war with a powerful nation. Our forefathers were Englishmen, inhabitants of a little island beyond the great water, and being distressed for land, they came and settled here. As long as we were young and weak, the English whom we had left behind, made us carry all our wealth to their country, to enrich them; and, not satisfied with this, they at length began to say we were their slaves, and should do whatever they ordered us. We were now grown up and felt ourselves strong; we knew we were free as they were, that we came here of our own accord and not at their biddance, and were determined to be free as long as we should exist. For this reason, they made war on us.

Jefferson continued with a statement that, while brimming with bravado, was the kind of talk that he believed the Indian chief expected to hear. The British, Jefferson said, "have waged that war six years, and have not yet won more land from us than will serve to bury the warriors they have lost."

Even with the enemy practically at his door, Jefferson had an extraordinary sense of confidence about the war's outcome. Later, his critics would cite his actions during this time as those of a coward on the run. But in Jefferson's remarks to the chief, he did not sound like a man afraid of the British. To the contrary, he sounded certain that victory was inevitable. The United States had been joined by the French, the Spanish, and other nations, while "the English stand alone, without a friend to support them, hated by all mankind because they are proud and unjust." The Americans alone "have a right to maintain justice in all the lands on this side [of] the Mississippi." This was how Jefferson viewed his world at the darkest moment of the war: not a collection of former colonies about to be retaken by the British, but an ever-growing independent nation.[14]

Jefferson did not mention in his speech that the British had occupied Richmond, destroyed plantations, plundered property, and forced him and his fellow legislators to flee to Charlottesville, although Ducoigne surely knew that the British were on the march. Ducoigne's loyalty, like that of so many Indian chiefs who struck deals with American leaders, would eventually be betrayed. The once-great nation of the Kaskaskia would wither and ultimately be forced to move far from their native lands. But for now, Chief Ducoigne, carrying his little son Jefferson, was greatly impressed by the governor, who oversaw such vast lands. The chief left, carrying the medal and other gifts, just two days before the British invaders swept into the valley.

A MASSIVE BRITISH FORCE was now headed in the direction of Charlottesville. On their way, the British captured "horses, saddles & bridles . . . whatever provisions they wanted," wrote diarist Robert Honyman.[15] In the Hanover County neighborhood close to where Honyman was living, a number of gentry who had estates in the Tidewater had set up a small community near Ground Squirrel Bridge, located roughly twenty miles northwest of Richmond and right on the main road of the British invasion force. Cornwallis set up temporary headquarters at one of the homes, known as The Retreat and owned by Ann Cary Nicholas, the widow of Virginia's former colonial treasurer, Robert Carter Nicholas.

Having hidden her plates and jewels in the chimney, Ann Nicholas greeted Cornwallis with trepidation. Cornwallis was said to have "demeaned himself with courtly consideration" of her, and he or his aides convinced a child at the home to reveal where the valuables were hidden. The British troops pulled down the fences, seized the cattle, hogs, sheep, and chickens for their meals, and left "pieces of flesh all in a putrefying state scattered over the plantation." Cornwallis and his lieutenants stayed inside the house, where the ill Mrs. Nicholas also remained. The residents everywhere were "dreadfully alarmed & sending off their families, Horses & most valuable effects," wrote Honyman, who visited the Nicholas home and wrote of the devastation. The attack on the Nicholas home would later be notable for another reason: Ann Nicholas's son George would play a key role in calling for an investigation into whether Jefferson was responsible for allowing the British to invade Virginia so easily.[16]

During this time, one of the most horrific but little-noted acts of British terror took place. Two soldiers in the Queen's Rangers, the force that included Loyalist Virginians, were robbing a local home when they came upon a nine-year-old girl. According to contemporaneous journals and letters, the soldiers "ravished" the girl. The commander of the Queen's Rangers, John Graves Simcoe, investigated the incident and wrote to Cornwallis on June 2 that "I have not the least doubt but that Jonathan Webster & Lewis Terrpan . . . of the Queen's Rangers, were guilty of a rape on Jane Dickinson yesterday." After a brief trial, apparently held in the vicinity of the Nicholas estate, the two men were given an hour "to prepare for their death." By order of Cornwallis, the men were then hanged "in the presence of the whole army." Word of the crime spread quickly, further terrifying Virginians.[17]

Cornwallis, having taken all the livestock and crops from the Nicholas estate, now led most of his men toward an even greater source of plunder—Jefferson's Elk Hill plantation, located about twenty-nine miles southeast of Monticello.

Tarleton's cavalry, meanwhile, was ordered to continue on to Charlottesville to find Jefferson and the legislators.

Tarleton's Green Dragoons galloped west in a noisy, thundering herd, clearing the road of Virginians, who gathered in their homes and hiding places. Daniel Trabue, the militiaman who had fought at Petersburg, heard Tarleton's forces barreling down a nearby road. "British! British!" someone yelled, just in time for Trabue to escape. Later, he accidentally ran into some of Tarleton's men, but escaped once again, running into a dense wood.[18]

ONE OF THOSE IN FLIGHT FROM TARLETON was Eliza "Betsy" Ambler, the daughter of Rebecca Burwell, whom Jefferson had unsuccessfully courted in Williamsburg nearly three decades earlier, and Jacquelin Ambler, the treasurer of Virginia. The family had fled Richmond when Cornwallis approached the capital. While her father hid in a carriage that moved from place to place, Eliza cowered in a "miserable little hovel" in the village of Louisa Court House. Suddenly a "terrible clatter of horses" approached Eliza's hideout. Fearing it was the British, she opened the door to find "a parcel of miserable militia," which had come to warn the family that the enemy was approaching. The family fled anew, believing that "the nearer the mountains the greater the safety." They traveled through "byways and brambles" until they reached a neighborhood called Springs, where they stayed at a friend's house. No sooner had they settled upon their pallets than the owner of the house arrived, breathless, and told them that "Tarleton and his men had just passed, and would catch the Governor before he could reach Charlottesville."[19] Tarleton was indeed very close. The British force stopped at the crossroads, entering Cuckoo Tavern in Louisa, forty miles east of Charlottesville. As the soldiers ordered food and drink, they were observed by a young man who happened to be a member of the militia, Jack Jouett. Jouett stood six foot four and weighed 220 pounds, a flamboyant twenty-six-year-old who wore a feathered hat and fancied himself one of the best riders of the Blue Ridge. Jouett's father ran the Swan Tavern in Charlottesville, where legislators had been meeting and dining for several days, and was a commissary to the Continental army, selling beef from his farm. Jouett's older brother, Matthew, had been killed in 1777 in the Battle of Brandywine. Two younger brothers also served in the militia.[20]

Jouett quickly guessed Tarleton's intentions and became concerned that the legislators might be targeted. The Jouett family knew Jefferson well, not just as the master of Monticello and governor but also from having served him at the

Swan Tavern. Jouett was aware that Jefferson had returned to Monticello after hours of meetings in Charlottesville, while many of the legislators remained in the town. He decided to warn them, first going to Monticello and then heading to Charlottesville.

It had been a dark, rainy day, but now the skies cleared to reveal a bright, nearly full moon. Around 10:00 p.m., Jouett mounted his horse and took back roads and mountain trails the forty miles to Monticello, hoping to avoid Tarleton's troops on the main road.

The town of Charlottesville is cradled in a peaceful valley watered by the Rivanna River, with the double peaks of the Southwest Mountains standing sentinel on the northeastern boundary, while the smaller part of the range, on which Monticello was perched, rose from the south. On the outskirts of this idyllic and isolated setting, a number of vast plantations were scattered around the countryside, many owned by Jefferson's friends. As Tarleton traveled the road to Charlottesville, he stopped at a number of these mansions in hopes of finding legislators and preventing the inhabitants from warning others of his approach.

One of the houses along the way was on the fifteen-thousand-acre plantation of Castle Hill in the shadow of the Southwest Mountains and owned by Dr. Thomas Walker. As Tarleton approached, Walker was hosting several illustrious Virginia officials, including Irish-born Peter Lyons, a large man who was a judge on the General Court and who, eighteen years before, had been the lawyer for James Maury in the famous Parson's Cause case; Colonel John Syme, the half-brother of Patrick Henry and a House delegate; and Newman Brockenbrough, also a member of the Virginia House of Delegates.

The guests at Castle Hill had been warned the British might be nearby, but Syme, who had been in the area longer than the others, assured them they were safe and that the legislature would be undisturbed in Charlottesville. In fact, Syme told the others on June 3, "the Assembly was under so little apprehension of a visit from the enemy, that it was to meet there again" on the following morning. Furthermore, a scout had been sent down the main roads and saw no sign of the British. As a result, Lyons later recalled, "we indulged the thought of being far from the enemy, and the pleasure of a good night's repose." What they did not know was that a note had been sent to Dr. Walker warning him of Tarleton's approach, and that the note was intercepted by Tarleton's men, thus alerting the British force that they would find a valuable catch at Castle Hill.

After a fine evening's meal and a night's sleep in their chambers, the guests of Castle Hill were suddenly awakened before dawn by their host. The British had arrived. Lyons crept from his bed and peeked through a curtain. "Looking out of the window, I saw the yard and house surrounded with soldiers, so that an attempt to get away was useless," he wrote. Brockenbrough went downstairs, where he found Tarleton in command of the house. He asked the young British commander to release him on account of bad health. But Brockenbrough was a delegate to the House, too valuable to be let go. He and a number of other legislators staying at Walker's home were taken prisoner and forced to ride to Cornwallis's camp.

Judge Lyons, meanwhile, was taken from his room before he had finished dressing and pushed unceremoniously into the yard, where the appearance of the enormously fat man "provoked gales of laughter from the assembled dragoons," according to one account. Tarleton was said to have sized up Lyons and, determining that he was not a delegate and would be too much trouble to carry as a prisoner, let him go.[21]

One of Tarleton's soldiers, Captain David Kinloch, found his cousin hiding at the Walker home; he was a South Carolina delegate to the Continental Congress, Francis Kinloch, who was unceremoniously taken away. Ambrose Rucker of Amherst County, a heavyset legislator, managed to escape by horseback, whipping his powerful steed forward and jumping a fence just as the British approached.[22]

According to family tradition, the Walker family did its part to save Jefferson. Dr. Walker had been the physician for Jefferson's father, Peter, and upon Peter's death had helped care for Thomas. A plot was hatched. Walker's chef, Dinah, cooked fried chicken for Tarleton, delaying his departure by crucial minutes.

Just before reaching Charlottesville, Tarleton's cavalry encountered a small militia force whose mission was to warn legislators if the British were approaching and then to try to stop the invaders. The militia, however, scattered at the sight of the overwhelming force, leaving Tarleton a clear path to the village and the legislators who had gathered there. Then, at a nearby estate called Pen Park, a man identified only as Mr. A. was staying as a guest when he saw the British approach. Mr. A. mounted his horse and attempted to escape, but was shot and carried off by Tarleton's men. The mistress of Pen Park, Eliza Gilmer, angrily went after Tarleton's forces in an effort to help her injured guest. She made her way past "drunk and disorderly troopers" and managed to plead her case to Tarleton, according to a family history. The cavalry commander was so "filled with admiration at her courage" that he sent his surgeon to attend to Mr. A., who returned to the Gilmer residence and recovered from his wounds.[23]

AS TARLETON APPROACHED CHARLOTTESVILLE, Jefferson informed
the legislative leaders who had stayed at Monticello that his duties as governor
were ended. His term expired at the beginning of June, and he did not intend
to serve again. Jefferson previously had mentioned his intention to some legislators; others, however, were unaware of his plan, and no succession had been
arranged. At such a crucial moment, Jefferson insisted, it was best for Virginia
that he be replaced by someone with military qualifications. He explained his
decision some time later in blunt terms, referring to himself in the third person.
"His office was now near expiring, the country under invasion by a powerful
army, no services but military of any avail, unprepared by his line of life and
education for the command of armies, he believed it right not to stand in the
way of talents better fitted than his own to the circumstances under which the
country was placed."

Jefferson suggested that Yorktown planter and militia leader Thomas Nelson should be appointed governor. Moreover, it would be necessary for Nelson
to assume the governorship and full command of the state's military resources,
a proposal at odds with Jefferson's earlier view against the concentration of so
much military and political power in the hands of one man. Jefferson knew he
did not have the luxury of sticking to such principle at a time when the British
were storming through the countryside. A "union of the civil and military power
in the same hands, at this time would greatly facilitate military measures," he
wrote.[24]

The change demonstrates how deeply Jefferson was affected by the invasion,
which would leave a deep impact on his thinking about executive power for
years to come. Several legislators were dismayed that Jefferson's decision left
the state without a chief executive. The full legislature would have to meet
again to elect a new leader. But there was no time. The British were nearly in
Charlottesville.

JOUETT'S MOONLIGHT RIDE now took him to the forested slope of Monticello. Spurring on his horse, Jouett ducked the oncoming branches but was
barbed repeatedly, which streaked his face with blood and gave him scars that
would be visible for the rest of his life. Finally, at 4:30 a.m., Jouett emerged from
the woods and ascended the path to Jefferson's home.

Jefferson had believed he would be safe at Monticello. The Continental
troops and militia would cut off the British advance. The Marquis de Lafayette
would arrive. The little mountain above Charlottesville would be a refuge, with
the citizenry below ready to alert them of any danger, and the approach of the

British easily spotted from a distance. Then came a knock at the door. It was Jouett, warning Jefferson that the British were coming.

Jefferson insisted that the mountains would delay the enemy and that there was time for breakfast. His plantation overseer, Edmund Bacon, would remark later that he never saw Jefferson ruffled. No matter what happened, Jefferson "always maintained the same expression . . . his countenance was perfectly unmoved."[25] Such serenity was a Jeffersonian trait, although in this case it suggested hubris.

Jefferson recalled taking a series of measured, prudent steps. "I ordered a carriage to be ready to carry off my family." Unwisely, the legislators headed back to Charlottesville, putting them directly in the path of the approaching British. Wisely, Jefferson's wife and daughters prepared to head south, away from the enemy.

Jefferson's wife, Martha, was in a frail state, physically and emotionally, as she boarded her carriage. She still had been recovering from the difficult birth the previous November of Lucy Elizabeth when the infant died in April. Nonetheless, she followed her husband's instructions, bundling up their two daughters, eight-year-old Patsy and two-year-old Maria, as she took the road to the southwest, stopping at an estate called Enniscorthy, fourteen miles from Charlottesville.

With his family and the legislators now gone, Jefferson tried to discover whether the British were indeed coming. He walked from the front of his home to a nearby ridgeline, looking toward Charlottesville and the cluster of buildings nestled in the valley below. He could get a better view of the roads leading into Charlottesville by going to the top of an adjoining mountain, which Jefferson called Montalto, and which was also known as Carter's Mountain. He ordered that a newly shod horse be brought to Thoroughfare Gap Road, which ran alongside Montalto. As his great-granddaughter wrote years later, Jefferson then "walked over to Carter's Mountain, whence he had a full view of Charlottesville." Jefferson's grandson gave a similar account in an unpublished manuscript, writing that Jefferson traveled "along the crest of the range, commanding a view of the road on both sides," and then reached a point "commanding a full view of Charlottesville."[26]

Montalto's summit is 1,230 feet, compared to the 850-foot height of Monticello, providing one of the most stunning panoramas in Virginia. Jefferson had acquired 483 acres on Montalto in 1777 and at one time envisioned putting a one-hundred-foot-tall observation tower at the peak. The tower was never built, but he noted that he could still see "10 or 12 counties" from near his house, most likely referring to the Montalto summit.[27] Jefferson had long marveled at how he was able to see small distant objects with such clarity from the mountain, likening it to the ability of a seafarer to spy a distant ship on the horizon, a phenomenon called "looming." The principal effect of looming was "to make distant objects appear larger, in opposition to the general law of vision, by which they are diminished," Jefferson wrote. He could see three miles away in Charlottesville, distinguishing the courthouse and Swan Tavern, owned by John Jouett Sr., the father of the young man who had just come to his door.

Jefferson planned his escape route carefully. Some rough trails wound through the woods around Montalto, providing a low road beneath a forest canopy through which Jefferson could travel to meet his family. No one knew this world of narrow trails and river crossings better than Jefferson, who would often spend three hours a day on horseback inspecting his property. He was confident that this knowledge, combined with his extraordinary riding skills, would keep him from capture.

At the mountain crest, Jefferson took out a folding telescope to scan the landscape. He owned a particularly precise instrument, one of the finest in world, made of mahogany and silver plating by the renowned Jesse Ramsden of London. The telescope collapsed to 7¼ inches and extended in three draws to 20½ inches. At some point, the family had Jefferson's name etched into the silver plating that encircled the instrument. He peered through the spyglass but did not see a single English soldier. Perhaps it was all a false alarm.

As he turned back, however, Jefferson's small sword cane fell from its sheath to the ground. As Jefferson went to retrieve the sword, he took one last look at Charlottesville. This time he noticed something glinting in the sun. Tarleton's dragoons were approaching the village.[28]

Jefferson still thought he had time.

JOUETT DESCENDED FROM MONTICELLO and arrived in Charlottesville shortly before the British. Jouett went from door to door, finding some legislators at the Swan Tavern, the courthouse, and a boardinghouse. He implored them to leave, to go west or south, but he was met with disbelief. Again, Jouett insisted they leave with all speed. Benjamin Harrison recalled that some legislators were "so incredulous" at Jouett's warning that "it was with much difficulty they could be prevailed on to adjourn." It was only with Jouett's "extraordinary exertions" that the legislators finally departed. Without that warning, "not one man of those in town would have escaped," wrote Harrison a few days later.[29]

The legislators rushed through a resolution to abandon Charlottesville and head over the Blue Ridge for the frontier town of Staunton, "there being reason to apprehend an immediate incursion of the enemy's cavalry to this place, which renders it indispensable that the General Assembly should forthwith adjourn to a place of greater security." Most of the legislators leaped onto their horses or into their carriages, heading west. A few insisted on remaining for a few minutes more, trying to pack up vital state papers or to hide gunpowder and other supplies. They waited too long.

AS TARLETON PREPARED TO STORM into Charlottesville, he was unsure whether Jefferson was in the village with the other legislators or still on the little mountain above the valley. Every building in Charlottesville needed to be inspected, every road explored. Tarleton decided to take the bulk of his troops into Charlottesville and go after the legislators in town. He ordered an aide, Captain Kenneth McLeod, to race up a winding road to see if Jefferson and the leaders of the House and Senate were at Monticello. Tarleton gave orders to McLeod with the "object of taking me prisoner with the two Speakers of the Senate and Delegates who then lodged with me," Jefferson wrote later.[30]

Tarleton's main cavalry thundered into Charlottesville, kicking up dirt and quickly surrounding the legislators who had tarried. The British ransacked the village and destroyed one thousand muskets, four hundred barrels of powder, clothing, tobacco, and county records. The wisdom of Jefferson's decision to remove the prisoners of war from the Albemarle Barracks prison camp became apparent. The British prisoners had been moved north to Maryland, and the Hessians who remained at the barracks had been ordered to move away earlier in the year. About twenty prisoners who had managed to remain in the area made their way out of the woods to join up with Tarleton's force. This was but a token number compared to the several thousand who might have done so had they been allowed to remain at the barracks. The British strike at Charlottesville put an end to the idea that the area was remote enough for a large and lightly guarded prison.

After urging the legislators to leave, Jouett had remained in Charlottesville. He was accompanied by Daniel Boone, the frontiersman who at the time was serving as a western representative in Virginia's legislature. The two men, trying to pass as innocent civilians, had hoped to prevent the British from seizing records stored in Charlottesville. They strolled around in a purposely lackadaisical manner, attempting not to attract attention, but the British stopped them, holding them briefly for questioning. Dressed in their frontier clothes, Boone and Jouett convinced the British interrogators that they were just passing through. Then, according to an account from Boone's son, Jouett unwittingly gave them away.

"Wait a minute, Captain Boone, and I'll go with you," Jouett said.

"Ah, is he a captain?" the British officer said, taking Boone prisoner.[31]

Boone spent the night in a coal house that served as a prison. He emerged smeared with black dust, further adding to his frontier appearance. Boone "pretended contentment and sung songs" and explained that he was called a captain because of his role in the wars against the Indians. The British, unaware of the role he had played in opening contested western lands to white settlement, eventually let him head west and join the legislators in Staunton.

British Horse Came to Monticello

JEFFERSON WAS A METICULOUS MAN, keeping thousands of documents and books carefully organized at his home. Now, with just minutes before he had to flee Monticello, he collected some of his most valuable papers, perhaps remembering how his family had lost precious items when his childhood home of Shadwell accidentally burned eleven years earlier. He stuffed papers into his saddlebags and pockets, misplacing labels in his haste. "In preparing for flight," Jefferson wrote, "I shoved in papers where I could."[1]

It was around this time that a twenty-three-year-old Virginia lieutenant named Christopher Hudson happened to be traveling on the road about four miles east of Monticello, on his way to join Lafayette's army. Hudson knew Jefferson, having been in Richmond during Arnold's invasion and observed how Jefferson was "constantly on duty." As Hudson continued along the road, he met a man named Mr. Long, who anxiously discussed the movements of British soldiers in the area. Long mentioned that Jack Jouett had gone to Charlottesville to warn the legislators about Tarleton's advance toward the village. Hudson asked whether Jouett had gone to Monticello to inform Jefferson of the danger. Long replied that he did not know.

Seized with alarm, Hudson tugged at his horse's reins and switched direction, determined to warn Jefferson of the approaching danger. Galloping up the hill, he arrived at the mountaintop and went inside Monticello. "I found Mr. Jefferson, perfectly tranquil, and undisturbed," Hudson recalled. He noticed that Monticello, normally teeming with laborers and craftsmen, was eerily silent and nearly empty. Jefferson would have no way to fend off an attack. "I was convinced his Situation was truly critical since there was only one man (his gardener) upon the Spot." Hudson told Jefferson that the enemy was ascending the hill of Monticello. Jefferson was still not quite ready to leave. Hudson again beseeched Jefferson to depart; Tarleton's horsemen were minutes away. Finally, "at my earnest request he left his house," Hudson recalled.[2]

Jefferson mounted his favorite horse, Caractacus. The six-year-old stallion, named after a first-century chieftain from Britain who led the resistance against the Romans, was one of the fastest horses in Virginia. Jefferson kicked with his heels and whipped Caractacus through a dense forest dominated by chestnut trees. He "knew that he would be pursued if he took the high road," so he "plunged into the woods of the adjoining mountain," as he later put it. He

raced around Montalto on rough trails as he headed toward the public road on
which he had sent Martha and the children. After a few miles, he overtook his
family's carriage, and galloped ahead to make sure no British were patrolling
the road.[3]

Jefferson must have been filled with dread. He had spent much of the last
dozen years planning and constructing Monticello. During the previous six
months, Virginia had witnessed the burning of its cities, the destruction of
its navy, and the plundering of plantations. Tarleton's reputation was widely
known. It was not just Jefferson in flight, but much of Virginia. For months,
Virginians had been fleeing their homes, burying their treasure, heading westward. The British seemed unstoppable. If Virginia was lost, so, too, might be
the revolution.

Charlottesville had not proven the haven Jefferson had promised. No longer
governor, however, he focused on his family's safety. While the legislators
headed west, he would head south. He quickly made a prosaic notation about
the day's extraordinary events for his memorandum book: "June 4. British horse
came to Monticello."[4]

Merely five minutes after Jefferson had left Monticello, Captain McLeod
and his men arrived at the house. Two of Jefferson's slaves, Martin Hemings, a
butler, and Caesar, were hiding pieces of silver in a storage area covered by some
planks. The storage area was under the bow of the parlor, which had been
added without a full basement. Caesar was in the storage area, receiving the
plates, when Martin Hemings saw the British arrive. He quickly replaced the
planks, covering both the dishes and Caesar, who, according to Jefferson family
lore, "remained in the dark and without food for three days and three nights."

One of the British soldiers cocked his gun and put it against Hemings's
chest, asking where Jefferson was. If Hemings refused to respond, the soldier
said, he would fire. "Fire away, then," Hemings responded.[5] The British soldiers let Hemings go. Inside the house, meanwhile, British soldiers searched
for Jefferson. Instead, they found some of Jefferson's finest wine, which they
consumed. Perhaps they raised a toast to King George III, for it so happened
that the raid on Monticello coincided with the monarch's forty-third birthday.
The soldiers remained for eighteen hours but did not disturb the home, returning the courtesy with which Jefferson had treated British prisoners who
until recently had been quartered at Charlottesville.

Jefferson and his family, meanwhile, arrived at the Enniscorthy estate, owned
by a friend, John Coles. Set upon the Green Mountains, the two-story mansion was one of the largest in Albemarle County. Still, with British patrolling
the area, Jefferson soon decided it was too dangerous either to stay overnight at

Enniscorthy or to return to Monticello. Instead, he decided to take the family and head toward the home of another friend, Hugh Rose, who lived forty miles farther to the southwest. It would be a difficult trip along mountain roads that might be cut off by the British at numerous junctions.

Rose had long been close to Jefferson and his family. Rose's father, Robert Rose, had been a parson who rode throughout Virginia preaching the Anglican faith, often stopping at a log structure called the Mountain Chapel near Jefferson's childhood home, Shadwell. Jefferson's father, Peter, had surveyed lands with Robert Rose and been an executor of his will. The elder Rose and Jefferson passed vast property on to their sons, Hugh and Thomas, thus putting both men at the center of Virginia's elite. Hugh and Thomas remained close over the years, visiting each other and taking leadership roles in the revolution, with Rose serving as a member of the House of Delegates and militia leader while Jefferson was governor.

The journey to the Rose home was an onerous one under the best of conditions. Jefferson normally preferred to travel by longer routes if it meant he could avoid taking his carriage on bumpy mountain roads, especially when traveling with his wife and daughters, but there was no time for such a luxury. The fastest route would take the Jeffersons along mountainous byways, over fast-moving streams, and through dense forests. At this time of year, a violent rainstorm could make creeks impassable, while a midday ride in the sun would leave the passengers covered with sweat and dust. A similar trip to Poplar Forest, taken some years later, was memorably recorded by Jefferson's granddaughters. On that later trip, Jefferson's carriage traveled over a high, rickety bridge made of logs. Suddenly one of the wheels sank, going halfway through a gap in the bridge, putting the Jeffersons "in great danger of going down carriage & horses & all."[6]

Now, as the Jeffersons continued their flight from Monticello, they traveled Secretary's Road, along which giant barrels of tobacco were rolled to the nearest river port by teams of horses or oxen. The Jeffersons crossed the Hardware River, and then traveled beside the Green Mountains. A few hours later they reached the Rockfish River, where the rushing waters could only be forded by horse and carriage at a few points. Jefferson headed to a tavern called Joplin's Ordinary, which served those passing across Joplin's Ford, several miles north of where the mouth of the Rockfish met the James River. Large boulders were scattered in the river, as if hurled from the precipices. Joplin and his slaves guided carriages and passengers safely across the ford.

Jefferson stayed overnight at a house by the Rockfish River, although accounts differ slightly as to how he found lodgings at a moment when the local population was concerned that his presence would endanger them. Jefferson's grandson Thomas Jefferson Randolph wrote that Jefferson initially was refused entry at one house by the Rockfish River. The owner, a man named Thomas, "refused to take him in, fearing he might be pursued and he punished for harboring him." Jefferson went a mile farther up the river, where he found Joplin, who took him in. But after supper Joplin said Jefferson "was of too much consequence to the country to risk his capture." Joplin insisted on "going with him three miles into the Mountains to a friend's house," where Jefferson would be safe.[7] Another version of the family story has Jefferson remaining at Joplin's while Joplin went alone into the mountains.

In either case, Jefferson recorded in his account book that he paid £45, which could have been for food and supplies at Joplin's Ordinary as well as for covering the fee for help in crossing the ford on the Rockfish River. After completing the crossing at Joplin's Ford, Jefferson traveled over a series of small mountain ranges, eventually approaching the entrance to Findlay's Gap. From the bridle seat of the carriage, the entrance to the gap must have seemed inviting. After a winding, hilly ride, the Jeffersons entered a valley at an elevation of about five hundred feet, surrounded by mountains on either side that rose to more than one thousand feet. The carriage rolled through these two parallel ranges into a scene of splendid isolation. Then the gap widened, providing a view of the great peaks of the Blue Ridge.

As the Jeffersons ascended a road along Findlay's Gap, they came upon an ordinary operated by a settler named Abraham Warwick, a colonel in the local militia. Here the Jeffersons stopped again, likely having dinner and possibly staying overnight. The Jeffersons then continued southwest on the main carriage road, through what was then called Amherst Court House, and across the Tye River. Then the narrow, rock-strewn road descended to a ford in the Piney River before rising again toward land owned by Hugh Rose.[8]

The road seemed clasped to the hillsides at points, as the Blue Ridge came closer into view. Soon, the Jeffersons approached Rose's house, known as Geddes, a narrow, one-and-a-half story structure spread across the land like a meeting house turned on an axis. In the distance, to the left, rose the peak known as the Priest. To the right stood the massif of Three Ridges Mountain. Acres of fields spread from the house to the mountains and down to the Piney and Tye rivers. Slave cabins lay beyond a copse of trees, near the abundant spring water. The house and fields seemed placed there by Providence, the Rose family believed, with the mountains serving as far-flung wings in a seemingly infinite landscape.

Even in the great anxiety of the moment, Jefferson could savor the scene, the remoteness providing a sense of security and wonder. Geddes was nothing like the Palladian elegance of Monticello, but the home was sturdy and tidy, built in a modest vernacular style. Composed of two smaller houses joined together by an entryway, it had been constructed from logs sawed from the towering virgin timber that once covered the region. The smooth pine flooring reflected the glow from brick fireplaces that warmed the house in winter, and a narrow stairwell ran upstairs to a hipped-roof attic with dormer windows, where some of the Rose children slept. Jefferson and Rose must have had an extraordinary discussion that night, with Jefferson explaining how he had fled the British, and Rose, in his role as local militia leader, expressing anxiety about the need to protect a nearby arms depot. What neither man realized was that at that moment the whole of Cornwallis's army was converging on an estate owned by Jefferson—not Monticello, but Elk Hill.[9]

TWENTY-NINE MILES SOUTHEAST OF MONTICELLO, the lush fields of Jefferson's Elk Hill plantation rolled gently toward the banks of the James River. The plantation house had none of Monticello's grandeur; it was a modest farmhouse with a pitched roof, set on a breezy eminence overlooking the plantation's 307 acres. In the little valley below, some of Jefferson's finest breeding horses were quartered in their stables. Barns were filled with corn and tobacco, slave cabins were scattered along the creeks, and cattle and sheep roamed through the grasses.

Jefferson normally visited Elk Hill a few times a year, overseeing the planting and going on long hunts. The property, acquired from Martha's family, was among his most profitable ventures, ideally situated for cultivation and transportation.[10] He knew that it would be a prime target of the British. In early May, Jefferson had gone to Elk Hill and removed most of his valuables, leaving his slaves, livestock, and farm implements.[11] But he was not prepared for the massive influx of British that followed.

HAVING FAILED TO ENGAGE the retreating Lafayette outside Richmond, Lord Cornwallis headed west and decided to rest his men by the banks of the James River, some twenty-five miles away from Lafayette's force. So it was that he arrived at Elk Hill in early June with the bulk of the seven thousand British troops. For ten days, Cornwallis's men camped in Jefferson's corn and tobacco fields. Cornwallis himself made his headquarters in Jefferson's house. Sitting at Jefferson's table, dating his letters as coming from "Jefferson's Camp," he signed orders that sent his men raiding across the Piedmont.

Cornwallis's army required an enormous supply of food and water, both of which Elk Hill had in abundance. The British, Loyalist, and Hessian soldiers scavenged across the landscape, stripping the fields bare and entering homes in search of a meal or plunder. In addition to the soldiers, there were hundreds of camp followers. There were also the thousands of former slaves who had been freed by Cornwallis's army during the marches across the Carolinas and Virginia and now worked for Cornwallis's officers and soldiers.

"The army appeared similar to a wandering Arabian or Tartar horde," wrote Johann Ewald. He was appalled that Cornwallis allowed the officers and soldiers to indulge themselves by turning the freed slaves into personal servants. Even among the Hessians, he wrote, "every officer had four to six horses and three or four Negroes, as well as one or two Negresses for cook and maid. Yes, indeed, I can testify that every soldier had his Negro, who carried his provisions and bundles." By Ewald's count, there were four thousand former slaves accompanying Cornwallis's army alone. The combination of the soldiers, camp followers, and former slaves created a massive caravan that, wherever it camped, created the largest city in Virginia. "Any place this horde approached was eaten clean, like a swarm of locusts," Ewald wrote.

After all the years of slavery in Virginia, the sight of so many "free" blacks was, as Cornwallis intended, alarming to many. They marched amidst the massive British army, walking or riding on horses, often wearing the suits, wigs, and hats of their former masters. Ewald was appalled. "When I first beheld this train, I could not grasp it, and I wondered as much about the indulgent character of Lord Cornwallis as I admired him for his military qualities. I wished that I could reconcile those qualities."[12]

Yet for many former slaves, the freedom was all too brief. Far from their homes, mixing with thousands of people, many were exposed to diseases that may have killed more people in Virginia during the invasion of 1781 than all the bullets, bayonets, and cannonballs.

A CONNECTICUT SOLDIER NAMED JOSIAH ATKINS was among those marching south as part of a Continental army unit coming to reinforce Lafayette's army. Atkins was a Patriot who wanted to oust the British, but the farther he went into Virginia, the more disturbed he became that he would, in effect, be protecting a system that gave vast wealth to the gentry and enslaved hundreds of thousands of blacks. As it happened, Atkins's march to Richmond took him through land owned by Washington, his commander in chief. He wrote in his diary that he was troubled that "some men in these parts, they tell me, own 30,000 acres of land for their patrimony, and many have two or three hundred negroes to work on it as slaves." Atkins thought it unjust, and in a sentence summed up the inconsistency of the revolution: "Alas! That persons who pretend to stand for the *rights of mankind,* for the liberties of society, can delight in oppression." He questioned his motivation for joining the war, asking God why he had left behind his pregnant wife, Sarah, and their one-year-old daughter, Sally, in order to carry "the cruel and unwelcome instruments of war" on behalf of these "strangers in a strange land."

After a march of nearly six hundred miles, as he neared Richmond, Atkins came upon an appalling sight. The roadsides were scattered with the putrefying, smallpox-ridden bodies of former slaves who had fled from their Virginia masters. Some believed the British had sent the slaves forward as part of a malicious plot to infect American soldiers. An infected person, or one purposely given the disease as part of an effort at inoculation, was supposed to be quarantined for many days to make sure the smallpox was not spread to others. Many blacks who came from Cornwallis's army had been infected but received no such quarantine. "These poor creatures, having no care taken of them, many crawled into the bushes about and died," Atkins wrote in his diary. "This is a piece of Cornwallisean cruelty."

Atkins questioned the morality of both the Virginians for keeping slaves and the British for freeing them and then using them to spread disease. After praying for guidance, he decided that instead of firing the "instrument of war" that he carried on his shoulder, he would volunteer as an assistant to an army surgeon, a job that increased his own risk of infection but satisfied "the feelings nature has given me for the sick and wounded."[13]

Atkins was part of a major buildup of Continental forces in the state. The Continental army and Virginia militia were still outmanned by Cornwallis, but the numbers were getting closer. Lafayette, for all his complaints about the militia and the lack of horses, had an overriding sense of confidence about the battles to come. He urged Congress not to overestimate the strength of Cornwallis's army. "You can be entirely calm with regard to the rapid marches of Lord Cornwallis," he wrote in a letter that was said to have been captured by the British, and is quoted in Ewald's diary. "Let him march from St. Augustine to Boston. What he wins in his front, he loses in his rear. His army will bury itself without requiring us to fight with him."[14]

This was confidence to the point of bravado. Indeed, Lafayette was in flight from Cornwallis shortly after writing this, to avoid likely defeat. However, Cornwallis did seem to be reverting to the same pattern that had doomed him in South Carolina, launching raids far from his base and being unable to hold the ground. Tarleton's foray into Charlottesville was not meant to occupy the village; his men left after a day. So long as Virginians could outrun the British, they could hold the enemy at bay. This, indeed, was the greatest accomplishment of the much-maligned Virginia forces: while they retreated with regularity, they were never defeated en masse, unlike the 5,500 Americans who surrendered at Charleston. Throughout the invasion of 1781, the Virginians skirmished with the British, giving the invaders a series of mostly Pyrrhic victories and drawing ever larger forces of the enemy into the state. It was hardly a preconceived strategy, but without such efforts the dénouement of Yorktown might not have been possible.

AS CORNWALLIS SAT IN JEFFERSON'S HOUSE at Elk Hill plantation, he drew up plans that he hoped would cripple Virginia's ability to fight. Informants told him that Virginia had established a string of arms depots west of Richmond, in hopes that the supplies would be safe from British invaders. The biggest depot was just six miles upriver from Elk Hill, at the confluence of the James and Rivanna rivers, at a place called Point of Fork. The defense of Point of Fork had been left to Baron von Steuben, who was no longer in charge of the troops in Virginia. Steuben believed that his primary mission at the Fork was to train soldiers in preparation for a march to South Carolina, not to guard Virginia's military supplies. Given the rapid movement of the British invaders, the location was no longer considered safe. "The Point of Fork is an improper place" because it was too "insecure," wrote the state's quartermaster, Captain Henry Young. He urged that Jefferson order supplies moved over the Blue Ridge Mountains to Staunton. "The governor is the best man in the world, and, if I mistake not, open to conviction," Young wrote to one of Jefferson's military aides. "Were you to use your influence with him I think he might be prevailed on to give up this Point of Fork that will one day damn the exertions of the state." Jefferson wrote two weeks later to Davies that legislators had agreed that the supplies should be moved, perhaps to Scottsville. Indeed, Jefferson understood the risk, having recently removed the most precious items from his nearby house at Elk Hill due to concern about British raids. Some weapons were moved from Point of Fork, but legislators and state officials waited too long to make a final decision, and many arms in need of repair and other supplies remained at the depot.[15]

Steuben had about six hundred men at Point of Fork, many of them newly recruited and poorly equipped. Learning that Cornwallis was near, he feared he would be overrun by the full force of the enemy, and ordered the supplies moved or hidden in the river. In fact, Cornwallis had detached John Graves Simcoe, the leader of the Queen's Rangers, with a unit of only five hundred men, many of them weakened from weeks on the march, including fifty who were barefoot. It was just days after two of Simcoe's men had been executed before the entire army for raping a young girl. The British dragged one cannon with them.

Simcoe was a master of the ruse. Knowing that Steuben feared a full army, he strung out his men to make them appear like a far larger force. A number of women who served as cooks were sent to a wooded hillside and ordered to bang their pots, which sounded from a distance like a huge corps of British. Then the British fired one shot from their cannon. Fifty of the Virginians guarding the depot fled from their post amidst the confusion, returning only when Steuben threatened them with severe punishment.[16]

The next morning, Steuben learned that the British had established a temporary bridge across the Rivanna River (the north fork of the James), a logistical breakthrough that put his men in greater danger. Steuben decided to retreat, leaving some supplies behind, and explaining later, "I thought it absurd to be making a bravado with a small number of bad troops against such a force."[17]

Steuben's retreat nonetheless outraged Virginia's legislators, who believed that he had lost three thousand arms. Speaker Harrison wrote that Steuben's conduct "gives universal disgust and injures the service much."[18] Some talked of hanging the Prussian. Steuben maintained that he had dispersed most of the supplies, saved his force from being captured, and left behind only some weapons in disrepair. It would be several months before Virginians realized that Steuben's losses were modest and that he had indeed managed to save many supplies by hiding them in the river. The real loss was that some of Steuben's men had deserted during the retreat as news of the setback further demoralized Virginians.

SEQUESTERED AT HUGH ROSE'S PLANTATION in Amherst County, Jefferson decided it was time to return to Monticello. It was one of the lowest points of the war in Virginia, and even the remote area where Jefferson was staying was deemed unsafe. So many Amherst County militia had failed to turn out that a court-martial of "delinquents" was planned.[19] Rose, a county militia leader, wrote letters urging local men to protect nearby arms depots and to send intelligence about the enemy's whereabouts.[20] Legislators discussed whether negotiations with the British would be necessary to end the war.

Despite the danger that British might be patrolling the road to Charlottesville, Jefferson insisted that he must return to see what had happened to his beloved home. He bade goodbye to his wife and children and retraced his escape

route in reverse, once again fording the Rockfish River and stopping at ordinaries along the way.

As Jefferson reached the top of his little mountain, all seemed normal at
Monticello. Nothing had been disturbed except some bottles of wine. The
British had occupied Charlottesville for one day when a violent rainstorm
threatened to flood the Rivanna, prompting Tarleton to ford the rising river
and leave the town.[21]

For three days, Jefferson went about his usual routine at Monticello, riding
to his quarter farms of Tufton, Shadwell, and Lego. On one of these days, he
gazed south toward the James, some twenty miles away. From his vantage
point, Jefferson had an extraordinary view of the devastation being wrought by
the British along the James River. Jefferson distinctly saw "the smokes of conflagration of houses and property on that river, as they successively arose in the
horizon at a distance of twenty-five or thirty miles."[22]

One of the properties was Elk Hill. Learning that Cornwallis had occupied
his plantation, Jefferson rode to inspect the property sometime shortly after
the British army had departed. Cornwallis had destroyed the corn and tobacco
that was under cultivation, burned the barns that contained crops harvested
during the prior year, and confiscated "all my stocks of cattle, sheep & hogs for
the sustenance of his army." Jefferson did not quarrel with Cornwallis's right
to feed his men with the spoils of war. But he was angry that Cornwallis had
allowed his troops to ruin nearly everything. The British had "carried off all the
horses capable of service." They had also cut the throats of the young horses, his
treasures, Jefferson wrote bitterly, and then "burned all the fences on the plantation so as to leave it an absolute waste."

While many plantations in the area had been plundered, Elk Hill suffered
the worst. Cornwallis had acted against him in a "spirit of total extermination
with which he seemed to rage over my possessions." Jefferson became particularly angry when he thought of Cornwallis sitting at his Elk Hill house, making
no effort to stop the destruction. "It was all done under his eye, the situation of
the house in which he was, commanding a view of every part of the plantation,
so that he must have seen every fire."

Jefferson later wrote that Cornwallis had "carried off" thirty slaves at Elk
Hill, twenty-seven of whom died of disease. If Cornwallis only meant to give
the slaves their freedom, Jefferson said, "he would have done right. But it was
to consign them to inevitable death from small pox and putrid fever, then raging in his camp."[23]

Jefferson's notation in his farm book, however, provides what is probably a
more accurate assessment. He wrote that he lost twenty-three slaves from three

plantations, including as many as eleven from Elk Hill. Jefferson meticulously noted in his farm book that these slaves variously "fled to the enemy," "joined enemy," or ran away. Some of Jefferson's slaves, such as those in Richmond, were taken but returned and survived. Some who fled to the British eventually returned to Jefferson's plantations and died, while still others came back and infected five more slaves who died.[24] Based on his own losses and those of other slave owners, Jefferson estimated that thirty thousand slaves had fled their owners in Virginia, due mostly to Cornwallis's entreaties, and that one hundred thousand had fled from all of the states. "History will never relate the horrors committed by the British army in the *southern* States of America," he wrote.[25]

Some historians believe Jefferson overestimated the number of fleeing slaves by a factor of five, with one study suggesting that the number of Virginia blacks who fled was less than six thousand and that the total throughout the United States during the Revolutionary War was closer to twenty thousand.[26] Jefferson may have exaggerated the number of slaves taken from all plantations in Virginia to bolster the complaints of Virginians who had difficulty paying debts to the British stemming from prewar agreements. Indeed, in referring to a debt he owed to British merchants, Jefferson wrote six years after Cornwallis laid waste to Elk Hill that "the useless and barbarous injury he did me in that instance was more than would have paid your debt, principal and interest." At the least, Jefferson argued, he shouldn't be charged interest for an eight-year wartime period.[27]

Whatever the total number of slaves freed by the British, many thousands who fled eventually made it to freedom, while others who were briefly free were returned to their masters at the end of the war. Years later, Jefferson remained angry at Cornwallis, whom he considered to have violated the war's code of honor, but he wrote almost fondly of Tarleton, whose reputation is usually portrayed in harsh terms but who had ordered that Monticello be left unscathed. "He behaved very genteelly with me," Jefferson wrote in a letter years later about Tarleton. "He gave strict orders to Capt. McLeod to suffer nothing be injured."[28]

With control of the region continuing to fluctuate between the British and local militia, Jefferson traveled back to Hugh Rose's home and informed his family that it was too dangerous to return to Monticello. So, on the morning of June 13, Jefferson paid Rose £150 for corn and prepared to move farther south. He had decided to take his family to the most remote of his three plantations, Poplar Forest, a place he had not visited in eight years.

The Unfortunate Passages in My Conduct

AS JEFFERSON FLED SOUTH, legislators raced westward over the Blue Ridge Mountains, dashing through the forests in small groups to avoid detection. One group, including Patrick Henry, Benjamin Harrison, and John Tyler Sr., stopped at a small home in the mountains. Henry explained to a woman who answered the door that they had been "obliged to fly" from Charlottesville "on account of the approach of the enemy." The startled woman fed the legislators and sent them on their way.[1]

The men arrived a few days later in Staunton, where the legislature renewed its session. The mood was strongly against Jefferson, as shown in letters written at the time by a number of legislators and militia leaders. Indeed, with Cornwallis roaming the countryside at will, the leaders of Virginia seemed in a state of panic. "We have now no Executive in the State," Harrison wrote to Joseph Jones, a Virginia delegate of the Continental Congress, three days after Tarleton's raid on Charlottesville. "For want of a Senate the governor will act no more, and the remainder of the council will not get together." Virginians were "in a most distressed condition from the sea to the mountains."[2]

Some of Virginia's militia commanders were unaware that Jefferson was no longer governor and bemoaned the lack of authority to repair arms and call enough men to service. One such commander, Josiah Parker, felt compelled to order the repair of arms even though he lacked sufficient authority. He complained bitterly to Harrison that he had sought help from Jefferson but received no reply. "I fear my Dear Sir the root of Springs of Government is rotten," Parker wrote "and I dread the Consequence."[3]

Richard Henry Lee told Washington that Virginia was "without Government at a time when the most wise and vigorous administration of public affairs can alone save us from the ruin determined for us by the enemy." Lee joined the chorus for Washington to take charge of his state as a virtual dictator. "Our country is truly, sir, in a deplorable way, and, if relief comes not from you, it will probably come not at all," Lee wrote.[4]

The legislators who had managed to escape from the British now assembled in the old Trinity Church in Staunton. At Henry's urging, delegate George Nicholas, the representative of Jefferson's own Albemarle County and the son of the late state treasurer, took the lead. Nicholas's family home had been the one taken over a few weeks earlier by Cornwallis and the British army, and

Nicholas himself may have been at or near the scene. It was near the Nicholas home that the nine-year-old girl had been raped by two British soldiers. The events could not have failed to make a deep impression on the young man.

Nicholas stood in the church pew and urged that Jefferson's actions be investigated. He introduced a resolution that required "an inquiry be made into the conduct of the Executive of this State for the last twelve months" in order to determine whether Jefferson and his government were responsible for enabling the British to wreak havoc across the state. This was no idle exercise. Approval of the motion alone was considered tantamount to a form of censure.

Nicholas next proposed that Virginia needed not a governor but "a dictator . . . who should have the power of disposing of the lives and fortunes of the Citizens thereof without being subject to account." He suggested Washington for the job. Five years had passed since legislators defeated a proposal that the governorship have dictatorial powers during Henry's term. Instead, the authority of the governorship had been weakened. Now Henry said he did not care whether the leader was called a dictator or governor. What was needed, Henry said in supporting Nicholas's motion, was that the state's chief executive be "armed with such powers necessary to restrain the unbridled fury of a licentious enemy."[5] The motion for a dictatorship was hotly debated and eventually defeated by a six-vote margin among the forty or so legislators. But the effort to investigate Jefferson's action as governor was approved. Jefferson's friends hurried to get word to him that his honor was at great risk.

ON JUNE 14, Jefferson and his family maneuvered their carriage and horses onto John Lynch's ferry to cross the James River. Lynch was a Quaker, whose religion had required him to free his slaves and forbade him from serving in the military; he would donate the land that would become the city of Lynchburg. Once across the river Jefferson traveled another ten miles, arriving at Poplar Forest. Here, he hoped, he would be safe deep amid the Blue Ridge Mountains, in the shadow of the Peaks of Otter. Many Virginians, not to mention the British, did not know Jefferson owned the property. He had inherited the 4,819 acres of Poplar Forest from his father-in-law, John Wayles, in 1773, but had left it in the hands of overseers. No one was expecting him. There was no proper home for a gentlemen and his family.

Poplar Forest was watered by the Bear and Tomahawk creeks and dominated by a stand of enormous tulip poplars. Years later, Jefferson would build a retreat here, creating an elegant octagonal structure with triple-sash windows and Palladian porticoes. The property at this point, however, had only barns, slave cabins, and a two-room dwelling occupied by the overseer, Thomas Bennett. An unused overseer's cabin may have also been standing. In one of these cabins Jefferson and his family apparently lived for the next five weeks. It was as far as Jefferson could have gotten from the comforts of Monticello, but also as far as he could get from the British, so it suited him.

Shortly after arriving at Poplar Forest, Jefferson received a formal letter from the House of Delegates informing him that he was under investigation due to the allegation that he had left Virginia without a proper defense during his governorship. Jefferson also learned about the proposal to create a dictatorship in Virginia. While the motions were introduced by Nicholas, Jefferson quickly concluded that the man behind the efforts was Henry. Nicholas should be the "subject of pity," Jefferson wrote, and his "natural ill temper was the tool worked with by another hand." Nicholas was like a minnow that goes into a whale, Jefferson wrote, "but the whale himself was discoverable enough by the turbulence of the water under which he moved."[6] Jefferson had been "in perfect concert" with Henry until the British invaded Virginia. The comity between them ended as a result of the censure effort. While Henry had been the first man to push the "ball of revolution," Jefferson later told Henry's biographer, his judgment in other matters "was inaccurate . . . he was avaritious & rotten hearted."[7] Henry's defenders would say it was never proven that he had written the legislation introduced by Nicholas. But Jefferson clearly believed Henry was responsible. Fairly or not, during the remaining forty-four years of his life, he frequently railed against Henry.

Jefferson, tapping his background as a lawyer, responded to the investigation into his conduct by seeking more information about the charges against him. He wrote to Nicholas and asked, with a trace of sarcasm, for specific examples of "the unfortunate passages in my conduct" so that he might prepare a proper defense. Three days later Nicholas wrote back, asserting that he was not "an accuser" but rather was "the representative of free Men" who deserved an account of "our numberless miscarriages and losses." He insisted that he would "exhibit no charges" against Jefferson. He nonetheless outlined a general complaint, saying there was a "total want of opposition to Arnold on his first expedition to Richmond." Militia had not been called out in a timely manner. The state had sustained a "great loss" in arms and other supplies.

Around the same time that Jefferson reviewed these accusations, he received a letter from Lafayette that conveyed a congressional request that he represent the United States on a commission in Paris. The idea of living in France and representing the cause of his country had great allure to Jefferson. But, realizing the seriousness of the accusations against him, he told Lafayette he had to turn down the offer. His inability to take the Paris post gave him more morti-fication than almost "any occurrence of my life," Jefferson wrote. He lamented missing the chance to go to a country that he had long admired for its "im-provements in science, in arts, and in civilization." But Jefferson said he had to disprove the allegation that he had acted with "misconduct" during the inva-sion. He would argue that he had been hampered by a lack of state funds and the "disobedience" of militiamen. "Suggestion and fact are different things," Jefferson wrote of the charges against him.[8]

As Jefferson prepared a detailed response to the legislature, he fell from his horse, Caractacus, while riding at Poplar Forest. The injury required two visits to a doctor to set Jefferson's broken wrist. He could not ride for weeks, so he decided to use his confinement productively. For the next month, he worked on a long-delayed letter to a French diplomat who had inquired about life in Virginia. His broken wrist now wrapped, he sat down to organize his thoughts in the overseer's cabin at Poplar Forest, unsure whether the British from whom his land had declared independence would soon be at his door.

It was five years after the signing of the Declaration of Independence. Jef-ferson made no mention of the anniversary in his account book, noting only that he bought corn, brandy, and chickens. After all the tumult of the last five years—the outbreak of war, the gathering of the Continental Congress, the governorship, the invasion, the flights from Arnold and Tarleton—Jefferson would finally use this opportunity to think and write, laying the foundation for all the achievements he hoped would come. He would alternate between a reverie about the beauty of Virginia and a white-hot dismissal of those who had questioned his actions as governor.

The project turned into Jefferson's only full-length published book, *Notes on the State of Virginia.* Even the title was an act of defiance: as England battled to keep Virginia a colony, the former governor was writing about Virginia as a state. It seems clear that even as he was fleeing the British, Jefferson was com-posing the outline of the book in his head. The ride to Poplar Forest had wound through mountain gaps, towering forests, and over rushing rivers. His life was in peril, but he was in the absolute thrall of his surroundings.

Jefferson rhapsodized about geography. The "natural bridge," a 90-foot-wide fissured arch rising 215 feet above Cedar Creek, was "the most sublime of Nature's works." Jefferson purchased the arch and surrounding property as a re-treat. Few men, Jefferson wrote, "have resolution to walk" over the bridge "and look over into the abyss. You involuntarily fall on your hands and feet, creep to the parapet and peep over it . . . it is impossible for the emotions, arising from the sublime, to be felt beyond what they are here." Jefferson was even more rhapsodic about the passage of the Potomac River through the Blue Ridge Mountains, which "is perhaps one of the most stupendous scenes in nature." Describing its confluence with the Shenandoah, he continued, "You stand on a very high point of land. On your right comes up the Shenandoah, having ranged along the foot of the mountain an hundred miles to seek a vent. On your left approaches the Patowmac, in quest of a passage also. In the moment of their junction they rush together against the mountain, rend it asunder, and pass off to the sea." He described being at one with the scene, riding the river, the "terrible precipices hanging in fragments over you," then the river "inviting you, as it were, from the riot and tumult roaring around, to pass through the breach and participate of the calm below."

This worked as well as a metaphor for Jefferson's experience—the invasion and the flight from the British, the calm of an inevitable American victory. The scene at the confluence of the Shenandoah and Potomac was "worth a voyage across the Atlantic." But, Jefferson continued, there are people who live within six miles of similar stupendous scenes of nature "and have never been to survey these monuments of a war between rivers and mountains, which must have shaken the earth itself to its center." As he wrote *Notes,* Jefferson could not imagine a greater scene than that spread before him in Virginia.[9]

Notes continues with detail about cascades, minerals, crops, and animals. It is telling, then, that when Jefferson described the state of Virginia's military, he believed that the most basic accounting would absolve him of what had happened during the first six months of 1781. Every free man in Virginia between the ages of sixteen and fifty was to be enrolled in the militia, in which Jefferson had placed all of his trust but which had disappointed him regularly. Every militia member was supposed to provide himself "with arms usual in the regular service. But this injunction was always indifferently complied with," Jefferson wrote. The militia in the lower part of Virginia were "entirely disarmed," while in the middle part of Virginia "a fourth or fifth part of them may have such firelocks as they had provided to destroy the noxious animals which infest their farms." It was only among the sparse militia from the western side of the Blue Ridge, where the men had to know how to shoot a bear from a distance or a running squirrel in a tree, that rifles were regularly carried. Combined with the movement of Virginians to join Continental forces in the north and south, this created a force that, he said with understatement, is "constantly on the change."[10]

Jefferson was even more dismissive when it came to assessing the state of what he had once called "our miserable navy." Having spent pages detailing the flora and fauna of Virginia, his chapter titled Marine Force consisted of a single, derisive paragraph:

> Before the present invasion of this State by the British, under the command of General Phillips, we had three vessels of 16 guns, one of 14, five small gallies, and two or three armed boats. They were generally so badly manned as seldom to be in condition for service. Since the perfect possession of our rivers assumed by the enemy, I believe we are left with a single armed boat only.[11]

In other words, Jefferson wrote from his little cabin at Poplar Forest, he had been trying to defeat the British with a ragtag militia that was lucky to have a small number of men with real muskets, and a single armed boat. It was with this force that he, a man with no military training, was supposed to fight the greatest army and navy in the world? The defense proffered in *Notes on the State of Virginia* would mesh with his response to the legislature, shifting blame away from him and putting it on the state's meager resources and the failure of militia to turn out.

The most controversial part of *Notes,* in retrospect, would be the inconsistency between his declaration that "all men are created equal" and his denigration of blacks. Jefferson had used one chapter in *Notes* to offer a defense of Indians, for whom he had respect, notwithstanding the fact that he wanted to take their land, turn them into farmers, and convert them into Christians. But when it came to blacks, slave or free, his opinion seemed inalterably hostile, a view that is particularly glaring in light of the evidence that he later had a sexual relationship and children with Sally Hemings. Even as his thirty slaves at Poplar Forest performed forced labor for him, he wrote a scathing criticism of their appearance, their work habits, their intelligence, and even their manifestations of love. He wrote that "they are more ardent after their female: but love seems with them to be more an eager desire, than a tender delicate mixture of sentiment and sensation." Blacks, he said in effect, were not created equal: "I think one could scarcely be found capable of tracing and comprehending the investigations of Euclid." Jefferson suggested the way to end slavery was to send blacks to another land, paying their expenses to help them start new lives. To Jefferson, this was an enlightened idea. It was not possible, he said, for blacks and whites to live in harmony if the slaves were freed and allowed to remain in Virginia. The reason, he wrote, was "deep rooted prejudices entertained by the whites; ten thousand recollections, by the blacks, of the injuries they have sustained; new provocations; the real distinctions which nature has made; and many other circumstances, will divide us into parties, and produce convulsions which will probably never end but in the extermination of the one or the other race."

In writing of these "deep rooted prejudices," Jefferson bluntly acknowledged sharing them. Jefferson sought to justify his denigration of blacks—and his ownership of them—by dehumanizing them. In Jefferson's view, slaves were noncitizens, and thus less than equal; they could be excluded from the liberties he said were due all men.[12]

Over time, he would call slavery a "moral depravity" and a "hideous blot." But he knew his effort to justify slave ownership would be viewed as hypocrisy. Countless critics of slavery, from his Quaker friends in Virginia to John Adams of Massachusetts, chided him over the issue. Nearly forty years after writing *Notes,* Jefferson was still pushing his idea of removing blacks to another land, writing that "there is not a man on earth who would sacrifice more than I would to relieve us from this heavy reproach, in any practicable way." But he saw little chance of it happening anytime soon, acknowledging, "We have the wolf by the ear, and we can neither hold him, nor safely let him go. Justice is in one scale, and self-preservation in the other." The division over slavery in the United States, Jefferson said, was like a "firebell in the night" that "awakened and filled me with terror." The firebell was "hushed" for the moment, he wrote in a letter late in his life, "but this is a reprieve only, not a final sentence."[13]

EVEN AS JEFFERSON WORKED ON *NOTES* in the seclusion of his cabin, the war seemed to be getting closer. The nearest significant town to Poplar Forest was New London, three miles to the southeast, which had about sixty structures, including a major militia arsenal. It was this arsenal that Loyalist conspirators had tried to rob two years earlier, leading Jefferson to congratulate Charles Lynch for arresting them. Now British troops were marching toward the arsenal, bringing the enemy once again on Jefferson's trail.

Worse, the local militia of Bedford County was anything but reliable. James Callaway, a local leader, wrote to Jefferson that the militia was unable to meet a demand to raise two companies despite a month of effort. Some men who were court-martialed for failing to serve escaped their guards. Another forty who enlisted for eighteen months "have long since deserted," Callaway wrote.[14] Rumors spread that some of Jefferson's Bedford County neighbors wanted to come to terms with the British.

By mid-July, the British decided to test the strength of the Patriots in Bedford County. Lieutenant Colonel Tarleton, using the same men who had raided Charlottesville, now moved his forces in the direction of Poplar Forest. As they headed west, Tarleton's men plundered homes for treasure, "ripped open feather-beds, broke mirrors," and set on fire at least one house, which was doused by a sudden rainstorm.[15] Arriving in Bedford County, Tarleton headed toward New London, the town near Poplar Forest. Hugh Rose, who had hosted Jefferson at his home a month earlier, considered it "a matter of first importance" to stop Tarleton's approach. He successfully rallied the local militia and made sure the arms stored at New London were hidden. Tarleton either became concerned about the gathering of the militia or was unable to determine where the arms were stored, and he headed back east to link up with Cornwallis's army. Once again, Jefferson had escaped the British threat.[16]

THE FORCES OF THE MARQUIS DE LAFAYETTE, encamped twenty-five miles from Lord Cornwallis's army, were getting stronger every day. "Mad Anthony" Wayne finally arrived with his eight hundred Pennsylvanians. Smaller units also trickled in, including the one with Joseph Atkins of Connecticut. A seemingly motley assortment of Virginia militia streamed into camp as well, some of them shoeless, wearing ragged hunting shirts and pants held together with an assortment of colorful patches. By the end of June, Lafayette commanded about 5,600 men, finally giving him enough men to engage Cornwallis's army of 7,700. If Lafayette caught the British crossing a river or an unfamiliar area, he could try to outflank the enemy. For the first time during the 1781 invasion, the Americans prepared to be the aggressors.

One of those at Lafayette's camp was Thomas Nelson Jr. The legislature in Staunton had accepted Jefferson's suggestion and appointed him governor and leader of the state's military. Several months earlier, the legislature had balked at Jefferson's request for more power to compel militia turnout. Now the legislature went far beyond what Jefferson had initially requested and gave Nelson an array of powers to enable him to turn out militia. The new governor was authorized to confiscate property of those who opposed the effort to call up militia, and to impose the death penalty against deserters. After several years in which Jefferson and other Virginia leaders had worried about giving too much power to a governor, the adoption of these extraordinary measures marked a sea change. To prevent an abuse of power, the legislature insisted that Nelson could invoke the powers only with the approval of the Governor's Council, which was composed of legislative leaders. Nelson often ignored even this attempt at oversight, ordering the seizure of property on his own accord when he believed it was impractical to consult the Council. His aggressive actions would lead to charges by some legislators that he had abused his powers, but he was cleared of the accusation.[1]

Most importantly, the legislature also approved measures to encourage a better turnout among the militia, ensuring that the pay of militia members would be the same as that of Continental soldiers, and that it would be increased to make up for depreciation of Continental currency. The legislators agreed that the militia, who typically had been on three-month terms, would serve only for two months at a time "and in no case to continue longer, unless the relief should be prevented from coming in time by some unavoidable accident."[2] Many deserters returned to duty and pleaded for mercy, anxious to avoid the tough new penalties. Separately, a number of local officials all but ignored efforts to draft Virginians for the Continental army, signaling to wary militia that they wouldn't face the threat of double duty if they showed up to protect Virginia.

Governor Nelson's whereabouts were unknown for several weeks, panicking his aides in the poorly defended and nearly deserted capital of Richmond. "I think we shall be swept off one of these days," Commissioner of War William Davies wrote on July 12 to Steuben, who himself was out of action due to a lengthy illness. "I see nothing in the world to prevent it. There is nobody here [who] knows where the Governor is, nor have we heard the least tittle from him or about him since he left Charlottesville. I hardly know how to account for it."[3] Four days later, Nelson showed up at the capital, but he did not stay long. He preferred a military role and went back to the battlefield.

Cornwallis, meanwhile, abruptly ended his western raids. He left Elk Hill on June 13, briefly occupied Richmond, crossed the Chickahominy River, and marched to Williamsburg. He believed he had succeeded in his primary mission in Virginia, which was to destroy the military supply system that had been hurting his efforts in South Carolina. He wrote to Clinton that he had destroyed five thousand arms and six hundred barrels of gunpowder while spreading fear across Virginia and putting the governor and legislature on the run. While Cornwallis's move toward Williamsburg struck some Virginians as a retreat, he viewed it as a tactical maneuver that would give him time to regroup and await orders from Clinton.

Those orders soon arrived. Clinton was worried about protecting his base in New York. The British commander had sent some of his men to reinforce Cornwallis and now feared he was exposed to attack. Clinton's fear was underscored when spies captured a letter from Washington to Lafayette that appeared to outline an allied American-French plan to attack New York. The letter actually was part of a ruse to deceive Clinton into hunkering down with his forces in New York. But Clinton, upon reviewing the letter, believed he was vulnerable. Clinton worried that his force of nearly eleven thousand would be overwhelmed by an American army of Continentals and militia of at least twenty thousand led by Washington. He ordered Cornwallis to establish a defensive post and then send as many troops as possible to New York.[4]

A major factor in Clinton's calculations was the influence of Arnold, who had returned from his five months in Virginia and now was a regular presence at British headquarters in New York. Arnold used his influence with Clinton to argue for his proposal to seize the Congress in Philadelphia. Cornwallis advised against it, writing to Clinton that an attack on Philadelphia "would do more harm than good to the cause of Britain," especially if Arnold did no more than plunder the city and then depart. Clinton was torn by indecision. William Smith, the chief justice of New York, who met frequently with Clinton, described him as "very unfit for his Station" and "very changeable."[5] Arnold's proposal was to recall four thousand of Cornwallis's men, whom Arnold would meet in Maryland. The men would then march to Philadelphia, oust the Congress, and seize the supplies of the Continental army. Clinton initially approved the idea but then reconsidered because of the threat that Washington might attack New York. Arnold was "disgusted at the Inactivity" in New York and tried to convince Clinton that Washington was too weak to attack the city. "General Arnold is discouraged," Smith wrote in his diary. "He despairs from the Defect of a Spirit of Enterprise, and Indecision. He can get nothing done." Clinton, meanwhile, was "all Misery, seems to approve but changes and resolves nothing."[6]

Indeed, Clinton worried that Virginia would be a lost cause if the Americans were reinforced by a French fleet. The citizenry of the Old Dominion hardly seemed submissive. "If we have not their hearts—which I fear cannot be expected in Virginia—there is reason to believe" that Virginians would "revolt again." Unless Loyalists rose up in Virginia, Clinton wrote to Lord George Germain, "we may conquer [but] we shall never keep."[7]

HAVING RECEIVED CLINTON'S ORDER to send as many men as possible to New York, Cornwallis marched from Williamsburg to Jamestown, preparing to cross the James River. His goal was to reach Portsmouth, send some transports loaded with men to New York, and then determine where to establish a defensive base. Cornwallis knew that Lafayette was trailing him and would try to attack his force while it was strung out across the river, so he set a trap. A large part of Cornwallis's force would hide in the woods, while giving Lafayette the impression that the men had crossed the river. Then, when Lafayette tried to attack Cornwallis's exposed rear, the men hiding in the trees would ambush the Americans.

Lafayette fell for the trap, sending Wayne with five hundred men to attack. The British sprang from the woods while Wayne, living up to his reputation, repeatedly risked his life while directing his men and exposing himself to fire. In the ensuing battle, at least twenty-eight Americans were killed, ninety-nine were wounded, and twelve were missing, while the British suffered about half that many casualties. The Americans also lost two of their prize pieces of field artillery. It was Lafayette's greatest loss of men as a commander. But Lafayette managed to portray it as a success. As the British crossed the river, Lafayette's men took over the battlefield, enabling the Frenchman to depict the enemy as being in retreat. "It will look well in a gazette," Lafayette said. As Lafayette's biographer wrote, "every patriotic American, including Lafayette, came to believe that Cornwallis ran because Lafayette chased him, though in actuality Lafayette chased him because he ran."[8]

As Cornwallis reached the south side of the James River and marched to Portsmouth, Virginians exulted that the enemy seemed to have entirely abandoned the northern portion of Virginia. The area from Yorktown to Richmond to Charlottesville and beyond was cleared of the British invaders. Then the force led by Tarleton, which had conducted raids that went nearly as far to the southwest as Poplar Forest, left to link up with Cornwallis, removing the British from that portion of the state. In a matter of a few weeks, Cornwallis had gone from loosely controlling a vast portion of Virginia to isolating his force at Portsmouth.

Jefferson, learning of the British withdrawal, considered it safe to end his five weeks of seclusion at Poplar Forest. Bidding goodbye to the overseer whose cabin had served as their home, Jefferson and his family climbed into a carriage for the hundred-mile ride back to Monticello. With Lafayette being hailed across Virginia, Jefferson wrote to the marquis to express his "private esteem" and "public gratitude."[9] Confident that it would be "impossible" for Cornwallis to escape from Virginia, Jefferson concentrated on clearing his name and then returning to private life.

"I have taken my final leave of everything of [a public] nature, have retired to my farm, my family and books from which I think nothing will ever more separate me," Jefferson wrote to James Monroe. But Jefferson had one more public task. He said he had "a desire to leave public office with a reputation not more blotted than it has deserved." Thus, he would seek a seat in the House of Delegates "with a single object": to defend his actions as governor, after which he would resign his seat.[10]

CORNWALLIS NOW FACED a momentous decision about what to do in Virginia. For weeks, Cornwallis corresponded with Clinton, the British commander who was still hoping that Cornwallis could send half of his men northward for reinforcement. Cornwallis believed it was essential to remain in Virginia in order to stop the flow of supplies to the American armies. Cornwallis had arrived in Portsmouth but was unenthusiastic about remaining with a depleted force at a swampy area that was a breeding ground for sickness. After several more weeks, Cornwallis decided to abandon Portsmouth, acting on what he believed to be an order from Clinton to establish bases near the mouth of the York River, at Yorktown on the south, and at Gloucester on the north. Clinton insisted that he had left it up to Cornwallis as to where to put his force. The two men would bicker for the rest of their lives about why Cornwallis wound up on the banks of the York River.[11]

The departure of the British from Portsmouth was just what Loyalists in the area had feared. Several months earlier, Johann Ewald had asked a leading Loyalist why more people did not turn out to support the British. The Loyalist had responded that people could never be certain the British would remain to protect them. Now, as the British abandoned Portsmouth and the Loyalists who lived nearby, Ewald wrote in his diary, "How will this look to the loyal subjects there? Have we not made enough people unhappy already?"[12]

The withdrawal, combined with the plundering of the countryside that was necessary to feed a huge army, turned yet more Virginians against the British. Cornwallis "is further from the conquest of Virginia than when he enter'd it. I don't believe ten Men have join'd him," Governor Nelson wrote to Washington. "They have made Whigs of Tories."[13] In fact, Nelson was more worried about Tory sympathizers to the British than he admitted; he ordered the arrest of his own brother-in-law, Phillip Grymes, who was among a group of men who had conspired against "the interests of the United States."[14]

But help was finally on the way. On August 14, Washington received assurances that the French admiral François-Joseph de Grasse would sail his fleet from the West Indies to Chesapeake Bay. As a result, Washington finally felt it was safe to heed months of urgent requests from Virginians and ordered his troops to Virginia to meet Cornwallis.

Clinton should have realized that Washington and his French ally, the Comte de Rochambeau, were heading south. The British had learned that the Continental army had ordered forage to be ready for a march through New Jersey. At the same time, an American woman who was a mistress to a French officer—and under surveillance by a British spy—was being sent to Trenton, "where she is to await the arrival of the army." This information was given to Clinton by a Hessian officer, Lieutenant Colonel von Wurmb. Clinton nonetheless still believed that Washington planned to attack New York.[15] Two weeks after receiving the intelligence report, Clinton was clearly confused by what he feared were Washington's feints. "I cannot well ascertain Mr. Washington's real intentions," he wrote, while suggesting that he might send fresh troops to Virginia were he certain of the American plans. Cornwallis, in the meantime, had no alternative but to work feverishly to fortify Yorktown.

In London, meanwhile, senior British officials wondered why so much emphasis had been put on remaining in Virginia. Richard Oswald, a British diplomat, went to the Tower of London, where the former president of the Continental Congress, Henry Laurens, was being held prisoner. The South Carolinian had been caught by the British during a mission to Europe. Oswald wound his way through the warrens of the old prison and entered the cell of Laurens, whom he had known from the days when South Carolina was a reliable colony. Oswald presented Laurens with a series of queries about conditions in America and finally asked Laurens what would happen if Virginia and the South were in submission. "Don't you think the Colonies to the Northward would give way?" Oswald asked. "I believe not," Laurens replied. "They would be obstinate and a scene of much blood and confusion would in all probability be still continued."

Returning to his quarters, Oswald prepared a lengthy report, which came to be known as "Mr. Oswald's Memorandum on the Folly of Invading Virginia." He thought it foolish for Cornwallis to expend his efforts on "that skirmishing War in Virginia" and recommended he return to the Carolinas. "If he should not, I think he ought to have Orders to do so." He inveighed against "the impropriety of this Virginia Invasion," which left British troops isolated and difficult to reinforce. "If I thought he had any chance of Success in that Country, it would be far against my inclination of his being interrupted." But Oswald despaired about the chance of success. He suggested that Cornwallis leave a small fleet at Portsmouth, guarding the mouth of Chesapeake Bay, and return to the Carolinas. The recommendation was sent on August 17, 1781, too late for the British ministers to enact a change in their Virginia strategy.[16]

ALL THE PIECES NOW WERE IN PLACE for the dénouement at Yorktown. Admiral de Grasse headed from the West Indies with his fleet of twenty-eight ships to Chesapeake Bay, where he defeated the British fleet of Admiral Thomas Graves, thus cutting off Cornwallis's access to the Atlantic. Clinton, finally convinced that Washington was headed south, belatedly promised to arrive with reinforcements. He planned to meet Cornwallis in Yorktown but left too late to participate in the battle. Washington's army joined with the French forces of the Comte de Rochambeau and marched to Virginia, where an emotional reunion was held in Williamsburg with Lafayette. "Never was more joy painted in any countenance than theirs," wrote an eyewitness, St. George Tucker.

"The Marquis rode up with precipitation, clasped the General in his arms, and embraced him in an ardor not easily described." The two men, accompanied by Governor Nelson, inspected the troops who overflowed the fields outside Williamsburg. Then Washington took his quarters at the home of George Wythe, Jefferson's former teacher, and planned his assault.[17]

In Yorktown, Cornwallis oversaw the construction of ten redoubts, lined with sixty-five cannons, including some from the *Charon,* the ship that Arnold had been on when he arrived in Virginia nine months earlier. But the combined force of 8,880 French (with another 15,000 on nearby ships) and 11,133 Americans vastly outnumbered the 9,725 British. The allied force brought 375 siege cannons, mortars, and other large guns, which they fired at an average rate of one shell every 1.2 seconds, shattering the redoubts and shaking the ground.[18]

Many of the major players in the 1781 invasion of Virginia converged at the scene. Cornwallis oversaw the battle from the village of Yorktown, while Tarleton and Ewald operated across the river at Gloucester.

On the American side, Washington gave the honor of overseeing one of the three divisions to Baron von Steuben, whose illness had kept him out of most of the summer fighting and whose reputation had been, in Washington's view, unfairly tarnished during his service in Virginia. The other divisions were given to Lafayette and to General Benjamin Lincoln, who wanted to avenge his surrender to Cornwallis at Charleston, South Carolina.

The Virginia militia, having borne so much criticism during the invasion, finally had the weapons and support it needed to be an effective force. About 3,200 of the Americans at Yorktown were from Virginia, under the overall command of Nelson in his adjunct role as the state's military leader. Nelson knew that his home in Yorktown was occupied by some British officers. Nelson, according to family legend, was said to have told the men firing the siege guns not to spare his home. Nelson's home was hit but survived, but the nearby residence of his uncle was destroyed.[19]

The increasingly desperate British could not stable or feed their hundreds of horses, so they were slaughtered and dragged into the York River, only to be brought back by the tide "as if they wanted to cry out against their murder after their death," Ewald wrote. The British and Hessian soldiers also no longer could feed or care for the slaves to whom they had promised freedom. So the British "drove back to the enemy all of our black friends . . . we had used them to good advantage and set them free, and now, with fear and trembling, they had to face the reward of their cruel masters."[20]

A number of Jefferson's slaves who had been seized by Arnold's forces in Richmond were with the British nearly until the end. Isaac was under British control at least through July and he recalled remaining so until October at Yorktown. (He later provided a contradictory chronology of the latter part of that tumultuous year when he was about six years old, leaving open the possibility that his memory of Yorktown was based on what he was told.) A "great many colored people died" at Yorktown, Isaac said, "but none of Mr. Jefferson's folks." As the Americans fired their siege cannons, Isaac said there was tremendous noise and smoke, which "seemed like heaven and earth was come together." He said he jumped every time the great guns fired, and heard the cries of wounded men screaming in pain. When the smoke blew away, "you see the dead men lying on the ground." Isaac and some other surviving slaves returned to Monticello, where Jefferson was "mighty pleased to see his people come back safe and sound," Isaac said. Isaac would work for Jefferson for many years, making nails and tin cups and performing other tasks. In 1847, he was a free man working as a blacksmith in Petersburg when a visitor recorded his memories for posterity.[21]

EWALD CAME TO ADMIRE the fighting skill, intelligence, and dedication of the American soldier. As one of the most astute observers of warfare, Ewald marveled that doctors, ministers, and farmers had "made themselves into excellent officers, putting to shame so many of our profession who have grown gray under arms." These Americans "did not choose military service as a refuge, as the nobility generally does, nor as a house of correction for an ill-bred son who would not learn anything at the academies, as is often the case among the middle classes" of Europe. Instead, the Americans became soldiers due to their "firm resolution ... of serving their country usefully, and of pushing themselves forward by their merits."

Ewald was astonished at how many captured Americans had carried military books in knapsacks that otherwise mostly contained "a few shirts and a pair of torn breeches." Volumes such as *Instructions of the King of Prussia to His Generals* and *Field Engineer,* translated into English, "came into my hands a hundred times through our soldiers." By contrast, the finely dressed and coifed British officers carried baggage filled with "bags of hair-powder, boxes of sweet-smelling" hair ointment called pomatum, playing cards, and "on top of all, some novels or stage plays."[22]

The Americans, Ewald concluded, were fighting for their lives and defending their country, while the British and Hessians were fighting for their royal leaders in a remote and hostile land. The Americans were willing to go "nearly naked and in the greatest privation." Such conditions would cause the best

European soldiers to "run away in droves," while the "poor fellows" of America were motivated by one thought: "Liberty!"[23]

JOSIAH ATKINS, the Connecticut soldier who saw the putrefying bodies of former slaves as he marched into Virginia and became a surgeon's assistant, had become increasingly ill as his unit neared Yorktown. Having attended to many dying soldiers under his care, Atkins contracted an illness that became grave enough for him to be discharged and sent homeward. He did not make it far. On October 15, he made a final entry in his diary, writing that his "fever is very severe at the present." Six days later, he died.

Atkins had been a devoutly religious man, outraged at the abuses of war and the mistreatment of blacks in Virginia, writing in his diary that he believed God would protect him. Yet he prepared for death in Virginia. He wrote a note accompanying his diary that he hoped would be read by whoever might find him dead. The person who found his body was welcome to his watch, silver shoe buckles, and stone sleeve buttons. "These I give you freely," he wrote. He asked only one favor: "To use best your utmost endeavor to send this book with its contents to my dear wife, whom [I] have left at home to mourn my misfortune." Concerned that an enemy might find the book and discard it, he provided his assurance that "I ever was while in life, the friend and well-wisher of all the soldiers." Atkins's last wish was granted by an unknown patron, who made sure that Sarah Atkins received her husband's diary. She treasured the volume, reading it aloud to their daughter, Sally, and to the son whom Josiah Atkins never met, born just days after the Connecticut soldier died in Virginia.[24]

AMERICANS SAW SPLENDOR in the bursting of bombs at Yorktown, each blast bringing the battle closer to conclusion. At nighttime, the cannonballs "appear like fiery meteors with blazing tails, most beautifully brilliant, ascending majestically to a certain altitude, and gradually descending to the spot where they are destined to execute their work of destruction," wrote James Thacher, an American surgeon who had spent much of the war operating on American victims of British shelling. Now he described the power of the American and French bombardment, which caused "fragments of the mangled bodies and limbs" of British soldiers to be "thrown into the air."[25]

On October 11, shortly after the American and French guns began firing in earnest, Cornwallis wrote a desperate dispatch to Clinton, who had failed to fulfill his promise to bring four thousand reinforcements. The American and French assault was so powerful that "we cannot hope to make a long resistance." Nothing but the arrival of Clinton's fleet on the York "can save me." Seventy British and Hessian soldiers had been killed, and the defenses were heavily damaged. A few hours later, Cornwallis wrote a postscript: "Since the above was written, we have lost thirty men." The following morning, he added another postscript: "We continue to lose men very fast." A French officer described the horrific scene in the following days, saying Yorktown was "riddled by cannon fire . . . One could not take three steps without running into some great holes made by bombs . . . with scattered white or negro arms or legs, some bits of uniforms."[26]

Cornwallis met with his council of war, which unanimously advised him to give up. On October 20, Cornwallis sent his final battlefield communiqué to Clinton: "I have the mortification to inform Your Excellency that I have been forced to give up the posts of York and Gloucester and to surrender the troops under my command by capitulation." The surrender agreement was co-signed by Thomas Symonds, the naval commander who had accompanied Arnold on the mission to Virginia and repeatedly clashed with him over the division of prizes and plunder. Clinton learned of the defeat as he sailed to Chesapeake Bay on his delayed rescue mission. It would be another two years before a peace treaty was signed, but the surrender at Yorktown effectively ended British hopes of winning the war.[27]

The invasion of Virginia, which had begun ten months earlier with such great hopes and easy conquests by Arnold, which had forced the flight of Jefferson and spread fear throughout the state, had ended with the inexorable siege of great guns fired by a superior army against a diminished enemy hiding behind battered mounds of earth on an indefensible peninsula. Three months later, Cornwallis returned to England on a ship that also carried Arnold, who would fruitlessly urge King George III to send him back to America to command an army.

Jefferson, learning of the victory, wrote a brief note of congratulations to Washington from Monticello. If it were not for his "state of perpetual decrepitude to which I am unfortunately reduced," Jefferson wrote, "I should certainly have done myself the honour of paying my respects to you personally." He did not want to "interfere" at Washington's encampment at such a moment.[28] Washington, Lafayette, Steuben, Wayne, and Nelson were feted across the newly freed state of Virginia. Jefferson, meanwhile, remained at Monticello, collecting affidavits in defense of his actions as he prepared to seek a seat in the House of Delegates, the platform he hoped to use to regain his honor.

ON DECEMBER 12, 1781, Jefferson, newly elected as the delegate from Albemarle County, prepared to address the charges against him. It had been six tumultuous months since the legislature demanded an investigation into his conduct during the invasion. Now, with the British defeat at Yorktown and Jefferson's return to the public stage, the matter could be settled. The delegates, however, no longer wanted to challenge the author of the Declaration of Independence. The war was all but over. The assembly preferred to pass a resolution thanking Jefferson for his service and drop the matter.

Jefferson was dismayed. He had spent months preparing to respond to what he believed were malicious accusations. George Nicholas, whom Jefferson believed had instigated the matter at Patrick Henry's behest, was absent. Henry was silent. No one was willing to prosecute the charges. "I came here in consequence of it, and found neither accuser nor accusation," Jefferson wrote later.[1]

Rising from his chair, he demanded the right to address the assembly. If no one would read the allegations against him, he would do it himself and provide answers he had drawn up during the summer. So Jefferson began to question himself. One by one, he went down a list of questions, and in each case he provided a defense.

What did he say about the charge that Washington had warned that the enemy was embarked upon an invasion of Virginia? Washington had written Jefferson on December 9, 1780, three weeks before Arnold arrived in Virginia, that "I am this Moment informed from New York, another embarkation is taking place...supposed to be destined Southward." The letter did not say that Arnold was leading the fleet, nor provide anything more specific than that the ships were headed south, leaving it unclear whether the ships intended to invade relatively tranquil Virginia or head farther south to the Carolinas, where warfare was rampant. "The truth is that Gen. Washington always considered it his duty to convey every rumor of embarkation," Jefferson said. At one time, Jefferson said, Virginia responded to such warnings by calling out the militia and other defenses at great expense, which "went far towards the ruin of our finances that followed." There wasn't enough evidence of an invasion to warrant setting up a costly defense in this case, he said.

Why had Jefferson failed to order riders to survey the coast and warn of an invasion? Again, Jefferson said he couldn't order the riders to their horses every time Washington warned of an invasion. "Those letters [from Washington] were no more than we had received upon many former occasions, and would have led to a perpetual establishment of post riders."

The next question, however, seemed to put the blame squarely on Jefferson. After being told that a fleet of ships had appeared at the Capes of Virginia, why had he failed to put enough men on the march from Williamsburg to protect the capital of Richmond? Jefferson had received a message telling him that a fleet had arrived on the coast, clearly indicating the possible threat, but Jefferson delayed calling out the militia because he was not certain whether the ships were French or British. Knowing the reluctance of the militia to turn out, he waited for better information. "It is denied that [the militia] were few or late," Jefferson said. He had called up 4,700 men "the moment an invasion was known to take place . . . on Tuesday, Jan. 2."

This was Jefferson's weakest response. It supposed it was wrong to call for a full defense unless there was unimpeachable intelligence, which is often unavailable during times of war. Jefferson knew the militia would be angry at a false alarm, and thus he delayed his reaction until information was certain. To Jefferson, this was the prudent course to follow. Had the war turned out differently in Virginia, however, the response would have prompted great scrutiny.

Why had there been no lookouts? "There had been no cause to order lookouts more than has ever been existing," Jefferson responded.

Why had the state not had adequate artillery that could be quickly moved on carriages? Jefferson blamed the Board of War and the Continental Congress, which failed to provide the necessary money. "We have even been unable to get those heavy cannon moved . . . by the whole energy of government."

The questions continued: Why had Jefferson not provided better defense on the approach to Richmond? Why had the militia been undermanned? To all of these questions, he responded that he had done what he could with threadbare intelligence, a nearly empty treasury, and an often disobedient militia. The only way to protect the entrance to the James River, Jefferson argued, would have been to keep a large force, possibly against their will, at the ready. "Would it be approved to harass the militia with garrisoning them?" Jefferson asked rhetorically.[2]

The bottom line, as many legislators appreciated, was that Virginia had been wholly unprepared for an invasion, that the militia system had been unreliable, and that the governor had had limited powers. It was also true that Jefferson was unsuited to be a military commander, as he said so himself on many occasions.

The matter was now nearly at an end. All that remained was for the assembly to apologize to Jefferson and thank him for his work. The matter had been referred to a committee, which said it convened to examine "some rumors" about Jefferson. No explanations of the rumors were given in the House journal. No one came forward with information to support them. Instead, the committee issued a one-sentence statement that it hoped would end the matter: "*Resolved, that it is the opinion of this committee,* That the said rumors were groundless."

Then another motion was made, amounting to a blanket apology and offer of gratitude to Jefferson. It was the equivalent of a legislature on bent knee, asking forgiveness.

> *Resolved,* That the sincere thanks of the General Assembly be given to our former Governor, Thomas Jefferson, Esq. For his impartial, upright, and attentive administration of the powers of the Executive, whilst in office; popular rumors gaining some degree of credence, by more pointed accusations, rendered it necessary to make an inquiry into his conduct, and delayed that retribution of public gratitude, so eminently merited; but that conduct having become the object of open scrutiny, tenfold value is added to an approbation, founded on a cool and deliberate discussion. The Assembly wish therefore, in the strongest manner, to declare the high opinion which they entertain of Mr. Jefferson's ability, rectitude and integrity, as Chief Magistrate of this Commonwealth; and mean by thus publicly avowing their opinion, to obviate all future, and to remove all former, unmerited censure.[3]

The measure was approved unanimously by the House and then the Senate. Jefferson, duly satisfied, resigned his seat as a delegate. But the experience continued to embitter him. The legislators had acknowledged that the accusation "was founded on *rumours* only, for which no foundation can be discovered," he wrote disdainfully to a friend, Isaac Zane.[4] Nonetheless, in the same letter Jefferson made clear that he wished to put the matter behind him, focusing on what he hoped would fill the remainder of his life: pursuits of the mind and examinations of the earth and the sky. He told Zane that he looked forward to discussing questions that were "mathematical, meteorological, geographical, physiological." He accepted an appointment to be counselor to the American Philosophical Society.

The state of Jefferson's mind at this time was particularly evident when he took up his pen to write to western military commander George Rogers Clark. Unlike his prior communication with Clark about Indian wars, Jefferson now had a scientific request. Having learned that the bones of a previously unknown and perhaps prehistoric "giant animal" had been found in the Ohio River area, Jefferson asked Clark if it was "possible to get a tooth of each kind, that is to say, foretooth, grinder." He urged Clark to secure the teeth in a box and arrange wagon transport as soon as possible. "The retirement into which I am withdrawing has increased my eagerness in pursuit of objects of this kind."[5]

Jefferson believed his public life was over. His desire now was to be a farmer on his mountain, a philosopher, a student of the sciences, examining the bones and teeth of prehistoric creatures, playing his violin, and perusing his books, all as he remained by the side of his Martha and their two daughters.

THE REVOLUTION HAD RID VIRGINIA of its British rulers, established greater toleration of religions, prompted freer trade around the world, and led to numerous other changes. But many of the gentry who had held high positions in Virginia before the revolution remained in power. Benjamin Harrison, whose plantation had been plundered by troops of Benedict Arnold, was named governor. With the British emancipation of slaves voided, slavery became even more deeply entrenched as a key part of the state's economy. The militiamen and Continental soldiers returned to their farms and families, with some collecting enlistment bonuses that enhanced their lives and others spending decades trying to collect compensation. The western lands claimed by Indians more rapidly fell into the hands of white settlers.

Mary Byrd retained her seat at Westover, once again demonstrating her diplomatic skills by welcoming into her home a group of French officers who had defeated the British at Yorktown. They included the Comte de Rochambeau and his erstwhile aide-de-camp, Baron Ludwig von Closen. Even as Byrd told the British she was nearly broke, Closen noted that Westover was still "maintained like a palace" and had "magnificent" furnishings. Closen marveled at the plantations lining the James River, "one more beautiful than the other," which were overseen "by the aristocracy" that remained very much in evidence. The aristocrats of Virginia "are fond of society, and abandon themselves to it, perhaps with too much relish, thinking only of amusing themselves," Closen wrote. He was appalled that the revolution had done nothing to change the system of slavery, describing the "large number of negro slaves" who were treated "cruelly" and "are not considered to be much better than animals." He observed that there were relatively few black slaves in New England, while in the south nearly all of the blacks were still slaves. "In general," Closen concluded, "despotism and aristocracy are the rule in Virginia more than elsewhere."[6]

During the same tour of Virginia, Rochambeau and Closen headed west to meet Jefferson. After crossing the Rivanna River and climbing up the mountain road, Closen and Rochambeau arrived at Monticello in midafternoon on

February 21, 1782. Jefferson, who had reluctantly passed up the opportunity
to be an American representative in France, was delighted that this group of
Frenchmen, who had played an integral role in ousting the British from Virginia, were paying their respects to him. Closen found Jefferson to be "a great
philosopher" who was "well read in literature, history and geography" and had
an "incomparable knowledge" of America. They discussed Jefferson's role in
the revolution and the war, including Tarleton's raid on Charlottesville, which
had "much alarmed his family," Closen wrote. Jefferson took the Frenchmen
on a tour of the mountains, pointing out the site of the former Albemarle Barracks to the north, the James River to the south, and the Blue Ridge to the west.
Jefferson told the story of how his experiment in viticulture had failed at the
nearby Colle estate when the horses of Baron von Riedesel trampled the vineyards. The Frenchmen settled into Monticello, perusing Jefferson's library and
spending the night. They "very regretfully" left on the following morning, having found him "very interesting and [his] family very agreeable."[7]

Jefferson's reputation now seemed rehabilitated. His role as the author of
the Declaration of Independence, which had not received great publicity at the
time, was becoming more widely known. In an ironic turn, a number of members of the Virginia House of Delegates now wanted Jefferson back in power,
arranging his election as a delegate, the position in which Jefferson had served
only briefly in order to respond to the inquiry into his conduct. Not only was
Jefferson suddenly expected to return to Richmond, but the new Speaker of the
House, John Tyler Sr., suggested that Jefferson might be "seized" and arrested
if he failed to show up. Tyler wanted Jefferson to take his place as Speaker of
the House, a position that some considered more powerful than the governorship. Tyler pleaded with Jefferson, telling him that "if the able and good
withdraw themselves from society, the venal and ignorant will succeed."[8] Jefferson might have supposed that the latter words referred to Henry, who had
reemerged as a legislative leader and tangled harshly with Tyler. The feud escalated when Henry backed a proposal renewing relations with Loyalists, which
prompted a stunned Tyler to ask how Henry, "above all other men, could think
of inviting into his family an enemy from whose insults and injuries he had suffered so severely."[9]

Jefferson, having just beaten back Henry's inquiry into his conduct, had no
interest in battling against him in the House. "I do not accept" the appointment, Jefferson wrote on May 6. He also had personal reasons for declining the
post. His wife was about to give birth, a condition that was bound to increase
her frailty. Two days later, Martha delivered her sixth child. The Jeffersons
named the baby Lucy Elizabeth, the same name given to their last child, who

had died thirteen months earlier during the invasion of Virginia. Martha's recovery was even more difficult than usual, confining her to bed.

Increasingly concerned about Martha's health, Jefferson wrote one of the most emotional letters of his life to his close friend James Monroe. Jefferson could not, must not, serve again in the legislature. While he was "always mortified when any thing is expected me which I cannot fulfill," he said he had "examined well my heart" and found that he was "thoroughly cured of every principle of political ambition." No "particle" of desire for political life remained. "Every fibre of that passion was thoroughly eradicated." He had allowed his private affairs "to run into great disorder and ruin" and had "a family advanced to years which required my attention and instruction." He had wanted nothing more from public service than "the affection of my countrymen." Instead, he "had even lost the small estimation" he once held. Even though the legislature had cleared his name, he believed his public image had been irreparably damaged. "I felt that these injuries . . . had inflicted a wound on my spirit which will only be cured by the all-healing grave," Jefferson wrote.[10]

Martha's condition quickly deteriorated. In June, legislators wrongly were told that she had died. Throughout the summer, Jefferson remained by Martha's side, "never out of calling," their daughter Patsy later recalled. "When not at her bed side he was writing in a small room which opened immediately at the head of her bed." Together, they shared memories of a favorite novel, *Tristram Shandy*. First, Martha took pen to paper:

> *Time wastes too fast: every letter*
> *I trace tells me with what rapidity*
> *Life follows my pen. The days and hours*
> *of it are flying over our heads like*
> *clouds of windy day never to return*
> *more everything presses on . . .*

Martha stopped writing. Jefferson, using a darker ink, completed the transcription:

> *. . . and every*
> *Time I kiss thy hand to bid adieu, every absence which*
> *follows it, are preludes to that eternal separation*
> *which we are shortly to make!*

After four months of "tormenting pain," Martha died on September 20. Jefferson was led from the room "almost in a state of insensibility," Patsy recalled. It was with great difficulty that the family ushered Jefferson into the library, "where he fainted and remained so long insensible that they feared he would never revive." Jefferson walked "incessantly night and day" and otherwise kept to his room for three weeks. He then poured his grief into long rides on horseback along remote trails or straight through the woods, often taking along ten-year-old Patsy. "In those melancholy rambles, I was his constant companion, a solitary witness to many a violent burst of grief," she wrote later.[11]

The loss of Martha was "unmeasurable," Jefferson wrote two weeks after her death. He could not conceive when he might emerge from "this miserable kind of existence," he told Martha's sister Elizabeth. Life only seemed worth continuing because of the "sacred charge left to me"—his daughters, Patsy, Maria, and the infant Lucy Elizabeth. The death of his thirty-three-year-old wife, Jefferson wrote, meant that "all my plans of comfort and happiness [were] reversed by a single event."[12]

Jefferson's friend and former neighbor, Philip Mazzei, attributed Martha's death partly to the horrific events of the invasion of the Virginia, during which she endured repeated flights from Richmond, the death of the first Lucy Elizabeth, the escape to Monticello, and the further flight to the home of Hugh Rose and onward to Poplar Forest. The innumerable rough rides on short notice and the narrow escapes from the British, combined with her frail health, had eventually taken their toll. "His angelic wife's death," Mazzei believed, "was the aftermath of her fright."[13]

Jefferson had sworn off public life. But in seeking escape from his grief, he accepted a new offer to serve as an American representative in Paris. He eventually found that he had much more than a "particle" of ambition and did re-enter politics, seeking the presidency, only to find that his clash with Patrick Henry and the events of the invasion of 1781 would haunt him once again.

JEFFERSON HAD BARELY SETTLED into his job as an America's representative in Paris in 1784 when he received news from home. Henry had won election to the governorship and, to Jefferson's alarm, intended to revise Virginia's
constitution. Writing in code due to concern his letter might be intercepted,
Jefferson expressed his disbelief to James Madison. "While Mr. Henry lives another bad constitution would be formed, and saddled forever on us," Jefferson
wrote, referring to laws that governed Virginia. "What we have to do I think is
devoutly pray for his death."[1]

In particular, Henry had proposed a tax to fund Christian denominations,
an effort all the more striking given that two decades earlier Henry had come
to prominence in a court case that centered on a tax that supported the Anglican Church. Henry argued that his tax proposal was different because citizens
could choose any Christian denomination to support, not simply the Anglicans. But the "General Religious Assessment" excluded payments to non-
Christian faiths and would build strong ties between church and state.

Henry's proposal came at a time when those who considered themselves
Deists were under attack. Deists believe that God created the universe and
governs by natural law but does not intervene directly in the life of humans;
they reject miracle stories and sacred revelations that are central to many religions. Jefferson shared many of these Deist beliefs. Years later, he underscored
his view by compiling his own book of Jesus' moral teachings extracted from the
gospels, while excising parts that he found unbelievable, including mentions
of miraculous or supernatural events (an assemblage that became known as the
"Jefferson Bible"). This would lead some of Jefferson's critics to accuse him of
being a nonbeliever, which Jefferson denied. Henry, meanwhile, believed the
Bible was "worth all the books that were ever printed," and thus he supported
the taxation of Virginians to teach the Christian faith. He thought that "religion [is] of infinitely higher importance than politics." He would rather be
considered a Tory—a British Loyalist—than viewed as "no Christian."[2]

One of Jefferson's aims had been to create what was later called a wall of separation between church and state. Some of Jefferson's revolutionary brethren
wanted to maintain the ties between church and state. As a House delegate and
governor, Jefferson had first proposed what would become known as the Virginia Statute for Religious Freedom, which called for an absolute separation,

but failed to win passage for the measure. Jefferson hoped Henry's effort would remind Virginians what was at stake. Indeed, he wrote, it would be helpful if Anglicans showed "their teeth and fangs. The dissenters had almost forgotten them." He left it to Madison to act as his proxy in the Virginia legislature. Arguing that religion "must be left to the conviction and conscience of every man," Madison won approval for Jefferson's statute in 1786. It was one of Jefferson's greatest accomplishments and later influenced the First Amendment clause that Congress shall make no law respecting the establishment of religion.[3]

JEFFERSON AND HENRY TANGLED INTERMITTENTLY for years. At first, both men were on the same side of a battle that would dominate early debate, sharing the anti-Federalist view that America should be a loose confederacy of powerful states. Federalists such as Washington believed a strong national force was necessary for defense against foreign invaders. Jefferson and Henry worried that a large army would result in tyranny.

Henry became the leading opponent of a federal constitution, which, proponents said, was necessary to end the threat of civil war. In the five years since Britain had signed the treaty conceding that the United States was independent, the fragile confederation of states was often in anarchy and disorder, with little cooperation between the states and a continuing refusal to pay bills owed by the federal government as a result of the war.

Jefferson, meanwhile, sought to mollify both sides in the debate. He wrote from Paris that were he in America, he would urge nine states to pass it but urge that the other four withhold their support until assurances were made that a Bill of Rights was attached to it. This approach prevailed, as Jefferson hoped, providing for the inclusion of the right of free speech and a free press as well as a prohibition against any law regarding the establishment of religion. When Jefferson returned to Virginia a year later, in 1789, however, he found that the state was still roiling in anti-Federalist sentiment. Jefferson insisted he was no Federalist, saying that his experience in France had left him "10,000 times more" of an enemy to monarchs "since I have seen what they are." He then served as President Washington's secretary of state, constantly battling with Alexander Hamilton, who tried to give his Treasury Department extraordinary national powers. When Jefferson left his job as secretary of state in 1793, he announced that he was deeply disenchanted with Federalists. But when Jefferson prepared to run for president in 1796, anti-Federalists doubted he was on their side and urged Henry to oppose him. "Most assiduous court is paid to P.H," Jefferson wrote, adding that some hoped Henry's candidacy would create a "schism" in Virginia. Jefferson believed that Henry's backers hoped to see him in the vice presidency but wrote that Henry "has been offered everything which they knew he would not accept." Henry, indeed, declined to run.[4]

Federalists, for their part, sought to undermine Jefferson's presidential candidacy by another means: they revived the controversy over his actions as wartime governor. One critic called Jefferson the "coward of Carter's Mountain," a reference to the area he had traversed when fleeing Monticello. A congressman from South Carolina named William Loughton Smith said Jefferson deserved little credit for his revolutionary writing because of how he had acted "in times of danger." Smith also demeaned Jefferson's famous written works of the revolution, arguing that "there is no great merit in composing . . . essays on civil rights, which are frequently done to obtain popularity, and without risk of personal convenience."[5]

Jefferson felt compelled once again to address the charges, which he described as "volumes of reproach . . . sung in verse, and said in humble prose."[6] He readily conceded his lack of military experience, but asked rhetorically why he should have been expected to stay and fight at Monticello against well-armed British cavalry. "I declined a combat, singly against a troop," Jefferson explained. Just before the election, a number of witnesses gave depositions meant for public consumption that backed Jefferson's account, including the testimony of Daniel L. Hylton, who swore that Jefferson had acted courageously in preserving arms and documents during Arnold's occupation of Richmond.

The attacks against Jefferson may have harmed his chances of winning the election. John Adams, a Federalist, was elected president and Jefferson, as the runner-up, became vice president. The office offered little influence, and Jefferson spent much of his tenure at Monticello.[7]

IT WAS DURING THIS TIME that Jefferson's final clash with Henry occurred. Henry changed his political views and began expressing Federalist sympathies. In the aftermath of the French Revolution, he feared that the United States would have to fight a resurgent France and worried that the nation had a weak federal army. At the same time, he considered Jefferson too much of a Francophile. He used a double entendre to accuse Jefferson of neglecting his "native victuals," suggesting Jefferson had too much of a taste for French cuisine as well as the new French government. At the same time, Washington and other Federalists were critical of Jefferson, believing that he wanted to go too far in weakening federal power. Washington won over Henry with a series of personal entreaties, writing that it was of "immense importance at this crisis" that Henry run for a seat in the Virginia legislature as a Federalist. If Jefferson had his way, the country would dissolve into civil war and be unable to defend itself against foreign invaders, his critics charged.

On March 4, 1799, Henry appeared at a polling place and told the gathered crowd that he was concerned that the nation was on the brink of civil war. He was calling not for a return for all-powerful monarchy-like powers, he stressed, but for unity. "United we stand, divided we fall. Let us not split into factions which must destroy the union upon which our existence hangs. Let us preserve our strength for the French, the English, the Germans, or whoever shall dare invade our territory."[8]

After delivering the speech, Henry felt increasingly ill and needed assistance to his carriage. He made a grueling twenty-mile ride to his home in southwestern Virginia, Red Hill, where he later learned he had won the election. But the great orator had spoken his last public words. He was sixty-three years old. On June 9, 1799, Henry refused a final offer of medicine and died. He was buried, as requested, at a gravesite at Red Hill with a tombstone that reads: "His fame his best epitaph."

Jefferson never believed Henry's rationale for becoming a Federalist, accusing him of "apostasy" for switching sides. He suspected that Henry hoped to profit from Federalist currency policies, a charge that Henry denied.[9] Jefferson never seemed to get over his bitterness, telling Henry's biographer that Henry "descended to the grave with less than its indifference, and verified the saying of the philosopher, that no man must be called happy till he is dead."[10] Six months after Henry died, the Virginia legislature considered a proposal to honor Henry for his "unrivalled eloquence and superior talents." The assembly, firmly in Jefferson's corner, rejected the measure.[11]

Jefferson continued his attacks on Henry for the remainder of his life, another twenty-seven years. There would be no chance for the kind of reconciliation that Jefferson eventually had with another adversary, John Adams. Yet the harshness of Jefferson's words—some of which he never intended to become public—must be balanced by his repeated praise of Henry's leadership in the early days of the rebellion. Henry had "been the idol of his country, beyond any one that ever lived," Jefferson said. He acknowledged there was more to Henry than an ability to gain followers. In 1824, nearly two years before his death, Jefferson told a visitor that while Henry was a man of "little knowledge," his role in the revolution had been vital. "It is not now easy to say what we should have done without Patrick Henry. He was far before all in maintaining the spirit of revolution."[12]

Indeed, while Jefferson had long been jealous of Henry's popularity and dismissive of his intellect, Jefferson had followed Henry's path throughout much of the revolution, and the relationship only diverged into deep antagonism after the controversy over Jefferson's governorship. The investigation into Jefferson's actions during the invasion had prompted him to tell friends he was through with politics. Yet the final clash with Henry over Federalism helps explain why Jefferson saw it as his duty to rejoin the political fray and once again seek the presidency.

Jefferson worried that the Federalists were too hungry for war, too anxious to take on the French and the British. The Federalists, Jefferson wrote, formed "an Anglican monarchial and aristocratical party" that wanted a large, standing army and a national bank, and did not tolerate dissent. His arguments against these powerful institutions enabled him to win the presidency in 1800, a triumph he viewed as nothing less than a second American revolution, ending what he called a "reign of witches" and returning power to the people. Jefferson declared the country was now united. "We are all Republicans," Jefferson said, referring to his anti-Federalist party. "We are all Federalists."[13]

In his eight years as president Jefferson was guided by the lessons he had learned from his experience as a wartime governor. Jefferson had authored the Declaration of Independence and welcomed war with Britain. Yet what happened in Virginia had deeply influenced him, and he constantly worried that Federalists would goad the country into battle unnecessarily. He withstood efforts by members of Congress to draw the United States into war against European powers, using declarations of neutrality, naval blockades, and economic embargoes to avoid the call to arms. "I think one war enough for the life of one man," he wrote. While he famously said that the "tree of liberty must be refreshed from time to time with the blood of patriots and tyrants," he made clear that the cost of sustained warfare should be weighed with the utmost care: "I abhor war and view it as the greatest scourge of mankind." Nonetheless, he assured Americans during his presidency that should war be necessary, they would wage it "like men."[14] He authorized ships to attack the pirate fleet of the Barbary States, whose leaders had seized an American ship for a month and constantly demanded tribute from vessels for safe passage in the Mediterranean Sea. It was the first time an American president had sent forces overseas to conduct warfare.

Jefferson emphasized the nation's need for a strong system of defense, and it was under his presidency that a national military academy was established at West Point. Arnold had, of course, intended to seize West Point when he defected to the British. While Arnold didn't capture West Point, he did easily invade Virginia because the state lacked a strong defense at places such as Hood's Point. Jefferson used his presidential powers to appoint military leaders who shared his philosophy. As part of the Military Peace Establishment Act, he hoped that a corps of engineers trained at West Point would be deployed to create a national network of forts that would prove far more effective than those that failed to stop the British in Virginia.[15]

Significantly, Jefferson told one of his successors in the governorship that he should not worry about gaining approval for every action in the event of an invasion. Such a delay "might produce irretrievable ruin," he wrote. Jefferson did not believe that the framers of the Constitution intended that its words should be followed so rigidly "that the constitution itself and their constituents with it should be destroyed" due to the lack of authority to repel invaders. Thus, Jefferson concluded, "an instant of delay in Executive proceedings may be fatal to the whole nation. They must not therefore be laced up in the rules of the judiciary department."[16]

Jefferson, of course, had been responsible for considerably more than "an instant of delay" when the British invaded Virginia, but, he insisted, he had acted when necessary. Jefferson's Federalist enemies would say Jefferson failed to learn the lesson of the invasion, namely, that a larger federal force was needed. Jefferson, however, believed the system had somehow succeeded, with the militia eventually turning out and the British defeated with help from the Continental army and French forces.

JEFFERSON SPENT THE REST OF HIS LIFE defending his actions as governor. He was pleased when a number of prominent defenders made declarations of support. George Nicholas, who had brought the charges against Jefferson at Henry's request, became a Jefferson defender in 1798. He wrote to a friend that he had "changed the unfavorable opinion, which, I once formed of [Jefferson's] political conduct, and that I consider him, as one of the most virtuous, as well as one of the ablest, of the American patriots." Jefferson excused Nicholas for being misled by those who had "half informed opinions."[17]

But as Jefferson won reelection to the White House in 1804, his Federalist critics continued to make an issue of his wartime actions, and eventually paired the attacks with stories that said he had fathered children with Sally Hemings. One such critic, James Thomson Callender, published articles in the *Richmond Recorder,* a Federalist newspaper. Another, who signed his name as Thomas Turner, wrote that Jefferson had been in such a rush to take "flight from Monticello" that he broke his wrist when he stumbled from his horse. (In fact, the accident occurred several weeks after Jefferson fled Tarleton's forces.) Jefferson enlisted Thomas Paine, the author of *Common Sense,* to come to his defense. Paine wrote an article for the *Repertory,* a Boston newspaper, in which he said it was "nonsense" for Jefferson to be criticized for abandoning "the seat of government when a country is invaded. The seat of government then is wherever government sit. Perhaps in a village; perhaps in a barn; perhaps in the open air."[18]

Jefferson's severest critic was a onetime ally, Henry "Light Horse Harry" Lee, the brilliant cavalry leader. In 1809, as Jefferson ended his second term as president, Lee was in a jail cell for failing to pay some debts. He used the time to write an autobiography in which he mercilessly attacked Jefferson. Lee believed that Jefferson had put Virginia at risk by failing to call out the militia in a timely fashion. Had he been leading the forces in Virginia, Lee wrote, he could have easily stopped Arnold. The state had more than enough militiamen "to have crushed any predatory adventure like that conducted by Arnold." He mocked Jefferson for being driven out of Richmond and being "forced to secure personal safety by flight."[19]

Jefferson called Lee's book a parody, "a tissue of errors from beginning to end."[20] As a Federalist, it was in Lee's interest to portray Jefferson as having been a poor military leader during his governorship, demonstrating the need for a system that could tax Americans directly in order to raise an army.

But the attacks on Jefferson's action only increased. Jefferson had tried to influence the writing of history by contacting Henry's biographer, William Wirt, sending him derogatory statements about the orator. Jefferson then embarked on a years-long effort to influence historical works that dealt with the invasion. Jefferson opened his home and files to Louis Girardin, the co-author of the seminal *History of Virginia,* which essentially vindicated Jefferson's actions as wartime governor. He similarly sought to influence the writing of William Johnson, a biographer of Nathanael Greene, the commander of southern forces of the Continental army. Jefferson was convinced that Johnson's work would ensure that Lee's memoir would be discredited and "removed from the shelf of History."[21] Lee died in 1818, but an anguished Jefferson wrote in 1822 that Lee's book was seen as legitimate and "had begun to be quoted as history." It had been forty-one years since the invasion, and Jefferson still recoiled at the thought that his flight from the British was seen by some as a stain on his honor.[22]

There Is Not a Truth Existing Which I Fear

IN NOVEMBER 1824, forty-three years after the invasion of Virginia, the Marquis de Lafayette arrived in Charlottesville as part of a celebratory tour across America. Traveling in a carriage drawn by four horses, Lafayette headed up the mountain road to Monticello. A gathering of citizens and cavalry lined the ellipse on the eastern portico of Jefferson's home. Lafayette proceeded along the circle as Jefferson descended the steps to greet the man he still regarded as Virginia's savoir.

Without Lafayette, the invasion of Virginia would not have been repulsed so effectively, nor the British bottled up at Yorktown so completely. Jefferson had renewed his relationship with Lafayette while serving in Paris and helped his friend during the French Revolution. Over the years, Lafayette was jailed and sent into exile, though he eventually returned and was celebrated for his accomplishments. Then, as his fortunes in France faded once again, he returned to America, greeted by seventy-five thousand in Boston, feted from New York to Yorktown, and making his emotional reunion at Monticello.

Jefferson was "feeble and tottering with age," while Lafayette was "permanently lamed" from injuries, according to a Jefferson grandson who witnessed the reunion. The two men shuffled toward each other. "Ah, Jefferson!" "Ah, Lafayette!" they exclaimed, embracing, crying with joy, before heading inside Monticello.[1]

Lafayette visited the university in Charlottesville designed by Jefferson, attended a banquet in his honor in the college's unfinished rotunda, and spent countless hours reminiscing about the revolution. Jefferson used his influence to convince Congress to pass legislation granting Lafayette $200,000 for his services to America. No such reward was given to Jefferson himself, nor did he seek it, though half that sum would have resolved Jefferson's own grave financial problems, which would later force his family to sell Monticello.

One day during Lafayette's visit, the two friends were riding in a carriage, deeply engaged in a conversation overheard by one of Jefferson's slaves, Israel. Lafayette remarked that "the slaves ought to be free; that no one could rightfully hold ownership in his brother man; that he spent his money in behalf of the Americans freely because he felt they were fighting for a great and noble principle." Jefferson responded that the slaves would one day be free. In fact, Jefferson had given up on solving what he called the greatest anxiety of his life.

Ending slavery, he wrote, would be "the work of another generation." He urged that every experiment to end slavery be tried. As for his own slaves, he freed two in his lifetime, manumitted another five in his will, and let at least three run away without seeking their capture. Shortly after Jefferson's death, his family would place an advertisement announcing the auction of 130 of his "valuable" slaves.[2]

In the aftermath of Lafayette's departure and the anticipation of the fiftieth anniversary of the Declaration of Independence, Jefferson's veneration seemed secure. Another guest who visited around this time found the eighty-one-year-old former president riding on horseback, bundled against the December cold in a long gray coat and scarf. Jefferson was as engaged as ever, recounting his reading of Greek literature and telling a visitor, "When I can neither read nor ride, I shall desire very much to make my bow."[3] A few revolutionary leaders still remained, including John Adams, who would die on the same day as Jefferson, and his close friend, James Madison. But most of the other players in the great drama of the invasion had taken their bow, or soon would do so.

Thomas Nelson Jr., the militia leader who signed the Declaration of Independence, succeeded Jefferson as governor, and helped finance the revolution, was among those who had died years earlier. Like a number of Virginia's revolutionary leaders, Nelson had won freedom from the British but not from his debts, and much of his property had to be sold off.

Benedict Arnold, who departed Virginia believing the state firmly in British control, insisted for many months afterward that the war could still be won. After failing to convince commanders in New York to let him capture the Congress in Philadelphia, he boarded a ship to London, where he failed in an effort to win command of the British army and complained that he never received appropriate compensation for switching sides. Following the path of many American Loyalists, he moved to Canada, but eventually fled after a mob burned an effigy of him that was labeled "traitor." Returning to England, belittled by those on both sides of the revolution, he died in 1801, leaving his wife, Peggy, to pay off his debts.

Lord Cornwallis, captured as a result of his disastrous defeat at Yorktown, was freed in a prisoner-of-war exchange and, despite harsh criticism of his actions in Virginia, continued to be one of Britain's most valued officers. He became governor-general of India and lord lieutenant of Ireland, overseeing a number of military victories against rebellious factions.

Few of the key players in the invasion could match the survival skills of Mary Willing Byrd, who remained at Westover for the rest of her life. She issued pleas for financial reimbursement as a result of the war to both the British and

Virginia governments. After the British said they would not pay for the loss of her forty-nine slaves, she submitted a new bill seeking compensation for other "immense" losses. "I am reduced from the greatest affluence to a state in which I know the want of many of the conveniences of life," she wrote in a letter to British officials who examined American Loyalist claims, thereby once again suggesting that her sympathies were with London.[4] Cornwallis tried to help her receive compensation, writing in 1784 that reimbursement was "justly due to her" and in 1789 that "her case is particularly deserving."[5] But the payments apparently were not made. At the same time, Byrd sought reimbursement from Virginia, saying she had provided food for militiamen, fodder for their horses, and a ferry on which hundreds of soldiers crossed the river.[6] Westover was sold upon her death in 1814. The Byrd family legacy thrived, however, producing a U.S. senator and Virginia governor, Harry Flood Byrd, and the famed polar adventurer Richard E. Byrd.

Byrd's neighbor, Benjamin Harrison, who signed the Declaration and served as Speaker of the House during much of Jefferson's governorship, became governor himself. His son William Henry Harrison worked closely with Jefferson as governor of a large Indian territory and served as president of the United States for a month before dying of pneumonia, the shortest tenure of any president in history. William's grandson, another Benjamin Harrison, later assumed the presidency as well, in 1889. The Harrison estate, damaged by the troops under Arnold's command, was sold and later became a major staging ground for troops during the Civil War.

Baron von Steuben, who was appalled at Jefferson's lack of preparedness but eventually was relieved of his command of Virginia forces, briefly faced the prospect of an investigation of his own conduct during the invasion. But Lafayette and Washington were convinced that Steuben was maligned, and he was given a prominent role in the battle at Yorktown. Granted American citizenship and a substantial pension, he lived more extravagantly than his finances would allow. At his death, in 1794, the memory of his service under Washington ensured that he was celebrated as one of the most indispensable men of the revolution.

Steuben's Prussian adversary, Johann von Ewald, defeated in Virginia but admiring the spirit of Americans, returned to his native land, where he felt he was not properly recognized or promoted for his service. He left for Denmark, where a grateful crown prince gave him a title and put him in charge of an elite corps. In his new role, he fought against the British, whom he once served so well. He produced a series of highly regarded treatises on the conduct of warfare, but his diary, one of the most important documents of the American Revolution, seemed lost to history until it was discovered by an American officer serving in Europe shortly after World War II.

John Champe, the soldier who tried unsuccessfully to capture Arnold and later escaped from the British invasion force, married and settled on land near Middleburg, Virginia, where he made a sparse living. Eventually, he moved westward and, while in search of more fertile land, he became ill and died in 1798 at a fort near the banks of the Monongahela River, where he was buried in an unmarked grave. Champe's family spent decades trying to get a proper pension for his service. Nearly a century after Champe arrived aboard Arnold's fleet in Virginia, a bill was introduced in Washington that declared that Champe's services had never been suitably recognized. It would be many more years before proper monuments were erected in his name.[7]

Jack Jouett, who rode through the night to warn Jefferson about the British plot to capture him, was hailed by the Virginia assembly for countering "the designs of the enemy." The assembly awarded Jouett a pair of pistols in 1783, but it was a sign of Virginia's destitute finances that it took twenty years to fulfill a promise to present him with an "elegant sword." He moved west and became a leader in Kentucky's separation from Virginia. Two decades after Jouett delivered his warning at Monticello, and with Jefferson newly elected as president, Jouett sought his old friend's influence to win an appointment to the important job of marshal in Kentucky. "I ask for this office with some Degree of Confidence you having Known me all my life," he wrote Jefferson. After friends wrote letters attesting that Jouett had given up "his former attachment to that accursed practice of gambling," Jefferson included Jouett on a list of candidates for the job, but the post may have gone to another man. Jouett did become a legislator in his adopted state, and his family eventually prospered there. In Virginia, it is said that had Jouett been celebrated by a worthy poet, as Paul Revere's ride was by Longfellow, the Jouett name would be among the most remembered in American history.[8]

IN 1826, JEFFERSON WAS INVITED to Washington to celebrate fifty years of independence. Too ill to make the journey, he regretted being unable to join "the remnant" of surviving revolutionary leaders. He wrote to the organizers that he felt confident that the Declaration of Independence would live on. "All eyes are opened, or opening, to the rights of man."[9]

Yet even with his hours dwindling, Jefferson made time for one last effort to set the record straight about his conduct during the invasion of Virginia. He had recently received a series of letters from Henry Lee, whose late father of the same name had written an autobiography excoriating Jefferson's conduct. Knowing of Jefferson's complaints about the memoir, the younger Lee said he would welcome Jefferson's thoughts for a new edition. "There is not a truth existing which I fear, or would wish unknown to the whole world," Jefferson responded.[10] In one of the last letters of his life, he provided a richly detailed account to Lee of what happened during the invasion. He invited Lee to Monticello to examine his papers and interview him on the subject.

Lee accepted the offer and on the morning of June 29, 1826, arrived at Monticello. Lee was ushered inside the entrance hall, adorned with buffalo skins, elk horns, and other mementos. Jefferson's daughter Patsy (also known as Martha), greeted Lee, regretfully informing him that her father was too ill to see anyone. But Jefferson learned Lee had arrived and insisted on his being allowed to enter.

Lee entered a pair of rooms separated by an alcove, which snugly held a bed on which Jefferson was resting. A clock, framed by two obelisks, hung from the wall at the foot of the bed. An Arabian sword also hung from one of the walls. Jefferson looked up from his bed and greeted Lee warmly. Lee was shocked at Jefferson's appearance. "There he was extended, feeble, prostrate," Lee wrote. Jefferson expressed regret that Lee should find him "so helpless." He alluded to his death "as a man would to the prospect of being caught in a shower, as an event not to be desired, but not to be feared." Still, there was a moment when Jefferson smiled and perhaps even laughed, and "the fine and clear expression of his countenance was not obscured."

Jefferson was prepared to talk once more about those days of his governorship and war; there were still things to clear up. He had spent hours in the previous months going over his records of the invasion, sorting the scraps of paper that he had taken with him as he fled on horseback from Arnold's approach to Richmond. It was all there, clear evidence of Jefferson's proper conduct. Lee could not bring himself to conduct a tiring interview with an ill man. He would come back on another day. "Well, do," Jefferson said. "But you dine here today." Lee insisted he would defer the pleasure until Jefferson recovered. Jefferson waved his hand, repeating impatiently, "You *must* dine here. My sickness makes no difference."[11] Lee consented.

After finishing his meal and bidding goodbye to Jefferson's daughter, Lee descended the hill. Jefferson would recover, Lee concluded. On another day, soon, Lee would go over the documents of the invasion of Virginia, with Jefferson as his guide. But Lee was the last visitor to Jefferson at Monticello. Only Jefferson's family, servants, and physician remained by his side thereafter. Jefferson had six days left to live, days of quietude and solemn voices. The bedroom window was left open, ushering in the mountain breeze, carrying scents from the summer garden, as Jefferson went in and out of consciousness.

JEFFERSON'S FLIGHTS from Richmond and Monticello were the lowest points of his public life. He had vowed after reaching such a depth never to enter politics again. Instead, the events leading up to the disasters and victories of 1781 shaped the political figure that Jefferson became. The bitterness associated with the British invasion initially convinced him to forswear politics, but the hard lessons of that war, and his belief that he was uniquely suited to keep peace in America, eventually brought him back.

It would often be suggested that if Jefferson was wrong, America was wrong, but if he was right, America was right. That seems too absolute. Jefferson's record was both remarkable and unsatisfactory, filled with contradictions—such as the way he favored equality while overseeing slavery, and his role as a war leader while acknowledging that he was unqualified to practice the art of war. Jefferson once urged a grandson to absorb the wisdom of sages while avoiding the false attractions around him. Such judgments shaped a man. So it has been for Jefferson and his country—the sands of his life shifted, his wisdoms absorbed, his faults better understood.

Ideas would be Jefferson's epitaph. He decided that his tombstone would commemorate him as the "Author of the Declaration of Independence [and] of the Statute of Virginia for religious freedom & Father of the University of Virginia." He saw no reason to mention that he had been president, as is often noted. Another omission seems equally striking: that he had served as his state's second governor.

Instead, Monticello itself would serve as a monument to Jefferson's ability to overcome such a dark period of his life. For generations, visitors have walked admiringly through the rooms, passing by the bed where Jefferson died, gazing at a display that includes a folding telescope, perhaps the one that Jefferson used to spot British horsemen on their way to his home.

Six days after Lee left Jefferson's bedside, on the fiftieth anniversary of the Declaration of Independence, Jefferson breathed his last. He was buried beside his wife, Martha, and near his childhood friend Dabney Carr on a gentle slope by his home, fulfilling his wish that never again would he be forced to leave his beloved mountain.

ACKNOWLEDGMENTS

THE EVENTS DESCRIBED IN THIS BOOK took place more than two centuries ago. But they seem very alive in the fiery letters by Jefferson, in the faded copies of the *Virginia Gazette,* and amid a landscape that has been remarkably preserved, from Williamsburg to Monticello. The story of Jefferson's life has attracted historians nearly from the country's founding. As I researched these events, however, I was encouraged at every turn by those who said that this period—invariably described as the "nadir" of Jefferson's career—warranted a fuller treatment.

I received extraordinary help, inspiration, and wisdom from those who know Jefferson best: the scholars at the International Center for Jefferson Studies, which, along with Monticello, is overseen by the Thomas Jefferson Foundation. The center granted me a fellowship that allowed me to live and study in the shadow of Monticello, immerse myself in Jefferson's world, and study in the glorious Jefferson Library. The center's director, Andrew O'Shaughnessy, welcomed the prospect of a journalist who wanted to tackle this period of history, patiently shared his extraordinary knowledge of Jefferson, and provided innumerable valuable suggestions for the manuscript of this work. The center's research historian, Gaye Wilson, generously shared her wealth of keen understanding of Jefferson as well. Gary Sandling, Monticello's director of interpretation, shared his extraordinarily detailed comprehension of this subject, and his enthusiasm for telling it, from beginning to end, and provided crucial input for the manuscript. Joan Hairfield encouraged my application for a fellowship and welcomed my many return visits. Monticello curator Susan Stein and architectural historian William L. Beiswanger helped me understand Jefferson's vision of his home. Monticello's Liesel Nowak provided images and other assistance. Lucia Stanton, co-editor of Jefferson's memorandum books and a volume on slavery, and Sarah Allaback provided important insights. I learned something new on each of my numerous tours of the house from knowledgeable guides.

I benefited from the work of those who have transcribed the letters written and received by Jefferson, a task that continues at Princeton University and at Monticello. The early volumes of the papers were particularly important for this study, and their value was greatly enhanced by the editing and detailed footnotes. I owe a debt to the early editor of the project, Julian P. Boyd, and many others who worked on the papers. At Monticello, J. Jefferson Looney and Lisa A. Francavilla of the Papers of Thomas Jefferson project pointed me in the proper direction on numerous occasions.

At the Jefferson Library of the International Center for Jefferson Studies at Monticello, I am deeply indebted to Jack Robertson, Anna Berkes, Eric Johnson, and Endrina Tay, all of whom shared their knowledge and enthusiastically helped me find resources. I learned much in my conversation with a number of the center's fellows: John Ragosta provided guidance on the role of Virginia's religious dissenters, and I also received advice and assistance from Tao Wei, Liam Paskvan, R. S. Taylor Stoermer, Carrie Douglas, and Sandra Rebok. Peter Hatch, Monticello's director of gardens and grounds, obliged my request to retrace Jefferson's steps from the Rivanna River to Monticello. Professor Peter S. Onuf of the University of Virginia also generously shared his knowledge. Cartographer and historian Rick Britton also provided assistance.

Edward Ayres, historian of the Jamestown-Yorktown Foundation, let me see Yorktown and the Revolutionary War era through his eyes, and provided many crucial suggestions as a result of his careful reading of the manuscript.

I was helped by staff of the University of Virginia's Albert and Shirley Small Special Collections Library, the Library of Virginia, and the Virginia Historical Society. I spent many hours at the Library of Congress, where I conducted research in the inspiring surroundings of the Main Reading Room in the rotunda of the Jefferson Building, as well as in the special collections and manuscript rooms, where I was assisted by Gerald Gawalt. I also spent many productive hours at a gem of a library at the Society of the Cincinnati in Washington, under the guidance of Ellen McCallister Clark and with the assistance of Elizabeth Frengel. The vast library of the Daughters of the American Revolution was another valuable resource. I received important documents and assistance from the David Library of the American Revolution; Bloomsburg University and archivist Robert Dunkelberger; the Naval Historical Center and Dennis Conrad; the Massachusetts Historical Society; the New-York Historical Society; and the British National Archives.

One of the glories of writing about the Revolutionary War in Virginia is that so many of the sites have been preserved and so many people are dedicated to promoting the heritage of those sites. Frederick and Inge Fisher graciously walked me through the grounds and house at Westover. Norman and Joanna Harris allowed me to spend several memorable hours at Geddes, to which Jefferson initially fled. Gail Pond of Poplar Forest devoted much time to ensuring that I understood the history of that plantation, owned by Jefferson. Val Matthews allowed me to roam the estate of Blenheim. A kind citizen walked with me through the woods to find the remnants of the works of Hood's Point.

I spent many days wandering the streets and buildings of Colonial Williamsburg and at the foundation's John D. Rockefeller Jr. Library. Among those who helped my research at this extraordinary cultural and research institution were Kevin Kelly, Linda

Rowe, Thomas Hay, and Doug Mayo. I was also assisted at the Earl Gregg Swem Library of the College of William and Mary.

I received assistance from Peggy Haile McPhillips, Norfolk city historian; Eric Price, an interpreter in Portsmouth; Alan Flanders, a Portsmouth historian; and the Portsmouth Naval Shipyard Museum. Judith Ledbetter, a Charles City County historian, provided valuable help. Robert Selig provided insights about the role of Hessian soldiers.

Jack Farrell, a longtime colleague, read a first draft of the manuscript and provided a wealth of suggestions and consistent encouragement.

My editors at the *Boston Globe,* where I serve as a Washington correspondent, were enthusiastic about this project. Former Washington bureau chief Peter Canellos, former political editor James Smith, and editor Martin Baron granted my request to take leave during some relatively quiet months of the 2008 presidential campaign. Moreover, the *Globe* repeatedly encouraged my efforts to research and write long-form narratives of presidential candidates over the past decade, which led me to spend many hours at archives and in the reading of history. That work mingled the disciplines of journalism and biography, and greatly influenced my decision to pursue this story of Jefferson.

My agent, David Black, played a crucial role as he steered me through the literary world and guided me deftly through the writing of a proposal for the book.

At Oxford University Press, my editor, Tim Bent, seized on this project from the beginning and saw it through to the end, providing peerless counsel and suggesting many improvements that are reflected throughout this work. Oxford's Dayne Poshusta helped in innumerable ways as the project went forward. Production editor Christine Dahlin patiently saw the manuscript through completion. Copy editor Sue Warga provided valuable review. Oxford sales representative Gary Kallman, a passionate student of history, provided important support. I am extraordinarily grateful to all.

During my childhood, my mother, Allye Kranish, and my father, Arthur Kranish, took me on countless trips to the Blue Ridge Mountains of Virginia, including a trip to Monticello, and provided me with a biography of Jefferson and an enthusiasm for history, both of which I retain.

Finally, this work would not have been possible without the love, patience, and understanding of my wife, Sylvia, and my daughters, Jessica and Laura, all of whom encouraged me to follow my Jeffersonian interests, read my words, provided countless valuable suggestions, and listened every time I wanted to share my latest discovery. To them, I give my deepest thanks.

For more information, and to contact me, please visit my Web site, www.michael kranish.com.

Prologue

1. Thomas Jefferson (TJ) to James Monroe, May 20, 1782, in *The Papers of Thomas Jefferson* (henceforth *PTJ*), ed. Julian P. Boyd (Princeton: Princeton University Press, 1952), 6: 184–87.

Williamsburg

The Gentleman Has Spoken Treason

1. Sarah N. Randolph, *The Domestic Life of Thomas Jefferson* (New York: Frederick Unger, 1958), 31–32.
2. Thomas Jefferson Randolph, "Memoirs," ed. James Adam Bear, University of Virginia Library Special Collections, MSS 5454-c.
3. TJ to John Harvie, January 14, 1760, *PTJ* 1:3.
4. William Wirt Henry, *Patrick Henry: Life, Correspondence and Speeches* (New York: Charles Scribner's Sons, 1891), 16.
5. Ibid., 19.
6. Ibid., 19–20.
7. TJ to William Wirt, August 14, 1805, quoted in Henry Mayer and James M. Elson, *Patrick Henry and Thomas Jefferson* (Brookneal, VA: Descendants' Branch of the Patrick Henry Memorial Foundation, 1997), 27–32.
8. Thomas Jefferson, *Notes on the State of Virginia,* ed. William Peden (Chapel Hill: University of North Carolina Press, 1982), 150–53.
9. Mayer and Elson, *Patrick Henry and Thomas Jefferson,* citing Daniel Webster's recollection of conversation with TJ, 61.
10. Lucille Griffith, *The Virginia House of Burgesses, 1750–1774* (Birmingham: University of Alabama Press, 1970), 3.
11. Henry, *Patrick Henry,* 24–27.
12. Ibid., 15.

13. Patrick Henry to Rev. John Camm, Dec. 12, 1763, John Fontaine, and James Maury, *Memoirs of a Huguenot Family* (New York: G. P. Putnam, 1853), 421.

14. Henry, *Patrick Henry,* 39–41.

15. Ibid., 41 (recollection of Capt. Thomas Trevilian).

16. Marion Tinling, ed., *The Correspondence of the Three William Byrds of Westover, Virginia, 1684–1776* (Charlottesville: University Press of Virginia, 1977), 2:604.

17. Alden Hatch, *The Byrds of Virginia* (New York: Holt, Rinehart and Winston, 1969), 136.

18. Byrd family letter book, Virginia Historical Society, Mss1 B9968 a, 21.

19. David Meade, "Autobiography of David Meade," *William and Mary Quarterly* 13, 2 (October 1904): 73–102.

20. Sophia Cadwalader, *Recollections of Joshua Francis Fisher* (Boston: D. B. Updike, 1929), 94–97.

A Determination Never to Do What Is Wrong

1. Randolph, *Domestic Life,* 24.

2. Dumas Malone, *Jefferson, the Virginian* (Boston: Little, Brown, 1948), 58.

3. Jane Carson, *James Innes and His Brothers of the F.H.C.* (Charlottesville: University Press of Virginia, 1965), 68; Malone, *Jefferson, the Virginian,* 106.

4. Jefferson Papers, University of Virginia Library Special Collections, Series 1, #857, no. 17.

5. *The Writings of Thomas Jefferson,* ed. Andrew A. Lipscomb and Albert E. Bergh (Washington, DC: Thomas Jefferson Memorial Foundation, 1903), 14:231.

6. TJ to Thomas Jefferson Randolph, November 24, 1808, Thomas Jefferson and Thomas Jefferson Randolph, *Memoir, Correspondence, and Miscellanies, from the Papers of Thomas Jefferson* (Boston: Gray and Bowen, 1830), 117–20.

7. "Journal of a French Traveller in the Colonies, 1765," *American Historical Review* 26, 4 (July 1921): 726–47.

8. TJ to Thomas Jefferson Randolph, November 24, 1808, Jefferson and Jefferson Randolph, *Memoir,* 117–20.

9. Anne Willis, "The Master's Mercy: Slave Prosecutions and Punishments in York County, 1700–1780," master's thesis, College of William and Mary, 1995.

10. Ibid., 81n.

11. 1765 York County prosecutions, York County records, Rockefeller Library, Colonial Williamsburg. See also Willis, "Master's Mercy," 79–80, 244.

12. Jefferson, *Notes on the State of Virginia,* 142.

13. George F. Willison, *Patrick Henry and His World* (Garden City, NY: Doubleday, 1969), 3.

14. Henry, *Patrick Henry,* 47.

15. Ibid., 81.

16. Ibid., 86.

17. TJ to Wirt, August 14, 1814, *The Writings of Thomas Jefferson,* ed. Paul Leicester Ford (New York: G. P. Putnam's Sons, 1898), 9:470.

18. Henry, *Patrick Henry,* 89–93.

19. Willison, *Patrick Henry and His World,* 9.

20. "Journal of a French Traveller," 746–47.

21. *Colonial Williamsburg Journal,* Winter 2001–2.

22. TJ to Wirt, August 14, 1805, in Ford, *Writings of Thomas Jefferson* 9:466.

23. *Virginia Gazette* (Purdie and Dixon), July 18, 1766.

24. Ibid., July 25, 1766.

25. Ibid., July 11, 1766.

26. Leo Lemay, "Robert Bolling and Colonel Chiswell," *Early American Literature* 6 (1971): 100–101.

27. *Maryland Gazette,* October 30, 1766.

28. Ibid.

29. *PTJ* 10:27. Jefferson believed that Virginia owed between £2 million and £3 million to Britain after the Revolutionary War, as much as the other states combined.

30. Lemay, "Robert Bolling and Colonel Chiswell," 142n.

What Is to Become of Children—Divided?

1. TJ to Wirt, April 12, 1812, in Ford, *Writings of Thomas Jefferson,* 338–45.

2. Henry Stephens Randall, *The Life of Thomas Jefferson* (New York: Derby & Jackson, 1858), 40.

3. Henry, *Patrick Henry* 1:127.

4. Ibid., 183, 197.

5. Kevin J. Hayes, *The Library of William Byrd of Westover* (Madison, WI: Madison House, 1997), 96. Historians believe Jefferson significantly underestimated the value of Byrd's library. Thomas Jefferson, *Jefferson's Memorandum Books,* ed. James Bear and Lucia Stanton (Princeton: Princeton University Press, 1997), 1:46.

6. Francis Walker Gilmer, *Reports of Cases Decided in the Court of Appeals in Virginia, from April 10th, 1820 to June 28th, 1821* (Richmond: Pollard-Franklin, 1821), 105–23; Byrd mortgage, August 12, 1769, Charles City County court records. Extracts of the Byrd mortgage records were accessed at Charles City County (Virginia) Historical Society, and online at www.charlescity.org. The records are recorded in Benjamin B. Weisiger, *Charles City County, Virginia Records, 1737–1774* (Richmond: B. B. Weisiger, 1986).

7. *PTJ* 2:69–71.

8. Frank L. Dewey, *Thomas Jefferson, Lawyer* (Charlottesville: University Press of Virginia, 1986), 30–44.

9. Ibid., 65.

10. Ibid., 67–69.

11. Frank L. Dewey, "Thomas Jefferson and a Williamsburg Scandal," *Virginia Magazine of History and Biography* 80, 1 (1981): 44–63; Jefferson notes on the case are at the Library of Congress, Jefferson Papers. The description of Henry in court wearing a black suit and tie-wig comes from St. George Tucker, in "William Wirt's Life of Patrick Henry," *William and Mary Quarterly* 22, 4 (April 1914): 255. Tucker, who first met Henry in 1772, disputed Wirt's suggestion that Henry's appearance was "clownish," saying instead that Henry had "the awkwardness of a modest Gentleman, not of a Clown."

12. Dewey, *Thomas Jefferson, Lawyer,* 64.

13. TJ to David Campbell, January 28, 1810, *PTJ, Retirement Series,* 2:187.

All Men Are Born Free

1. *Virginia Gazette* (Purdie and Dixon), September 7, 1769.

2. Lucia Stanton, *Slavery at Monticello,* Monticello monograph series (Charlottesville: Thomas Jefferson Memorial Foundation, 1996), 23–26.

3. Ford, *Writings of Thomas Jefferson* 1:373–81.

4. Paul Finkelman, *Slavery and the Founders: Race and Liberty in the Age of Jefferson* (New York: M. E. Sharpe, 2001), 137–39.

5. *Virginia Gazette* (Purdie and Dixon), August 16, 1770.

6. John E. Selby, *The Revolution in Virginia, 1775–1783* (Williamsburg: Colonial Williamsburg Foundation, 1988), 24.

7. Evarts Boutell Greene and Virginia D. Harrington, *American Population Before the Federal Census of 1790* (Baltimore: Genealogical Publishing Co., 1993), 152.

8. Anthony Benezet, *Some Historical Account of Guinea, Its Situation, Produce, and the General Disposition of Its Inhabitants; An Inquiry into the Rise and Progress of the Slave Trade, Its Nature and Lamentable Effects* (London: J. Phillips, 1788), 70–71.

9. Patrick Henry to Robert Pleasants, June 18, 1773, in George Morgan, *The True Patrick Henry* (Philadelphia: J. B. Lippincott, 1907), 246–47.

10. *Autobiography of Thomas Jefferson* in Ford, *Writings of Thomas Jefferson* 1:4–5.

11. *Somerset v. Stewart,* June 22, 1772, Opinion of Lord Mansfield, *Great Opinions by Great Judges,* ed. William Snyder (New York: Baker, Voorhis, 1883), 112–15.

12. *Virginia Gazette* (Rind), May 25, 1769; *Virginia Gazette* (Purdie and Dixon), May 16, 1771.

13. Annette Gordon-Reed, *The Hemingses of Monticello* (New York: W. W. Norton, 2008), 69.

14. Randall, *Life of Thomas Jefferson* 1:63.

15. TJ to Robert Skipwith, August 3, 1771, *PTJ* 1:76–81.

16. Stanton, *Slavery at Monticello,* 13. The largest slaveholder was Edward Carter.

17. Randolph, *Domestic Life,* 44–45.

18. TJ to Skipwith, August 3, 1771, *PTJ* 1:76–81.

19. TJ to Martha Jefferson Randolph, *PTJ* 16:300.

Revolution

With What Majesty Do We Ride There Above the Storms!

1. Thomas Jefferson (TJ) to Maria Cosway, October 12, 1786, in *The Papers of Thomas Jefferson* (henceforth *PTJ*), ed. Julian P. Boyd (Princeton: Princeton University Press, 1952), 10:447.

2. B. L. Rayner, *Sketches of the Life, Writings, and Opinions of Thomas Jefferson* (New York: A. Francis, 1832), 44–45.

3. Lord Dunmore to Lord Dartmouth, March 31, 1773, in *Revolutionary Virginia,* comp. William Van Schreeven (Charlottesville: University Press of Virginia, 1973), 2:8.

4. Philip Mazzei, *Philip Mazzei: My Life and Wanderings,* ed. S. Eugene Scalia and Margherita Marchione (Morristown, NJ: American Institute of Italian Studies, 1980), 27.

5. Ibid., 203–5, 212.

6. Ibid., 206–7.

7. Ibid., 208–10.

8. Philip Mazzei, *Philip Mazzei: Selected Writings and Correspondence,* ed. Margherita Marchione (Prato: Edizioni del Palazzo, 1983), 1:68.

9. John F. Kennedy, in his book *A Nation of Immigrants,* cited Mazzei as the inspiration for Jefferson's phrase "All men are created equal," and a congressional resolution similarly gave Mazzei credit. Many Jeffersonian scholars, however, cite other inspirations.

10. *Virginia Gazette,* January 26, 1775.

11. Thomas Jefferson, *Jefferson's Memorandum Books,* ed. James Bear and Lucia Stanton (Princeton: Princeton University Press, 1997), 1:369–70; Thomas Jefferson, *Garden Book, 1766–1824,* Coolidge Collection of Thomas Jefferson Manuscripts, Massachusetts Historical Society, 18.

12. John E. Selby, *The Revolution in Virginia, 1775–1783* (Williamsburg: Colonial Williamsburg Foundation, 1988), 26.

13. Resolution of the House of Burgesses, May 24, 1774, *PTJ* 1:105–7; Jefferson's description of the resolution being "cooked up" is in ibid., 106n.

14. Washington to George William Fairfax, June 10, 1774, in *Writings of George Washington,* ed. John Clement Fitzpatrick (Washington, DC: U.S. Government Printing Office, 1931), 3:223.

15. Woody Holton, *Forced Founders: Indians, Debtors, Slaves, and the Making of the American Revolution in Virginia* (Chapel Hill: University of North Carolina Press, 1999), 118.

16. William Wirt Henry, *Patrick Henry: Life, Correspondence and Speeches* (New York: Charles Scribner's Sons, 1891), 1:120.

17. Resolution by association of members of the late House of Burgesses, May 27, 1774, *PTJ* 1:107–8.

18. *Colonial Williamsburg Journal,* Spring 2003.

19. Jefferson, *Jefferson's Memorandum Books* 1:374.

20. *PTJ* 1:121–35.

21. Thomas Jefferson, *Notes on the State of Virginia,* ed. William Peden (Chapel Hill: University of North Carolina Press, 1982), 169.

22. Thomas Jefferson, *Autobiography of Thomas Jefferson,* in *The Writings of Thomas Jefferson,* ed. Albert Ellery Bergh (Washington, DC: Thomas Jefferson Memorial Foundation, 1907), 1:11.

23. The manuscript that came to be known as *Summary View,* and quoted herein, is in *PTJ* 1:121–37. It has been reprinted in many forms.

24. Jefferson, *Autobiography* 1:12.

25. *PTJ* 1:119–43.

26. Jefferson, *Autobiography* 1:12.

27. Worthington Chauncey Ford, ed., *Journals of the Continental Congress, 1774–1779* (Washington, DC: Government Printing Office, 1904), 1:75–80.

The War Is Actually Begun!

1. George F. Willison, *Patrick Henry and His World* (Garden City, NY: Doubleday, 1969), 267.
2. Ivor Noel Hume, *1775, Another Part of the Field* (London: Eyre & Spottiswoode, 1966), 34–35.
3. Van Schreeven, *Revolutionary Virginia* 2:369.
4. Ibid., 2:375.
5. Ibid., 2:376.
6. Ibid., 3:3.
7. Ibid., 3:5.
8. "Deposition of Dr. William Pasteur. In Regard to the Removal of Powder from the Williamsburg Magazine," *Virginia Magazine of History and Biography* 13, 1 (July 1905): 48–50.
9. Benjamin Waller deposition, Committee on the Late Disturbances, Report, June 14, 1775, *Journal of the House of Burgesses, 1773–1776*, 232.
10. Lyon Gardiner Tyler, *Williamsburg, the Old Colonial Capital* (Richmond: Whittet & Shepperson, 1907), 66.
11. *Virginia Gazette* (Dixon and Hunter), May 5, 1775.
12. John Page, *Memoirs,* reprinted in *Virginia Historical Register,* III (Richmond: Macfarlane & Ferguson, 1850), 142–51.
13. Dunmore to Dartmouth, March 14, 1775, in Jane Carson, *James Innes and His Brothers of the F.H.C.* (Charlottesville: University Press of Virginia, 1965), 80.
14. *Virginia Gazette* (Dixon and Hunter), May 13, 1775; Willison, *Patrick Henry and His World,* 270–75.
15. TJ to William Small, May 7, 1775, *PTJ* 1:166n.
16. *Virginia Gazette* (Purdie), May 19, 1775.
17. *Virginia Gazette* (Pinkney), April 28, 1775, supplement; Selby, *Revolution in Virginia,* 41–42.
18. Mazzei, *Philip Mazzei: My Life,* 215.
19. *PTJ* 1:171.
20. Jefferson, *Jefferson's Memorandum Books* 1:405. See also Sandor Salgo, *Thomas Jefferson, Musician and Violinist* (Charlottesville: Thomas Jefferson Memorial Foundation, 2000), 39.
21. Dartmouth to Dunmore, July 5, 1775, in *Naval Documents of the American Revolution* (Washington, DC: U.S. Government Printing Office), 1:1311–13 (hereafter *NDAR*).

The Horrid Disposition of the Times

1. John Adams to Timothy Pickering, August 6, 1822, in *The Works of John Adams, Second President of the United States,* ed. Charles Francis Adams (Boston: Little, Brown, 1856), 2:512.
2. Sir Henry Clinton, *The American Rebellion: Sir Henry Clinton's Narrative of His Campaigns, 1775–1782,* ed. William B. Wilcox (New Haven: Yale University Press, 1954), 19.

3. TJ to Francis Eppes, June 26, 1775, *PTJ* 1:174–75. Washington's comment to Henry is in Henry, *Patrick Henry* 1:298.

4. Marion Tinling, ed., *The Correspondence of the Three William Byrds of Westover, Virginia, 1684–1776* (Charlottesville: University Press of Virginia, 1977), 2:812.

5. Otway Byrd to William Byrd III, Feb. 10, 1775, ibid., 2:803.

6. William Byrd III to Ralph Wormeley, October 4, 1775, Ralph Wormeley Letters, UVA, Special Collections, Mss 1939.

7. T. T. Byrd to Thomas Gage, July 11, 1775, Tinling, *Correspondence* 2:818n.

8. Kevin P. Kelly, "The White Loyalists of Williamsburg," *The Colonial Williamsburg Interpreter* 17, 2 (Summer 1996): 2.

9. *Virginia Gazette* (Pinkney), July 20, 1775.

10. Ibid., August 24, 1775.

11. *Virginia Gazette* (Dixon and Hunter), October 26, 1775.

12. TJ to William Wirt, September 29, 1916, attachments, *Pennsylvania Magazine of History and Biography,* 32, 4 (1910), 414.

13. Comments of "Cato," cited in Henry, *Patrick Henry* 1:313n.

14. Van Schreeven, *Revolutionary Virginia* 3:402–3.

15. TJ to John Randolph, August 25, 1775, *PTJ* 1:240–43.

16. *Virginia Gazette* (Dixon and Hunter), September 23, 1775.

17. Willison, *Patrick Henry and His World,* 289.

18. Margaret Willard, *Letters of the American Revolution* (Port Washington, NY: Kennikat Press, 1968), 221, cites an October 28, 1775, letter published on December 22, 1775, in the *Morning Chronicle and London Advertiser.*

We Must Be Prepared to Destroy It

1. TJ to John Page, October 31, 1775, *PTJ* 1:250–51.

2. Page to TJ, November 11, 1775, *PTJ* 1:259.

3. Sprowle will, as cited in Alan Flanders, "Sprowle's Gosport Built on British Blueprint," *Virginian Pilot,* January 5, 1996.

4. John F. D. Smyth, *A Tour in the United States of America: Containing an Account of the Present Situation of That Country* (London: G. Robinson, 1784).

5. William Byrd II, *The Westover Manuscripts, Containing the History of the Dividing Line* (Petersburg: Edmund and Julian Ruffin, 1841), 10.

6. *Norfolk Intelligencer,* August 16, 1775, in Van Schreeven, *Revolutionary Virginia* 3:414–15.

7. Virginia Committee of Safety, November 11, 1775, in *NDAR* 2:993–94.

8. John Macartney to Paul Loyall, *Virginia Gazette,* August 30, 1775, in Van Schreeven, *Revolutionary Virginia* 3:431.

9. Van Schreeven, *Revolutionary Virginia* 3:473.

10. Ibid., 3:433.

11. William Cowley to George Washington, October 4, 1775, *NDAR* 2:293–94.

12. *Virginia Gazette* (Pinkney), September 14, 1775.

13. *Virginia Gazette, or Norfolk Intelligencer,* September 6, 1775, accessed at Norfolk Public Library.

14. Dunmore to Secretary of State, October 5, 1775, cited in H. S. Parsons, "Contemporary English Accounts of the Destruction of Norfolk in 1776," *William and Mary College Quarterly Historical Magazine,* 2nd ser., 13, 4 (October 1933): 219–24.

15. Dunmore to Mayor et al., of Norfolk, published in Victor Hugo Paltsits, *John Holt: Printer and Postmaster* (New York: New York Public Library, 1920), 9–10.

16. TJ to Wirt, September 29, 1816, included in Henry Mayer and James M. Elson, *Patrick Henry and Thomas Jefferson* (Brookneal, VA: Descendants' Branch of the Patrick Henry Memorial Foundation, 1997), 52–53.

17. Carson, *James Innes and His Brothers,* 1–2.

18. Ibid., 60.

19. Ibid., 42.

20. Edmund Pendleton to William Woodford, December 24, 1775, in *The Letters and Papers of Edmund Pendleton, 1734–1803,* ed. David John Mays (Charlottesville: University Press of Virginia, 1967), 140–41.

21. Washington to Joseph Reed, March 7, 1776, *The Papers of George Washington: Revolutionary Series* (Charlottesville: University Press of Virginia, 1983), 3:428–29.

22. Henry Mayer, *A Son of Thunder: Patrick Henry and the American Republic* (New York: F. Watts, 1986), 284.

23. TJ to John Eppes, November 7 and 21, 1775, *PTJ* 1:252, 264.

24. Ackiss's death is cited in a November 17, 1775, report in the *Virginia Gazette;* Page to TJ, November 24, 1775, *PTJ* 1:264–66.

25. Helen Calvert Maxwell Read and Charles Brinson Cross, *Memoirs of Helen Calvert Maxwell Read* (Chesapeake, VA: Norfolk County Historical Society, 1970), 54–56.

26. Dunmore to Major General Howe, November 30, 1775, *NDAR* 2:1209–11.

27. *Virginia Gazette* (Purdie), November 17, 1775.

28. *Virginia Gazette* (Dixon and Hunter), November 25, 1775.

29. December 13, 1775, proclamation, in Van Schreeven, *Revolutionary Virginia* 5:125.

30. Van Schreeven, *Revolutionary Virginia* 5:3–11; Woodford to Page, December 11, 1775, in ibid., 108–9. A Virginian reported to Colonel William Woodford that the British loss was "102 Killed & Wounded." This has in some accounts been shortened to 102 killed. Dunmore's account of seventeen killed, as noted herein, appears to have referred only to British regulars.

31. Van Schreeven, *Revolutionary Virginia* 5:386–87.

32. Dunmore to Major General Howe, November 30, 1775, *NDAR* 2:1209–11.

33. Washington to Richard Henry Lee, December 26, 1775, *Papers of George Washington: Revolutionary Series* 2:610–12.

34. William S. Forrest, *Historical and Descriptive Sketches of Norfolk and Vicinity* (Philadelphia: Lindsey and Blakiston, 1853), 84.

35. James Nicholson deposition, Norfolk Commission Report: Virginia Auditor of Public Accounts: Records of Commissioners to Examine Claims in Norfolk, 1777–1836, Library of Virginia archives, ref. APA 235.

36. Rogers deposition, Norfolk Commission.

37. Smythe deposition, Norfolk Commission.

38. Chisholm deposition, Norfolk Commission.

39. Forrest, *Historical and Descriptive Sketches,* 86–87.

40. William Ivey deposition, Norfolk Commission.

41. Pendleton to Woodford, January 16, 1776, in Mays, *Letters and Papers of Edmund Pendleton,* 148.

42. Van Schreeven, *Revolutionary Virginia* 5:308–33, 354–57, 396–431. For the order on "house to be demolished," see Proceedings of the Fourth Virginia Convention, January 16, 1776, reprinted in ibid., 5:515–17.

43. Norfolk Commission.

44. Forrest, *Historical and Descriptive Sketches,* 83.

Save Us from Ruin

1. Dunmore to Dartmouth, February 18, 1776, *NDAR* 3:1349–50.

2. Thomas Byrd to William Byrd III, Feb. 23, 1776, in Tinling, *Correspondence* 2:817.

3. Dunmore to Germain, March 30, 1776, *NDAR* 4:585.

4. *Virginia Gazette* (Purdie), March 29, 1776; *Virginia Gazette* (Dixon and Hunter), April 13, 1776.

5. Alden Hatch, *The Byrds of Virginia* (New York: Holt, Rinehart and Winston, 1969), 214.

6. Samuel Adams to James Warren, January 7, 1776, in *The Writings of Samuel Adams,* ed. Harry Alonzo Cushing (New York: G. P. Putnam's Sons, 1907), 3:253; Washington to Reed, January 31, 1776, *Reprint of the Original Letters from Washington to Joseph Reed During the American Revolution* (Philadelphia: A. Hart, 1852), 55–56.

7. Fawn M. Brodie, *Thomas Jefferson: An Intimate History* (New York: Bantam Books, 1974), 137–38.

8. Page to TJ, April 6 and 26, 1776, *PTJ* 1:287–90.

9. Willison, *Patrick Henry and His World,* 294–99.

10. *PTJ* 1:290–91.

11. Dunmore to Germain, March 30, 1776, *NDAR* 4:586.

12. Dunmore to Germain, June 26, 1776, *NDAR* 5:756–57.

13. Ibid.

14. William Fleming to TJ, June 22, 1776, *PTJ* 1:406.

15. Journal of Lieutenant John Trevett, *NDAR* 5:688n.

16. Dunmore to Germain, June 27, 1776, *NDAR* 5:757.

17. Page to TJ, July 6 1776, *PTJ* 1:454–55; Randolph to TJ, June 23, 1776, *PTJ* 1:407.

18. TJ to Fleming, July 1, 1776, *PTJ* 1:411–13.

19. Jefferson map of Gwynn's Island is in *PTJ* 1:566.

20. *Virginia Gazette* (Dixon and Hunter), July 20, 1776.

21. *Virginia Gazette* (Purdie), July 19, 1776.

22. *Virginia Gazette* (Dixon and Hunter), July 20, 1776

23. Dunmore to Germain, July 31, 1776, *NDAR* 5:1312–14.

24. *Virginia Gazette* (Dixon and Hunter), August 31, 1776.

25. Jefferson's "original Rough draught" of the Declaration of Independence, *PTJ* 1:423–28.

26. Patrick Henry to Richard Henry Lee, May 20, 1776, cited in Henry, *Patrick Henry* 1:411.

27. Philip Mazzei to Henry, June 16, 1776, cited in Mazzei, *Philip Mazzei: Selected Writings* 1:118–19.

28. Francis Eppes to TJ, July 3, 1776, *PTJ* 15:576.

29. James Adam Bear, Isaac Jefferson, and Hamilton W. Pierson, *Jefferson at Monticello* (Charlottesville: University Press of Virginia, 1967), 15–16.

30. Henry, *Patrick Henry* 1:506.

31. Jefferson, *Notes on the State of Virginia*, 126.

32. See Holton, *Forced Founders,* and Michael McDonnell, *The Politics of War: Race, Class, and Conflict in Revolutionary Virginia* (Chapel Hill: University of North Carolina Press, 2007); TJ to Page, August 5, 1776, *PTJ* 1:485–87.

33. TJ to Fleming, July 1, 1776, *PTJ* 1:411–13.

34. Fleming to TJ, July 27, 1776, *PTJ* 1:475.

35. Adam Stephen to TJ, July 29, 1776, *PTJ* 1:481.

36. Page to TJ, July 15 and 20, 1776, *PTJ* 1:461–62, 468–70.

He Lost Everything

1. Van Schreeven, *Revolutionary Virginia* 5:386–87.

2. Landon Carter, *The Diary of Colonel Landon Carter of Sabine Hall, 1752–1778,* ed. Jack P. Greene (Charlottesville: University Press of Virginia, 1965), 2:989.

3. TJ to Wirt, September 29, 1816, in Mayer and Elson, *Patrick Henry and Thomas Jefferson,* 53.

4. William Byrd to Wormeley, October 5, 1775, *Papers of Ralph Wormeley, 1773–1802,* Accession #1939, University of Virginia Library Special Collections.

5. *Virginia Gazette* (Dixon and Hunter), January 3, 1777.

6. Memoir by an unnamed granddaughter of Mary Byrd, Huntington Library, CA, and Library of Virginia.

7. *Virginia Gazette* (Dixon and Hunter), March 14, 1777. Byrd's library was bought in March 1778 by Isaac Zane for £2,000 and shipped on forty wagons to Philadelphia bookseller Robert Bell.

Fiery, Hot and Impetuous

1. TJ to Francis Eppes, October 24, 1775, and November 21, 1775, *PTJ* 1:248, 264.

2. TJ to Randolph, November 29, 1775, *PTJ* 1:269.

3. TJ to Thomas Nelson, May 16, 1776, *PTJ* 1:292–93.

4. Jefferson's notes on witness testimony in the investigation of the Canadian campaign are in *PTJ* 1:433–54.

5. Ibid.

6. TJ to Francis Eppes, August 9, 1776, *PTJ* 1:487–88.

7. Richard Henry Lee to TJ, November 3, 1776, *PTJ* 1:589.

8. Robert P. Davis, *Where a Man Can Go: Major General William Phillips, British Royal Artillery, 1731–1781* (Westport, CT: Greenwood Press, 1999), 32.

9. Russell M. Lea, *A Hero and a Spy: The Revolutionary War Correspondence of Benedict Arnold* (Westminster, MD: Heritage Books, 2006), 246–47.

10. John William Fortescue, *A History of the British Army* (London: Macmillan, 1902), 3:4.

11. John Harvie to TJ, September 15, 1778, *PTJ* 2:212.

12. Valentine C. Hubbs, *Hessian Journals: Unpublished Documents of the American Revolution* (Columbia, SC: Camden House, 1981), 1. Of the 17,000 troops sent to North America by the German state of Hessia, for example, 10,500 returned. An estimated 357 were killed in combat; 4,626 died of various causes. Another 2,949 of the Hessian soldiers deserted, many remaining in America or Canada.

13. Ibid., 1–3.

14. William Leete Stone, *Letters of Brunswick and Hessian Officers During the American Revolution* (New York: Da Capo Press, 1970), 128–29.

15. Ibid., 138–40.

16. August Wilhelm du Roi, *Journal of Du Roi the Elder, Lieutenant and Adjutant, in the Service of the Duke of Brunswick, 1776–1778,* trans. Charlotte S. J. Epping (Philadelphia: University of Pennsylvania Press, 1911), 151.

17. Philander D. Chase, "Years of Hardships and Revelations: The Convention Army at the Albemarle Barracks, 1779–1781," *Magazine of Albemarle County History* (Albemarle County Historical Society) 42 (1983): 19.

18. Du Roi, *Journal,* 146–61.

Who Would Have Expected All This Here?

1. Du Roi, *Journal,* 146–61.

2. William Finnie to John Jay, February 5, 1779, item 78, Papers of the Continental Congress, National Archives, as cited in Chase, "Years of Hardships," 25.

3. TJ to Henry, March 27, 1779, *PTJ* 2:237.

4. John Hammond Moore, *Albemarle, Jefferson's County* (Charlottesville: University of Virginia Press, 1976), 60–62; letter from Staunton, Virginia, in Stone, *Letters of Brunswick and Hessian Officers,* 182–83.

5. Thomas Anburey, *Travels Through the Interior Parts of America* (London: William Lane, 1789), 2:368.

6. TJ to William Phillips, April 1779, *PTJ* 2:261.

7. Mazzei, *Philip Mazzei: My Life,* 226–27.

8. TJ to Albert Gallatin, January 25, 1793, *PTJ* 25:92–93.

9. Frederika Charlotte Luise (von Massow) Riedesel, *Letters and Memoirs Relating to the War of American Independence,* trans. William L. Stone (Albany, NY: Joel Munsell, 1867), 155.

10. Sarah N. Randolph, *The Domestic Life of Thomas Jefferson* (New York: Frederick Unger, 1958), 50–55.

11. Riedesel, *Letters,* 159.

12. Baron von Riedesel to TJ, December 4, 1779, *PTJ* 3:212–13.

13. Peter Nicolaisen, "Thomas Jefferson and Friedrich Wilhelm von Geismar: A Transatlantic Friendship," *Magazine of Albemarle County History* 64 (2006): 27, 40. See also Salgo, *Thomas Jefferson.*

14. TJ to Richard Henry Lee, April 21, 1779, *PTJ* 2:255.
15. Friedrich Wilhelm von Geismar to TJ, February 26, 1780, *PTJ* 3:304.
16. Selby, *Revolution in Virginia,* 219.

The Conflagration in the Night

1. Ithiel Town, "A Detail of Some Particular Services Performed in America (Journal of Collier and Matthews's Invasion of Virginia)," *Virginia Historical Register and Literary Notebook* 4 (October 1851): 181–95.
2. Ibid., 188.
3. Ibid., 188, 193.
4. *Resolutions, Laws and Ordinances Relating to . . . the Offices and Soldiers of the Revolution* (Washington, DC: Thomas Allen, 1838), 431–34.
5. Henry to Sir George Collier, May 13, 1779, in Town, "Detail," 191–92.
6. Collier to Henry Clinton, May 16, 1779, in Clinton, *American Rebellion,* 406.
7. Ibid.
8. Town, "Detail," 194.
9. Ibid., 193.
10. Philip Mazzei, *Researches on the United States* (Charlottesville: University Press of Virginia, 1976), xiii.
11. Mazzei, *Philip Mazzei: My Life,* 230–35; Mazzei, *Philip Mazzei: Selected Writings,* 182–201. Mazzei returned briefly to Virginia in 1783 and eventually moved to Paris, where he renewed his friendship with Jefferson.
12. TJ to Page, June 2, 1779, *PTJ* 2:279.
13. *Virginia Gazette* (Dixon and Nicolson), June 5, 1779; TJ to Phillips, June 25, 1779, *PTJ* 3:14–15; TJ to Richard Henry Lee, June 17, 1779, *PTJ* 3:298.

The Enemy Will Commit Great Ravages

1. Marie Goebel Kimball, *Jefferson, War and Peace, 1776 to 1784* (New York: Coward-McCann, 1947), 55.
2. Fleming to TJ, May 22, 1779, *PTJ* 2:267–70.
3. TJ to Fleming, June 8, 1779, *PTJ* 2:288–89.
4. *Virginia Gazette* (Dixon and Nicolson), June 26, 1779; *Virginia Gazette* (Dixon and Nicolson), May 22, 1779.
5. *Virginia Gazette* (Dixon and Nicolson), June 5, 1779.
6. TJ to Fleming, June 8, 1779, *PTJ* 2:288–89.
7. Inventory of Furniture in the Governor's Palace, *PTJ* 2:296–97.
8. TJ to Phillips, June 25, 1779, *PTJ* 3:14–15.
9. Washington to Theodorick Bland, July 27, 1779, *Washington Papers,* Library of Congress.
10. TJ to Washington, July 17, 1779, *PTJ* 3:41.
11. Phillips to Bland, July 3, 1779, *The Bland Papers* (Petersburg: Edmund and Julian C. Ruffin, 1840), 141.

12. Friederich Adolphus Riedesel, *Memoirs, Letters and Journals, of Major General Riedesel, during his Residence in America,* trans. William L. Stone (Albany, NY: J. Munsell, 1868), 2:74; TJ to Riedesel, May 3, 1780, *PTJ* 3:368–69.

13. TJ to Phillips, June 25, 1779, *PTJ* 3:14–15.

Almost the Whole County Was Inflaim'd

1. Richard C. Bush, "Awake, Rouse Your Courage, Americans Brave: Companies Raised in Northumberland County for the Virginia Continental Line, 1776 and 1777," *Bulletin of the Northumberland County Historical Society* 29 (1992): 20.

2. George Gilmer, "Address of George Gilmer to the Inhabitants of Albemarle County," *Collections of the Virginia Historical Society,* 1887, n.s., 6:122.

3. Richard Henry Lee to TJ, April 29, 1777, *PTJ* 2:14; TJ to John Adams, May 16, 1777, *PTJ* 2:18; receipt for bounty money to John Jouett Jr., April 15, 1777, *PTJ* 2:11.

4. Henry to TJ, February 15, 1780, *PTJ* 3:293–94.

5. William Waller Hening, *Hening's Statutes at Large* [online at http://www.vagenweb.org/hening/], October 5, 1780, 10:331; L. Scott Philyaw, "A Slave for Every Soldier: The Strange History of Virginia's Forgotten Recruitment Act of 1 January 1781," *Virginia Magazine of History and Biography* 109, 4 (2001): 367–86.

6. TJ to Benjamin Harrison, December 11, 1780, *PTJ* 4:197.

7. TJ to Washington, September 23, 1780, *PTJ* 3:660–61.

8. Washington to TJ, October 10, 1780, *PTJ* 4:26–30.

9. James M. Elson, *Lynchburg, Virginia: The First 200 Years* (Lynchburg: Warwick House, 2004), 4–6.

10. TJ to Charles Lynch, August 1, 1780, *PTJ* 3:523.

11. Hening, *Hening's Statutes* 1:49.

12. Virginia State Library and H. J. Eckenrode, *A Calendar of Legislative Petitions, Arranged by Counties: Accomac-Bedford* (Richmond: D. Bottom, 1908), 28.

13. Theodorick Bland Sr. to Theodorick Bland Jr., October 21, 1780, *Bland Papers* 1:37.

14. Jefferson, *Notes on the State of Virginia,* 118.

15. Charlotte County petition, October 15, 1779, Library of Virginia, Reel 38, Box 53, Folder 6.

16. Jefferson, *Notes on the State of Virginia,* 159.

17. John A. Ragosta, "Fighting for Freedom: Virginia Dissenters' Struggle for Religious Liberty During the American Revolution," *Virginia Magazine of History and Biography* 116, 3 (2008): 227–61. Ragosta's work was expanded upon in a presentation attended by the author at the International Center for Jefferson Studies. Also see Jefferson, *Notes on the State of Virginia,* 157–61; Prince Edward County petition, October 11, 1776; "Ten-Thousand Name Petition," October 16, 1776, Library of Congress, Early Virginia Religious Petitions database.

18. *Tyler's Quarterly Historical and Genealogical Magazine* 9 (April 1928): 239.

19. TJ to Samuel Huntington, September 14, 1780, *PTJ* 3:647–48.

20. Richard C. Bush, "Revolution and Community in Northumberland, Virginia, 1776–1782," *Bulletin of the Northumberland Historical Society* 30 (1993): 18–19, citing Lewis

Peyton Little, *Imprisoned Preachers and Religious Liberty in Virginia* (Lynchburg, VA: J. Bell, 1938), 466.

21. McDonnell, *Politics of War,* 1.

22. Thomas Gaskins to TJ, February 23, 1781, *PTJ* 4:693.

This Dangerous Fire Is Only Smothered

1. TJ to Huntington, September 14, 1780, *PTJ* 3:647–48.
2. Thomas Nelson to TJ, October 21, 1780, *PTJ* 4:54–55.
3. James Innes to TJ, October 21, 1780, *PTJ* 4:55–57.
4. *Virginia Gazette* (Dixon and Nicolson), October 25, 1780.
5. TJ to Washington, October 22, 1780, *PTJ* 4:60–61.
6. TJ to Huntington, October 25, 1870, *PTJ* 4:67–68.
7. TJ to Virginia Delegates in Congress, October 27, 1780, *PTJ* 4:76–77; TJ to Washington, October 25, 1780, *PTJ* 4:68–69.
8. TJ to Thomas Sim Lee, October 26, 1780, *PTJ* 4:70–71.
9. TJ to Virginia Delegates in Congress, October 27, 1780, *PTJ* 4:76–77.
10. TJ to Horatio Gates, October 28, 1780, *PTJ* 4:77–78.
11. TJ to James Wood, November 1, 1780, *PTJ* 4:87–88.
12. TJ to Thomas Sim Lee, November 2, 1780, *PTJ* 4:89–90.
13. TJ to Huntington, November 10, 1780, *PTJ* 4:109–10.
14. TJ to Huntington, November 19, 1780, *PTJ* 4:128.
15. Henry A. Muhlenberg, *The Life of Major-General Peter Muhlenberg of the Revolutionary Army* (Philadelphia: Carey and Hart, 1849), 217–20.

Whom Can We Trust Now?

1. Beverley Robinson to Benedict Arnold, May 1779, in Lea, *Hero and A Spy,* 331–34.
2. *Pennsylvania Packet,* March 6, 1779, quoted in Willard Sterne Randall, *Benedict Arnold, Patriot and Traitor* (New York: William Morrow, 1990), 440.
3. Arnold to Washington, May 5, 1779, in Lea, *Hero and a Spy,* 330.
4. Randall, *Benedict Arnold,* 454, 458.
5. Ibid., 499.
6. Washington to Arnold, April 1780, in ibid., 387.
7. Lea, *Hero and a Spy,* 443.
8. Ibid., 444.
9. Ibid., 445–47.
10. Willard Mosher Wallace, *Traitorous Hero; The Life and Fortunes of Benedict Arnold* (New York: Harper, 1954), 251.
11. Arnold to Washington, September 25, 1780, in Lea, *Hero and a Spy,* 499–500.
12. Lea, *Hero and a Spy,* 501, 503.
13. James Thacher, *A Military Journal During the American Revolution* (Boston: Cottons and Barnard, 1827), 223.

14. Arnold proclamation, October 20, 1780, Library of Congress, Printed Ephemera Collection; Portfolio 111, Folder 2.

15. Washington to TJ, October 10, 1780, *PTJ* 3:26–30.

16. Ibid.

Bring Him Alive to Headquarters

1. Henry Lee, *Memoirs of the War in the Southern Department of the United States* (New York: University Publishing, 1869), 395.

2. Ibid.

3. Ibid., 396.

4. Ibid.

5. Wilbur C. Hall, "Sergeant Champe's Adventure," *United Service Journal* (December 1834): 438–52, as reprinted in *William and Mary Quarterly*, 2nd ser., 18, 3 (July 1938): 322–42. The account of Champe's adventure in Hall's article is drawn from the writing of a British officer named Captain Cameron, who said he was Champe's superior officer during the time that Champe was aboard Arnold's fleet. Cameron wrote that he happened upon Champe some time later and wrote an account of their discussion.

6. Hall, "Sergeant Champe's Adventure," 335.

7. Lee, *Memoirs*, 401.

8. Ibid., 394–411.

9. Ibid., 405.

10. Hall, "Sergeant Champe's Adventure," 333.

11. Washington to Henry Lee, Oct. 20, 1780, Lee, *Memoirs,* 408n.

12. Clinton, *American Rebellion,* 235–36.

13. Bartholomew James, *Journal of Rear-Admiral Bartholomew James, 1752–1828,* ed. John Knox Laughton and James Young Falkland Sulivan (London: Navy Records Society, 1896), 109.

14. Hall, "Sergeant Champe's Adventure," 341.

15. Lee, *Memoirs,* 410.

Invasion

Beyond All My Fears

1. Benedict Arnold to Henry Clinton, January 21, 1781, British National Archives, Reference PRO 30/11/99.

2. John Graves Simcoe, *Simcoe's Military Journal, a History of the Operations of a Partisan Corps, Called the Queen's rangers, Commanded by Lieut. Col. J. G. Simcoe, during the War of the American Revolution* (New York: Bartlett & Welford, 1844), 168. Simcoe wrote that "above forty horses had been thrown overboard." Arnold wrote that "about one-half of the cavalry horses were lost."

3. Johann von Ewald, *Diary of the American War: A Hessian Journal,* ed. Joseph P. Tustin (New Haven: Yale University Press, 1979), 258–59. The fleet is also described in the log of the *Fowey,* British National Archives, PRO, ADM, 52/1748.

4. Marie Goebel Kimball, *Jefferson, War and Peace, 1776 to 1784* (New York: Coward-McCann, 1947), 72; Thomas Jefferson, *Notes on the State of Virginia,* ed. William Peden (Chapel Hill: University of North Carolina Press, 1982), 91.

5. Charles Thomas Long, "Green Water Revolution," Ph.D. dissertation, George Washington University, 2005, 282.

6. Richard Henry Lee to Thomas Jefferson (TJ), July 8, 1779, in *The Letters of Richard Henry Lee,* ed. James Curtis Ballagh (New York: Macmillan, 1914), 2:83; TJ to Lee, July 17, 1779, in *The Papers of Thomas Jefferson* (henceforth *PTJ*), ed. Julian P. Boyd (Princeton: Princeton University Press, 1952), 3:39–40.

7. *PTJ* 3:40n.

8. TJ to Richard Henry Lee, July 17, 1779, *PTJ* 3:39–40.

9. TJ to John Jay, June 19, 1779, *PTJ* 3:5.

10. Robert Armistead Stewart, *The History of Virginia's Navy of the Revolution* (Baltimore: Genealogical Publishing, 1934), 72.

11. TJ to La Luzerne, August 31, 1780, *PTJ* 3:577–78.

12. Henry Stephens Randall, *The Life of Thomas Jefferson* (New York: Derby & Jackson, 1858), 1:288.

13. TJ to the County Lieutenants of Hampshire and Berkeley, *PTJ* 4:229–30.

14. William Waller Hening, *Hening's Statutes at Large* [online transcription, www.vagenweb.org/hening/], 10:377–80.

15. Jefferson, *Notes on the State of Virginia,* 217.

16. John Page to TJ, December 9, 1780, *PTJ* 4:191–93.

17. TJ to Francis Eppes, August 9, 1776, *PTJ* 1:487–88.

18. Clinton to Arnold, December 14, 1780, British National Archives, PRO, 30/11/4.

19. Clinton to Thomas Dundas and John Graves Simcoe, December 14, 1780, Clinton papers, 133:32, WLC.

A Fatal Inattention

1. Jacob Wray to Thomas Nelson, December 30, 1780, BR Box 11 (1)d, Huntington Library, San Marino, CA.

2. TJ to Wray, January 15, 1781, *PTJ* 4:377–78. Jefferson expressed displeasure that Wray had failed to identify the vessels as British, but Wray was not in position to have seen the ships and was only conveying what he was told by Commodore Barron, who apparently could not be sure of the origin. Jefferson nonetheless admonished Wray for not getting more information from Barron after his further reconnaissance mission.

3. William Tatham to William Armistead Burwell, June 13, 1805, *PTJ* 4:273.

4. TJ to Frederick William von Steuben, December 31, 1780, *PTJ* 4:254.

5. Bartholomew James, *Journal of Rear-Admiral Bartholomew James, 1752–1828,* ed. John Knox Laughton and James Young Falkland Sulivan (London: Navy Records Society, 1896), 93–96.

6. Ibid., 96–98.

7. Jefferson's certificate for Alexander Spotswood, September 12, 1798, *PTJ* 30:518.

8. Ewald, *Diary of the American War,* xix–xxxi.

9. Johann von Ewald, *Treatise on Partisan Warfare,* trans. Robert A. Selig and David Curtis Skaggs (New York: Greenwood Press, 1991), 25.

10. Ewald, *Diary of the American War,* 258–60.

11. Arnold to officer commanding the party on shore, Jan. 1, 1781, HCA 32/492, British National Archives.

12. H. R. McIlwaine, *Journals of the Council of the State of Virginia* (Richmond: Virginia State Library, 1932), 2:269.

13. Jefferson's 1816 version of the diary and notes of 1781, *PTJ* 4:262.

14. Tatham to Armistead Burwell, *PTJ* 4:273.

15. Nathaniel Burwell to TJ, January 2, 1781, *PTJ* 4:294.

16. Ewald, *Diary of the American War,* 260.

17. Arnold to the officer commanding the party on shore, Jan. 2, 1781, Baron von Friedrich Wilhelm Ludolf Augustin Steuben Papers, New-York Historical Society, 4:12.

18. Emory G. Evans, *Thomas Nelson of Yorktown: Revolutionary Virginian* (Charlottesville: Colonial Williamsburg Foundation, 1975), 126.

19. Ibid., 67.

20. Ewald, *Diary of the American War,* 261.

21. TJ to Benjamin Harrison, January 2, 1781, *PTJ* 4:296.

22. TJ to Abner Nash, January 16, 1781, *PTJ* 4:381.

23. James Fairlee to Steuben, January 3, 1781, Steuben Papers, New-York Historical Society.

The Most Wretched Situation That Can Be Conceived

1. John McAuley Palmer, *General Von Steuben* (New Haven: Yale University Press, 1937), 1–5.

2. Ibid., 50, 91–94.

3. Ibid., 1–5.

4. Ibid., 98–99.

5. *Steuben: Secret Aid for the Americans* (Berlin: Foundation for Prussian Cultural Property, 1981), 17.

6. Ibid., 31.

7. Steuben to Baron de Frank, July 4, 1779, in William Leete Stone, *Letters of Brunswick and Hessian Officers During the American Revolution* (New York: Da Capo Press, 1970), 239–55.

8. Palmer, *General Von Steuben,* 234–35.

9. Steuben to TJ, December 15, 1780, *PTJ* 4:210.

10. Steuben to TJ, December 16, 1780, *PTJ* 4:212–14.

11. Nelson to TJ, January 22, 1781, *PTJ* 4:427.

12. TJ to Steuben, January 4, 1781, *PTJ* 4:308.

13. TJ to George Mutter, February 18, 1780, *PTJ* 3:301–2.

14. Steuben to TJ, December 15, 1780, *PTJ* 4:209.

15. Simcoe, *Simcoe's Military Journal,* 160.

16. Ewald, *Diary of the American War,* 261.

17. James Maxwell to TJ, January 1, 1781, *PTJ* 4:290.

18. Nelson to TJ, January 4, 1781, *PTJ* 4:307.

19. Harrison to TJ, January 4, 1781, *PTJ* 4:307–8.

20. August Wilhelm du Roi, *Journal of Du Roi the Elder, Lieutenant and Adjutant, in the Service of the Duke of Brunswick, 1776–1778,* trans. Charlotte S. J. Epping (Philadelphia: University of Pennsylvania Press, 1911), 159–60.

21. "Autobiography of David Meade," *William and Mary Quarterly* 13, 2 (October 1904): 94.

22. Mary Byrd to TJ, February 23, 1781, *PTJ* 4:690–92.

23. Memoir of Mary Byrd's granddaughter, BR Box 274 (57), Huntington Library, San Marino, CA.

24. Ibid.

25. Ibid.

26. Mary Byrd to TJ, February 23, 1781, *PTJ* 4:690–92.

27. Mary Byrd to Sir Guy Carleton, June 5, 1783, *PTJ* 5:704–5.

28. Robert M. Owens, *Mr. Jefferson's Hammer* (Norman: University of Oklahoma Press, 2007), 11.

29. Joseph Jones to James Madison, January 17, 1781, in *Letters of Joseph Jones of Virginia, 1777–1787* (Washington, DC: Department of State, 1889), 67.

Seemed Like the Day of Judgment Was Come

1. Simcoe, *Simcoe's Military Journal,* 160–61; Henry Lee, *Memoirs of the War in the Southern Department of the United States* (Washington, DC: Printed by Peter Force, 1827), 192n.

2. Arnold to Clinton, January 21, 1781, *Documents of the American Revolution,* ed. Kenneth Gordon Davies (Great Britain: Irish University Press, 1981), 21:40–43.

3. Ewald, *Diary of the American War,* 266.

4. Simcoe, *Simcoe's Military Journal,* 161.

5. Harry M. Ward and Harold E. Greer, *Richmond During the Revolution, 1775–83* (Charlottesville: University Press of Virginia, 1977), 37–43.

6. Ibid., 53.

7. James Adam Bear, Isaac Jefferson, and Hamilton W. Pierson, *Jefferson at Monticello* (Charlottesville: University Press of Virginia, 1967), 4–9.

8. TJ to Charles Lee, May 15, 1826, in *The Works of Thomas Jefferson,* ed. Paul Leicester Ford (New York: G. P. Putnam's Sons, 1904), 12:277–81.

9. TJ to John Nicholas, November 10, 1819, in *Writings of Thomas Jefferson,* ed. H. A. Washington (Washington, DC: Taylor and Maury, 1954), 7:144.

10. TJ to Charles Lee, May 15, 1826, in Ford, *Works of Thomas Jefferson* 12:277–81.

11. Ewald, *Diary of the American War,* 267.

12. Ibid.

13. Simcoe, *Simcoe's Military Journal,* 162.

14. Bear, Jefferson, and Pierson, *Jefferson at Monticello,* 4–9.

15. Ibid., 8–9.

16. Tatham to Armistead Burwell, *PTJ* 4:273.

17. Bear, Jefferson, and Pierson, *Jefferson at Monticello*, 9; Thomas Jefferson, *Memoir, Correspondence, and Miscellanies, from the Papers of Thomas Jefferson*, ed. Thomas Jefferson Randolph (Charlottesville, VA: F. Carr, 1829), 39–40.

18. Benedict Arnold's letter to the inhabitants of Richmond, January 5, 1781, Virginia Historical Society, Mss2 Ar642 a 1.

19. Bear, Jefferson, and Pierson, *Jefferson at Monticello*, 9.

20. TJ to George Weedon, January 10, 1781, *PTJ* 4:335–36.

21. Simcoe, *Simcoe's Military Journal*, 163; Ewald, *Diary of the American War*, 268.

22. Ewald, *Diary of the American War*, 268–69.

23. Arnold to Clinton, Jan. 21, 1781, in Davies, *Documents of the American Revolution* 21: 40–43.

24. TJ to Charles Lee, May 15, 1826, in Ford, *Works of Thomas Jefferson* 12:277–81.

25. Steuben to TJ, January 6, 1781, *PTJ* 4:312.

26. Palmer, *General Von Steuben*, 249.

27. Ibid., 248.

28. Ewald, *Diary of the American War*, 269; Simcoe, *Simcoe's Military Journal*, 164. Simcoe said nine deserted or were captured, but he was counting only members of the Queen's Rangers.

29. Evans and Smallwood messages, January 6, 1781, Steuben Papers.

30. Mutter to TJ, January 7, 1781, *PTJ* 4:314–15.

31. Diaries of Arnold's Invasion, *PTJ* 4:258–70.

32. TJ to George Washington, January 10, 1781, *PTJ* 4:333–35; TJ to Weedon, January 10, 1781, *PTJ* 4:335–36.

The Enemy Mean to Overrun Us

1. Ewald, *Diary of the American War*, 268.

2. Benson J. Lossing, *Pictorial Field Book of the Revolution* (New York: Harper and Brothers, 1860), 2:238.

3. Pension application of William Seth Stubblefield, accessed at http://www.charlescity.org/rwr.

4. Simcoe, *Simcoe's Military Journal*, 167.

5. Nelson to TJ, *PTJ* 4:321.

6. Ewald, *Diary of the American War*, 269–70; Ewald, *Treatise on Partisan Warfare*, 128.

7. Ewald, *Diary of the American War*, 270.

8. Ibid., 270–71; Ewald, *Treatise on Partisan Warfare*, 78.

9. John Page to Theodorick Bland, January 21, 1781, *Virginia Historical Register* 4 (January 1851): 195–99.

10. Edmund Pendleton to Washington, February 16, 1781, in *The Letters and Papers of Edmund Pendleton, 1734–1803*, ed. David John Mays (Charlottesville: University Press of Virginia, 1967), 338–40.

11. Rev. James Madison to James Madison, March 9, 1781, in *The Papers of James Madison*, Congressional Series, ed. William T. Hutchinson and William M. E. Rachal (Chicago: University of Chicago Press, 1963), 3:9–11.

12. Steuben to Washington, January 11, 1781, in Jared Sparks, *Correspondence of the American Revolution* (Boston: Little, Brown, 1835), 3:205.

13. Nathanael Greene to Steuben, January 7, 1781, in *The Papers of General Nathanael Greene,* ed. Richard K. Showman, Dennis Michael Conrad, and Roger N. Parks (Chapel Hill: University of North Carolina Press, 1976), 7:68–69.

14. Steuben's Queries, *PTJ* 4:358.

15. Steuben to TJ, February 11, 1781, *PTJ* 4:584.

16. TJ to Steuben, February 12, 1781, *PTJ* 4:592–93.

17. Steuben to Washington, February 18, 1781, Steuben Papers.

18. Harrison to TJ, February 12, 1781, *PTJ* 4:589–90; Harrison to Washington, February 16, 1781, in *Calendar of Virginia State Papers* (Richmond: R. F. Walker, 1875), 1:523–24.

You Loyalists Won't Do Anything

1. Ewald, *Diary of the American War,* 274. Ewald wrote that Norfolk was a "blot" that "had been burned to the ground at the beginning of the war, except for a few houses."

2. Arnold to Clinton, January 21, 1781, in Davies, *Documents of the American Revolution,* 42.

3. Ewald, *Diary of the American War,* 286.

4. Ewald, *Treatise on Partisan Warfare,* 93.

5. Kevin P. Kelly, "The White Loyalists of Williamsburg," *Colonial Williamsburg Interpreter* 17, 2 (Summer 1996): 1–14.

6. Ewald, *Diary of the American War,* 286–87.

7. Ibid., 276–79.

8. William Gilpin, *Memoirs of Josias Rogers, Esq., Commander of His Majesty's Ship Quebec* (London: Printed for T. Cadell and W. Davies, 1808), 20–50.

9. James, *Journal,* 106.

10. Henry A. Muhlenberg, *The Life of Major-General Peter Muhlenberg, of the Revolutionary Army* (Philadelphia: Carey and Hart, 1849), 230.

Honor Is Like an Island

1. Dundas to Clinton, January 22, 1781, Clinton Papers, William L. Clements Library, University of Michigan.

2. Steuben to Washington, February 18, 1781, Steuben Papers 4:54.

3. Frederick Mackenzie, *The Diary of Frederick Mackenzie* (New York: New York Times Books, 1968), 465–66.

4. James, *Journal,* 103–4.

5. Arnold letters in the High Court of Admiralty, British National Archives, Public Records Office, Reference 238 32–299.

6. James Innes to TJ, March 6, 1781, *PTJ* 5:73.

7. Arnold to Simon Kollock, March 10, 1781, in *Report on American Manuscripts in the Royal Institution of Great Britain* (London: John Falconer, 1904), 255.

8. Mackenzie, *Diary of Frederick Mackenzie,* 540.

9. Ewald, *Diary of the American War,* 294–96.

10. Ibid., 250.

11. Ibid., 296.

12. Ibid., 298. The words about honor carried by Ewald were by the French poet Nicolas Boileau Despréaux (1636–1711).

13. Ibid., 296.

14. Isaac Newton Arnold, *The Life of Benedict Arnold* (New York: Arno Press, 1979), 347.

15. TJ to Washington, January 10, 1781, *PTJ* 4:335; TJ to J. P. G. Muhlenberg, January 31, 1781, *PTJ* 4:487–88.

16. Edward W. Hocker, *The Fighting Parson of the American Revolution: A Biography of General Peter Muhlenberg, Lutheran Clergyman, Military Chieftain, and Political Leader* (Philadelphia: Hocker, 1936), 110–11.

17. TJ to Muhlenberg, January 31, 1781, *PTJ* 4:487–88.

18. Muhlenberg, *Life of Major-General Peter Muhlenberg,* 239.

19. TJ to Nelson, January 16, 1781, *PTJ* 4:382.

20. Washington to Board of War, October 25, 1780, *Writings of George Washington,* ed. Worthington Chauncey Ford (New York: G. P. Putnam's Sons, 1889), 9:16–17.

21. *PTJ* 4:382n.

22. Beesly Edgar Joel to TJ, February 9, 1781, *PTJ* 4:569–70.

23. Nelson to TJ, February 7, 1781, *PTJ* 4:553–54.

24. TJ to Joel, February 14, 1781, *PTJ* 4:608–9.

25. Innes to TJ, February 21, 1781, *PTJ* 4:675–76.

26. George Corbin to TJ, February 28, 1781, *PTJ* 5:21–2; TJ to Corbin et al., March 13, 1781, *PTJ* 5:137.

27. TJ to the County Lieutenants of Berkeley and Frederick, February 16, 1781, *PTJ* 4:627–28.

28. TJ to Charles Lynch, February 15, 1781, *PTJ* 4:618.

29. TJ to George Rogers Clark, February 19, 1781, *PTJ* 4:653.

30. TJ to Steuben, February 24, 1781, *PTJ* 4:700–701.

31. The Affair of Westover, *PTJ* 5:679.

32. John Page to TJ, April 26, 1776, *PTJ* 1:288–90. A scalding attack on Byrd was published in June 10, 1775, and signed by "Voluntarious." Page told Jefferson that Innes's "bold attack" on Byrd and other Loyalists in the newspaper resulted in Innes's ouster as head usher of the William and Mary grammar school.

33. Innes to TJ, February 21, 1781, *PTJ* 4:675–76.

34. Nicholas to TJ, *PTJ* 4:668.

35. *Journal of the Council of the State of Virginia* (Richmond: Virginia State Library, 1932), 298.

36. Mary Byrd to Steuben, February 23, 1781, *PTJ* 5:689–91.

37. Steuben to Innes, February 25, 1781, *PTJ* 5:692.

38. TJ to Steuben, March 10, 1781, *PTJ* 5:117.

39. McIlwaine, *Journals of the Council* 2:302–3.

40. George Lee Turberville to Steuben, March 15, 1781, *PTJ* 5:699–700.

41. Turberville to Steuben, March 16, 1781, *PTJ* 5:701.

42. TJ to Mary Byrd, March 1, 1781, *PTJ* 5:31–32.
43. Memoir of Mary Byrd's granddaughter.
44. Sophia Cadwalader, *Recollections of Joshua Francis Fisher* (Boston: D. B. Updike, 1929), 100.
45. Charles Campbell, *History of the Colony and Ancient Dominion of Virginia* (Philadelphia: J. B. Lippincott, 1860), 712.

We Must Give It Up

1. TJ to the Speaker of the House of Delegates, March 1, 1781, *PTJ* 5:33–37.
2. TJ to the Speaker of the House of Delegates, March 9, 1781, *PTJ* 5:105n.
3. "Journal of the House of Delegates," March 1781 session, *Bulletin of the Virginia State Library* XVII (January 1928): 33–35.
4. Ibid., 41; E. M. Sanchez-Saavedra, *A Guide to Virginia Military Organizations in the American Revolution, 1774–1787* (Richmond: Virginia State Library, 1978), 134.
5. Steuben to TJ, March 9, 1781, *PTJ* 5:106.
6. "Journal of the House of Delegates," March 1781 session, 53–54.
7. George Elliott to Steuben, March 18, 1781, *PTJ* 5:155–56n.
8. Benjamin Greene to Richard Claiborne, March 7, 1781, *PTJ* 5:82–83n.
9. Steuben to TJ, March 9, 1781, *PTJ* 5:107.
10. TJ to Steuben, March 10, 1781, *PTJ* 5:119–20.
11. Harlow G. Unger, *Lafayette* (Hoboken, NJ: Wiley, 2002), 126.
12. Washington to Philip Schuyler et al., May 25, 1780, in Ford, *Writings of George Washington* 8:284.
13. Unger, *Lafayette,* 124.
14. *Writings of George Washington,* ed. Jared Sparks (Boston: Russell, Odiorne and Metcalf, 1835), 7:419.
15. TJ to Marquis de Lafayette, March 8 and 10, 1781, *PTJ* 5:92, 113.
16. Palmer, *General Von Steuben,* 256.
17. Steuben to Washington, April 14, 1781, *PTJ* 5:107n.
18. Ewald, *Diary of the American War,* 289–91.
19. A. T. Mahan, *The Major Operations of the Navies in the War of American Independence* (Boston: Little, Brown, 1968), 171.
20. James, *Journal,* 107.
21. Stewart, *History of Virginia's Navy,* 98; Lyon Gardiner Tyler, *Encyclopedia of Virginia Biography* (New York: Lewis Historical Publishing, 1915), 1049.
22. Lafayette to Washington, March 26, 1781, in *Lafayette in the Age of the American Revolution: Selected Letters and Papers,* ed. Stanley J. Idzerda (Ithaca, NY: Cornell University Press, 1977), 3:417–18.

Burnt All Their Houses

1. William Phillips to Clinton, April 15, 1781, in Sir Henry Clinton, *The American Rebellion: Sir Henry Clinton's Narrative of His Campaigns, 1775–1782,* ed. William B. Wilcox (New Haven: Yale University Press, 1954), 510.

2. Ewald, *Diary of the American War,* 296.

3. "Burnt All Their Houses: The Log of HMS *Savage* During a Raid up the Potomac River, Spring 1781," *Virginia Magazine of History and Biography* 99, 4 (October 1991): 513–30. Background on Lyles comes from Francis B. Heitman, *Historical Register of Officers of the Continental Army During the War of the Revolution, April, 1775, to December, 1783* (Baltimore: Genealogical Publishing Co., 1967), 361.

4. Mary V. Thompson, "Different People, Different Stories," delivered at Mount Vernon Ladies' Association symposium, "George Washington and Slavery," November 3, 2001, quoting "An Old Citizen of Fairfax County," *Mount Vernon Reminiscences, Alexandria Gazette,* January 18, 1876.

5. Ellen McCallister Clark, "A Wartime Incident," *Annual Report 1986* (Mount Vernon, VA: Mount Vernon Ladies' Association of the Union, 1987), 23–25.

6. Washington to Lund Washington, August 20, 1775, LOC.

7. François Jean Chastellux, *Travels in North America in the Years 1780, 1781 and 1782 by the Marquis de Chastellux* (New York, 1828), 282n.

8. Lafayette to Washington, April 23, 1781, in *Memoirs, Correspondence and Manuscripts of General Lafayette* (London: Saunders and Otley, 1837), 1:406.

9. Washington to Lund Washington, April 30, 1781, George Washington Papers, LOC.

10. TJ to John Skinker and William Garrad, April 14, 1781, *PTJ* 5:451.

11. Skinker to TJ, April 11, 1781, *PTJ* 5:406–7.

12. Thomas Gaskins to TJ, April 13, 1781, *PTJ* 5:430.

13. Commissioners for Collecting Taxes in Accomack County to TJ, May 15, 1781, *PTJ* 5:651–55; Corbin to TJ, May 31, 1781, *PTJ* 6:44–47.

14. Garret van Meter to TJ, April 11, 14, 20, 1781, *PTJ* 5:409–10, 455, 513–15.

15. Muhlenberg, *Life of Major-General Peter Muhlenberg,* 244–45.

16. Ibid., 246.

17. George Gilmer to TJ, April 13, 1781, *PTJ* 5:430–31.

18. Thomas Jefferson, *Jefferson's Memorandum Books,* ed. James Bear and Lucia Stanton (Princeton: Princeton University Press, 1997), 1:508.

19. TJ to David Jameson, April 16, 1781, *PTJ* 5:468.

Uncommon Dangers Require Uncommon Remedies

1. Robert Honyman, "News of the Yorktown Campaign: The Journal of Dr. Robert Honyman, April 17–November 25, 1781," ed. Richard K. MacMaster, *Virginia Magazine of History and Biography* 79 (1971): 390–91.

2. Ibid.

3. Ewald, *Diary of the American War,* 296; Phillips ship inventory, cited in Robert P. Davis, *Where a Man Can Go: Major General William Phillips, British Royal Artillery, 1731–1781,* Contributions in Military Studies, no. 179 (Westport, CT: Greenwood Press, 1999).

4. Innes to TJ, April 20, 1781, *PTJ* 5:506.

5. TJ to Innes, April 22, 1781, *PTJ* 5:533.

6. Innes to TJ, April 21, 1781, *PTJ* 5:521.

7. Samuel Graham, "An English Officer's Account of His Services in America," *Historical Magazine* (September 1865): 241–50.

8. Ibid.

9. Lafayette to TJ, April 17, 1781, *PTJ* 5:477.

10. Lafayette to TJ, April 21, 1781, *PTJ* 5:522–23.

No Wagons, No Intelligence, Not One Spy

1. Daniel Trabue, *Westward into Kentucky: The Narrative of Daniel Trabue,* ed. Chester Raymond Young (Lexington: University Press of Kentucky, 2004), 99–100.

2. Steuben to Nathanael Greene, April 25, 1781, in Showman, Conrad, and Parks, *Papers of General Nathanael Greene* 8:147.

3. Trabue, *Westward into Kentucky,* 99–100.

4. Ibid., 101.

5. Ibid., 102–3.

6. J. T. McAllister, *Virginia Militia in the Revolution* (Hot Springs, VA: McAllister Publishing, 1913), 129; Henry Howe, *Historical Collections of Virginia* (Charleston, SC: Babcock, 1845), 244.

7. Palmer, *General Von Steuben,* 267–68; Steuben to Nathanael Greene, May 15, 1781, in Showman, Conrad, and Parks, *Papers of General Nathanael Greene* 8:267–68.

8. Maxwell to TJ, April 26, 1781, *PTJ* 5:557–58.

9. Arnold to Clinton, May 12, 1781, in Clinton, *American Rebellion,* 520.

10. Randall, *Life of Thomas Jefferson* 1:324n.

11. Sanchez-Saavedra, *Guide to Virginia Military Organizations,* 173–74.

12. TJ to Van Meter, April 27, 1781, *PTJ* 5:566.

13. *PTJ* 5:590–92n.

14. TJ to Virginia delegates in Congress, May 10, 1781, *PTJ* 5:632–33.

15. Lafayette to Washington, May 4, 1781, in Sparks, *Correspondence of the American Revolution* 3:303–4.

16. John C. Dann, *The Revolution Remembered: Eyewitness Accounts of the War for Independence* (Chicago: University of Chicago Press, 1980), 406.

17. Lafayette to Nathanael Greene, May 3, 1781, in Idzerda, *Lafayette,* 80.

18. Lafayette to Washington, May 4, 1781, in Sparks, *Correspondence of the American Revolution* 3:303–4.

19. TJ to legislators, May 1, 1781, *PTJ* 5:585–86.

20. Lafayette to Washington, May 4, 1781, in Sparks, *Correspondence of the American Revolution* 3:303–4.

Bring Our Whole Force into Virginia

1. Quotes from the two previous paragraphs are from Lord Cornwallis to Phillips, April 24, 1781; Phillips to Cornwallis, May 6, 1781; Phillips to Matthew von Fuchs, May 6, 1781, in Davis, *Where a Man Can Go,* 176–78.

2. TJ to the Speaker of the House of Delegates, May 10, 1781, *PTJ* 5:626–29; TJ to William Fleming, *PTJ* 5:640. Joseph Prentis and Dudley Digges resigned from the Council. See Prentis to TJ, April 8, 1781, *PTJ* 5:383, and Digges to TJ, May 14, 1781, *PTJ* 5:644. John Tyler declined to take a seat on the Council; see Tyler to TJ, April 1, 1781, *PTJ* 5:316.

3. Edward Ayres, "The Impact of the Revolution on Agricultural Production in Eastern Virginia," in *Proceedings of the 2003 Conference* (North Bloomfield, OH: Association for Living History, Farm and Agricultural Museums, 2004), 26:52–57.

4. George Moffett to TJ, May 5, 1781, *PTJ* 5:603–5; Thomas Posey to William Davies, May 18, 1781, *PTJ* 5:605n.

5. Samuel McDowell to TJ, May 9, 1781, *PTJ* 5:621–23.

6. TJ to Robert Lawson, May 8, 1781, *PTJ* 5:613–14.

7. Michael McDonnell, *The Politics of War: Race, Class, and Conflict in Revolutionary Virginia* (Chapel Hill: University of North Carolina Press, 2007), 460.

8. L. P. Jackson, "Virginia Negro Soldiers and Seaman in the American Revolution," *Journal of Negro History* 27, 3 (July 1942): 247–87; Lewis Hinton pension application, S10831, National Archives.

9. Lafayette to Washington, July 20, 1781, in Idzerda, *Lafayette* 4:256.

10. Madison to Joseph Jones, November 28, 1780, in *The Writings of James Madison,* ed. Gaillard Hunt (New York: G. P. Putnam's Sons, 1900), 1:106.

11. Alexander Dick to the Speaker of the House of Delegates, May 11, 1781, Box 2, Executive Communications, Library of Virginia.

12. Quotes from the three previous paragraphs are from Mann Page to TJ, May 13, 1781, *PTJ* 5:640–43n, with enclosures of Prince William County court records.

13. Mann Page to TJ, May 13, 1781, *PTJ* 5:640–43, with enclosures of Prince William County court records.

14. June 14, 1781, *Journal of the House of Delegates of the Commonwealth of Virginia* (session starting May 1781) (Richmond: Thomas W. White, 1828), 11–12, 17.

15. Jefferson, *Notes on the State of Virginia,* 155.

16. May 10, 1781, *Journal of the House of Delegates* (session starting May 1781), 3.

17. TJ to Lafayette, May 14, 1781, *PTJ* 5:644–45.

18. Cornwallis to Lord George Germain, August 21, 1780, in *Correspondence of Charles, First Marquis Cornwallis,* ed. Charles Derek Ross (London: John Murray, 1859), 1:492–95.

19. Banastre Tarleton, *Campaigns of 1780 and 1781 in the Southern Provinces of North America* (North Stratford, NH: Ayer Co., 2001), 30, 77–79, 83–84.

20. Ibid., 80.

21. Cornwallis to Lt. Col. Cruger, August 18, 1780, in Ross, *Correspondence of Charles* 1:56–57.

22. TJ to Horatio Gates and Edward Stevens, September 3, 1780, *PTJ* 3:588, 593.

23. Mark Mayo Boatner III, *Encyclopedia of the American Revolution* (New York: David MacKay, 1974), 575–83.

24. Ibid., 460–71.

25. TJ to John Campbell, November 10, 1822, in *The Jeffersonian Cyclopedia,* ed. John P. Foley (New York: Funk & Wagnalls, 1900), 123–24.

26. Cornwallis to Clinton, April 10, 1781, in Ross, *Correspondence of Charles* 1:86.

27. Davis, *Where a Man Can Go,* 34. Phillips also had two children with another woman, Catherine Cure. He also may have earlier been married to a third woman.

28. Cornwallis to Phillips, April 10, 1781, Cornwallis Papers, PRO 30/11/85.

29. Ross, *Correspondence of Charles,* 91.

30. Tarleton, *Campaigns of 1780 and 1781,* 290.

31. Ewald, *Diary of the American War,* 299.

32. Tarleton, *Campaigns of 1780 and 1781,* 341–42.

33. Lafayette to Washington, May 24, 1781, in Idzerda, *Lafayette* 4:130–31.

34. Tarleton, *Campaigns of 1780 and 1781,* 291.

35. Cornwallis to Banastre Tarleton, May 25, 1781, in ibid., 342.

36. Henry Lee, *Memoirs of the War in the Southern Department of the United States* (New York: University Publishing, 1869), 410.

37. Cadwalader, *Recollections,* 100.

38. Cornwallis to Clinton, May 26, 1781, in Ross, *Correspondence of Charles,* 101.

39. William Smith, *Historical Memoirs of William Smith, 1778–1783,* ed. William Henry Waldo Sabine (New York: New York Times Books/Arno Press, 1971), 418.

40. Louis Reichenthal Gottschalk, *Lafayette and the Close of the American Revolution* (Chicago: University of Chicago Press, 1942), 234–35.

41. Pendleton to Madison, May 28, 1781, in Mays, *Letters and Papers of Edmund Pendleton* 1:359–60.

42. Gottschalk, *Lafayette and the Close of the American Revolution,* 229.

43. Paul David Nelson, *Anthony Wayne, Soldier of the Early Republic* (Bloomington: Indiana University Press, 1985), 130.

44. Gottschalk, *Lafayette and the Close of the American Revolution,* 235.

45. Ross, *Correspondence of Charles,* 100.

46. TJ to Washington, May 28, 1781, *PTJ* 6:32–33; Washington to TJ, June 8, 1781, *PTJ* 6:82–83.

47. Honyman, "News of the Yorktown Campaign," 397.

48. William Meade, *Old Churches, Ministers and Families of Virginia* (Philadelphia: J. B Lippincott, 1878), 109.

49. Honyman, "News of the Yorktown Campaign," 397.

50. Cornwallis to Clinton, June 30, 1781, in Clinton, *American Rebellion,* 535–36.

Flight from Monticello

A Terrible Clatter of Horses

1. John Maass, "To Disturb the Assembly," *Southern Campaigns in the American Revolution* [online magazine, www.southerncampaign.org] 2, 3 (March 2005): 6.

2. Harrison speech, May 28, 1781, *Journal of the House of Delegates of the Commonwealth of Virginia, 1781* (Richmond: Thomas W. White, 1828), 4.

3. Thomas Jefferson (TJ) to Speaker of the House of Delegates, May 10, 1781, in *The Papers of Thomas Jefferson* (henceforth *PTJ*), ed. Julian P. Boyd (Princeton: Princeton University Press, 1952), 5:626–27.

4. May 26, 1781, *Calendar of Virginia State Papers,* ed. W. P. Palmer (Richmond: Virginia State Library, 1881); facsimile edition (New York: Kraus Reprint Corp., 1968), 2:122.

5. TJ to Marquis de Lafayette, May 29, 1781, *PTJ* 6:35.

6. Samuel Patteson and David Ross to William Davies, May 27, 1781, *PTJ* 6:22–23.

7. May 29, 1781, legislative order, *Journal of the House of Delegates of the Commonwealth of Virginia, 1781,* 5–6.

8. Merrill D. Peterson, *Thomas Jefferson and the New Nation* (New York: Oxford University Press, 1970), 219.

9. Woody Holton, *Forced Founders: Indians, Debtors, Slaves, and the Making of the American Revolution in Virginia* (Chapel Hill: University of North Carolina Press, 1999), 37.

10. Anthony F. C. Wallace, *Jefferson and the Indians: The Tragic Fate of the First Americans* (Cambridge, MA: Belknap Press, 1999), 71–79.

11. State of Indiana and Logan Esarey, *Governors' Messages and Letters* (Indianapolis: Indiana Historical Commission, 1922), 115.

12. Jefferson speech to Jean Baptiste Ducoigne, June 1, 1781, *PTJ* 6:60–62.

13. Robert Scot invoice and footnotes, *PTJ* 4:35–37. This description comes from a medal made in 1780; Jefferson asked the same engraver to make the same medal for Ducoigne on May 30, 1781. See TJ to Scot, May 30, 1781, *PTJ* 6:43.

14. Jefferson speech to Ducoigne, June 1, 1781, *PTJ* 6:60–62.

15. Robert Honyman, "News of the Yorktown Campaign: The Journal of Dr. Robert Honyman, April 17–November 25, 1781," ed. Richard K. MacMaster, *Virginia Magazine of History and Biography* 79 (1971): 399.

16. Louise Pecquet du Bellet, Edward Jaquelin, and Martha Cary Jaquelin, *Some Prominent Virginia Families* (Lynchburg, VA: J. P. Bell, 1907), 313; Honyman, "News of the Yorktown Campaign," 399–402.

17. Honyman, "News of the Yorktown Campaign," 400; John Graves Simcoe, *Simcoe's Military Journal, a History of the Operations of a Partisan Corps, Called the Queen's Rangers, Commanded by Lieut. Col. J. G. Simcoe, During the War of the American Revolution* (New York: Bartlett & Welford, 1844), 212; Mary Beacock Fryer and Christopher Dracott, *John Graves Simcoe, 1752–1806: A Biography* (Toronto: Dundurn Press, 1998), 75.

18. Daniel Trabue, *Westward into Kentucky: The Narrative of Daniel Trabue,* ed. Chester Raymond Young (Lexington: University Press of Kentucky, 2004), 107.

19. Eliza Jacquelin Ambler to Mildred Smith, June 5, 1781, "An Old Virginia Correspondence," *Atlantic Monthly* (October 1899): 538–39. After Jefferson's flight from the British became known, Ambler later wrote to a friend about the "laughable ... account we have of our illustrious Governor, who, they say, took neither rest nor food, for man or horse, 'til he reached" the neighboring mountain. This letter would be quoted for years to mock Jefferson; it was particularly cutting given that Jefferson had unsuccessfully courted Eliza's mother, Rebecca. Yet Eliza and her family had made a similarly hasty dash, as shown in the letter quoted within.

20. Jack Jouett page, *The Jefferson Encyclopedia,* Monticello [online, http://wiki.monticello.org/mediawiki/index.php/Jack_Jouett%27s_Ride].

21. John Cook Wylie, "New Documentary Light on Tarleton's Raid: Letters of New Brockenbrough and Peter Lyons," *Virginia Magazine of History and Biography* 74, 4 (October 1966): 452–61.

22. Sudie Rucker Wood, *The Rucker Family Genealogy* (Richmond: Old Dominion Press, 1932), 69.

23. George Gilmer, "Papers, Military and Political, 1775–1778, of George Gilmer, M. D., of Pen Park, Albemarle County," *Collections of the Virginia Historical Society* 6 (1887): 73.

24. Diary of Arnold's Invasion, *PTJ* 4:260–61.

25. James Adam Bear, Isaac Jefferson, and Hamilton W. Pierson, *Jefferson at Monticello* (Charlottesville: University Press of Virginia, 1967), 71.

26. Sarah N. Randolph, *The Domestic Life of Thomas Jefferson* (New York: Frederick Unger, 1958), 55–56; Thomas Jefferson Randolph, *Memoirs of Thomas Jefferson Randolph,* unpublished manuscript, University of Virginia Library Special Collections, MSS 5454-c, 1874, 16–17.

27. TJ to William Gordon, July 16, 1788, *PTJ* 13:362–64.

28. Randolph, *Domestic Life,* 55–56.

29. Joseph Jones to George Washington, June 20, 1781, citing Benjamin Harrison letter, *Letters of Joseph Jones of Virginia, 1777–1787* (Washington, DC: Department of State, 1889), 82.

30. TJ to Gordon, July 17, 1788, *PTJ* 13:362–64.

31. Nathan Boone, Olive Van Bibber Boone, Lyman Copeland Draper, and Neal O. Hammon, *My Father, Daniel Boone: The Draper Interviews with Nathan Boone* (Lexington: University Press of Kentucky, 1999), 73. The story of Boone's capture and questioning by Tarleton has been retold in various forms, and some Boone stories are subject to question, but there is no doubt Daniel Boone was a Virginia legislator at the time and would have had reason to be in Charlottesville.

British Horse Came to Monticello

1. TJ to William Fleming, June 9, 1781, *PTJ* 6:84.

2. Deposition of Christopher Hudson, July 26, 1805, Jefferson memorandums on invasion, *PTJ* 4:256–76.

3. Jefferson notes on invasion of Virginia, *The Works of Thomas Jefferson,* ed. Paul Leicester Ford (New York: G. P. Putnam's Sons, 1904), 10:49.

4. Thomas Jefferson, *Jefferson's Memorandum Books,* ed. James Bear and Lucia Stanton (Princeton: Princeton University Press, 1997), 1:510.

5. Randolph, *Domestic Life,* 56.

6. Cornelia J. Randolph to Virginia J. Randolph, August 17, 1817, Monticello Family letters collection, accessed at http://retirementseries.dataformat.com.

7. Randolph, *Memoirs of Thomas Jefferson Randolph,* 17.

8. Jefferson, *Jefferson's Memorandum Books* 1:510–11. This account of Jefferson's flight is based primarily on Jefferson's notations in his memorandum books. The author sought to reconstruct the route on several visits, using contemporary and current maps, keyed to Jefferson's notations of payments for food, lodging and ferriage fees. The footnotes in *Memorandum Books* were invaluable in compiling the route.

9. The description of Geddes is based on an author visit and the "National Register of Historic Places Inventory Nomination Form" for Geddes, filed February 24, 1983.

10. Ellie Weeks, "Elk Hill: Thomas Jefferson's Plantation on the James," *Goochland County Historical Society Magazine* 3, 1 (1971): 6–11. The Jeffersons used the land after signing papers for it in 1774 but the acquisition was not finalized until 1778.

11. TJ to Gordon, July 17, 1788, *PTJ* 13:362–64.

12. Johann von Ewald, *Diary of the American War: A Hessian Journal*, ed. Joseph P. Tustin (New Haven: Yale University Press, 1979), 305–6.

13. Joseph Anderson, Sarah J. Prichard, and Anna Lydia Ward, *The Town and City of Waterbury, Connecticut* (New Haven: Price and Lee Co., 1896), 471–79. The idea that Cornwallis was sending infected blacks into the American army was buttressed by a letter from a British general, Alexander Leslie, to Cornwallis, which suggested that seven hundred blacks infected with smallpox would be distributed among rebel plantations. Leslie to Cornwallis, July 31, 1781, British National Archives, PRO 30/11/6.

14. Ewald, *Diary of the American War*, 302. The letter from Lafayette was captured by British troops and recorded by Ewald in his diary. Ewald usually is a reliable source and thus the letter is quoted herein. However, the letter does not appear to have survived. Ewald was frustrated at Cornwallis's strategy, writing in his diary, "We hold no more ground than our cannon can reach. . . . What good are our victories which have been so dearly bought with our blood?"

15. Henry Young to Davies, May 13, 1781, in Minnie Lee McGehee, "Point of Fork Arsenal in 1781," *Bulletin of the Fluvanna County Historical Society* 25 (October 1977): 12; TJ to Davies, May 31, 1781, *PTJ*, 648–49n.

16. Simcoe, *Simcoe's Military Journal*, 213–18.

17. "Baron Steuben's Account of His Transactions in Virginia," *Historical Magazine* 4 (October 1860): 301–3.

18. Harrison to Joseph Jones, quoted in letter of Jones to Washington, June 20, 1781, in *Letters of Joseph Jones*, 82.

19. Alexander Brown, *The Cabells and Their Kin* (Cambridge, MA: Riverside Press, 1895), 195.

20. Hugh Rose to William Cabell, June 9, 1781, in Brown, *Cabells and Their Kin*, 193–94.

21. TJ to Gordon, July 16, 1788, *PTJ* 13:362–64.

22. TJ to Henry Lee, May 15, 1826, in Ford, *Works of Thomas Jefferson* 12:277–81.

23. TJ to Gordon, July 16, 1788, *PTJ* 13:362–64.

24. Thomas Jefferson, *Farm Book*, 1774–1824, Collidge Collection of Thomas Jefferson Manuscripts, Massachusetts Historical Society, 29.

25. TJ to Gordon, July 16, 1788, *PTJ* 13:362–64.

26. Cassandra Pybus, "Jefferson's Faulty Math: The Question of Slave Defections in the American Revolution," *William and Mary Quarterly* 62, 2 (2005): 243–64.

27. TJ to William Jones, January 5, 1787, *PTJ* 11:14–18.

28. TJ to Gordon, July 16, 1788, *PTJ* 13:362–64.

The Unfortunate Passages in My Conduct

1. Alexander Gurdon Abell, *Life of John Tyler* (New York: Harper & Bros., 1843), 10.

2. The Harrison letter is quoted in Joseph Jones to Washington, June 20, 1781, in *Letters of Joseph Jones,* 82.

3. Josiah Parker to Benjamin Harrison, June 9, 1781, *PTJ* 6:83–84.

4. Richard Henry Lee to Washington, June 12, 1781, in *The Letters of Richard Henry Lee,* ed. James Curtis Ballagh (New York: Macmillan, 1914), 83.

5. Archibald Stuart to TJ, September 8, 1818, *PTJ* 6:85n.

6. TJ to Isaac Zane, December 24, 1781, *PTJ* 6:143.

7. Henry Mayer and James M. Elson, *Patrick Henry and Thomas Jefferson* (Brookneal, VA: Descendants' Branch of the Patrick Henry Memorial Foundation, 1997), 27.

8. TJ to Lafayette, August 4, 1781, *PTJ* 6:111–12.

9. Quotations from the previous two paragraphs are from Thomas Jefferson, *Notes on the State of Virginia,* ed. William Peden (Chapel Hill: University of North Carolina Press, 1982), 19, 24–25.

10. Ibid., 88–90.

11. Ibid., 91.

12. Ibid., 137–43.

13. TJ to John Holmes, April 22, 1820, in *The Writings of Thomas Jefferson,* ed. Paul Leicester Ford (New York: G. P. Putnam's Sons, 1898), 12:158.

14. James Callaway to TJ, June 4, 1781, *PTJ* 6:77.

15. William Meade, *Old Churches, Ministers and Families of Virginia* (Philadelphia: J. B Lippincott, 1878), 459–50n.

16. Brown, *Cabells and Their Kin,* 197.

Liberty!

1. Emory G. Evans, *Thomas Nelson of Yorktown: Revolutionary Virginian* (Charlottesville: Colonial Williamsburg Foundation, 1975), 103–6.

2. Brown, *Cabells and Their Kin,* 195.

3. Davies to Steuben, July 12, 1781, *PTJ* 6:78n.

4. Henry Clinton to Cornwallis, June 11, 1781, in Sir Henry Clinton, *The American Rebellion: Sir Henry Clinton's Narrative of His Campaigns, 1775–1782,* ed. William B. Wilcox (New Haven: Yale University Press, 1954), 529–30.

5. Cornwallis to Clinton, May 28, 1781, in Clinton, *American Rebellion,* 522–23; William Smith, *Historical Memoirs of William Smith, 1778–1783,* ed. William Henry Waldo Sabine (New York: New York Times Books/Arno Press, 1971), 357.

6. Cornwallis to Clinton, June 30, 1781, in Clinton, *American Rebellion,* 535; Smith, *Historical Memoirs,* 428–29.

7. Clinton to Lord George Germain, June 9, 1781, in Clinton, *American Rebellion,* 528–29.

8. Louis Reichenthal Gottschalk, *Lafayette and the Close of the American Revolution* (Chicago: University of Chicago Press, 1942), 267–71.

9. TJ to Lafayette, August 4, 1781, *PTJ* 6:112.

10. TJ to James Monroe, September 16, 1781, *PTJ* 6:117–18.

11. See the correspondence of June through August 1781 between Cornwallis and Clinton, in *Correspondence of Charles, First Marquis Cornwallis,* ed. Charles Derek Ross (London:

John Murray, 1859), and in the appendix of Clinton, *American Rebellion.* The matter is also covered in Benjamin Franklin Stevens, *Clinton-Cornwallis Controversy* (London: B. F. Stevens, 1888).

12. Ewald, *Diary of the American War,* 323.

13. Thomas Nelson to Washington, July 27, 1781, in H. R. McIlwaine, ed., *Official Letters of the Governors of the State of Virginia* (Richmond: Virginia State Library, 1926), 3:13–14.

14. Nell Moore Lee, *Patriot Above Profit: A Portrait of Thomas Nelson, Jr.* (Nashville, TN: Rutledge Hill Press, 1988), 451–54.

15. Bruce E. Burgoyne, *Enemy Views: The American Revolutionary War as Recorded by the Hessian Participants* (Bowie, MD: Heritage Books, 1996), 459.

16. Richard Oswald, *Memorandum on the folly of invading Virginia, the strategic importance of Portsmouth, and the need for civilian control of the military; written in 1781 by the British negotiator of the first American treaty of peace,* ed. Walter Stitt Robinson (Charlottesville: University of Virginia Press for the Tracy W. McGregor Library, 1953).

17. Lyon Gardiner Tyler, *Williamsburg, the Old Colonial Capital* (Richmond: Whittet & Shepperson, 1907), 58.

18. Mark Mayo Boatner III, *Encyclopedia of the American Revolution* (New York: David MacKay, 1974), 1230–49.

19. Lee, *Patriot Above Profit,* 464, 472.

20. Ewald, *Diary of the American War,* 335–36.

21. Bear, Jefferson, and Pierson, *Jefferson at Monticello,* 10. Isaac provided conflicting information about when he returned to Monticello. Although he said he was at Yorktown in October and then returned to Monticello, he also said he was with the British for six months and returned to Monticello while Jefferson was at Poplar Forest, which would have meant Isaac returned in July and was not at Yorktown. In either case, his memory of the events in Richmond corresponds to what happened there, and his discussion of Yorktown correlates with that battle, whether he saw it as a six-year-old or was told about it.

22. Edward Jackson Lowell, *The Hessians* (New York: Harper, 1884), 226–27.

23. Ewald, *Diary of the American War,* 341.

24. Anderson, Prichard, and Ward, *Town and City of Waterbury,* 480–81.

25. James Thacher, *A Military Journal During the American Revolution* (Boston: Cottons and Barnard, 1827), 284.

26. Cornwallis to Clinton, October 11, 1781, in Ross, *Correspondence of Charles,* 124; Ludwig Closen, *The Revolutionary Journal of Baron Ludwig von Closen, 1780–1783,* ed. Evelyn Martha Acomb (Chapel Hill: University of North Carolina Press, 1958), 155.

27. Clinton, *American Rebellion,* 581–87.

28. TJ to Washington, October 28, 1781, *PTJ* 6:129–30.

Time Wastes Too Fast

1. TJ to Zane, December 24, 1781, *PTJ* 6:143.

2. Charges advanced by George Nicholas, with Jefferson's Answers, *PTJ* 6:106–8.

3. December 12, 1781, *Journal of the House of Delegates of the Commonwealth of Virginia, 1781.*

4. TJ to Zane, December 24, 1781, *PTJ* 6:143.

5. TJ to George Rogers Clark, December 19, 1781, *PTJ* 6:139.

6. Closen, *Revolutionary Journal of Baron Ludwig von Closen,* 186–87.

7. Ibid., 182–83.

8. John Tyler to TJ, May 16, 1782, *PTJ* 6:183–84.

9. George F. Willison, *Patrick Henry and His World* (Garden City, NY: Doubleday, 1969), 377.

10. TJ to Monroe, May 20, 1782, *PTJ* 6:184–87.

11. *PTJ* 6:196, 198–200n., citing Randolph to James Madison, September 20, 1782, *Papers of James Madison,* 5:150–51; and, Reminiscences of Thomas Jefferson by Martha Randolph, University of Virginia, Randolph collection.

12. TJ to Elizabeth Wayles Eppes, October 3 (?), 1782, *PTJ* 6:198.

13. Philip Mazzei, *My Life and Wanderings,* ed. S. Eugene Scalia, and Margherita Marchione (Morristown, NJ: American Institute of Italian Studies, 1980), 283.

Devoutly Pray for His Death

1. TJ to Madison, December 8, 1784, *PTJ* 7:557–59.

2. Willison, *Patrick Henry and His World,* 458, 472.

3. TJ to Madison, December 8, 1784, *PTJ* 7:557–59. "Memorial and Remonstrance Against Religious Assessments," in James Madison, *The Writings of James Madison,* ed. Gaillard Hunt (New York: G. P. Putnam's, 1901), 2:183–191.

4. TJ to Monroe, July 10, 1796, *PTJ* 29:147–48.

5. William Loughton Smith, Oliver Wolcott, William Vans Murray, and Peter Force, *The pretensions of Thomas Jefferson to the presidency examined: and the charges against John Adams refuted: addressed to the citizens of American in general, and particularly to the electors of the president* (Philadelphia, 1796), 33.

6. *PTJ* 4:265.

7. TJ to Monroe, July 10, 1796, *PTJ* 29:147–48.

8. Willison, *Patrick Henry and His World,* 479.

9. Ibid., 470–78.

10. TJ to William Wirt, August 4, 1812, in Ford, *Writings of Thomas Jefferson* 9:345n.

11. William Wirt, *Sketches of the Life and Character of Patrick Henry* (Philadelphia: Desilver, Thomas, 1836), 413.

12. Mayer and Elson, *Patrick Henry and Thomas Jefferson,* 59–62. Jefferson was speaking to Daniel Webster, whose oratory would later be compared to that of Henry.

13. Online at http://wiki.monticello.org/mediawiki/index.php/Election_of_1800.

14. Thomas Jefferson and John P. Foley, *The Jeffersonian Cyclopedia* (New York: Funk & Wagnalls, 1900), 683, 915, 917.

15. Christine Coalwell, "West Point: Jefferson's Military Academy," *Monticello Newsletter* 12, 2 (Winter 2001): 1–3. Despite his concerns about overreaching federal authority, Jefferson sometimes took actions as president that went far beyond the powers given to the executive. When the opportunity arose to purchase the Louisiana Territory from the French for $15 million, he authorized the deal without approval from Congress.

16. TJ to James Barbour, January 22, 1812, *PTJ, Retirement Series,* 4:332–34.

17. *PTJ* 4:268n.

18. Thomas Paine, "Mr. Jefferson Defended by Thomas Paine!!" *The Repertory* (Boston), August 30, 1805.

19. Henry Lee, *Memoirs of the War in the Southern Department of the United States* (New York: University Publishing, 1869), 300.

20. *PTJ* 4:264–65.

21. TJ to William Johnson, October 27, 1822, in Ford, *Works of Thomas Jefferson* 12:119–22.

22. Ibid.

There Is Not a Truth Existing Which I Fear

1. Randolph, *Domestic Life,* 390–91.

2. Fawn M. Brodie, *Thomas Jefferson: An Intimate History* (New York: Bantam Books, 1974), 623–26.

3. George Ticknor, *Life, Letters, and Journals of George Ticknor* (Boston: Osgood, 1876), 349.

4. British National Archives, American Loyalists Claims, Public Record Office/AP/12/117.

5. Ross, *Correspondence of Charles,* 166, 455.

6. Janice L. Abercrombie and Richard Slatten, *Virginia Publick Claims, Lunenburg County* (Athens, GA: Iberian Publishing, 1992), 8. The claims file suggests Byrd was paid but is not definitive on the subject.

7. By some accounts, Washington later sent for Champe to head an infantry corps but was mistakenly told he was dead. The story of Champe's later years is told in petitions written over a number of years from his family to Congress. Champe died at Prickett's Fort, near what is today Fairmont, West Virginia. It was not until April 22, 2001, that a gravestone was unveiled at the site in memory of Champe.

8. Jack Jouett to TJ, January 12, 1801, *PTJ* 32:451–52.

9. TJ to Robert C. Weightman, June 24, 1826, in *The Writings of Thomas Jefferson,* ed. Albert Ellery Bergh (Washington, DC: Thomas Jefferson Memorial Foundation, 1905), 15:181.

10. TJ to Henry Lee, May 15, 1826, in Bergh, *Writings of Thomas Jefferson* 15:172–81.

11. Merrill D. Peterson, *Visitors to Monticello* (Charlottesville: University Press of Virginia, 1989), 108–10, citing Lee's letter of August 19, 1826, in *Niles' Weekly Register,* November 25, 1826.

SUGGESTED READING

THIS BOOK HAS RELIED HEAVILY on primary sources, but it is, of course, influenced by a legion of Jefferson and Revolutionary War scholars. For the Jefferson enthusiast, there is no greater resource than volumes of the Papers of Thomas Jefferson, which continue to be produced at Monticello and at Princeton University. Jefferson wrote more than nineteen thousand letters in his lifetime and received thousands, providing an extraordinary wealth of material. One can only regret that Jefferson destroyed the letters to and from his wife, Martha, and that he wrote only a cursory autobiography.

Among the many biographies of Thomas Jefferson, I have found the following to be particularly helpful: *Jefferson, War and Peace*, Marie Goebel Kimball; *Jefferson the Virginian*, Dumas Malone; *Thomas Jefferson: An Intimate History*, Fawn M. Brodie; *Thomas Jefferson: A Life*, Willard Sterne Randall; *Thomas Jefferson and the New Nation*, Merrill D. Peterson; *Jefferson and the Indians*, Anthony F. C. Wallace; *Thomas Jefferson*, R. B. Bernstein; *Jefferson and Monticello: The Biography of a Builder*, Jack McLaughlin; and *The Life of Thomas Jefferson*, Henry Stephens Randall. I also consulted a vividly illustrated work, *Thomas Jefferson's Monticello*, William L. Beiswanger, Peter J. Hatch, Lucia Stanton, and Susan R. Stein.

Patrick Henry's story is told in *Patrick Henry and His World*, George F. Willison, and *A Son of Thunder: Patrick Henry and the American Republic*, Henry Mayer. A compendium of Jefferson writings about Henry is included in *Patrick Henry and Thomas Jefferson*, Henry Mayer and James M. Elson. Also helpful are *Sketches of the Life and Character of Patrick Henry*, William Wirt; and *Patrick Henry: Life, Correspondence and Speeches*, William Wirt Henry.

The story of William and Mary Byrd can be traced in *The Correspondence of the Three Williams Byrds of Westover*, Marion Tinling; *The Byrds of Virginia*, Alden Hatch; and numerous archival sources.

The early years of the revolution in Virginia are recorded in *Revolutionary Virginia*, William Van Schreeven; *The Revolution in Virginia, 1775–1783*, John E. Selby; *The Revolution in Virginia*, Hamilton J. Eckenrode; and *Naval Documents of the American Revolution*. The contemporary sources include *Hening's Statutes*, the *Journals of the*

Council of the State of Virginia, the *Calendar of Virginia State Papers,* and the *Journal of the House of Delegates.*

John McAuley Palmer wrote the essential biography *Baron von Steuben.* Many of the Steuben papers are at the New-York Historical Society.

John Graves Simcoe, the British officer, told his version of the invasion in *Simcoe's Military Journal,* and the fuller story of his life is told in *John Graves Simcoe, 1752– 1802,* Mary Beacock Fryer and Christopher Dracott.

The Marquis de Lafayette left behind letters, papers, and a memoir. The standard biography dealing with the invasion is *Lafayette and the Close of the American Revolution,* Louis Reichenthal Gottschalk.

Thomas Nelson Jr., the militia leader, is profiled in *Thomas Nelson of Yorktown: Revolutionary Virginian,* Emory G. Evans. The role of the college fraternity at the College of William and Mary is described in *James Innes and his Brothers of the F.H.C.,* Jane Carson.

For more on Jefferson's motivations for the revolution, see *Forced Founders: Indians, Debtors, Slaves, and the Making of the American Revolution in Virginia,* Woody Holton. For more on the role of the lower classes in the revolution and draft riots, see *The Politics of War: Race, Class, and Conflict in Revolutionary Virginia,* Michael McDonnell.

The archives of the *Virginia Gazette* at the Colonial Williamsburg Foundation provide a rich source of material about Jefferson and his world. Vital documents are available through the University of Virginia, the College of William and Mary, the Library of Virginia, the Virginia Historical Society, the Library of Congress, the British National Archives, and other sources cited in the notes and acknowledgments.

A number of soldiers and officers left behind journals and diaries of their experience in Virginia. One of the most valuable is *Diary of the American War* by the Hessian officer Johann von Ewald. I hope my book does its small part in highlighting the extraordinary contribution of Ewald, who provided the closest thing to contemporary journalism that we have about the invasion of Virginia in his vivid descriptions of the events. Oftentimes Ewald wrote down his impressions immediately after battle. Ewald's diary was acquired in 1948 by an American officer named Joseph P. Tustin, who then translated and edited the journal. I have also cited a number of other journals and memoirs that, as far as I can tell, have received little or no notice in accounts of the invasion of Virginia. These include the journal of the Connecticut soldier Josiah Atkins, the journal of Rear Admiral Bartholomew James, and the memoir of Josias Rogers.

A number of officers, including Benedict Arnold, Henry Clinton, and Baron von Steuben, wrote accounts of the invasion in letters. In addition to the Jefferson papers, I have also consulted the papers of Americans George Washington, Nathanael Greene, Philip Mazzei, Richard Henry Lee, James Madison, John Page, George Mason, John Adams, Daniel Webster, and Joseph Jones, as well as British officers Henry Clinton, William Smith, Lord Cornwallis, Banastre Tarleton, and others.

For more on the slavery issue, see *The Hemingses of Monticello,* Annette Gordon-Reed; *Epic Journeys of Freedom,* Cassandra Pybus; *Slavery at Monticello,* Lucia Stanton; and *Rough Crossings: Britain, the Slaves, and the American Revolution,* Simon Schama.

Among the many scholarly journals that I consulted are the *Virginia Magazine of History and Biography* and the *William and Mary Quarterly.*

INDEX